A Fine Tuning

Studies of the Religious Poetry
of Herbert and Milton

medieval & renaissance texts & studies

VOLUME 64

A Fine Tuning
Studies of the Religious Poetry
of Herbert and Milton

edited by

MARY A. MALESKI

medieval & renaissance texts & studies
Binghamton, New York
1989

Library of Congress Cataloging-in-Publication Data

A Fine Tuning : Studies of the Religious Poetry of Herbert and
Milton / edited by Mary A. Maleski.
    p. cm.—(Medieval & Renaissance texts & studies ; v. 64)
Includes Index.
ISBN 0–86698–048–2 (alk. paper)
  1. English poetry—Early modern, 1500–1700—History and criticism.
2. Christian poetry, English—History and criticism. 3. Theology in
literature. 4. Summers, Joseph H. (Joseph Holmes). 1920- .
I. Maleski, Mary A.
PR545.R4F56 1989
821′.3′09382—dc19
                                88–39951
                                   CIP

FTW
AFF 3902

Contents

Illustrations

The Following are Found Between Pages 240 and 241

Preface

This *festschrift* for Professor Joseph H. Summers culminates a celebration which began at a symposium in his honor, the Sixth Annual Le Moyne Forum on Religion and Literature: "Theology and the Poetry of Seventeenth-Century England." Scholars young and old, fledgling and famous, submitted excellent papers to fete Summers at that conference; given the ordering of topics, not even all of the *best* could be chosen. Essays in this volume have been selected from those delivered at the Forum, then revised and updated. The first piece, a tribute to Professor Summers, was written and presented by his colleague, Russell A. Peck, at the symposium banquet. Articles by the keynote speakers Louis L. Martz and Barbara Lewalski respectively lead the discussions here of Herbert and Milton, the two authors about whom Summers wrote seminal studies.

I thank all who supported these commemorations, particularly Roger Lund, Chair of the English Department, and Rev. Frank Haig, S.J., former President of Le Moyne College. Funds granted by the Research and Development Committee of the College allowed me to have word processing done by two most competent typists, Patricia Weller and Barbara Poole. Frank Huntley and Anthony Low have earned my gratitude through their reading of the book for the Press, though any mistakes of judgment or composition are, of course, my own. As Director and General Editor of MRTS, Mario Di Cesare gave this publication his usual careful attention, which I deeply appreciate. My greatest debt, though, is to my husband, John Fruehwirth, who meticulously proofread this text; he selflessly and generously supports me always.

Joseph H. Summers

A Fine Tuning

Studies of the Religious Poetry of Herbert and Milton

Introduction

Theological Approaches
to Seventeenth-Century Poetry

MARY A. MALESKI

S tudies emphasizing the Protestant nature of seventeenth-century religious poetry have proliferated since Barbara Lewalski published her seminal work, *Donne's "Anniversaries" and the Poetry of Praise* (1973).[1] That book developed from Lewalski's interest in "biblical poetics" as well as her dissatisfaction with the then-usual approaches to Donne's great epideictic poems. Her 1979 *Protestant Poetics and the Seventeenth-Century Religious Lyric*[2] deepened, refined, and extended the former study to show how contemporary Protestant theology particularly and peculiarly influenced the poetry of Herbert, Vaughan, Traherne, and Taylor, as well as Donne. Richard Strier's *Love Known: Theology and Experience in George Herbert's Poetry* treats the canon of that one poet in depth, and exemplifies the best of the scholarship following Lewalski.[3]

Certainly the most influential of the earlier critical approaches, which Lewalski's studies contest, Louis Martz's book *The Poetry of Meditation* (1954; rev. 1962)[4] began with his wondering about the usual formal construction of, yet again, John Donne's *Anniversaries*. Martz discovered that the meditative tradition, as expressed especially in the *Spiritual Exercises* of St. Ignatius Loyola and the works of St. Bernard, profoundly affected the structure and hence the sense of the poems; Lewalski discerned instead the emergence of a distinctly Protestant poetics. Intersecting in their central analyses of the *Anniversaries*, these two major critics represent even today the polarities of theological interpretations of seventeenth-century literature. Thomas Roche's review of Anthony Raspa's *The Emotive Image: Jesuit Poetics in the English Renaissance*, for instance, embodies the still divergent views on these issues. After arguing against the notion of *any* sort of religious (or other) poetics à la Lewalski, Roche concludes his piece with "Viva Louis Martz."[5] Martz's ideas do indeed live, and so do Lewalski's, together in this present volume. These authors, as well as several other contributors, here augment our knowledge and engage our curiosity about the knotty theological issues we must continue to investigate if we wish fully to understand religious poets like Donne, Herbert, and Milton.

In the lead essay, Louis Martz reveals "The Generous Ambiguity of Herbert's *Temple*." He shows how George Herbert's religious attitude changed as he progressed from the early version of his *Temple* in the Williams manuscript to that of the final 1633 edition. Citing John Henry Newman's controversial commentary on the Thirty-nine Articles of the Church of England, Martz manifests the vagueness of these tenets as opposed to the trenchant doctrine of predestination expressed by the Lambeth Articles. Such openness, Martz remarks, probably explains Donne's propensity for the Articles despite his Roman Catholic upbringing. As he analyzes an array of Herbert's poems, Martz counters those who would assert that Herbert thoroughly espouses the Calvinist doctrine of the Lambeth Articles. "It would appear," Martz argues, "that, as Herbert's ordination in the Church approached (he was ordained deacon near the end of 1624), he drew closer to the eucharist and its images." Indeed Herbert included several eucharistic poems in the 1633 edition which spoke to and of a "Lord of Love" rather than a Calvinist "Lord of Power." And especially in the poem "The Judgement" he wittily and boldly dramatizes his apprehension of God as "a Friend." Herbert remained a firmly Protestant and became a clearly Anglican poet, and Martz shows us that his poetry offers an attractive ambiguity which makes it accessible and acceptable to a very wide audience.

While Martz surveys the whole *Temple*, Sidney Gottlieb concentrates on "The Two Endings of George Herbert's 'The Church,'" a precise comparison of only the conclusions of the Williams and the 1633 productions. His findings strongly reinforce Martz's arguments. He notes the speaker's varying moods in the Williams manuscript; the persona moves quickly from a friendly rapport with God to a loss of dignity, an immature clinging to God expressed in a "hysterical, hallucinating style."

Even though he returns to optimism, that return is not rightly introduced. But the additions to, and the revisions of, the later edition bolster the speaker's continuous sense of assurance that man indeed has hope for a new life with his loving God. Gottlieb cautions us to recognize that, although Herbert's religious thinking clearly changes from Puritan to Anglican, he was at times either liberal or Puritan both early and later in life.

Herbert uses the stuff of secular poetry to signal his relationship with God in "The Dedication" to *The Temple*. He addresses God as his patron and requests, Michael Schoenfeldt tells us, divine protection and acceptance. Transforming the usual opposition in Renaissance poetry of patronage, he struggles with his own difficulty as a maker who humbly submits to that Creator who has supreme power over all. As Schoenfeldt says, "paradoxically, the act of submission requires the very dialectic between self and other which it attempts to eradicate." So while he exercises all apparent humility, Herbert cleverly and necessarily displays his talent. The tension between him and the Creator is productive, though, and Herbert manages to maintain a properly Protestant attitude which recognizes that a poet's ability to form and re-form comes always from God.

In "Altering the Text of the Self: The Shapes of the Altar," Thomas Hester further illuminates Herbert's drive toward re-formation *in imagine Dei*. Hester guides us through the meditative and dramatic act whereby Herbert comes to realize the visual shape of the altar of praise and sacrifice and thus comes to understand himself. Again we witness how an act of submission and sacrifice requires a praise of the maker which ultimately reverts to the poet. Hester carefully unfolds a sense of the altar from the Augustinian perspective so congenial to Herbert: the poet must exercise that higher memory which returns him to contemplation, to colloquy with God. "The final shape of 'The Altar' is *both* an altar and an *I*—an image of the speaker's self and his Christ. . . . The final couplet carefully retains the paradox of man's shape; for until the final transfigurative re-writing of God, all poets and readers must 'see through a glass darkly,' or in Augustine's terms, 'see through a mirror enigmatically.' Until then, man can do no more than 'frame' himself as an enigmatic image of Christ."

Diane Kelsey McColley's essay demonstrates how Herbert's re-forming and re-tuning of the self depended upon the resonant rhythms of the psalms, hymns and canticles which Renaissance Protestants typically sang as they prayed together publicly in churches and privately at home. As she felicitously puts it, "Herbert's poems, begotten in liturgy, are borne on the wings of music." She provides and elucidates examples of the musical patterns of Gibbons, Byrd, and Weelkes which Herbert would have known. In such light, she analyzes Herbert's two Antiphons and his Easter poem with its choral song of men and angels. Moreover, she moves us to hear Herbert's poetic voices singing individually and in harmony, in "concent"—"heart," "I," and "God."

In all his conflict, his emblems, and his musical configurations, Herbert seeks unity with God. He seeks that rest denied man by his Creator in "The Pulley." Writing about the poem, Chauncey Wood illuminates the Augustinian basis for the seventeenth-century idea of "rest." After positing a variety of possible sources, he establishes Herbert's knowledge of Augustine's *Confessions* and especially the pertinent "our hearts are restless" passage. Both Augustine and Herbert focus attention on the Creation: Augustine knows that he was created by God for union with him and that thus he will be restless until he returns to him. In "The Pulley," Herbert poetically examines God's withholding rest from mankind; he sees that pulley (mentioned only in the title) as a device by which his restless action causes a movement upward toward rest in and with God. As Wood shows, Augustine shares that very sense of the mechanics of man's rise to God: "In Augustine's metaphysics, the natural direction of the heart is upwards, towards God, with love as the efficient cause." Furthermore, Wood agrees with and reinforces Richard Strier's conclusion that the "goodnesse" of the poem refers to God rather than to man. Yet Wood allows the potential for a subdued secondary meaning of goodness as well—but God gave and he controls the pulley.

The second group of essays here offer fresh perspectives on the theology and poetry of John Milton. Concerned with both text and context, Professor Barbara Lewalski argues that Milton drew upon a multiplicity of literary forms when he conceived the God of *Paradise*

Lost. And she shows that Milton expresses a rationale which allows such a portrayal in his *De Doctrina Christiana*: although we cannot grasp the totality of God with our limited intellects, we can know him as he wished — through biblical images. "Moreover, though the portrayal of God and his Son in *Paradise Lost* draws heavily upon biblical language and literature, the fact that, for Milton, the Bible itself offers only accommodated images of God evidently sanctions for him the use of other literary accommodations so long as they accord with and help to expand the biblical images." To evidence her point, Lewalski centers her analysis on the Dialogue in Heaven between God and his Son (3.56–348), a scene consonant with the theology of *De Doctrina*. She shows us Milton's multiple figures and modes from both classical and biblical sources, and she reveals how Milton and his God expand and transform those sources. The effect of this kaleidoscope vision is to demonstrate the individual attributes of God — as much as we can know them — and paradoxically at the same time to indicate his ineffable transcendence.

Despite Milton's enormous theological and literary resources, he seemed literally unable to write directly about the Passion of Christ. Exploring reasons for this inability, William Shullenberger and Marshall Grossman examine Milton's early poem on the Passion and again the *De Doctrina Christiana* for responses. Shullenberger sees the theological idea of the poem informing, that is, providing a deep structure for the piece. Espousing the heresy of mortalism in the *De Doctrina*, Milton, Shullenberger tells us, believed that the whole Christ, like any man, would die until his resurrection. In that case, to create the Passion of Christ in a poem would be to obliterate the Word and so to disallow the poem itself. While other early poems like *Lycidas* and the Nativity Ode can, because of their theological ideas, "triumph," a poem on the Passion is "a self-consuming artifact."

Like Shullenberger, Grossman closely analyzes Milton's notion of the hypostatic union(s) in *De Doctrina Christiana*: "The union is ineffable and the Scriptural mode of suggesting it through metaphor must be understood as accommodated speech." Because language is bound by limits of time, it cannot extend to express *both* of Christ's natures simultaneously. Grossman, though, probes the nature of Milton's special problem in dealing with Christ's Passion. Again an answer involves temporal limitations. The moment of the Passion is the point of Christ's transcendence to eternity: "The scene of the Passion is a 'horizon' that divides, yet joins time and eternity, death and life, humiliation and exaltation." Milton will not again attempt portrayal of the Crucifixion in his poetry. While they stand at different vantage points to view Milton's problems with writing about the Passion, and while they proceed along different paths of argument, Shullenberger and Grossman conclude that, for Milton, language simply has not the power positively to express the moment of the Crucifixion.

Alinda Sumers further focuses our perception of Milton's Christ when she studies sixteenth- and seventeenth-century Protestant commentaries (as well as Milton's *De Doctrina*) to demonstrate that in *Lycidas* the "Pilot of the Galilean lake" must represent Christ rather than St. Peter. She finds that the two-handed engine standing at the door refers to human conscience and, her sources would argue, definitely *not* to Christ. In this light, the notion of the smiting engine translates readily to be the evil, and so inimical, conscience of the untrue clergy who are struck into a hell of their own making. And they fall in opposition to Lycidas, Edward King, whose clear bright conscience stands "the Genius of the shore." In her analysis, Sumers brings clarity to a passage so often thought insoluably enigmatic.

While Milton lines up with his Protestant peers, then, in his portrayal of Christ the keeper of the keys, Fannie Peczenik demonstrates how he severely criticizes "prevailing contemporary beliefs" in his depiction of Eve's creation in *Paradise Lost*. She searches Rabbinic and Christian exegeses, including those of Luther and Calvin, to learn their understanding of the nature of Adam's sleep during which Eve was created from a rib of his side. Milton has Adam's sleep follow a natural tiredness after much conversation with divinity. Unlike even Luther, Milton uses the dream as a vehicle for the creation, and his language is that of the love poets of his time. At her making, Eve is for Adam "the source and center of all beauty and love in Eden." But at the fall, Adam revises his story of her creation and, his vision impaired, sees her as literally part of himself and so somehow a lesser being. But Eve, after all, bears responsibility for tempting rather than inspiring him to yet higher beauties. By taking us through the hexaemeral commentaries and showing us Milton's iconoclastic presentation, Peczenik disabuses us of some of our notions about that poet. She demonstrates that Milton was not misogynist in his portrayal of Eve's creation; on the contrary, he clearly showed that only the fallen Adam embraced a hierarchical view of woman.

Indeed Adam's prelapsarian response to Eve in his love song corresponds to the lush liberality, Noam Flinker tells us, of the Ranters' doctrine on Canticles. When Milton's Adam is yet sinless, he remains committed to a healthily-blended erotic and spiritual love for Eve as well as a profound love for God. With sin, he loses the perspective and the freedom of his prelapsarian mode. Flinker suggests that we read Canticles as an intertext for Adam's song wherein Milton purposefully and positively parallels Ranter antinomian texts. Flinker notes too that Christopher Hill has already studied Milton's Satan in relation to Ranter doctrine.

Christopher Grose's essay helps us comprehend the nature of that insidious tempter in *Paradise Regained*. Martin Luther conceived of the "white devil" as one who disguised himself as a bringer of grace and all good things, one who knows and who perversely uses the Words of Scripture to charm and disarm us. In Milton's brief epic, that type of disguised Satan "can be said to displace the narrator as the purveyor of the story in its external aspect—the visible world of *Paradise Regained*." Ironically, although he remembers so much of Christ's part, he seems to forget his own hellish reality—perhaps to try to make hearers likewise forget that. Even at the end of Book Four, a passage which Grose closely analyzes, the text itself is disturbingly ambiguous. Who is carried up on that "floating coach" by angels? Christ, of course—although the pronoun might *seem* grammatically to refer to Satan. But if readers are at all hoodwinked by that "white devil," Grose assures us that Christ is not. Milton, in fact, stresses the Savior's superiority when he shows him outwitting Satan, that smooth and sleazy talker.

With the exception of the piece on Herbert's Augustine, whose influence upon the reformers is so pervasive that he *seems* their contemporary, each essay in this volume somehow explores seventeenth-century religious contexts. As vital and important as these studies are, however, considerable work yet needs to be done. We should, I think, attend more closely to the continental writers, especially contemplatives like John of the Cross and Teresa of Avila,[6] whose work had extraordinarily wide-ranging influence. We might indeed discover Roman Catholics on the continent practicing some aspects of meditation which we are tempted to call peculiarly Protestant. Together with such broadening of our scope within the Renaissance, I think it is crucial that we more extensively take advantage of information available from our contemporary theologians and historians, so that we might better read the reformers and be able to separate their prejudices from the truth, and to admit our own literary and theological biases as well.

Notes

1. Barbara Kiefer Lewalski, *Donne's "Anniversaries" and the Poetry of Praise* (Princeton: Princeton University Press, 1973).

2. Barbara Kiefer Lewalski, *Protestant Poetics and the Seventeenth-Century Lyric* (Princeton: Princeton University Press, 1979).

3. Richard Strier, *Love Known: Theology and Experience in George Herbert's Poetry* (Chicago: University of Chicago Press, 1983). See Lewalski's review of the book in *George Herbert Journal* 8 (1985): 45–49. See also Donald R. Dickson, "The Complexities of Biblical Typology in the Seventeenth-Century," *Renaissance and Reformation*, n.s., 11 (1987): 253–72, and Donald R. Dickson, *The Fountain of Living Waters* (Columbia: University of Missouri Press, 1987).

4. Louis L. Martz, *The Poetry of Meditation: A Study in English Renaissance Literature of the Seventeenth Century*, rev. ed. (New Haven: Yale University Press; London: Oxford University Press, 1962).

5. Thomas P. Roche, Jr., review of *The Emotive Image: Jesuit Poetics in the English Renaissance*, by Anthony Raspa, *George Herbert Journal* 9 (1985): 57.

6. See Anthony Low, *Love's Architecture: Devotional Modes in Seventeenth-Century English Poetry* (New York: New York University Press, 1978).

A Tribute to Joseph Holmes Summers

RUSSELL A. PECK

St. Bonaventure, writing in a hallowed patristic tradition, claimed that the Arts were handmaidens of Theology. But, as sometimes happens in history, patterns get reversed, and Theology fosters the Arts. So it came to pass in Summers's lineage. Joseph Summers's grandfather, Elliott West Summers, was a Baptist minister in Kentucky. He had two sons who followed their father's footsteps and became Baptist ministers also. But in the second generation, Joe's father, Hollis Spurgeon Summers (the middle name came from an admired Baptist minister in 19th century England), sired two sons who devoted their lives to literature rather than religion. The older, Hollis Jr., grew up to be a poet and novelist; his younger brother, Joseph Holmes Summers, became the distinguished critic and Christian humanist celebrated in this *festschrift*.

In his semi-autobiographical novel *Brighten the Corner* (1952), Hollis Summers tells how he and little Joe, their parents having just moved to a new parish in Kentucky, overhear their father talking with a parishioner about God's omnipresence. The boys admire the big word and try it out:

"I'll give you a omnipresent for Christmas," Joe says.
"I'll omnipresent you day after tomorrow," his brother replies.

Later their father tells them that "omnipresent" means "everywhere"; "God is everywhere. He is in this house." As soon as the boys are alone, Joe, who is about four years old, invents a game of "sitting on God" everywhere they can in the strange new place—on the sofa, in dark corners behind the couch, leaping to lie on Him in mid-air, and resting upon Him in the sunlight in the garden. The real Joseph Summers has vouched that this story is essentially true. As children they did play that game. Those who know Joe in later life and have read his books know that the game has continued. In truth, Professor Summers—critic, friend, and horticulturist—has been playing in God's garden since he first began to form sentences.

In his recent autobiographical essay on his writing of *George Herbert: His Religion and Art*, Joe tells of the profound effect of his first encounter with Herbert's poetry in Graduate School at Harvard.

> Herbert seemed to speak to me more directly and authentically of the Christian life than any other poet I had read; and he also seemed the most consummate artist in the lyric that I had ever known. My childhood training and early reading made a number of things in *The Temple* seem obvious. . . . I was given my own copy of the Bible when I was six years old, and I insisted on joining the church shortly thereafter. By reading three chapters every weekday and five on Sundays one can read through the Bible within a year. I finished reading it for the first time shortly after my seventh birthday, and I continued annual readings for a number of years, finishing my eighth reading when I was fifteen. Those readings, coupled with what I had picked up from sermons, hymns, and various meetings (the regimen was formidable: Sunday School, Young People's Union, and both morning and evening services every Sunday; prayer meetings every Wednesday; innumerable special meetings and at least two weeks of twice-a-day evangelical 'protracted meetings' every year) meant that I recognized immediately a large number of Herbert's scriptural and doctrinal references; with no scholarly self-consciousness at all, I heard echoes and saw the kinds of relationships that would have been commonplaces for most seventeenth-century readers of Herbert.

Bible study has been part of Joe's life from earliest days. Even in his 60's, he continues the exercise of daily Bible reading aloud with his wife U. T. Over the years they have progressed through virtually every English

translation of the Bible, and now they are reading those sections desig-
nated by the daily lectionary from the *Book of Common Prayer* in French
and Italian as well.

But, fortunately, despite Erik Erikson's assertion that our adult pat-
terns are established by the time we are four years old, it is not neces-
sary in the diagnosis of human behavior to trace everything back to
childhood experience. Joe's autobiographical statement about Herbert's
power to unlock whole segments of his life reflects not just his reli-
gious sensibility. He also speaks in the passage of Herbert's consum-
mate artistry. By the time he encountered Herbert the craftsman, he
had completed four years of undergraduate study as an English major
at Harvard, where he so enjoyed his work and mastered his discipline
that he graduated *magna cum laude*. His mentors were Walter Hough-
ton, who Joe says had the greatest influence on him by teaching him
to read closely; Douglas Bush, with whom he studied Milton and of
whom Joe writes, "probably the most learned scholar in Renaissance
and Classical literature that I have known"; and F. O. Matthiessen, who
after the war was a very close friend of the Summers until his prema-
ture death. But lest we as college teachers deem ourselves something
more than cultivators of talents already deep-rooted in receptive under-
graduates, and with no intention of diminishing the significance of Joe's
Harvard experience, I would recall the other side of Joe's childhood
governance—his mother, Hazel Holmes Summers, to be sure, a minister's
wife (tactful, generous, quietly pious and influential, but fiercely loyal
to and supportive of her children). His mother was a part-time librari-
an. She nourished her children on books as well as motherlove. Both
Joe and Hollis were eager subjects to her literary persuasion. Joe was
a voracious reader in his youth, and he still is, especially of twentieth-
century fiction and poetry. To satisfy his boyish impulses for acquisi-
tion and accomplishment, he kept written records of his readings—not
just lists of books he had read last summer, but notes on the books
as well. So compulsive was his desire for mastery of the elements of
his literary world that he even graded his authors: Rex Stout ... A;
Feodor Dostoevski ... B-.

Knowing of Joe's childhood, we can readily foresee in the youth the
distinguished seventeenth-century scholar he has become. But to com-

ment only on the religious and bookish side of his youth is to ignore a third side which runs as deep as the other two. Sitting through church congregational meetings, hearing debates for or against the minister (which inevitably he took personally), witnessing prejudices by parishioners against blacks in the name of religion, being censured by association if his parents took a stand in the name of decency and conscience, Joe grew up with an acute sensitivity to social issues. At Harvard he did his senior essay on Louis MacNeice, the "first modern poet" he felt he "really understood." MacNeice's poetry combined a richness of classical allusion and biblical stuff with burning social issues of the late 1930s — the Spanish Civil War, Hitler, conscience, and the impending World War. When the war broke out, Joe took the lonely and extremely unpopular stand of conscientious objector. He was drafted for "alternative service" at a Quaker-run Civilian Public Service Camp in New Hampshire, which was under the jurisdiction of the Forestry Service. There he mostly cut wood and maintained his sanity by reading medieval mystics — *The Cloud of Unknowing, Theologica Germanica*, and Quaker publications such as Brother Lawrence's "The Practice of the Presence of God." His one contribution to human history at this time was, he says, to serve as a human guinea pig in a louse experiment for the testing of DDT. Toward the end of the war he was moved to Mt. Weather, Virginia, a camp run by the Brethren for the Weather Bureau, where he was made chief cook, dietitian, and supplier, a job for which he says he had neither talent nor training and which led him to the verge of despair. After the war, he worked with the National Committee on Conscientious Objectors, a subsidiary of the American Civil Liberties Union, to help get CO's out of jail and back into society.

The conscientious side of Joe's character has not flagged. Politically he remains an old-fashioned liberal, outspoken on public issues and America's perpetually imperialistic foreign policy. His three children have grown up sharing his keen sense of political issues. Mary, a Harvard graduate who is trained in the medical profession, has been active for several years in ward-level politics in Cleveland, supporting liberal candidates and working in ghetto areas to get out the vote. In the spring and summer of 1984 she served as campaign strategist and the principal speech writer for Jesse Jackson in his bid for the Presidential nomination. His son, Joseph, went into American Studies at the University of Michigan; he has been active in the social mission of the Christian church, working as a voice in support of oppressed peoples whether in Chile, El Salvador, or Detroit. In the fall of 1984 he entered Yale Divinity School. Hazel took her degree in English from the University of Rochester and now lives in St. Louis with her husband. They have given Joe and U. T. three lovely granddaughters. Hazel has a master's degree in social work and works with the elderly—mainly the lower income population of St. Louis' Northside.

Joe's sense of pastoral care touches all areas of his life and accounts nearly as much for his love of literature as for the profession he has chosen. His response to literature springs not simply from theory or aesthetic delight but also from deep conviction. One never feels with Joe that literary study is some form of escapism. But neither is it a religion. Rather, it is an intense encounter with basic issues and their rhetoric. Joe includes several selections from Milton's treatises on civil liberties in his undergraduate course on Milton. In recent years, he has taken to reading the English writings of authors in Asia, Africa, and the Caribbean—V. S. Naipaul and Derek Walcott from the West Indies, Chinua Achebe and Wole Soyinka from Nigeria, R. K. Narayan and Salman Rushdie from India, and Athol Fugard from South Africa. Joe got his start reading anti-colonial writers in 1972, when he was teaching at the University of Kent in England. One evening at a faculty dinner, a British colleague challenged Joe: "You Americans claim to care about modern literature, but you don't have available in paperback the fiction of the best novelists now writing in English." He was referring to V. S. Naipaul, whose works at that time were not in print in the U.S. But that deficiency soon was remedied, not only for Joe but for students in the Literature of Asia, Africa, and the Caribbean courses which he has introduced in recent years at the University of Rochester.

After the war and his stint with the ACLU, Joe returned to Harvard where he finished his graduate work and tutored in history and literature. He looks back on those years as among the happiest of his life. He was engaged in 1941 to U. T. Miller, an alumna of Vassar who was in graduate school at Radcliffe. They had been separated for sometime during the war. Although they had been married in 1943, this was their first opportunity to enjoy a normal life together. Much of their happiness derived from the intensity and busy-ness of their lives. U. T. had a job at Houghton Mifflin, and Joe worked at his courses and dissertation. They developed many lasting friendships in a circle of young intellectuals and poets that included the likes of Richard Wilbur and, through U. T.'s job, Elizabeth Bishop, who was living at that time in New York.

Joe's first full-time teaching job was at Bard College, where he taught for two years. The memorable event of that period (1948–50) was a poetry conference which the poet Theodore Weiss organized with the encouragement and assistance of younger members of the department like Joe and James Merrill. They brought together a host of rising stars and some who were already at their zenith—William Carlos Williams, Louise Bogan, Elizabeth Bishop, Lloyd Frankenberg, Jean Garrigue, Richard Wilbur, Richard Eberhart, Kenneth Rexroth, and Robert Lowell, all on a budget of $125. The banquet was potluck, but the real feast was akin to Plato's *Symposium.*

In 1950 the Summers moved to the University of Connecticut, where Joe progressed upward into the ranks of tenure. There Joe rewrote his dissertation, which Chatto & Windus and Harvard University Press agreed to publish as *George Herbert: His Religion and Art.* In 1952–53, on a grant from the Fund for the Advancement of Learning, he spent a year in Italy in a picturesque flat in Fiesole, learning Italian and absorbing Renaissance culture. It was there, he says, that architecture became to him a meaningful art. Joe next began work in earnest on Milton, for which project he was awarded a fellowship by the John Simon Guggenheim Foundation in 1957–58. He spent his Guggenheim year in Cambridge.

In 1959 the Summers family moved West, where Joe became Professor of English at Washington University in St. Louis. He returned to the Northeast for a year as visiting professor at Amherst in 1962–63, but then returned to Washington to serve as chairman of the department. While at Washington he published his Laurel Poets edition of Andrew Marvell's poetry, served as general editor for the D. C. Heath series entitled "Discussions of Literature," and edited selected papers from the English Institute on *The Lyric and Dramatic Milton* (Columbia

University Press, 1965). But his signal achievement of those years was his publication of *The Muse's Method: An Introduction to Paradise Lost* (Chatto & Windus; Harvard University Press, 1962), a book which, like the Herbert book, remains a landmark in seventeenth-century studies — twice reprinted and twice pilfered for chapters in collections of essays on Milton. In 1966 Joe accepted an appointment at Michigan State which he began with a year's leave as a Fulbright Professor and Visiting Fellow at All Souls College, Oxford. During this time the New American Library published his edition of Herbert's English poems.

In 1969 he came to the University of Rochester where he has ever since greatly enriched the intellectual life of the institution as a teacher, scholar, and colleague. In his years at Rochester he published numerous essays, and, in 1970, his third book on the seventeenth-century poets, *The Heirs of Donne and Jonson* (Oxford University Press, 1970). His professional influence now came into full sway as he began serving on several national committees: The Phi Beta Kappa Committee for the Christian Gauss Award, the Executive Committee for Religious Approaches to Literature Division of the Modern Language Association, the Milton Society, for which he recently served as President, and the ACLS Fellowship Selection Committee. His career at Rochester has been filled with honors and accolades. In 1972 he was appointed by Molly Mahood to be visiting Professor at the University of Kent in Canterbury. In 1976 he was a Senior Fellow at the Folger Shakespeare Library and was also named to the Roswell S. Burrows chair at the University of Rochester. In 1980–81 he was an NEH-Huntington Library Fellow. In the spring of 1983 he was made a fellow of the American Academy of Arts and Sciences, a rare honor indeed. In his retirement year he has published his book on Shakespeare's plays, entitled *Dreams of Power and Love* (Oxford University Press, 1984). Doubtless the new book will bring him further glories, if there are glories left to be had. In his discussions of Prospero, Lear, and Leontes we see Joe at his most wise, as one who has come to know the passions and to understand their languages.

In looking over the Summers bibliography one is struck by the number of books, chapters, and articles which have been reprinted. His criticism is read. Moreover, it appeals to a wide audience — undergraduates, graduate students, specialists, practicing poets, and intelligent people in all walks of life. There is simplicity about his criticism. He always works from basic questions of the text. Seldom does he speculate on methodology or critical theory. His own method of reading is lively and just without calling attention to itself. To know Joe is to recognize in his person that poetry is always with him: he may burst forth with a poem by MacNeice or Wilbur as readily as one by Herbert or Donne. This immediacy of poetry to his life is always evident in his writing. The one criterion he insists upon for sound criticism is honesty of response combined with the stipulation that an author be allowed his say before the critic judges him. He often relies upon his feelings in sounding out a text but warns against confusing feeling with prejudice. In his essay published in *The Christian Scholar*, 47 (1964), he writes:

> As Christian literary scholars we have taken a more or less definite position in relation to life and experience. It is inevitable that a good deal of our scholarship should be concerned with the patterns and meanings that are most significant to our lives. This is not, I believe, a real limitation of our scholarly roles; we have the advantage of being conscious of our position and our traditions, and we should therefore more easily avoid the usual scholarly pitfall: the unconscious projection of an individual's private obsessions and desires upon the literary evidence. (94)

A scholar's first obligation, Summers insists, "is the discovery and communication of truth," not the expending of critical energy as "religious or moral cops and judges, rapping knuckles and heads, assigning sentences" (99). "We should recognize," he writes, "our prime duty to be as informed and as intelligent and as honest as we can and to make (and communicate) fairly subtle discriminations. As convinced Christians, we should not find any contradiction between our scholarly commitment to truth and our religious aims. We do not, surely, believe that God requires us to tell lies for Him. We are committed to the discovery, the preservation, and the communication of truth, and we have faith the truth will make us free" (95). If there were a textual civil liberties union, Summers would be its negotiator.

In conclusion, I would make two other points about Joe's approach to literature, one regarding his commitment to seventeenth-century literature as a field and another regarding his sense of himself as a reader of literature. In his essay on "Christian Literary Scholars," from which the previous extended quotation was taken, Summers goes on to designate an additional primary duty of the Christian Scholar, besides being honestly and subtly discriminating, namely, "to try to make evident and available to those living in our own age the achievements of the Christian literature of the past" (95). Summers has a passionate affinity for the seventeenth century. As we have seen, when he first came upon its literature at Harvard, he saw that it had a special power to move him and that he had a special background to respond. But it was not simply a matter of seeing himself through that voice (or rather, those voices). In fact, he warns against the dangers of fiendish empathy which imposes monolith "Christian" doctrine (that is, one's own) upon all forms of Christian literature:

> When we attempt to deal with an authentic work of religious literature from the past, our first responsibility is not to "correct" its doctrine, however fragmentary, strange, or imperfect we may find it. It is rather, to attempt to answer accurately a few questions: what does it say? how does it "work"? Perhaps other questions will follow: how was it possible for intelligent and creative men to believe such doctrines? what did the doctrines *mean* for the life of the individual and the community? what was the relation between the doctrines and that literary creation which can still speak to other men? We may, of course, wish to continue with more stringent criticism of the work and its limitations, but we should reverence the life that we find within it. It is possible to identify and condemn the dehumanizing, the deadening, the evil within any civilization or literary work of man, and still to recognize that, insofar as each truly "exists," the work and the will of God lives within it. (96)

Summers insists that a scholar betrays Christian values if he approves literature simply because he knows that its author is Christian; the scholar also betrays Christian values if he tries to present popular non-Christian works as "essentially Christian" merely because he wants Christianity to be popular (96).

To be a critic like Summers, one needs to have a strong sense of self. (That is not a prerequisite for reading him, of course.) It is his own firm sense of critical presence that makes his essays so attractive. Readers go to his books because they want to know what Summers says. I do not mean to imply that he writes about himself. Readers do not flock to his books to see Summers prance. Indeed, few personalities I have known have been less given to romanticism. But Joe is, nonetheless, a man of powerful feelings, and as critic he speaks out of love of his subject. His readers discern in his articulate style what it is they also have felt and sometimes seen, though now more richly. And they also see what they had ignored or never seen, and are grateful.

In his review of Stanley Fish's *Self-Consuming Artifacts: The Experience of Seventeenth-Century Poetry*, Summers, though he finds much that is admirable in Fish's various readings, particularly his notions about literature "which has designs on the reader," objects to the assumption prevalent in Fish's argument that "admirable literary designs on the reader should always be antagonistic, tricky, or evangelical; that the ultimate recognition the best seventeenth-century works provide is the distrust of any sort of reliance on the 'self' or human reason; and what they bring the reader to, again and again, is the recognition both of their own and their readers' inadequacies before divine revelation and the inexplicable will of God" (406). Summers points to numerous instances in the literature of the period which are directly, or upon second or third readings, deeply founded in a profound confidence of the self, a confidence that lies at the heart of Christian thought and expresses itself in celebration rather than in cynicism. "In emphasizing 'self' as opposed to or separate from God," Fish, Summers argues, "almost ignores that emphasis on self as accepting and accepted by God which made religious poetry possible for Herbert" (412).

It seems to me that the point Summers makes about acceptance in the religious poets of the seventeenth century might also be said about his own criticism. He writes out of a confidence in his sensibilities—a marvelous trust which is not too different from the naiveté of his childhood game of sitting on God—that yields a celebratory quality to his discussions that is refreshing and quite different from his more theoretically or thesis-bound cohorts. He gets on just fine with Being and

Presence, both in himself and in poetry. At the end of his review essay entitled "Notes on Recent Studies in English Literature of the Earlier Seventeenth Century," *MLQ* 26 (1965), Joe summarizes his views on what we as scholars should be up to:

> A humane ideal would be for everyone to read more and to publish less. Only slightly less utopian would be the suggestions that scholars should feel obligated not only to cite or summarize secondary material but also to try to make sense of it, that critics should read most of a writer's works before they start writing on his individual poems, and that scholars and critics alike should attempt to write as clearly, simply, and readably as possible and should go to some lengths to avoid jargon. The simple fact, though, in seventeenth-century studies as elsewhere, is that there are no substitutes for attention or for love. Granted only the average in human intelligence and academic training, a scholar or a critic who cares enough about a poem, a book, an author or an issue to give it his full attention for some period of time will probably avoid most of the common faults — including dullness. If the quality of his attention rises to love, there is at least a chance that what he writes may provide true illumination for a number of his readers. (149)

That is a credo to which critics of all persuasions can say "Amen."

The Published Writings of Joseph H. Summers

Books, Editions, and Major Collaborative Works

George Herbert: His Religion and Art. London and Cambridge, Mass.:
Chatto & Windus and Harvard University Press, 1954. Reprinted
1968; Reprinted Binghamton, N.Y.: Medieval & Renaissance Text
& Studies, 1981. Chapter IV, "The Conception of Form." Reprint-
ed in *The Metaphysical Poets: Key Essays on Metaphysical Poetry and
the Major Metaphysical Poets*. Ed. Frank Kermode. New York: Faw-
cett, 1969, 230–51; and in *The Metaphysical Poets: A Selection of Crit-
ical Essays*. Ed. Gerald Hammond. London: Macmillan, 1974, 157–81.
Chapter VI, "The Poem as Hieroglyph." Reprinted in *Seventeenth-
Century English Poetry: Modern Essays in Criticism*. Ed. William Keast.
New York: Oxford University Press, 1962, 215–37. Rev. ed. 1971,
225–47; and in *George Herbert and the Seventeenth-Century Religious
Poets*. Ed. Mario Di Cesare. New York: W. W. Norton, 1978,
255–70.

Andrew Marvell (Selected Poems). Ed. J. H. S. New York: Dell, Laurel
Poets, 1961.

The Muse's Method: An Introduction to "Paradise Lost." London and Cam-
bridge, Mass.: Chatto & Windus and Harvard University Press, 1965.
Reprinted 1970. Reprinted New York: W. W. Norton, 1978.
Reprinted Binghamton, N.Y.: Medieval & Renaissance Text &
Studies, 1981.

Chapter V, "The Pattern at the Centre." Reprinted in *Milton's Epic Poetry*. Ed. C. A. Patrides. Harmondsworth: Penguin, 1967, 179–214.

Chapter VIII, "The Final Vision." Reprinted in *Milton: A Collection of Critical Essays*. Ed. Louis L. Martz. Englewood Cliffs, N.J.: Prentice-Hall, 1966, 183–206.

The Lyric and Dramatic Milton. Selected Papers from the English Institute. Ed. J. H. S. New York and London: Columbia University Press, 1965. Author of Foreword and "*Samson Agonistes*: The Movement of the Drama," 153–75.

General Editor, *Discussions of Literature*. 25 vols. Boston: D. C. Heath, 1960–66.

George Herbert: Selected Poetry. Ed. J. H. S. New York and London: New American Library, 1967.

The Heirs of Donne and Jonson. London and New York: Chatto & Windus and Oxford University Press, 1970.

"Donne and Jonson" (part of Chapter I). Reprinted in *Ben Jonson and the Cavalier Poets*. Ed. Hugh Maclean. New York: W. W. Norton, 1974, 454–65.

Dreams of Power and Love: Essays on Shakespeare's Plays. New York and London: Oxford University Press, 1984.

Articles

Translations of four Latin poems by George Herbert. *Quarterly Review of Literature* 6 (1951): 211–12.

"Herbert's Form." *PMLA* 66 (1951): 1055–72. Reprinted in *Essential Articles for the Study of George Herbert's Poetry*. Ed. John R. Roberts. Hamden, Conn.: Archon, 1979, 87–104.

"Herbert's 'Trinitie Sunday.'" *The Explicator* 10 (1952): item 23. Reprinted in *The Explicator Cyclopedia* 2. Chicago: Quadrangle Books, 1969, entry 342.

"Marvell's 'Nature.'" *ELH* 20 (1953): 121–35. Reprinted in *Andrew Marvell: A Collection of Critical Essays.* Ed. George DeF. Lord. Englewood Cliffs, N.J.: Prentice-Hall, 1968, 42–54; in *Andrew Marvell: A Critical Anthology.* Ed. John Carey. Harmondsworth and Baltimore: Penguin, 1969, 137–50; in *Marvell: Modern Judgements.* Ed. Michael Wilding. London: Macmillan, 1969, 141–54; and in *George Herbert and the Seventeenth-Century Religious Poets.* Ed. Mario Di Cesare. New York: W. W. Norton, 1978, 326–37.

"'Grateful Vicissitude' in *Paradise Lost.*" *PMLA* 59 (1954): 251–64.

"The Masks of *Twelfth Night.*" *The University of Kansas City Review* 22 (1955): 25–32. Reprinted in *Shakespeare: Modern Essays in Criticism.* Ed. Leonard F. Dean. New York: Oxford University Press, 1957, 128–37; rev. ed. 1967, 134–43. Also reprinted in *Comedy: Plays, Theory, and Criticism.* Ed. Marvin Felheim. New York: Harcourt Brace, 1962, 258–62; in *Discussions of Shakespeare's Romantic Comedies.* Ed. Herb Weil. Boston: D. C. Heath, 1966, 111–18; and in *Twentieth-Century Interpretations of "Twelfth Night."* Ed. Walter N. King. Englewood Cliffs, N.J.: Prentice-Hall, 1969, 15–23. Excerpted in *The Reader's Encyclopedia of Shakespeare.* Ed. O. J. Campbell and E. G. Quinn. New York: Crowell, 1966, 908.

"The Arts in Italy: The Burden of the Past." *The Yale Review* 54 (1955): 373–87

"The Voice of the Redeemer in *Paradise Lost.*" *PMLA* 70 (1955): 1082–89.

"Milton and the Cult of Conformity." *The Yale Review* 46 (1957): 511–27. Reprinted in *Milton: Modern Judgements.* Ed. Alan Rudrum. London: Macmillan, 1968, 29–43.

"Commemorative note on Edwin Muir." *Books Abroad* 24 (1960): 123.

"The Achievement of Edwin Muir." *The Massachusetts Review* 2 (1961): 140–60.

"The Two Great Sexes in *Paradise Lost.*" *Studies in English Literature* 2 (1962): 1–26.

"Marvell's Political Poetry." Abstract of a 1962 MLA paper. *Seventeenth-Century News* 21 (Spring and Summer 1963): 21.

"Christian Literary Scholars." *The Christian Scholar* 47 (Summer 1964): 94–99. Reprinted in *Religion and Modern Literature: Essays in Theory and Criticism*. Ed. G. B. Tennyson and Edward E. Ericson, Jr. Grand Rapids: Eerdmans, 1975, 108–13.

"Notes on Recent Studies in English Literature of the Earlier Seventeenth Century." *Modern Language Quarterly* 26 (1965): 135–49.

"The Embarrassments of *Paradise Lost*." In *Approaches to "Paradise Lost": The York Tercentenary Lectures*. Ed. C. A. Patrides. London and Toronto: Edward Arnold and University of Toronto Press, 1958, 65–79.

Entry on Edwin Muir in *Encyclopedia of World Literature in the 20th Century*. Ed. W. B. Fleischman. New York: Frederick Ungar, 1969, 2: 429–30.

"Reading Marvell's 'Garden.'" *The Centennial Review* 13 (1969): 18–37.

"The Heritage of Donne and Jonson." *The University of Toronto Quarterly* 39 (1970): 107–26.

"Andrew Marvell: Private Taste and Public Judgement." *Metaphysical Poetry*. Stratford-upon-Avon Studies, Vol 11. Ed. Malcolm Bradbury and David Palmer. London: Edward Arnold, 1970, 180–209.

"Milton and Celebration." *Milton Quarterly* 5 (1971): 1–7.

"The Anger of Prospero." *The Michigan Quarterly Review* 12 (Spring 1973): 116–35.

"Stanley Fish's Reading of Seventeenth-Century Literature." *Modern Language Quarterly* 35 (1974): 403–17.

(With U. T. Miller Summers), Biography of Francis O. Matthiessen. *Dictionary of American Biography, Supplement Four, 1946–1950*. Ed. John A. Garraty and Edward T. James. New York: Charles Scribner's Sons, 1974, 559–61.

Response to Michael K. Ferber's "Simone Weil's *Iliad* and Literary Pacifi-
cism." In *Simone Weil: Live Like Her? A Technology and Culture Semi-
nar and Lecture Series.* Transcribed and edited by George A. White.
Cambridge, Mass.: The Technology and Culture Seminar, M.I.T.,
1976, 26–35.

"Some Apocalyptic Strains in Marvell's Poetry." In *Tercentenary Essays
in Honor of Andrew Marvell.* Ed. Kenneth Friedenreich. Hamden,
Conn.: Archon, 1977, 180–203.

"From 'Josephs coat' to 'A true Hymne.'" *George Herbert Journal* 2, no.
1 (1978): 1–12.

"Response to Anthony Low's address on *Simon Agonistes* (Le Moyne
College, May 4, 1979)." *Milton Quarterly* 13 (October 1979): 102–6.

Essays on Elizabeth Bishop, George Herbert, Henry King, and Richard
Wilbur. *Great Writers of the English Language: Poets.* Ed. James
Vinson and D. L. Kirkpatrick. London and New York: St. James's
Press and St. Martin's Press, 1979, 104–5, 484–86, 557, 1076 and
1077.

"'Look there, look there!' The Ending of *King Lear.*" *English Renais-
sance Studies Presented to Dame Helen Gardner in honour of her Seven-
tieth Birthday.* Ed. John Carey. Oxford: Clarendon Press, 1980, 74–93.

"Notes on Simone Weil's *Iliad.*" In *Simone Weil: Interpretations of a Life.*
Ed. George Abbott White. Amherst: The University of Massachusetts
Press, 1981, 87–93.

"*George Herbert: His Religion and Art*: Its Making and Early Reception."
George Herbert Journal 5 (Fall 1981-Spring 1982): 1–18.

Reviews

Poetry and Dogma by M. Y. Ross. *College English* 17 (1955): 63.

Contemporary Literary Scholarship (Merritt Hughes' chapter on the seven-
teenth century). *College English* 20 (1959): 197.

The Revival of Metaphysical Poetry by Joseph E. Duncan. *MLN* 75 (1960): 517–19.

The Imagination as a Means of Grace by Ernest L. Tuveson. *College English* 21 (1961): 443.

A Critique of "Paradise Lost" by John Peter. *JEGP* 61 (1962): 181–84.

European Metaphysical Poetry by Frank J. Warnke and *Baroque Lyric Poetry* by Lowry Nelson, Jr. *The Yale Review* 52 (1962): 122–26.

John Donne's Lyrics by Arnold Stein. *Criticism* 5 (1963): 376–79.

Edwin Muir by P. H. Butter. *Studies in Scottish Literature* 1 (October 1963).

The Return of Eden: Five Essays on Milton's Epics by Northrop Frye. *JEGP* 46 (1967): 146–49.

The Poetry of Grace: Reformation Themes in Seventeenth-Century Poetry by William H. Halewood. *Modern Language Quarterly* 33 (1972): 195–97.

Hieroglyphics: The History of a Literary Symbol by Liselotte Dieckmann. *English Language Notes* 12 (1974): 238–41.

The Rhetoric of Renaissance Poetry from Wyatt to Milton. Ed. Thomas O. Sloan and Raymond B. Waddington. *Criticism* 18 (1976): 77–82.

The Prophetic Milton by William Kerrigan. *Modern Philology* 74 (1977): 420–23.

Shakespeare's Mediated World by Richard Fly, *Shakespeare and the Mystery of God's Judgments* by Robert G. Hunter, and *Spirits Finely Touched: The Testing of Value and Integrity in Four Shakespearean Plays* by Harold Skulsky. *Shakespeare Quarterly* 30 (1979): 103–7.

George Herbert: An Annotated Bibliography of Modern Criticism, 1905–1974 by John R. Roberts. *Renaissance Quarterly* 32 (Autumn 1979): 440–42.

Foreshortened Time: Andrew Marvell and Seventeenth-Century Revolutions by R. I. V. Hodge. *CLIO* 10 (1980): 112–14.

The Call of God: The Theme of Vocation in the Poetry of Donne and Herbert by Robert B. Shaw and *The Shadow of Eternity: Belief and Structure in Herbert, Vaughn, and Traherne* by Sharon Cadman Selig. *Renaissance Quarterly* 36 (Spring 1983): 151–55.

Herbert

The Temple . . . reflects Herbert's belief that form was that principle by which the spiritual created existence out of chaos, and Herbert assumed that that process could be rationally apprehended.

—*George Herbert: His Religion and Art*

George Herbert. From the drawing by Robert White.
By permission of the Houghton Library, Harvard University.

The Generous Ambiguity of Herbert's Temple

LOUIS L. MARTZ

In the year 1841 John Henry Newman, then still a member of the Church of England, caused a storm of controversy when he published his famous Tract No. 90, in which he argued that certain of the most important among the Thirty-nine Articles of the Church of England were capable of a Roman Catholic interpretation. He argued, for example, that Article XXV did not deny the existence of seven sacraments, but only affirmed that Baptism and the Lord's Supper, being ordained by the Gospels, were sacraments in a different sense from the traditional other five. So too with the problem of the action of grace — the crucial point of controversy between Catholics and Calvinists and all those who in Herbert's day were hovering, or struggling to hover, in between the strict adherents of these warring doctrines. Newman cited the words of Article XI: "That we are justified by Faith only, is a most wholesome doctrine." "The Homilies," Newman says, "add that Faith is the sole *means*, the sole *instrument* of justification." But, he continues, these statements do "*not* imply a denial of *Baptism* as a means and an instrument of justification. . . . When, then, Faith is called the sole instrument, this means the sole *internal* instrument, not the sole instrument of any kind." "There is nothing inconsistent, then," he concludes, "in Faith being the sole instrument of justification, and yet Baptism also the sole instrument, and that at the same time, because in distinct senses; an inward instrument in no way interfering with an outward instrument, Baptism may be the hand of the Giver [God], and Faith the hand of the receiver [the human being reaching out to God]."

Moreover, he even more daringly adds, "An assent to the doctrine that Faith alone justifies, does not at all preclude the doctrine of Works justifying also." "The only question is," he contends, "*What* is that sense in which Works justify, so as not to interfere with faith only justifying?" "A number of means go to effect our justification. We are justified by Christ alone, in that He has purchased the gift; by Faith alone, in that Faith asks for it; by Baptism alone, for Baptism conveys it; and by newness of heart alone, for newness of heart is the life of it."[1]

I stress all this to make two points: (1) Newman here in Tract 90 is only discovering, or uncovering, what the strict Calvinists had been pointing out all through the reign of Queen Elizabeth and on through the reigns of James I and Charles I—that the terms of the Thirty-nine Articles as set forth in 1563 were frequently, indeed pervasively, so vague, so guarded, so ambiguous that people of an anti-Calvinist persuasion could and did, in good conscience, swear allegiance to them, while making their own interpretations, as Newman here has done; (2) Newman's way of interpreting the article on Faith may suggest something like the reasoning by which people such as John Donne, with his strong Catholic upbringing, could nevertheless become a member of the Church of England. It would appear that the Thirty-nine Articles were left deliberately vague in order that as many people as possible might feel, in their consciences, that they could, with their own interpretations, swear to them. As Newman put it: "the Articles are not framed on the principle of excluding those who prefer the theology of the early ages to that of the Reformation. . . . their framers constructed them in such a way as best to comprehend those who did not go so far in Protestantism as themselves."[2]

I raise these points because there is now such a powerful tendency in studies of Herbert to read him as a strictly Calvinist poet, on the grounds that a "Calvinist consensus" existed in the English church of Herbert's day.[3] This tendency in scholarship seems to have arisen from the work of certain historians, especially Charles and Katherine George, who have shown that Calvinism rose to a dominant position among the leading English churchmen during the latter part of the sixteenth century and the earlier years of the seventeenth.[4] I am impressed by the evidence for this domination, but I am also impressed by the evidence that this domination represented, not a consensus, but an attempt to impose a consensus from the top down, while this effort met with opposition from the top down, in the government, the church, the universities, and among the common people.[5]

Consider, for example, what happened in 1595, when Archbishop Whitgift, the Bishop of London, and other prominent churchmen set forth the Lambeth Articles in a bold effort to settle the controversies then raging at Cambridge. I will quote all the articles here, for their precision gives the best possible definition of what it meant to be a true Calvinist in the England of Donne and Herbert; these are the tenets that the framers believed would underlie a truly Calvinist Church of England; and these are the tenets that would underlie a truly Calvinist "Church" of George Herbert:

I: God from eternity has predestined some men to life, and reprobated some to death.

II: The moving or efficient cause of predestination to life is not the foreseeing of faith, or of perseverance, or of good works, or of anything innate in the person of the predestined, but only the will of the good pleasure of God.

III: There is a determined and certain number of predestined, which cannot be increased or diminished.

IV: Those not predestined to salvation are inevitably condemned on account of their sins.

V: A true, lively and justifying faith, and the sanctifying Spirit of God, is not lost nor does it pass away either totally or finally in the elect.

VI: The truly faithful man — that is, one endowed with justifying faith — is sure by full assurance of faith of the remission of sins and his eternal salvation through Christ.

VII: Saving grace is not granted, is not made common, is not ceded to all men, by which they might be saved, if they wish.

VIII: No one can come to Christ unless it be granted to him, and unless the Father draws him: and all men are not drawn by the Father to come to the Son.

IX: It is not in the will or the power of each and every man
to be saved.[6]

When word of these Articles reached the top of the government,
Robert Cecil sent the following stern rebuke to the Archbishop: "Her
majesty . . . hath commanded me to send unto your grace that she mis-
likes much that any allowance hath been given by your grace and the
rest of any points to be disputed of predestination, being a matter tender
and dangerous to weak, ignorant minds, and thereupon requireth your
grace to suspend them." "I could not tell what to answer," Cecil wryly
adds, "but do this as her majesty's commandment, and leave the matter
for your grace who I know can best satisfy her in these things."[7] The
Archbishop knew: he at once wrote to Cambridge, exhorting his col-
leagues to observe her majesty's admonition that these matters are "ut-
terly unfit" to be "any ways" "publicly dealt with, either in sermon
or disputation" or in any form of "publication."[8]

Meanwhile, within the Church, Lancelot Andrewes had written a
commentary on the Lambeth Articles, because, as the Georges say in
their carefully qualified and judicious book, he "had certain anxieties
about the predestinarian argument," and, the Georges add, "the sig-
nificance of his anxieties is all the greater since the majority of his con-
temporaries and successors tended to share them to some extent."[9]

To this lack of consensus one should add the sort of testimony cited
by Patrick Collinson, who calls attention to the report of a godly minister
of this era in Kent, concerning a parish of four hundred communicants.
"Marveiling that my preachinge was so little regarded," Josias Nichols
took it upon himself "to conferre with everie man and woman." When
asked "whether it were possible for a man to live so uprightlie, that
by well doeing he might winne heaven," there was "skarse one, but did
affirme, that a man might be saved by his own wel doing: and that
he trusted he did so live, that by Gods grace, he should obtaine everlast-
ing life by serving of God & good prayers, &c."[10] This stubborn ten-
dency of human nature to think that "good life" must in some way
be rewarded was the everlasting enemy of Calvinism.

To come closer to the poets, one should ponder this passage from
a sermon by John Donne, cited in part by the Georges as an example

of an aberration from what they regard as the Calvinist norm; the whole passage needs to be quoted, because it shows Donne's mind firmly set against the exclusive tenor of the theology represented by the Lambeth Articles and by the chief representative of English Calvinist theology, William Perkins:

> They are too good husbands, and too thrifty of Gods grace, too sparing of the Holy Ghost; that restraine Gods generall propositions, *Venite omnes* [Mat. 11.28], Let all come, and *Vult omnes salvos* [1 Tim. 2.4], God would have all men saved, so particularly, as to say, that when God sayes *All*, he meanes some of all sorts, some Men, some Women, some Jews, some Gentiles, some rich, some poore, but he does not meane, as he seemes to say, simply All.[11] Yes; God does meane, simply All, so as that no man can say to another, God meanes not thee, no man can say to himselfe, God meanes not me. *Nefas est dicere, Deum aliquid, nisi bonum praedestinare*; It is modestly said by S. *Augustine*, and more were immodesty; There is no predestination in God, but to good. And therefore it is *Durus sermo*, They are hard words, to say, That God predestinated some, not onely *Ad damnationem*, but *Ad causas damnationis*, Not onely to damnation because they sinned, but to a necessity of sinning, that they might the more justly be damned . . .

After thus pushing the doctrine of reprobation to its inevitable conclusion, Donne turns to explain why he finds this aspect of Calvinism impossible to accept:

> Christ wept for the imminent calamities, temporall, and spirituall, which hung over Jerusalem; and *Lacrymae Legati doloris*, saies S. *Cyprian*, Teares are the Ambassadours of sorrow; And they are *Sanguis animi vulnerati*, saies S. *Augustine*, Teares are the bloud of a wounded soule; And would Christ bleed out of a wounded soule, and weepe out of a sad heart, for that, which himselfe, and onely himselfe, by an absolute Decree, had made necessary and inevitable?[12]

Donne is dealing here with the tension between the "Lord of Power" and the "Lord of Love" that represents the central problem of Calvinism, the central problem in the controversies that beset the Church of England in the days of Donne and Herbert, a problem that runs throughout George Herbert's *Temple*, and a problem which he, like Donne, resolves in favor of Love, as in "The Flower." But we have two versions of *The Temple*, the final version of 1633, and the early version in the manuscript now in Dr. Williams's Library, London, which contains only 69 of the 164 poems in the final version, plus six more that were discarded.[13] This early version seems more strongly imbued with Calvinism than the ultimate version, partly because it lacks most of the strongly eucharistic poems that appear in 1633, and partly because some of its phrasing, later revised, and some of its poems, later removed, have a Calvinist ring, or deal with Calvinist issues.

It contains, for example, the poem "Perseverance," which by its title brings up one of the problems that troubled Lancelot Andrewes in the Lambeth Articles[14]—the problem of the "Perseverance of the Saints"— that is, whether or not one can fall from grace. The Lambeth Articles (see Item V) make it clear that grace, once given, cannot be withdrawn. Herbert is not so sure:

> My God, the poore expressions of my Love
> Which warme these lines, & serve them up to thee
> Are so, as for the present, I did move
>   Or rather as thou movedst mee.

Note the theological correction: as "I did move / Or rather as thou movedst mee." The latter would be the right Calvinist position. Since "Perseverance" comes near the end of Herbert's "Church" (sixth poem from the end), reference to "these lines" seems to apply to all the foregoing poems in the book; the opening stanza suggests a tentativeness in "these lines" written "as for the present." Much more remains to be done, as the next two stanzas imply:

> But what shall issue, whither these my words
> Shal help another, but my iudgment bee;
> As a burst fouling-peece doth save the birds
>   But kill the man, is seald with thee.

> For who can tell, though thou hast dyde to winn
> And wedd my soule in glorious paradise;
> Whither my many crymes and use of sinn
> May yet forbid the banes and bliss.

This speaker lacks the "full assurance of faith" that is a mark of the "truly faithful man," according to the Lambeth Articles (Item VI): he fears that his own sins may yet forbid the banns that might announce his welcome to the marriage-supper of the Lamb. What is important here is the sense of personal responsibility in a highly contingent universe where one's fate seems not predetermined, but seems "yet" to hang in the balance, dependent in some measure upon "my words," which may help to save another and yet lead to the speaker's own damnation:

> Onely my soule hangs on thy promisses
> With face and hands clinging unto thy brest,
> Clinging and crying, crying without cease
> Thou art my rock, thou art my rest.

This is a cry of deep anguish seldom seen so nakedly in Herbert's poetry; but it represents an effort at assertion of Faith quite in line with Article XVII of the Church of England, "Of Predestination and Election," which, unlike the Lambeth Articles, overtly speaks only of "Predestination to Life" as "the everlasting purpose of God, whereby (before the foundations of the world were laid) he hath constantly decreed by his counsel secret to us, to deliver from curse and damnation those whom he hath chosen in Christ out of mankind." The "godly consideration" of this Predestination, the article goes on to say, "is full of sweet, pleasant, and unspeakable comfort to godly persons," but on the other hand, "for curious and carnal persons, lacking the Spirit of Christ, to have continually before their eyes the sentence of God's Predestination, is a most dangerous downfal, whereby the Devil doth thrust them either into desperation, or into wretchlessness of most unclean living, no less perilous than desperation." The thought of possible reprobation stands as a warning for carnal persons; God is here not made responsible for reprobation in explicit terms. Then, after almost presenting a Calvinist position on this matter, the article adds the following paragraph: "Furthermore, we must receive God's promises in such wise, as they be generally set forth to us in holy Scripture: and, in our doings, that Will of God is to be followed, which we have expressly declared unto us in the Word of God." That sounds very much like a codicil added to satisfy dissenting members of a committee: it leaves the whole matter open to personal interpretation according to the Scripture.

Thus Herbert clings to the scriptural Promises after his own fashion. But he removed this poem from the final version of *The Temple*. Why? Perhaps because it raised a controversial issue. Perhaps because its outcry seemed to conflict with the mood of assurance that dominates the last twelve or fifteen poems in the final version, especially the poems that follow after the twin eucharistic poems, "The Invitation" and "The Banquet." Still, one could wish that Herbert might somehow have found a place for the poem earlier in his book; for, unlike the other five discarded poems, this is a strong piece of work, dramatizing an aspect of religious experience that is not elsewhere fully represented in *The Temple*.

Whatever the reasons, removal of the poem is fully in accord with Herbert's effort to resolve within the human heart, without controversy, the paradoxical issues involved in the concepts of divine Power and divine Love. I tend to read *The Temple* in its final form as a composition analogous to, and indeed representing, dramatizing, the tense and delicate equilibrium that prevailed in the Church of England for most of Herbert's lifetime. It contains poems that are, here and there, capable of a Calvinist interpretation, though I would argue that such poems have, like the Thirty-nine Articles, a Calvinist *tone*, as Conrad Russell would say, rather than a firm and distinctly Calvinist doctrine, as in the Lambeth Articles.

Herbert's poem "The Water-course" provides a striking example of his mode of resolution, since this poem has often been taken as evidence for Herbert's acceptance of the full Calvinist doctrine of double predestination.[15]

> Thou who dost dwell and linger here below,
> Since the condition of this world is frail,

Where of all plants afflictions soonest grow;
If troubles overtake thee, do not wail:

For who can look for lesse, that loveth $\begin{cases} \text{Life?} \\ \text{Strife?} \end{cases}$

But rather turn the pipe and waters course
To serve thy sinnes, and furnish thee with store
Of sov'raigne tears, springing from true remorse:
That so in purenesse thou mayst him adore,

Who gives to man, as he sees fit, $\begin{cases} \text{Salvation.} \\ \text{Damnation.} \end{cases}$

Calvinist in tone? Perhaps, but Calvinist in doctrine? Not quite. For notice: "Who gives to man, as he sees fit"—either salvation or damnation. This is not the wording of the Lambeth Articles, where man is predestined by "the will of the good pleasure of God."[16] But "as God sees *fit*"—*suited, appropriate*—to what? To God's eternal plan? To God's foreknowledge? To man's remorse for his sins, in some measure? Perhaps. The rest of the poem seems to indicate that this remorse may have some effect. Does the judge then consider the circumstances of man's life? Does man perhaps after all have something to do with his own salvation?

Perhaps the poem "Redemption" will be less ambiguous; it has been taken as Calvinist because the speaker receives the answer to his "suit" before he has even asked for it.[17]

Having been tenant long to a rich Lord,
        Not thriving, I resolved to be bold,
        And make a suit unto him, to afford
A new small-rented lease, and cancell th' old.
In heaven at his manour I him sought:
        They told me there, that he was lately gone
        About some land, which he had dearly bought
Long since on earth, to take possession.
I straight return'd, and knowing his great birth,

>   Sought him accordingly in great resorts;
>   In cities, theatres, gardens, parks, and courts:
>   At length I heard a ragged noise and mirth
>   Of theeves and murderers: there I him espied,
>   Who straight, *Your suit is granted*, said, & died.

But what, exactly, is the nature of the suit that has here been granted, and what is the meaning of this discovery of the Crucifixion, enacted on this earth before the speaker's eyes? The speaker has asked for a new lease that will make the payment of his rent possible, and for cancellation of the old lease that he has found impossible to pay. The old lease of course suggests the Law of the Old Testament, and the new lease the mode of redemption offered in the New Testament, the lease made possible by the sacrifice of Christ. This new lease is "small-rented"; payment will be easier, but presumably some payment on man's part remains to be made. The sonnet does not say all this, but neither does it say that the tenant is saved by irresistible grace, or that the property is granted rent-free. One should note a further possibility, in the fact that the speaker finds the Crucifixion being enacted before him. Someone such as Newman might take this to represent the eternal presence and re-enactment of the sacrifice in the Mass.[18] There is nothing in the poem to prevent a reader from reading the conclusion in this way, if his own theological presuppositions lead him to take it in this direction. But a strict Calvinist could also read it as proof of the doctrine of imputed righteousness and assume that the speaker's suit was granted in a measure beyond his asking. In such ambiguity lies the source of Herbert's popularity and acceptance by Christians of all creeds and by advocates of reader-response theory in our own day. His generous ambiguity is implicit in the words of his eucharistic "Invitation," where he seems to agree with Donne that when God says All, he means All:

>   Lord I have invited all,
>   And I shall
>   Still invite, still call to thee:
>   For it seems but just and right
>   In my sight,
>   Where is All, there All should be.

Another mode of ambiguity, or inclusive doubleness, may be found in "The Priesthood," where Herbert contemplates with awe the possibility of becoming a priest. I doubt whether a strict Calvinist would have used the term "Priesthood" so plainly and with such awe at the traditional powers attributed to that order:

> Blest Order, which in power dost so excell,
> That with th' one hand thou liftest to the sky,
> And with the other throwest down to hell
> In thy just censures; fain would I draw nigh,
> Fain put thee on, exchanging my lay-sword
>   For that of th' holy Word.

The Word of God comes first, in a way appropriate to reformed religion; interpreting and preaching the Word, carrying out the mission that descended upon the apostles in the tongues of fire—this is the awesome responsibility that first gives the speaker pause:

> But thou art fire, sacred and hallow'd fire;
> And I but earth and clay: should I presume
> To wear thy habit, and severe attire
> My slender compositions might consume.
> I am both foul and brittle; much unfit
>   To deal in holy Writ.

He begins to reassure himself with the image of the potter, who by "force of fire" makes "curious things" out of "wretched earth." Then comes the daunting thought of another great responsibility:

> But th' holy men of God such vessels are,
> As serve him up, who all the world commands:
> When God vouchsafeth to become our fare,
> Their hands convey him, who conveys their hands.
> O what pure things, most pure must those things be,
>   Who bring my God to me!

The last two lines here, as Hutchinson notes,[19] echo the fourth book of *The Imitation of Christ*, the eucharistic book, in Herbert's time usually omitted from Protestant translations. After this echo of ancient tra-

dition, Herbert views the problems that face the priesthood in this present
day, when the church seems to shake under the shocks of controversy:

> Wherefore I dare not, I, put forth my hand
> To hold the Ark, although it seem to shake
> Through th' old sinnes and new doctrines of our land.
> Onely, since God doth often vessels make
> Of lowly matter for high uses meet,
>   I throw me at his feet.

And so, by a willed act of submission, he hopes to become worthy.
The inclusive nature of Herbert's reformed theology, in its mature form,
is here fully expressed.

"But he doth bid us take his bloud for wine," cries the discontented
voice in Herbert's "Divinitie," in a slyly obtuse reversal of the usual
form of the argument over the eucharist: in what way does the wine
represent his blood? Herbert, in accord with the whole poem, dismiss-
es all such "curious questions":

> Bid what he please; yet I am sure,
> To take and taste what he doth there designe,
>   Is all that saves, and not obscure.

This will serve well as an attack on excessive doctrinal controversy—
but assertions will not solve the basic problem: what does God there
design?

Herbert wrestled with the problem,[20] first in a surprisingly clumsy
and uneasy poem found only in the early Williams manuscript: "The
H. Communion." Herbert opens by asking whether the Lord is present
in these "gifts," the bread and wine, only by his usual omnipresence,
or whether that presence is more particular, as the doctrine of transub-
stantiation argues, leaving only the appearance of bread and wine, not
their essential elements:

> O Gratious Lord how shall I know
> Whether in these gifts thou bee so
>   As thou art evry-where;
> Or rather so, as thou alone

> Tak'st all the Lodging, leaving none
>   For thy poore creature there.

He then attempts to dismiss the problem by heavy-handed sarcasm:

> First I am sure, whether bread stay
> Or whether Bread doe fly away
>   Concerneth bread not mee.
> But that both thou, and all thy traine
> Bee there, to thy truth, & my gaine
>   Concerneth mee & Thee.

But what does it mean to say that "thou, and all thy traine" are there in the sacrament? *Traine* apparently means all the traditional benefits that accompany the taking of the sacrament. The vagueness seems deliberate, for the next stanza is even more evasive.

> And if in comming to thy foes
> Thou dost come first to them, that showes
>   The hast of thy good will.

Here Herbert seems to be conceding the possibility that the Zwinglians may be right: grace comes directly to the human beings ("thy foes") taking the sacrament; grace is not mediated by the sacrament. But then the traditional view may also be right to some extent:

> Or if that thou two stations makest
> In Bread & mee, the way thou takest
>   Is more, but for me still.

That is to say, the grace or spirit of Christ may have two stopping-places; the journey is thus made longer, but the result is the same. Herbert has no doubt, however, that the doctrine of transubstantiation is wrong: he cannot believe that the physical body of Christ is really present in the sacrament, replacing the physical elements:

> Then of this also I am sure
> That thou didst all those pains endure
>   To' abolish Sinn, not Wheat.
> Creatures are good, & have their place;

> Sinn onely, which did all deface
> Thou drivest from his seat.

The remaining four stanzas do not make Herbert's position any clearer, nor does the quality of the poetry improve.

Replacing this piece in *The Temple* is quite a different work entitled "The H. Communion," a double poem, in which the first part deals subtly, delicately, and exactly with the doctrinal issues, and then the second part transforms an early poem entitled "Prayer" into an expression of gratitude for the sacrament:

> Thou hast restor'd us to this ease
> By this thy heav'nly bloud;
> Which I can go to, when I please,
> And leave th' earth to their food.

It is noteworthy that in the Williams manuscript the corresponding (final) stanza of this poem lacks this explicit reference to the restoring blood and relies instead upon the "word":

> But wee are strangers grown, o Lord,
> Lett Prayer help our losses,
> Since thou hast taught us by thy word,
> That wee may gaine by crosses.

The "ease" of the second part is guaranteed by the doctrinal security of the first part, where Herbert opens by asserting his belief that the physical elements of the Communion are endowed with some degree of divine presence and efficacy:

> Not in rich furniture, or fine aray,
> Nor in a wedge of gold,
> Thou, who for me wast sold,
> To me dost now thy self convey;
> For so thou should'st without me still have been,
> Leaving within me sinne:

> But by the way of nourishment and strength
> Thou creep'st into my breast;

> Making thy way my rest,
> And thy small quantities my length;
> Which spread their forces into every part,
> Meeting sinne's force and art.

As the rest of the poem shows, the "small quantities" are the physical particles of the bread and wine, which have an important, though limited efficacy: only the spiritual presence of Christ can penetrate to the soul:

> Yet can these not get over to my soul,
> Leaping the wall that parts
> Our souls and fleshy hearts;
> But as th'outworks, they may controll
> My rebel-flesh, and carrying thy name,
> Affright both sinne and shame.

> Onely thy grace, which with these elements comes,
> Knoweth the ready way,
> And hath the privie key,
> Op'ning the souls most subtile rooms;
> While those to spirits refin'd, at doore attend
> Dispatches from their friend.

Herbert has here created a blending of the old and the new, in a poem that moves with graceful assurance to affirm a measure of the traditional efficacy of "these elements," while reserving the indispensable place for spiritual grace "which with these elements comes." How it comes, by what means, Herbert will not debate. The gift has been given, the sacrifice has been made: should we then contend about the meaning of so generous a gift? "Could not that Wisdome, which first broacht the wine, / Have thicken'd it with definitions?" ("Divinitie")

Remembrance of that gift runs throughout *The Temple* in the many poems that celebrate the Lord's Supper and the wounds of Christ, poems that infiltrate the Calvinist tone and move the whole book toward a middle way. It is notable that those who would argue for Herbert's strongly Calvinist bias tend to underestimate the significance and frequency of the eucharistic allusions in the final version of *The Temple*, as compared with the early version. A prime example of the difference may be found in the poem that now bears the title "Church-lock and key":

> I know it is my sinne, which locks thine eares,
> > And bindes thy hands,
> Out-crying my requests, drowning my tears;
> Or else the chilnesse of my faint demands.
>
> But as cold hands are angrie with the fire,
> > And mend it still;
> So I do lay the want of my desire,
> Not on my sinnes, or coldnesse, but thy will.
>
> Yet heare, O God, onely for his blouds sake
> > Which pleads for me:
> For though sinnes plead too, yet like stones they make
> His blouds sweet current much more loud to be.

As the poem finally stands, it represents a subtle account of how the prayer of the speaker is conveyed by means of the blood of Christ into the ear of God, so that God's ear may be unlocked and his hands may be unbound to guide the soul toward its salvation. In the central stanza here the speaker seems to rebuke himself for laying this situation upon the will of God. For this speaker, through the sacrifice of Christ, the situation caused by his sin is redeemable partly through the effect of his own cries, working within the sweet current of Christ's blood.

In the Williams manuscript the poem is quite different: it is here a poem in four stanzas entitled "Prayer." An additional (second) stanza emphasizes the speaker's sinful condition by stressing his lack of "Innocence or Fervencie"; and in the final stanza the blood of Christ is not mentioned: the implication is that all depends upon the direct action of the grace of God to make the speaker either "wholy guiltles" or "at least / Guiltles so far" that his prayer, uttered in "zele and purenes," may be allowed to reach the Deity.

> I know it is my sinn, which stops thine eares
> > And binds thy hands
> Outcrying my requests, drowning my teares;

Or els the chilnes of my faint demands.

If either Innocence or Fervencie
                              Did play their part
Armies of blessings would contend & vye
Which of them soonest should attaine my hart.

Yet as cold hands are angry with the fire
                              Mending it still:
So I doe laye the want of my desire
Not on my sinns or coldnes: but thy will.

O make mee wholy guiltles, or at least
                              Guiltles so farr;
That zele and purenes circling my request
May guard it safe beyond the highest starr.

Thus Herbert appears to have undergone considerable development and change in his religious outlook from his early years at Cambridge, prime center of strict Calvinism, up through his late ordination in the Church dominated at that time (1630) by the Arminian Bishop Laud. Such a development would accord with the dating (circa 1623)[21] usually given for Herbert's sequence of Latin poems on the Passion (*Passio Discerpta*), where devotion to the wounds of Christ is closer to Crashaw's epigrams than anything else in Herbert's works. It would appear that, as Herbert's ordination in the Church approached (he was ordained deacon near the end of 1624),[22] he drew closer to the eucharist and its images.

Such a movement is suggested by many of the poems that do not appear in the Williams manuscript. Thus in "The Agonie," inserted among the opening poems of "The Church," Herbert defines the nature of Sin and Love and their meaning for mankind by asking the reader to contemplate the Agony of Christ in the Garden and the final shedding of his blood on the Cross:

> Who would know Sinne, let him repair
> Unto Mount Olivet; there shall he see
> A man so wrung with pains, that all his hair,

His skinne, his garments bloudie be.
Sinne is that presse and vice, which forceth pain
To hunt his cruell food through ev'ry vein.

Who knows not Love, let him assay
And taste that juice, which on the crosse a pike
Did set again abroach; then let him say
   If ever he did taste the like.
Love is that liquour sweet and most divine,
Which my God feels as bloud; but I, as wine.

The last line does not deny the presence of Christ in the sacrament: it refers to the sensory impression felt by all partakers of the wine, whatever their theology. Avoiding controversy, Herbert throws the stress on the restorative power of wine as a cordial: the essential aspect of the eucharist is that it constitutes a sacrament of Love. And in this way Herbert, in the last two lines, is able to bind together four of the great thematic words that help to bind together his entire *Temple*: Love, sweet, blood, wine.

Then in "Conscience," the poem that begins the major group of poems inserted into the fabric represented by the Williams manuscript (eighty pages of poems, running from "Conscience" to "The Elixir"), Herbert transmutes this prime theme of Calvinist theology into a tribute to the power of the sacrament:

And the receit shall be
My Saviours bloud: when ever at his board
I do but taste it, straight it cleanseth me,
   And leaves thee not a word;
No, not a tooth or nail to scratch,
And at my actions carp, or catch.

Nothing could pay higher tribute to Herbert's mature belief in the efficacious power of the eucharist.

John Donne too, it would seem, underwent such changes in his beliefs, more complex than anything in Herbert. In his Holy Sonnets Donne seems to be pondering, with fearful anxiety, how he might come to terms with Calvinist orthodoxy,[23] while using essentially Jesuit methods of meditation as part of his quest for a solution. But in his late sermons preached before King Charles in 1629, he had clearly adopted an Arminian, anti-Calvinist position. In his second sermon on the Image of God he argues from the principle that the other creatures live under a law of necessity, but man, he says,

> lives under another manner of law; This you shall doe; that is, this you should doe, this I would have you doe; And *fac hoc*, doe this, and you shall live; disobey, and you shall die. But yet, the choise is yours: Choose ye this day life, or death. . . . In man [God's] administration is this, that he hath imprinted in him a faculty of will, and election; and so hath something to reward in him. . . . the free will of man God visites, and assists with his grace to doe supernaturall things.

He then goes on to discuss the operations of the three powers of the soul, memory, understanding, and will, those faculties which, according to the ancient principle of Augustine, constitute the interior trinity which is the Image of God in man. But Donne deals with the faculties in an unusual order, equating the will with the attribute of the second person of the Trinity, the Son of God, "which is Wisdome," for wisdom, says Donne, "is not so much in knowing, in understanding, as in electing, in choosing, in assenting." So important is the point that he repeats it: "Wisdome is in choosing, in Assenting."

> Make thine understanding, and thy will, and thy memory (though but naturall faculties) serviceable to thy God; and auxiliary and subsidiary for thy salvation. For, though they be not naturally instruments of grace; yet naturally they are susceptible of grace, and have so much in their nature, as that by grace they may be made instruments of grace: which no faculty in any creature, but man, can be. And doe not thinke that because a naturall man cannot doe all, therefore he hath nothing to doe for himselfe.[24]

All these terms, free will, choosing, assenting, reward, indicate a firmly Arminian view, and represent Donne's way of responding to mankind's natural tendency to believe that there must be *something* that he or she can do to assist in the work of salvation.

George Herbert seems to have reached a similar position, for a similar view of free will, choice, assent, and even reward, lies within the poem "Obedience," which appears in the Williams manuscript.[25] Here the legal imagery of contract and agreement between two parties implies two wills that must agree before the transaction can be successful.[26] The legal image is carried through from beginning to end, with subtle variations in attitude, but no basic change in the theological assumptions. Herbert begins, in his familiar way, by taking this very poem as a document by which the speaker agrees to transfer possession of his whole being to God:

> My God, if writings may
> Convey a Lordship any way
> Whither the buyer and the seller please;
> Let it not thee displease,
> If this poor paper do as much as they.
>
> On it my heart doth bleed
> As many lines, as there doth need
> To passe it self and all it hath to thee.
> To which I do agree,
> And here present it as my speciall Deed.
>
> If that hereafter Pleasure
> Cavill, and claim her part and measure,
> As if this passed with a reservation,
> Or some such words in fashion;
> I here exclude the wrangler from thy treasure.

Having thus agreed to "convey" himself to God, he now goes on to beg God to complete his part of the bargain, to make possible the conformity of man's will with God's will—the traditional aim of Augustinian Christianity:

> O let thy sacred will
> All thy delight in me fulfill!
> Let me not think an action mine own way,
> But as thy love shall sway,

Resigning up the rudder to thy skill.

Lord, what is man to thee,
That thou shouldst minde a rotten tree?
Yet since thou canst not choose but see my actions;
So great are thy perfections,
Thou mayst as well my actions guide, as see.

The thought of God's love has led to the thought of man's unworthiness, and from there to a rather whimsical argument based on the reality of God's power and omnipresence. Then, with a wry effect of associative afterthought, remembrance of Christ's sacrifice begins to guide the poem's movement:

Besides, thy death and bloud
Show'd a strange love to all our good:
Thy sorrows were in earnest; no faint proffer,
Or superficiall offer
Of what we might not take, or be withstood.

The last line here is difficult, perhaps even deliberately ambiguous. By itself it might be taken to indicate an offer that could not be "withstood"—an irresistible offer. But the whole stanza, and indeed the whole poem, will not support such a reading. He is talking about a "faint proffer," a "superficiall offer" that is not really meant to be accepted, and thus is hedged with conditions of things "we might not take," that is, things not included in the offer; if we attempted to take them, such efforts would "be withstood," and the negotiations would fail.[27] Christ's "sorrows were in earnest"—offering a contract of quite a different sort, seriously meant, and offered "in earnest" also in the legal sense of payment made to guarantee the fulfillment of an agreement, with the additional figurative sense suggested by the *OED*: "A foretaste, installment, pledge, of anything afterwards to be received in greater abundance."

"Wherefore," the speaker says in the following stanza, "I all forgo:" with only one stipulation: "To one word onely I say, No":

Where in the Deed there was an intimation

Of a gift or donation,
Lord, let it now by way of purchase go.

The speaker is here clarifying the terms of the Deed, to avoid any possibility of misunderstanding. He has spoken at the outset of the "buyer and the seller," but perhaps in the second stanza and the third there has been an implication that the speaker is making a gift. The memory of Christ's sorrows reminds him that the price for the "land" has already been offered; all that remains is for the seller to accept the price. And so he agrees, with the thought that this "paper" may stand as an example for others to follow, bringing benefits both to the writer of the Deed and to future followers of the same writing:

He that will passe his land,
As I have mine, may set his hand
And heart unto this Deed, when he hath read;
And make the purchase spread
To both our goods, if he to it will stand.

We are entering here into a world where one human being can receive "good" by providing a good example for another; this is perilously close to the ancient idea of reward! In any case, the hoped-for follower clearly lives in the world of the conditional "if"—he must choose whether or not to stand by such a Deed.

How happie were my part,
If some kinde man would thrust his heart
Into these lines; till in heav'ns Court of Rolls
They were by winged souls
Entred for both, farre above their desert!

Vaughan, in his famous response ("The Match"), shows himself to be that well-disposed and kindred spirit by declaring: "Here I joyn hands, and thrust my stubborn heart / Into thy *Deed*." This too is an act of human choice, an act of assent. Vaughan understood "Obedience" perfectly.

Finally, perhaps the clearest, certainly one of the most audacious, dramatizations of Herbertian theology is found in the witty poem

"Judgement," which appears near the close in both versions of *The Temple.* Here the speaker, pondering his future in the presence of God, calmly plans what he will choose to do on Judgement Day, when asked to present his "book" of accounts:

> Almightie Judge, how shall poore wretches brook
>   Thy dreadfull look,
>   Able a heart of iron to appall,
>   When thou shalt call
>   For ev'ry mans peculiar book?
>
> What others mean to do, I know not well;
>   Yet I heare tell,
>   That some will turn thee to some leaves therein
>   So void of sinne,
>   That they in merit shall excell.

The familiar ("I heare tell") manner of speech suggests his lack of real fear at the prospect, while his droll jibe at those who are, according to rumor, planning to rely on their good works ("merit") implies his firm Protestant affiliation. But now he reveals what he will choose to do at the "dreadfull" juncture: he will "decline" to present his own book of accounts and instead will turn the tables on the Judge by presenting him with a Book that will remind the Judge that he has taken upon himself the sins of the world:

> But I resolve, when thou shalt call for mine,
>   That to decline,
>   And thrust a Testament into thy hand:
>   Let that be scann'd.
>   There thou shalt finde my faults are thine.

Only someone speaking in the presence of a Friend could think of such a witty manoeuver; this is not the awesome Absolute of the Calvinist predestinarian. Yet a strict Calvinist could read the poem with satisfaction, for it makes Christ the sole agent of redemption. But then so could any Protestant, for the poem's witty theology says only that this speaker relies upon Christ to be his Savior. And indeed, the wit of Herbert's second stanza is so slyly hyperbolic that it tends to make the reader say, "Not me"; for who, in any church, would wish to be counted among those who commit the sin of pride by claiming to "excel" in "merit"? Thus even at the Day of Doom Herbert's imagination manages to maintain its attractive generosity.

Notes

1. John Henry Newman, *Tracts for the Times. Remarks on Certain Passages in the Thirty-nine Articles*. No. 90. 4th ed., rev. (London: Rivington, 1842), 12–13, 43–46.
2. Newman, 81–82.
3. See Barbara Kiefer Lewalski, *Protestant Poetics and the Seventeenth-Century Religious Lyric* (Princeton: Princeton University Press, 1979); A. D. Nuttall, *Overheard by God: Fiction and Prayer in Herbert, Milton, Dante and St John* (London and New York: Methuen, 1980); and Richard Strier, *Love Known: Theology and Experience in George Herbert's Poetry* (Chicago: University of Chicago Press, 1983).
4. Charles H. George and Katherine George, *The Protestant Mind of the English Reformation, 1570–1640* (Princeton: Princeton University Press, 1961).
5. See H. C. Porter, *Reformation and Reaction in Tudor Cambridge* (Cambridge: Cambridge University Press, 1958); Peter Lake, *Moderate Puritans and the Elizabethan Church* (Cambridge: Cambridge University Press, 1982), esp. Chap. 9 on "The theological disputes of the 1590s"; and the essay by Nicholas Tyacke, "Puritanism, Arminianism and Counter-Revolution," in *The Origins of the English Civil War*, ed. Conrad Russell (London: MacMillan, 1973). Tyacke's essay is especially important for the era of George Herbert, when, as Tyacke says, "English Arminians came to balance their rejection of the arbitrary grace of predestination with a new found source of grace freely available in the sacraments, which Calvinists had belittled" (130).
6. The articles were originally in Latin; I quote the translation by H. C. Porter, p. 371. See Porter's Chapter 16 for a full account of the genesis of the Lambeth Articles.
7. See Claire Cross, *The Royal Supremacy in the Elizabethan Church* (London: Allen and Unwin, 1969), 205–6.
8. Cross, 206–7.
9. Charles and Katherine George, 63–65.
10. Josias Nichols, *The Plea of the Innocent* (1602), 219–20. Patrick Collinson, *The Religion of Protestants* (Oxford: Clarendon Press, 1982), 202.
11. Compare William Perkins, *A Golden Chaine* (Cambridge, 1597), 201: discussing, among other texts, the two that Donne here cites, Perkins argues, "We may

understand by (*all*) of all sorts some, not every singuler person of all sorts." This is part of his Chapter 54, devoted to refuting "a new devised doctrine of Predestination, taught by some new and late Divines."

12. John Donne, *Sermons*, ed. George R. Potter and Evelyn M. Simpson, 10 vols. (Berkeley: University of California Press, 1953–62), 5:53–4. The sermon is based on the text of Acts 10:44: "While Peter yet spake these words, the Holy Ghost fell on all them, which heard the Word." The editors conjecture that it may be dated between 1618 and 1621.

13. The arguments for an early dating, beyond the extensive revision performed upon some poems, have been set forth by Amy Charles in the Introduction to the facsimile of the Williams MS published by Scholars' Facsimiles & Reprints, Delmar, N.Y., 1977.

14. See Charles and Katherine George, 64.

15. See, for example, the above-cited books by Lewalski (286) and Strier (85), and my review of Joseph Summers's *George Herbert* in the *George Herbert Journal* 5 (1981–82): 80, where I accepted this view.

16. H. C. Porter (369) notes that the phrase signifying "absolute and simple will of God" was modified during the course of composing the Lambeth Articles "to 'the will of the good pleasure of God,' *voluntas beneplaciti Dei*, a phrase which echoed not Calvin but St. Paul: 'Having predestinated us unto the adoption of children by Jesus Christ to himself, according to the good pleasure of his will'" (Ephesians 1:5).

17. See Nuttall, 33–34.

18. I owe this suggestion to Kathleen Lynch, a member of my recent seminar at the Folger Library.

19. *The Works of George Herbert*, ed. F. E. Hutchinson (Oxford: Clarendon Press, 1941), 534. All quotations from Herbert are taken from this edition, except for poems from the Williams MS, which have been based upon the facsimile cited in note 13, with "u" and "v" normalized and the initial "ff" recorded as "F," since the doubling of "f" is the normal way of indicating a capital "F" in Renaissance manuscripts.

20. See the essay by Jeanne Clayton Hunter, "'With Winges of Faith': Herbert's Communion Poems," *Journal of Religion* 62 (1982): 57–71.

21. See Amy Charles, *A Life of George Herbert* (Ithaca, N.Y.: Cornell University Press, 1977), 92–93; and *The Latin Poetry of George Herbert*, trans. Mark McCloskey and Paul R. Murphy (Athens: Ohio University Press, 1965), 178–79.

22. Charles, *Life of Herbert*, 112–17. Such a development corresponds with the rise of Arminianism within the Church of England: according to Tyacke this movement began to gain strength about 1610, though "as early as 1605 the views of Arminius were being cited with approval by anti-Calvinists in Cambridge." See esp. pp. 130–33 of Tyacke's essay, cited above, note 5. Calvinist domination, which had endured for about sixty years, was breaking up during the 1620s, especially after the accession of Charles in 1625.

23. See Lewalski, 264–73.

24. Donne, *Sermons*, ed. Potter and Simpson, IX, 75, 84–85.

25. See the different interpretation by Strier, 91–96.

26. See Bernard Kneiger, "The Purchase-Sale: Patterns of Business Imagery in the Poetry of George Herbert," *Studies in English Literature* 6 (1966): 111–24.

27. This interpretation seems to be reinforced by the Williams MS, which has no comma after "take": "Of what we might not take or be withstood."

The Two Endings of George Herbert's "The Church"

SIDNEY GOTTLIEB

The Williams Manuscript (*W*) of George Herbert's poems has most often been used to study the development of his craftsmanship. Even a quick look at the revisions in the poems and their order gives convincing evidence of Herbert's growing mastery of a variety of poetic skills. But this needs to be supplemented by a consideration of what may well be important doctrinal or at least temperamental and emotional changes in Herbert—or the persona he presents—that become visible when we compare the early and later arrangement of his lyrics. The fact that a substantial number of the poems at the beginning and end of "The Church" in *W* are also clustered in basically the same places in the later arrangement (in the Bodleian Manuscript [*B*] and the first printed edition of 1633) has led many critics to emphasize only the continuity between the two versions of "The Church." Richard Strier, for example, suggests that the opening and closing sequences "remained virtually constant through Herbert's enlargements and revision of his manuscript."[1] Amy Charles notices but downplays the differences; she concludes that "it is beyond question that the same basic order prevails in *W* and in *B* . . . When *W* was revised and became the basis of *B*, the original plan was retained as the foundation of a volume re-ordered, expanded, corrected, and refined."[2] But *W* is more than simply a rough draft containing the later sequence in outline or miniature form: it is a highly articulated volume representing Herbert's poetic techniques and ideas at a particular stage in his career. More attention needs to be paid to how the re-orderings, expansions, corrections, and refinements dramatically and substantively alter the way Herbert opens and, more to my present point, closes "The Church."[3]

A comparative reading of the two endings of "The Church," encompassing the last dozen or so poems in *W* and in the first printed edition, reveals a remarkable shift in focus and philosophy. To summarize briefly: in the later version we see a less imperious, more gentle and familiar God; instead of severity, legalism, sermonizing, and stiffness in the verse, there is a new emphasis on allowable pleasure, and playfulness, confidence, humor, and an overall awakening of the senses; certain strict notions of proper behavior and troublesome themes and catchwords are eliminated, and a deep sense of unworthiness and corresponding self-abasement give way to at least a tentative portrayal of the importance of human assent and action without denying one's basic dependence on God; there are more frequent uses of sacramental imagery and allusions to texts (such as the *Book of Common Prayer* and the *Imitation of Christ*) that establish a "high" rather than a "low" church context for these poems, and the quick and disturbing shifts in tone and mood so much in evidence in *W* are smoothed out as man's hope for perfection is no longer undermined.

These changes in Herbert's "sense of an ending" are worth taking into account not only in any analysis of the shape and structure of *The Temple*, but also in any study of the theological underpinnings of Herbert's poetry. We must not of course forget that the poems in question are lyric and dramatic artifacts, not direct statements of religious beliefs. Nevertheless, a comparison of the two endings of "The Church" may shed some light on the topic that is more and more interesting modern critics, Herbert's relationship—and I would suggest his shifting relationship—to two styles of religious belief and expression that we may call, for lack of better terms, Puritanism and Anglicanism.[4]

Let us first examine, however briefly, the poems that comprise the ending of "The Church" in *W*. The somber poem "Mortification" sets the tone for much of what follows, and unforgettably illustrates one of Herbert's important concluding themes. The opening exclamation "How soone does Man decay!" becomes the motto for a series of naked emblems detailing how each stage of life reinforces a single lesson, the insistent connection of "breath" and "death." Each stanza envisions a dramatic transformation of life into death, and Herbert very subtly makes the reader experience these transformations intimately. In the first few stanzas, the repeated reference to "them" keeps the reader somewhat distant from the subjects bound for death. But references in the next few stanzas to "his" and "him," individual and personal pronouns, reinforce the applicability of these scenes to the reader. The fact that we are each involved in the drama presented here is clinched by a sudden personal turn in the conclusion, one of Herbert's characteristic techniques which will also appear in the following poem: "Yet Lord, instruct *us* so to dye, / That all these dyings may be life in Death" (35–36; emphasis added).[5] Helen Vendler, underestimating the omnipresence of the *memento mori* tradition in the early seventeenth century, perhaps overstates the shock effect of the poem: "The grim metaphors of 'Mortification' are deliberately repugnant to common feeling: the preacher is imposing on his audience a blighted private vision."[6] The "solemnitie" put together by Herbert in this poem is not as intimidating as Vendler suggests; William Ames, for example, like many other Protestant divines, defined mortification technically as the "wasting away of sin," the first stage of the process of sanctification, a necessary prelude to vivification and glorification.[7] But for all its attempt to encourage human mastery of death,[8] "Mortification" is chilling and sobering, not triumphant or engaging.

The sermonizing tone and style of "Mortification" continue in "The Publican," where the main text expounded upon is simple and sad: "Man is a foolish thing, a foolish thing" (2)—a rare bit of repetition in Herbert, establishing not an emblematic wreath-like circle of perfection but rather a quick dead end. According to the sin-obsessed and over-righteous speaker, man is unwilling to hold up his end of the covenant, "The bargaine made to serve thee" (26). Thus, instead of praising God, man is hardly fit to serve the swine. "How shal infection / Presume on thy perfection?" (35–36) is one of the most strongly worded accusations in all of Herbert's poetry, and it rings in our ears throughout the concluding poems, especially "Perfection." The overwhelming force of the speaker's descriptions of man's unworthiness, weakness, and "strange pollutions" (13), elaborated in a poem that is unusually long for Herbert, is not mitigated even when the speaker is unmasked in the final lines as a Pharisee.[9] The concluding look within—"My God, I meane my selfe"—is honest and courageous, especially in a poem that seems to deny the possibility of even a glimmer of self-knowledge (cf. stanzas 9–11). This confession however does not cancel, but rather extends the range of the indictment of man as a "lump of flesh" (74): one more sinner acknowledges his corruption.

It is tempting to see the "easy quick access" to God at the opening of "Prayer" (II) as a consequence of the humble confession that closes "The Publican," but Herbert does not make this connection clear. Instead, "Prayer" (II) seems to be the first of several sudden interruptions or quick changes of mood evident in the concluding sequence in *W*. Quite in contrast to "The Publican," man now seems capable of dedicated service to God, and if he is but willing to lift his eyes in prayer, his "suit is made" (5). Perhaps echoing "The Publican," life is still described as "silly houre" (10) (interestingly, this is revised to "measur'd houre" when "Prayer" (II) no longer directly follows "The Publican," retitled "Miserie," in the later arrangement) but if man will renounce human attachments and achievements—"Wealth, fame, endowments, vertues, all should goe" (22)—he gains, not loses, by relying on God's "*Ease, Power,* and *Love*" (20).

The next few poems continue to develop the important and related themes of obedient service to God and renunciation of self. "Obedience" is written in the form of a legal contract to certify that the persona is willing to forswear all his pleasures, possessions, and ambitions in order to "lett thy sacred will / All thy delyte in me fulfill" (16–17). Man is described as ineradicably corrupt, "a rotten tree" (22), yet this proves to be almost inconsequential: it is precisely this "self" that is "passed" (8), resigned to "thy love," "thy skill," "thy perfections." As comforting as it may be, though, the complete renunciation of one's self is difficult to accomplish, and even as the speaker announces his obedience to God he almost instinctively tries to reclaim some power of his own. By his own admission, God cannot be "withstood" (30), yet he resists, for a moment, one article in the new contract, offering to give something in return to God: another man, similarly obedient.

The wish "How happy were my part / If some kind man would thrust his hart / Into these lines" (41–43) is poignant and well-intentioned (as Vaughan would attest), but also somewhat inappropriate. "Obedience" concludes by gently but emphatically reminding the speaker that human entrance into heaven, while a possibility, is "farr aboue their desert" (45). Several poems later, in "Perseverance," Herbert may very well want the reader to recall the conclusion of "Obedience" as he again questions the value of any human action, suggesting that even if one's "words / Shal help another" (5–6), they may literally blow up in one's face.

"Invention" continues the theme of writing from "Obedience" and further suggests that self-reliance is improper in aesthetic as well as moral matters. Like the classical and Renaissance rhetoricians — but unlike their more modern counterparts — Herbert defines true invention as a process of discovery rather than creation, and as in "The Publican" one's self is shown to be an undesirable obstacle to finding and serving God. Ironically, acceptable poetry and service begin only when the pointless hustle and bustle of human activity end, and though we should be careful not to accept it too quickly as a final and complete statement of Herbert's theory of poetry, this theme links "Invention" closely to the surrounding poems in W, which similarly dramatize the radical and often frustrating inequality of man and God. As difficult as its lesson is, though, "Invention" is a gentle and comforting poem, humbling but not humiliating, and by this point in the concluding sequence the required renunciation of the self seems more and more possible, acceptable, and even desirable. Who would not be swayed by a "friend" whispering:

> How wide is all this preparation!
> There is in love a sweetnes readie pennd:
> Coppy out that: there needs no alteration.
>
> (16–18)

"Perfection," a pivotal text in the sequence, follows and directly responds to the previous poems. The short lines here, contrasted with the long, winding lines used (and criticized) in "Invention," suggest that the advice to write in a simple and honest way has been adopted, and the opening stanza virtually rewrites the conclusion of the previous poem as a plea:

> Lord teach mee to referr
> All things I doe to thee
> That I not onely may not erre
> But allso pleasing bee[10]

Here human activity seems, for the moment, worthwhile and allowable as long as it is directed by and toward God, and there is great power in this service:

> A man that looks on glass
> On it may stay his eye:
> Or if he pleaseth, through it pass
> And then the Heav'en espy.
>
> (5–8)

The ambiguity of the phrase "if he pleaseth" is particularly heartening (although at the end of the poem it appears to have been misleading): man's will and God's judgment seem equally balanced, and whether or not man gains a glimpse of heaven is determined by his desire to do so as much as by God's evaluation of whether he is pleasing or not. The poem continues to make greater and greater claims. An earthly life of service is secure, as man is personally protected from the inevitable attacks of the devil (stanza 3), and pleasurable, as even "drudgerie" becomes "divine" (18), and we rise again quickly to the prospect of heaven:

> All may of thee pertake:
> Nothing can be so low,
> Which with his tincture (for thy sake)
> Will not to Heauen grow.
>
> (13–16)

However the vision of the transporting and transforming power of human action, powerfully conveyed by the alchemical figure, is only apparently climactic. The real conclusion of the poem is shocking and unexpected, even in a work by a poet whose endings frequently reverse his beginnings. Suddenly cut off from "perfections," the most man can now dare is to stand honestly before God, naked and virtually humiliated:

But these are high perfections:
Happy are they that dare
Lett in the Light to all their actions
And show them as they are.

The last stanza of "Perfection" marks a jarring interruption of an action that has been developing throughout this series of poems, as the persona seemed to be moving, however tentatively, from earth to heaven, from corruption to perfection, from self-abasement to fulfillment through divinely guided and supported activity. But this is not to say that here we catch Herbert "nodding." It is likely at this place in the concluding sequence that he means to remind his readers of something like the following: that, as John T. McNeill summarizes, "men are zealously to be urged to seek perfection; but the persuasion that they have attained it is a 'diabolical invention.'" The thought and final words are Calvin's, and they echo throughout the theological writings of the period, particularly those of the Puritans.[11]

The two poems that follow "Perfection" continue in the same discouraging way. Far from being in a position of calm confidence, the speaker of "The Knell" is an overwrought "servant" (2), a "perplexed Soule" (2) left "Strugling on th' hook" (6). God seems distant from man, and the resulting vulnerability is expressed with frightening intensity by a nearly hysterical, hallucinatory style more common to Donne than Herbert:

O help, my God!
See, they breake in
Disbanded humours, sorrows, troops of Sinn,
Each with his rodd.

(9–12)

The best one can do is "call on thee / ffor some relief" (17–18), but "Perseverance" immediately undermines even this source of comfort. In place of the "easy quick access" (1) of man to god via prayer ("Prayer" [II]) and the assurance that man's writings are aided by God ("Invention") and might at least help ratify their close connection ("Obedience"), "these my words" (5) in "Perseverance" are only "poore expressions of my Love" (1) and seem powerless to make God any less inscrutable to or distant from a suffering sinner. At this point in the sequence Herbert is apparently unable to accept the Reformation idea of the perseverance of grace, but neither is he able to leave off his attempt to penetrate this mystery.[12] Ironically, what perseveres in this poem is a sense of sinfulness, weakness, and doubt, and in the concluding stanza the speaker is reduced to infantile, if not hysterical, "clinging vnto thy brest / Clinging and crying, crying without cease" (14–15). The psalmic phrases that are the substance of his cries—"Thou art my rock, thou art my rest" (16)—perhaps look forward to but do not bring him any relief within the borders of this poem.

There is thus a disturbing split in the sequence: the earlier poems harshly censure man's prideful independence but then attempt to replace it with dignified dependence; the latter poems, however, picture man as ineffectual and panic stricken. It may well be that Herbert's plan was to put a sudden stop to man's far-reaching and perhaps premature confidence, and return the reader to a more sober perspective from which to contemplate the final and most important themes of life. Yet this sobriety is short-lived. The poems that follow "Perseverance" are joyous, hopeful, and reinstate man's strength and, above all, closeness to God.

"Death," for example, is remarkably optimistic. Like "Mortification," but in a far less ominous manner, it suggests that because of God's intervention death comes to life and is "Much in request, much long'd for as a good" (16). This readiness to welcome death accounts for the sense of urgency in "Dooms-day," as man is repeatedly invited to "Come away" and join in a heavenly chorus. Then in "Judgement" a potentially frightening situation—man's inability to justify himself—is resolved by a witty reversal: when God calls for "evry man's peculiar Book" (5) the speaker declines and offers instead God's own book, which promises that Judgment Day will be an occasion of mercy, not terror. And in the following poem, we see that there is sacred as well as human wit. Written as an echo poem, "Heaven" is structured so that even without the paraphernalia of alchemy or religious ritual, man's doubts and questions are instantly turned into comforting answers. For a moment at the close of "Perfection" it seemed as though heaven was the illusion and "drudgerie" the only reality for man; this is reversed in "Heaven" as "cares and businesse" fade while pleasure and leisure last forever (17–18).

Finally, particularly after a series of poems that describe man more or less stumbling toward heaven, it is infinitely refreshing to reach "Love" (III) and its tale of fully consummated holy love: "You must sitt downe, sayes Love, and tast my meat / So I did sitt and eat" (17–18). As in several of the preceding poems, Herbert once again affirms "I will serve thee" (16), but in fact it is God who serves him. Man is the favored guest, not a low, unworthy servant, and the meal he shares with God confirms their intimacy.

While even in the Williams Manuscript "The Church" ends somewhat triumphantly, the hesitancy and unevenness of the conclusion are unmistakable, and may reflect the fact that Herbert was still at that time struggling, not altogether successfully, with some blend of theological and personal strictness and insecurity, wrestling with the kind of severe understanding of God and human incapacity that we usually associate with Puritanism. The revised conclusion seems to show Herbert at a much different stage of development.

Interestingly, the revisions begin in the Williams Manuscript itself, where "Perfection" is marked over with corrections in Herbert's own hand. Helen C. White, Charles Molesworth, and Camille Wells Slights makes particularly valuable comments on the changes in the poem, but each seems to subscribe to Mary Ellen Rickey's general claim that in his revisions Herbert "did not, of course, completely reverse either his thinking or the exercise of his craft."[13] On the contrary, the revisions in "Perfection" and the re-ordering of the concluding sequence disclose a substantial change of heart and mind. One of the most crucial changes occurs even in *W* as the final stanza of "Perfection" is crossed out. The new conclusion fulfills rather than overturns the optimism of the earlier stanzas:

> This is the famous stone
> That turneth all to gold
> For that which God doth touch and owne
> Can not for less be told.[14]

The original version describes an alchemical process that fails, but in the revised version, retitled "The Elixir," Herbert no longer flees from the alchemical image and the promise it offers of achieved perfection. God is close, not "high" and far away; in fact he "touches" and "owns" us, and this contact insures that a power even greater than that of the legendary philosopher's stone can work in the daily life of every Christian acting "for thy sake." J. F. H. New uses "The Elixir" as "an illustration of the strain of perfectionism in Anglicanism in contrast to the characteristic Puritan emphasis on human depravity."[15] Ironically, the original version of the poem would illustrate exactly the opposite.[16] The textual revisions in *W* completely erase the split that is so glaring in the first version of the poem and make "The Elixir" more coherent, positive, and fully developed. But Herbert is of course not yet finished. The same motives that prompted the revisions in "Perfection" most likely led Herbert to reconstruct the entire concluding sequence, a process that we should now quickly examine.

Although some elements of the original conclusion are preserved, the revised conclusion begins with a series of poems that do not appear anywhere in *W* and may have been written specifically to fill this place.[17] Several of the new poems are in some ways functionally analogous to the old poems, but the differences are even more striking. "The Rose," like "Mortification," warns men against living too intensely in the physical world, which "biteth in the close" (24), but the argument is engaging rather than intimidating because it is expressed via a gentle emblem and loving gestures rather than sobering *memento mori*. The speaker is calm and self-assured, and we sense that his refusal of "pleasure here" (5) and "Worldly joyes" (26) stems from an awareness of pleasure, joy, and beauty awaiting him elsewhere, a theme developed further in later poems. The fact that he is capable of moderation (stanza 1) and responsible judgment—"But I health, not physick choose" (29)—suggests that he has an erected, not dismally infected, wit and will.

For this reason, as we see in the following poem, "Discipline" can be "gentle" (4). God's tremendous power is acknowledged, but he is identified primarily as the figure of Love, who can work on willing man without rod and wrath. The speaker is well aware that man "frailties hath" (30), and that every human action must be divinely supported: "Not a word or look / I affect to own, / But by book, / And thy book alone" (9–12). Still, however weak it seems in comparison to God's sacrifice for our sake, man's attempt to meet God at least part of the way by exercising his will and affections—"I aspire / To a full consent. . . . Though I fail, I weep: / Though I halt in pace, / Yet I creep / To the throne of grace" (7–8; 13–16)—counts for something.

By stressing the power of love and showing how God's bowing to man is answered by man's creeping humbly to God, "Discipline" anticipates the final meeting in "Love" (III). We may recall that "Love" (III) is curiously unsupported and unprepared for by the preceding poems in the Williams Manuscript; such is no longer the case in the revised conclusion. "The Invitation," for example, introduces the scene of a heavenly meal at which God is both an honored guest and the substance of the feast. The poem is aimed particularly at men of various pleasures "whom joy / Doth destroy" (19–20); the alternative is not to withdraw into asceticism, however, but to choose one's pleasures more carefully. By using sacramental imagery (which remains prominent until the end of "The Church") Herbert assures all that wine, joy, and love are essential, not alien, to religious experience, and he focuses on the almost indescribable bliss of a celebration which one may share not only with God but also with a larger, more inclusive community to whom the possibility of grace is proffered.[18]

Much in contrast with the austerity of the poems at the close of "The Church" in *W*, the new concluding poems dramatize a continual purifying and awakening of the senses. In "The Banquet," for example, obviously paired with "The Invitation," ecstatic "delight" is not incompatible with moderation and restraint—"neatnesse" (4), to use Herbert's word. Barely beneath the surface of both poems lies a gentle spirituality akin to the *Imitation of Christ*, based on a conviction, proved on the pulses, "That God is sweet above all things and in all things, to the soul that loves Him."[19] In "The Banquet," the Incarnation and Crucifixion, often terrifying and intimidating mysteries, are resolved into a more homely and comforting form—similar to Herbert's technique in "Discipline" with the figure of God as Justice—and via the sacramental ceremony are presented as means of perfuming man's heart and raising him to a face to face intimacy with God.

Yet man too plays a role in this elevating action. Perhaps the last lines here—"Hearken under pain of death, / Hands and breath; / Strive in this, and love the strife"—intentionally recall "The Water-course," usually cited as an example of Herbert's fundamental Calvinism, but only to go beyond its rather foreboding conclusion. The message there is that love of life is equated with love of strife, and the best man can hope for is to adore God via remorseful tears; God remains distant from man, and his distribution of salvation and damnation remains inscrutable and unaffected by human actions. At the conclusion of "The Banquet," however, those who "love the strife," who attempt through prayer and song to acknowledge "the wonder of his pitie" (49), participate in an effectual action that takes them upward.

"The Posie" continues to develop the theme of writing introduced in the final stanza of "The Banquet," a theme that Herbert also focuses on in virtually the same place in the original concluding sequence. But the differences between "Invention" and "The Posie" are striking. Stated most simply, the drama presented in "Invention" has long been resolved for the speaker of "The Posie": he stands apart from all the tempting contests of wit, and when the holy voice enters into his poem it is not a lesson or correction but a repeated affirmation he is in no danger of forgetting or disregarding. The evasive hustle and bustle so evident in the earlier poem can be stilled by a simple injunction—"Invention rest" (9)—because of the submission implicit in his posie: "Lesse than the least / Of all Gods mercies" (11–12). Anyone who may be liable to read this as a motto of self-abasement would do well to recall the full context of these words from Genesis 30:10 (explicated, for example, in a magnificent sermon by Donne), where it is clear that the emphasis is on how bountiful God has been to Jacob, his servant.[20]

Whereas "The Posie" shows that secular wit is inferior to even the simplest devotional phrase, the following poem, "A Parodie," suggests that such wit may be redirected and transformed. Throughout the new concluding sequence, Herbert's impulse has been to integrate rather than separate, to accept rather than spurn, to salvage rather than abandon, and writing a parody is akin to those actions.[21] What is only fashionable hyperbole in speaking of a Petrarchan mistress becomes literal truth when God seems withdrawn from sight: "No stormie night / Can so afflict or so affright, / As thy eclipsed light" (13–15). At first glance, "A Parodie" appears to be a disturbing and discordant poem in a sequence that is otherwise consistently cheerful and elevating. Strier notes that especially in the final stanza "Herbert dramatizes how far toward desperation God will allow the regenerate to fall,"[22] but this desperation seems attenuated when we compare "A Parodie" with such a poem as "Perseverance" in the original concluding sequence. The distressing scenes in "A Parodie" are presented only to be overcome. Unlike a typical love lyric, with its tale of continuing pain and unfulfillment, a sacred re-enactment and transformation of a secular lyric can and, Herbert seems to suggest, even must end happily. We feel calmed, but hardly surprised when the poem ends with "but while I grieve, / Thou com'st and doth relieve."

The transforming action of "A Parodie" leads directly into "The Elixir," which in its further revised form, including changes beyond those introduced in *W*, radiates an even more thorough-going confidence and assurance well suited to the new concluding sequence. The formality and timidity of the original opening lines disappear in favor of a more familiar style, a strong sense of the immediacy of God, and a positive desire to do good, not just avoid error:

> Teach me, my God and King,
> In all things thee to see,
> And what I do in any thing,
> To do it as for thee.

The second stanza is entirely new:

> Not rudely as a beast,
> To runne into an action;
> But still to make thee prepossest,
> And give it his perfection.

Interestingly, these lines re-introduce the word "perfection" which was so troublesome in the original version of the poem, and was avoided in the intermediate revision in W.[23] Here, far from being problematic, "perfection" encourages man; he can share it with God. This new stanza seems particularly indebted to the *Book of Common Prayer.* Even in the *W* version "The Elixir" (or "Perfection") may owe something to the Collect for Peace, and its claim that the service of God is "perfect freedom."[24] In the new stanza Herbert is perhaps echoing with some modifications the Collect for Grace: "grant that this day we fall into no sinne, nor runn into any kind of danger, but that all our doings may be ordered by thy governance, to do always that is righteous in thy sight: through Jesus Christ our lord."[25]

The final stanzas of "The Elixir" are not changed but are more forceful because of the way they are supported by the preceding poems. The key statement "All may of thee partake," for example, clearly recalls "The Invitation" and is further reinforced by a series of references to sacramental imagery in other poems. As in almost all the earlier poems, God is physically present, and as a result the note of joy is never far from the surface of "The Elixir." When God "touches" man at the conclusion of the poem Herbert compresses several important themes that have run through the entire sequence: God tests and judges man, as with a touchstone, but this "touch" is also a loving embrace that transforms us into something very valuable indeed.

When Herbert crossed out the original conclusion to "The Elixir" in *W* and rewrote the ending, he may have immediately projected a further change: "The Knell" and "Perseverance" would both seem quite out of place after a poem about man's wondrous transformation. As we might expect, these two disturbing and uneasy poems are excluded from the new conclusion, and in their place we find "A Wreath," which, like "The Elixir," shows how the poet's work and life may be transformed into a "crown of praise" (12) when "my wayes" (3) become "thy wayes" (10).

The final poems in the sequence are left unchanged, but they are strengthened because the poems that introduce them represent an unwavering, positive thrust toward heaven. "Death" seems to ring even more confidently with the promise of a new life after a series of poems that dramatize man's decisive action to live according to God. The call "Come away" in "Dooms-day" is even more welcome now as it recalls the similar appeal in "The Invitation" that precedes a glorious banquet.

And "Heaven" states clearly what all the previous poems hint: that "delight" is man's rightful province. But of these concluding poems, it is "Love" (III) that is most strongly reinforced. We now meet this poem with a great sense of recognition as well as relief. We have been introduced to this setting in "The Invitation" and "The Banquet" and are, like the persona, finally ready to sit and assent. When we reach "Love" (III) in the revised conclusion there is no serious doubt as to whether or not man can reach "high perfections." He is there.

It would be an oversimplification, however tempting, to conclude that the two endings of "The Church" portray two completely different poets: early Herbert, the rigid or troubled Puritan, and late Herbert, the flexible and secure Anglican. On the contrary, we should recall that some of Herbert's early poems, specifically the Latin epigrams *Musae Responsoriae* written against Andrew Melville, are directly and outspokenly critical of various Puritan attitudes, while some of the later poems (that is, poems not in the Williams Manuscript) such as "The Water-course," "Dotage," "Home," and "The Glance" seem very much in accord with key Puritan positions and are exactly the kind of poems taken to heart by such Puritans as Richard Baxter.[26] In addition, the poems that make the ending sequence in *W* so hesitant and uneven are not repudiated or discarded by Herbert (excepting only "The Knell" and "Perseverance") but preserved elsewhere in the revised "Church." These facts, coupled with the almost inevitable intractability and imprecision of such terms as Puritan and Anglican, urge a cautious conclusion, perhaps even one that retreats somewhat to emphasize only the local, technical achievement of Herbert's revisions and reorderings.

But the modifications in the closing sequence are unquestionably improvements that cannot adequately be measured by discussing poetic technique detached from the marked changes in vision and structure of belief and feeling that underlie the new conclusion. Although I hesitate to use the term Anglican normatively—as if to suggest that the closer Herbert's poems accord with this theology and characteristic mentality, the better they become—a close look at the two endings of "The Church" dramatizes how intimately the painstaking creation of what Martz describes as a "plateau of assurance" corresponds to the no doubt equally painstaking achievement and confirmation of what can broadly be called Herbert's Anglicanism.[27] This is not to pigeon-hole Herbert. Joseph Summers strikes exactly the right note in speaking of "George Herbert and Anglican Traditions": "The 'Anglicanism' of Herbert's poems was more than a matter of parochial, provincial, or even denominational allegiances. Within those poems, a master artist and rhetorician conveyed the recognizably authentic experiences of an individual's life within the church."[28] The breadth and inclusiveness of Anglicanism are crucial, and Summers' comments on "The Invitation" apply to the entire group in which this poem is embedded: "The true catholicity of a church filled with God's presence and all of human joy and to which all are invited surely represents the most important Anglican tradition of all."[29] This tradition animates the final much more than the original ending of "The Church," and makes it a fit and moving conclusion to Herbert's collection of lyrics.

Notes

Claude Summers and Ted-Larry Pebworth helped to reshape an earlier version of my essay, and more recently I am very grateful that I had the opportunity to discuss the ideas in this paper with Louis Martz and Barbara Lewalski, both of whom offered valuable advice that I have tried to follow. I would also like to thank Joseph Summers for looking over my essay, making numerous comments and suggestions, and sending me a copy of his unpublished lecture "George Herbert and Anglican Traditions," which reinforces one of the important subjects of *George Herbert: His Religion and Art*: the careful analysis of Herbert's Anglicanism and the strengths and weaknesses of the traditional Anglican approach to his poems.

1. Richard Strier, *Love Known: Theology and Experience in George Herbert's Poetry* (Chicago: University of Chicago Press, 1983), 48.

2. Amy M. Charles, "The Williams Manuscript and *The Temple*," in *Essential Articles for the Study of George Herbert's Poetry*, ed. John R. Roberts (Hamden, Conn.: Archon Books, 1979), 417, 422.

3. For two particularly interesting readings of the opening sequence of "The Church," see Strier, *Love Known*, 48–60, and Ilona Bell, "'Setting Foot into Divini-

ty': George Herbert and the English Reformation," in *Essential Articles for the Study of George Herbert's Poetry*, 63–83. A full study of the revisions and reordering of this opening sequence needs to be written. It would, I believe, underscore how carefully Herbert sought to deepen our awareness of the persona's sinfulness and general weakness at the beginning of "The Church"—a point well worth keeping in mind as I argue in the present paper that in the revisions and re-ordering of the closing sequence Herbert aimed at exactly the opposite effect.

4. The broad base of theological agreement in England during the late sixteenth and early seventeenth centuries is set out in great detail by Charles H. and Katherine George, *The Protestant Mind of the English Reformation, 1570–1640* (Princeton: Princeton University Press, 1961). Similarly, Barbara K. Lewalski emphasizes the common background shared by various Protestant poets in *Protestant Poetics and the Seventeenth-Century Religious Lyric* (Princeton: Princeton University Press, 1979). Nevertheless, I follow John F. H. New, *Anglican and Puritan: The Basis of Their Opposition, 1558–1640* (Stanford: Stanford University Press, 1964), focusing on the crucial differences in attitudes, beliefs, and religious psychology that set up two distinct "universes of discourse" (4) during this time period. In discussing the characteristics of and differences between the original and revised endings of "The Church," I adopt a number of the categories used by New to define and distinguish Puritan and Anglican. Nevertheless, I hope it is clear that I use these terms very tentatively and with many reservations. Christopher Hill warns that "The word 'Puritan' . . . is an admirable refuge from clarity of thought" because it has such a range of meanings; see "The Definition of a Puritan," in *Society and Puritanism in Pre-Revolutionary England* (New York: Schocken Books, 1972), 13–29. And Richard Strier reminds us that the term "Anglican" was not used in Herbert's day (*Love Known*, xv). It would be particularly convenient if I could simply use the term "Arminian" to refer to the positions that Herbert arrives at as he revises his poems, but this would overstate the case: what I am attempting to describe as Herbert's developing "Anglicanism" embraces some aspects of but is by no means limited to or identical with the ascendant Arminianism of the latter period of his life (1625–33), studied in impressive detail in Nicholas Tyacke, *Anti-Calvinists: The Rise of English Arminianism c. 1590–1640* (Oxford: Clarendon Press, 1987).

5. All quotations from *The Temple* are from *The Works of George Herbert*, ed. F. E. Hutchinson (1941; corrected repr., Oxford: Clarendon Press, 1945), and are indicated by line numbers only in the body of my essay. For the text and corrections of the poems from *W*, see *The Williams Manuscript of George Herbert's Poems*, ed. Amy M. Charles (Delmar, New York, Scholars' Facsimiles and Reprints, 1977). In quoting from *W* I have expanded all abbreviations.

6. Helen Vendler, *The Poetry of George Herbert* (Cambridge, Mass.: Harvard University Press, 1975), 170.

7. William Ames, *The Marrow of Theology*, trans. John Dykstra Eusden (Durham, North Carolina: The Labyrinth Press, 1983), 170.

8. Arnold Stein emphasizes such a mastery and conversion of "death" to "a stage

of life" in his reading of this poem in *George Herbert's Lyrics* (Baltimore: The Johns Hopkins Press, 1968), 156–69.

9. Stanley E. Fish, *Self-Consuming Artifacts: The Experience of Seventeenth-Century Literature* (Berkeley: University of California Press, 1972), 180. Strier contests this claim; see *Love Known*, 5, n. 10.

10. Though the thoughts behind this plea are of course commonplace in seventeenth-century theological works, shared by writers as diverse as William Perkins and Richard Hooker, the cool formality of Herbert's lines seems comparable to William Ames's manner in a comment from his discussion of "Good Works," translated from the original Latin as: "To be truly good an action must be referred to God as the chief end, at least in effect." See *The Marrow of Theology*, 233.

11. John T. McNeill, *The History and Character of Calvinism* (Oxford: Oxford University Press, 1973), 215–16, quoting Calvin from the *Institutes of the Christian Religion*, IV.i.20. Thomas Wilson, in *A Christian Dictionary* (London, 1612) inspired by Calvin, notes that there is such a thing as "An absolute fulnesse of grace, when there is not the least want" (356), but defines "perfection" in this world primarily as "A good degree of perfection in grace, and a striving towards the absolute fulnes of it, though still there may be many wants." He goes on to warn that those who "have taught an absolute perfection of inherent grace in this life" are dangerous and "rise up against the light of both Scripture and of their owne conscience, which doth witnesse the contrary to every man."

12. Strier notes in several places that Herbert believed in the perseverance of the saints (see *Love Known*, 84, 141–42, for example), but "Perseverance" is one of the few poems by Herbert not mentioned at all in his book, perhaps because it does not appear in the final version of *The Temple*.

13. Helen C. White, *The Metaphysical Poets: A Study in Religious Experience* (1936; repr., New York: Collier Books, 1966), 177–82; Charles Molesworth, "Herbert's 'The Elixir': Revision Towards Action," *Concerning Poetry* 5, no. 2 (1972): 12–20; Camille Wells Slights, *The Casuistical Tradition in Shakespeare, Donne, Herbert, and Milton* (Princeton: Princeton University Press, 1981), 240–42; Mary Ellen Rickey, *Utmost Art: Complexity in the Verse of George Herbert* (Lexington, Kentucky: University of Kentucky Press, 1966), 104.

14. See the second part of "The H. Communion" (titled "Prayer" in *W*) and "Whitsunday" for further examples of Herbert revising poems that were originally dramatically interrupted by a turn in the conclusion signaled by the word "But."

15. Noted by Slights, *The Casuistical Tradition*, 245, n. 49.

16. Strier disagrees, noting very quickly that the final version of "The Elixir" is not "as it once was, a poem about actually doing things well" (*Love Known*, 207).

17. In the new arrangement of the poems, Herbert relocates but also keeps together "Mortification," "The Publican" (retitled "Miserie"), "Prayer" (II), "Obedience," and "Invention" (retitled "Jordan" [II]), and they continue to function as a connected group.

18. In "Changing the Object: Herbert and Excess," *George Herbert Journal* 2, no. 1 (Fall 1978): 24–37, Strier objects to the prospect of Herbert inviting "all," sinners

included, to the Eucharist: "That the minister should call 'all' to God is perfectly 'just and right' in Protestant terms; that he should invite all to the Eucharist is not. The Reformed tradition insisted strongly on the need for both doctrinal and spiritual preparation for the Eucharist" (31). He then goes through a complicated argument to make "The Invitation" compatible with the Protestant doctrine of "worthy reception," suggesting that the poem is an ecstatic "testimony," not a real invitation (33–34). However "The Invitation" does not preclude careful preparation for the Eucharist, though it may not be described in the poem. Furthermore, the "problems" of the poem seen by Strier recede if we read it against the background not of a strict Protestant "concern to weed out the unworthy" but rather that of Anglican "willingness to dispense [sacraments] indiscriminately." See New, *Anglican and Puritan*, 69, and 13 for the Anglican belief that grace was "proffered to all if not conferred on all." Regarding the proper context of "The Invitation," Terry G. Sherwood notes that "The poem's title refers to the first step in the Anglican Communion Office (Invitation, Confession, Absolution, and Comfortable Words)." See "Tasting and Telling Sweetness in George Herbert's Poetry," *English Literary Renaissance* 12, no. 3 (Autumn 1982): 334.

19. Thomas à Kempis, *Of the Imitation of Christ*, trans. Abbot Justin McCann (New York: New American Library, 1962), 115 (Book III, chapter 34). For the basic affinity between Herbert and the *Imitation*, see Louis L. Martz, *The Poetry of Meditation: A Study in English Religious Literature of the Seventeenth Century* (1954; rev. ed. New Haven, Conn.: Yale University Press, 1962), esp. 282–87. We need not of course go as far as the *Imitation of Christ* for an expression of the great physical joy released by the Sacrament of the Body and Blood of Christ; see, for example, Richard Hooker's remarkably exuberant description of this experience in *Of the Laws of Ecclesiastical Polity* (London: J.M. Dent and Sons, 1965), II:330–31 (Book V, chapter 67).

20. John Donne, *The Sermons of John Donne*, ed. George R. Potter and Evelyn M. Simpson (Berkeley: University of California Press, 1953–1962), I:268–84. By compressing Jacob's statement—"I am not worthy of the least of all the mercies, and of all the truth, which thou hast shewed unto thy servant"—Herbert not only gains the brevity necessary for a "posie" but also avoids even raising the disturbing problem of man's worthiness. The only use of the word "worthy" in *The Temple* comes in "Love" (III), where the issue of man's worthiness is gently but finally resolved.

21. Rosemond Tuve's essay "Sacred 'Parody' of Love Poetry, and Herbert" (in *Essays by Rosemond Tuve: Spenser, Herbert, Milton*, ed. Thomas P. Roche, Jr. [Princeton: Princeton University Press, 1970], 207–51) presents an extremely useful warning against defining "parody" too loosely, but her definition of the term, I believe, is too limiting to account for the numerous acts of parody that seem particularly prominent in the concluding sequence of "The Church."

22. Strier, *Love Known*, 243.

23. In "Praise" (III), not in the Williams Manuscript and therefore perhaps a later poem, Herbert also uses the word "perfection" in very much the same way as in the revised version of "The Elixir." Addressing God directly, he notes: "When thou dost favour any action, / It runnes, it flies: / All things concur to give it perfection" (7– 9).

24. *The First and Second Prayer Books of Edward VI* (New York: E. P. Dutton and Co., 1957), 26.

25. *The First and Second Prayer Books of Edward VI*, 27.

26. C. A. Patrides, ed., *George Herbert: The Critical Heritage* (Boston: Routledge and Kegan Paul, 1983), 11.

27. Martz, *The Poetry of Meditation*, 309–20.

28. Joseph Summers, "George Herbert and Anglican Traditions," unpublished essay, 11.

29. Summers, "George Herbert and Anglican Traditions," 20.

"Respective Boldnesse": Herbert and the Art of Submission

MICHAEL C. SCHOENFELDT

Because the professed purpose of Herbert's "Dedication" is to defer attention from itself and its earthly maker in order to reveal God's act of authorship, the poem has appropriately received little close critical attention.[1] Yet the kinetics of this deferral are decidedly worthy of investigation. For "Dedication" also exhibits the verbal abilities of its human maker, and so calls attention to itself as an example of the highest form of art, the art "that appeareth not to be arte."[2] "Dedication" purports, even aspires, to be "self-consuming," to "let go" of the fiction of mortal fabrication for the greater glory of God. But at the same time the poem participates in a process of self-display that re-establishes the claims of human authorship apparently relinquished.[3] Despite the ingratiating power of its initial gesture of surrender, "Dedication" reveals upon close inspection a self that is demanding, assertive, even aggressive. The poem demonstrates how an act of authorship, even one declaring profound devotion and submission, may be subversive of the authority to which it submits.

The conventions of dedicatory address attract Herbert precisely because they equip him with the opportunity and the terminology to scrutinize the impediments implicit in his project of using art as a vehicle for submission to divine authority. In the Renaissance, dedications supply the medium through which a writer imposes a text upon the world; yet dedications also comprise a submission of self and text to that world. Dedications provide chances for self-display; but one of the talents most often displayed is the ability to engage in self-deprecation. The accomplishments of the self must be brandished even as they are relinquished in order for the gesture of capitulation to be meaningful. In his "Dedication" Herbert exploits these tensions inherent in the literature of clientage to create a succinct but complex account of the goals and obstacles of his own poetic project. When examined in the context of the discourse its governing metaphor invokes—the deferential yet cunningly coercive language with which a poet addresses his patron— "Dedication" emerges as a paradigm of Herbert's overriding concern with the problems of making art of his intercourse with God.

As the prefatory poem to a volume that exudes devout piety, "Dedication" surprisingly begins with the conventional language of a secular poet offering his work to a patron: "Lord, my first fruits present themselves to thee."[4] God is figured as a superior to whom the poet is suing for grace and protection. The following poems are thus rendered as gifts the poet would devote to his patron in the hope either of binding him to act beneficently, or of returning to him thanks for favors already granted. Yet in the second and third lines of his poem, it would seem that Herbert, in surrendering his role in the creation of his poems, also surrenders this patron-client model for his relationship with God: "Yet not mine neither: for from thee they came, / And must return." The speaker declares that those poems he would present to his Lord in the hope of ingratiating himself are the products of that Lord's action. A recognition of God's transcendent omnipotence appears to supplant the metaphor of clientage with which the poet in the first line structures the relationship among himself, his poems, and his God.

Such a renunciation of proprietary rights and creative responsibility, however, is itself part of the conventional discourse between a poet and his patron. As Eleanor Rosenberg observes,

> a dedication, even if it had not appeared in print, gave the patron not merely the right to possess the manuscript but in fact some measure of proprietary right in the text of the work addressed to him.[5]

Moreover, dedications commonly assert that the beneficence of the patron actually produces the artifact and so grants him a title to it. John

Reynolds's dedicatory epistle to his translation of Denys de Refuges's *A Treatise of the Court*, for example, declares: "I did it in your service, it is therefore yours by propriety, I did it out of mine owne private obligation to your immerited favours, it is therefore yours in the right of debt and requitall."[6] Similarly, Shakespeare's dedication of *The Rape of Lucrece* to the earl of Southampton proclaims "what I have done is yours, what I have to do is yours, being part in all I have, devoted yours."[7] The writer's statement that the credit belongs to the patron deferentially shifts all praise of the work itself from the writer to the patron. Within the patron-poet metaphor, Herbert's abandonment of proprietary rights can be read as a stock supplicatory tactic intended to ingratiate the poet with his benefactor.

Each of these statements attributing composition to the patron, however, requires a prior act of self-advertisement. The ascription of credit to the patron is not accomplished without a preliminary reminder of the writer's own artistic achievements. In the examples from Shakespeare and Reynolds, the performances of the self are paraded ("I did it," "What I have done") before being assigned ("it is therefore yours," "is yours") to the title of a benevolent patron. In a similar fashion, Herbert initially claims his fruits to be his own ("my first fruits") before declaring them to be the product of God's actions upon him: "Yet not mine neither: for from thee they came, / And must return." Furthermore, this appealing surrender of human agency is itself a consummate example of human craft: the rhetorical figure *metanoia*. George Puttenham appropriately terms this figure "the Penitent," and describes it as when

> we speake and be sorry for it, as if we had not wel spoken, so that we seeme to call in our word againe, and to put in another fitter for the purpose.[8]

Significantly, the speaker of "Dedication" does not behave toward his initial claim of authorship in the manner that Herbert describes in "Jordan (II)": "I often blotted what I had begunne." Rather, the original assertion is left to stand beside his revision of it, so that the speaker receives credit both for his artistic performance and for the deferential gesture of surrendering credit for this performance to his divine patron.

Even in the remainder of "Dedication," which appears to discard the social language of the first two-and-a-half lines, the discourse of patronage structures Herbert's supplication:

> Accept of them [my first fruits] and me,
> And make us strive, who shall sing best thy name.
> Turn their eyes hither, who shall make a gain:
> Theirs, who shall hurt themselves or me, refrain.

He is asking God to accept his works, and by this act of acceptance to control their reception. This would seem to be an act of which only an omnipotent being would be capable. Yet Eleanor Rosenberg reminds us that patrons, by accepting the dedication of a work of literature to them, "guaranteed license for printing and protection against carping critics."[9] Spenser's dedicatory sonnet to the earl of Oxford begins: "Receive most Noble Lord in gentle gree, / The unripe fruit of an unready wit: / Which by thy countenaunce doth crave to bee / Defended from foule Envies poisnous bit."[10] Herbert's anxiety over the project of writing religious poetry and releasing it to the world finds expression in the conventional language of a poet requesting the protection of a patron.[11] In asking God to control the reception of his work, Herbert is only exercising another aspect of the patron-poet metaphor with which he began. God's acceptance of Herbert's "fruits" will be an admission of Herbert into his service ("Accept of them and me"); such acceptance will also involve the formation of a "fit audience" for Herbert's poetry.

In "Dedication," then, Herbert utilizes to a startling degree the strategies and language with which a secular poet addresses his patron. But this is a language which has also been steeped in the waters of the Jordan. The gestures by which secular poets announce and renounce the claims of authorship allow Herbert to interrogate the religious doctrine implicit in his production of sacred poetry. By presenting this work to his Lord, Herbert attempts both to obligate his Lord and to remove himself from obligation. He desires to reciprocate in words for God's gift of the Word. But as Herbert observes in his "Briefe Notes on Valdesso's *Considerations*," one should not "presume . . . to merit, that is, to oblige God, or justify himselfe before God, by any acts or exercises of Religion" (312). In asserting his own possessory right over his fruits only to reveal them to be the product of his Lord's procreative power, Herbert replaces a declaration of the human capacity to perform works for God with the admission that the opportunity and capacity to perform are gifts of God. The impertinence of presenting these works to God is superseded by a reluctant recognition of the obligation to return to God what is already his ("for from thee they came, / And *must* return").[12] The illusion of human agency and the dream of reciprocating God's beneficence are replaced by a grudging acknowledgment of God's overwhelming omnipotence. "Herbert," remarks Barbara Lewalski, "wrestles constantly with the paradox of his responsibility to create poems of praise, yet his inability to do so unless God will enable him and participate with him in those praises."[13] Herbert's assertion and subsequent renunciation of his own creative action in "Dedication" powerfully dramatize this paradox.

The "onelie begetter" topos of secular dedications thus furnishes Herbert with a language able to convey a theological account of the production of his poems. The greatness of his own poetic creations (despite his disclaimers to the contrary) lies partly in his willing recourse to a language saturated by both the Jordan and the Thames. The phrase "first fruits," for example, is suffused with social and sacred meaning. It is "a commonplace of dedications," regardless of the age of the writer or the place of the work in a career.[14] It serves to demean the work, and so functions as a strategy by which a writer attempts to defuse charges of presumption for obtruding a work upon the world, and a self upon a patron. As we have seen, Spenser employs a variation on this topos in his dedication to the earl of Oxford when he calls *The Faerie Queene* "the unripe fruit of an unreadie wit." By so depreciating his own poetic labors, Spenser invites the earl to exercise a benevolence the poet makes no claims to deserve. The phrase "first fruits" suggests that if the work is accepted, other more substantial labor will follow. The phrase, however, derives from the Old Testament injunctions of God to the Israelites. There, God commands: "The first of the fruits of thy land thou shalt bring into the house of the Lord thy God."[15] These "first fruits" are a sacrifice of devotion and a sign of gratefulness. In *Abels Offering* (1621), John Wing suggests that the phrase denotes not our immature labors but "our choysest and chiefe, our first, and best, the prime and principall ... of our lives, of our selves."[16] Herbert's declared desire in "Dedication" to "sing best thy name" even while surrendering the act of authorship to God amplifies this sense of the phrase. Moreover, the first two poems of "The Church"—"The Altar" and "The Sacrifice"— reinforce the typological identification of Herbert's votive gestures with Old Testament sacrifice that is initiated in "Dedication."

Yet Herbert does not allow the religious echoes of this language to drown out its social resonance. Rather, he cultivates the gap between its social and religious reverberations to demonstrate simultaneously the necessity and the difficulty of employing art as an instrument for submission to God. The tension, for example, between the social and religious connotations of the phrase "first fruits," between a deferential depreciation of the poet's work and an exaltation of the work's primacy, provides Herbert with a vocabulary capable of expressing the inherent antagonism between the creative means and submissive ends of his devotional acts. Such acts issue in a submission which is concurrently humiliating and elevating. In order to be seen as an appropriate gift for the Lord of Lords, the poetry must be valued highly as a product of the poet's "utmost art"; yet in order that the act of human creation not be allowed to encroach upon divine power, the work must be denigrated, while whatever value it possesses is revealed to be a product of that Lord's action. This tension is present in the first two words of the poem: "Lord, my." The address to superior power is followed immediately by a word affirming the integrity and dominion of the poet. Paradoxically, the act of submission requires the very dialectic between self and other that it attempts to eradicate.

This tension between self-assertion and submission is embodied most fully in the shrewd craft and wit the poem displays. The well-balanced alliterative pattern of the first two lines—the manner in which "first fruits" is matched by "themselves ... thee," while "not ... neither" is redoubled by "For from thee they"—offers a *tour de force* of consonance. The phrase "make a gain," moreover, designates not only the spiritual profit available to Herbert's readers, but also the way in which the poetry may encourage them to be re-born, made again, and as a result to go on to "make again" the kind of poetry Herbert has engaged in here (a wish which Harvey, Crashaw, and Vaughan fulfilled[17]). This matrix of meanings is related to the plays on "turn" and "return," which imply that conversion (a "turning with" or "toward," as in "The Church-porch" and "The Elixir") of readers will be the "return" promised in the dedication. Yet the remunerative language—"gain," "present," and "return"—alludes to the primary motive for dedicating a work to a social superior: financial and/or political gain.

Herbert's wit here is almost imperceptible, yet its very subtlety displays the craft of the poet even as he disclaims any part in the production of his poems. By deploying words that suggest the creation or formal partition of poems—e.g., "sing," "turn" (Latin, *verso*), and "refrain"—Herbert's "Dedication" declares itself, and the poems that follow, to be the products of a master craftsman. Quite significantly, the word "make" is used twice in this short poem ostensibly surrendering the act of making to God. The word recalls both the artist's creative abilities (Sidney's sense of the poet as maker) and, of course, God's (the "author of this great frame" in "Love [I]").[18] But it also invokes God's coercive powers, suggesting that he not only "makes [Herbert and his fruits]" but also "makes [them] strive," forces them to behave in a particular way. The two meanings of "make" operative here imply that the one kind of making is related to and enables the other, that the power of coercion is a product of the act of creation. God's ability to control the conduct of his creatures is thus seen as a necessary adjunct to his prior act of creation.

The speaker's act of making, on the other hand—the product of which is a poem disclaiming any part in the creative process—announces the coercive potential of the rhetoric of social submission. By submitting himself and his poems to God, and revealing both to be a result of God's creative action, Herbert makes God responsible for him, his poems, and their reception. He binds God to him both by the ingratiating acknowledgment of God's power and by his subtle reminders of the "present," "return," and "gain" that this act of poetic devotion invites. Even the revelation of God's coercive power is stated as an imperative—"Make us strive"—blurring the distinction between supplication and command through which power and status are exhibited and sustained. In the act of showing how God makes him and his poems, then, Herbert also tries to "make" God behave in a particular way towards him.

Herbert's "Dedication" performs an earnest act of submission, rendering to God the praise for his poetic fruits by surrendering to God his own part in their making. But the language of this submission discloses a radically assertive self that displays its creative powers and demands recognition and remuneration for them. In "Dedication," we see Herbert engaged in the process he censures in "Jordan (II)"—weaving the self into the sense. Like an off-color thread in a seemingly uniform fabric, Herbert's repeated references to the ability and integrity of the self are apparent only on close inspection of the language of his submission. The very subtlety of these references, however, enhances rather than diminishes their authority, for as Castiglione's Sir Frederick comments:

> if the words that the writer useth bring with them a little . . .
> covered subtilitie, and not so open, as such as be ordinarily spoken,
> they give a certaine authority to the writing, and make the reader
> more heedfull to pause at it, and to ponder it better, and he taketh
> a delyte in the wittinesse and learning of him that wryteth.[19]

Paradoxically, then, the degree to which the references to the self and its abilities are submerged becomes a measure of the covert claims for authority being made by the self. In a poem ostensibly diverting praise for the act of making from the poet to God runs a counter-current demanding admiration for "the wittinesse and learning of him that wryteth." Through the "covered subtilitie" with which he states his own aspirations, Herbert regains for himself a "certaine authority" in the very act of submitting to superior authority. The disguise that the demands of the self assume in deference to superior power grants an authority to those claims.

In "Dedication" Herbert displays a sophisticated understanding of the arts of secular submission. He demonstrates that he was the kind of man he portrays in "The Pearl. Matth. 13. 45"—one who knew well

> the wayes of Honour, what maintains
> The quick returns of courtesie and wit:
> In vies of favours whether partie gains . . .

Herbert's early career was marked by a profound dexterity with this language of social obligation. He progressed through the academic hierarchy at Cambridge by exhibiting great promise not only in Latin but also in the modes of supplication and praise by which preferment was won in the seventeenth-century court. In a letter to his step-father expressing his desire for the position of University Orator at Cambridge, Herbert pledges that he will "work the heads to my purpose" (369), explicitly recognizing the manipulative motives that gestures of submission authorize and disguise. The duties Herbert performed after his bid for the post proved successful—winning the good graces of the powerful, thanking them for favors already granted, and persuading them to behave beneficently in the future—assume the same supplicatory prowess that Herbert directs toward God in *The Temple*.[20] Before sacred and secular authority, the ambitions of the self can be advanced only through discourse proclaiming praise and subordination.

By employing the tactics of social supplication in a poem submitting himself and his work to his Lord, Herbert certifies his own ability to engage in the delicate verbal subterfuges required in the disingenuous world of the court. As Puttenham reminds us, the disguising of one's own acquisitive motives was a prime requirement of courtly discourse; "the profession of a very Courtier," he observes, "is cunningly to be able to dissemble."[21] In a social world idealized as static but invigorated by merit and ambition, the ability to dissemble one's own assertions and demands, to insinuate them into one's proffers of submission, was psychologically as well as strategically imperative. "Offerings of devoted submission may be functionally ambiguous," remarks Louis Montrose.

> They may allow an oblique and limited expression of the aggression or independence that is being denied, and a purgation of the resentment that the submission entails.[22]

In "Dedication," the language of social submission functions in just this way, allowing Herbert to express indirectly the indignation that the necessity of subordination can include. The insinuation of such latent aggression into a poem advertising itself as an act of submission parallels Herbert's attempted insinuation of himself into his Lord's favor through a declaration of devotion. In both activities, an apparently self-demeaning stance sanctions covert self-advancement.

It is as if Herbert is at pains to show, even in the reader's "first en-trance" into *The Temple*, the paradox around which his poetic devo-tions to God perpetually revolve—how the very authority inherent in the act of writing can confound the submissive goals of his writing. The self-deprecatory surrender of proprietary right in the first two-and-a-half lines is disarmingly humble (as, indeed, dedications were intend-ed to be). It creates the illusion of ease in the act of submission to God. "Yet not mine neither: for from thee they came, / And must return," concedes the speaker, as if he has now gotten it right, as if the accom-plishment of a genuine submission only required the confession of God's benevolence and the speaker's own impotence. But Herbert understood that the problems of submission to God were far too complex to be dispersed simply by a display of humility and penitence achieved through the application of *metanoia*. His familiarity with the arts of secular sub-mission would have told him, as his good friend Francis Bacon remarks, that "excusations, cessions, modesty itself well governed are but arts of ostentation."[23]

In the *Ancilla Pietatis*, Daniel Featley considers the aesthetic dilemma confronted by the poet of *The Temple*. Featley criticizes those who

> court Almighty *God* with idle complements, . . . [who] cast up
> Prayers with strong lines to heaven, hoping thereby to drawe downe
> a blessing from God . . . [and who] discourse profoundly in their
> Prayer, as if they meant in good earnest to teach Almighty *God*
> what hee ought to doe.[24]

Featley determines to answer "these men in their own language," declaring that their methods of addressing God are "*playing*, not Praying . . . in sending up such prayers they burne not *incense* to God, but *incense* him rather" (20). Yet Featley also castigates those who

> affect a kinde of *Rhetorike*, which weedeth out all flowers of
> Rhetorike . . . Nothing pleaseth them in this kinde, but that which
> is spunne with an over course thread. (22)

Such supplicants, Featley argues, "should have considered better, that sharpnesse of wit, and true eloquence are gifts of *God*, and therefore best of all to bee employed in holy things" (23). To Featley, artful language is improper for religious devotion because it focuses attention not on God but upon the abilities of the mortal devotee. It attempts to manipulate God, to tell him what he ought to do. Yet a plain style of devotion is also indecorous, because it fails to envelop "heavenly conceptions" in the wit and eloquence that holy subjects deserve. Unadorned devotions cheapen the act of submission because they are accomplished at no expense to the devotee. "For my part," declares Featley, "I am resolved with *David never to offer that to God which costeth mee nothing.*"[25]

Featley resolves this dilemma not by delineating a *via media* between artfulness and artlessness but by directing attention to the necessarily imperfect nature of all acts of supplication:

> O what sinfull wretches are we, who need a large pardon, not onely for our profane and carnall, but even for our holy, and spirituall excercises? *Lord bee mercifull!* shall I say *to our sinnes*? Nay even to our best works which are not free from imperfections, Even when we pray against sinne, wee sinne in Praying, both in respect of the forme, and manner and end of Prayer. (25)

For Featley, the self continually contaminates the text of its genuinely devout attempts to submit to God. Whether through a studied plainness or displays of artfulness, the self engages in discourse that subverts its intended submission. The act of supplication for pardon is endlessly implicated in the imperfections of the self, and so engenders the necessity of another act of supplication begging pardon for the flaws of the previous supplication:

> My very prayers which I make unto thee for the supplying of all my wants, and the healing of all my infirmities, are accompanied with so many wants and infirmities, that I have neede to aske pardon for these my imperfect prayers. (398)

The cycle of infinite regress required by such intense scrutiny of one's own devotional performances is shattered only by the infinite progress of God's benevolence toward his creatures.[26]

Herbert's poetry engages in a similarly rigorous and incessant examination of the processes by which the self pollutes its own acts of submission. Throughout *The Temple*, Herbert does court God; he casts up prayers with strong lines to heaven, and discourses profoundly with his divine superior in the attempt to manipulate his behavior. By employing such potentially duplicitous tactics borrowed from the world of secular supplication, however, Herbert remains sincere to his project of representing the full complexity of the process of submitting the self and its fruits to God. Like the speaker of "Love Unknown," who slips his heart into a "dish of fruit" offered to his Lord only to discover that his "heart was foul," the speaker of "Dedication" insinuates his own imperfect desires into the text proffering his lyric fruits to his Lord.[27] By simultaneously identifying himself with and distancing himself from such speakers, Herbert affirms both his fervent desire to submit to God and his awareness of the difficulty of accomplishing this submission in a work of art.

In "A Litanie," Donne pleads: "When wee are mov'd to seeme religious / Only to vent wit, Lord deliver us."[28] Like Herbert, Donne is mindful of the possibilities of self-aggrandizement inherent in devotional discourse. But where Donne prays in verse to be cleansed of such motives, Herbert inspects such prayers for vestiges of the motives they seek to purge. "The inveterate human tendency to misrepresent what has happened is nowhere more strongly criticized than in Herbert," remarks Helen Vendler.

> Herbert knows that to appear pious is not to be pious; to pay formal tribute is not to love; servilely to acknowledge power is not to wonder; to utter grievances is not to pray. . . . We have a rich sense of social deception in human society and can detect a note of social falseness in a novel almost before it appears; but it sometimes does not occur to us that the same equivocations, falseness, self-justifications, evasions, and defensive reactions can occur in a poet's colloquies with his God.[29]

In "Dedication" and throughout *The Temple* Herbert displays profound and painful insight into the deception, evasion, and aggression lurking within his gestures of devotion. In "Prayer (I)," for example, Herbert calls prayer an "Engine against th'Almightie, sinners towre, / Reversed thunder, Christ-side-piercing spear," revealing the potential violence involved in the act of petitioning God. In "The Reprisall" and "Artillerie"

Herbert employs the imagery of warfare to portray the agonistic aspects of his transactions with God.[30] Even a poem like "Gratefulnesse" brags quite proudly about the strategic "art" that God's "beggar" employs in praising God's bounty to "make" his "gifts occasion more."

At the end of "The Priesthood," a poem about the dedication of the self to God's service, Herbert employs some paradoxical maxims from the world of social submission to explain his reasons for entering the ministry despite an overwhelming sense of unworthiness for such a task:

> The distance of the meek
> Doth flatter power. Lest good come short of ill
> In praising might, the poore do by submission
> What pride by opposition.

Here Herbert explicitly identifies the aggressive energies latent in the supplicatory language of "Dedication" and aligns them with the potentially submissive aspects of an act of opposition. The deferential observation of hierarchical distance functions as flattery of superior power—flattery whose goal is covert advancement of the self through winning the good graces of that superior. A posture of humility is thus revealed to be a strategy for self-promotion. The submission of the poor and the opposition of the proud are gestures very different in appearance but very similar in results. Both work to praise "might": the one by declaring the distance between the self and superior power in language so artful that it acquires a kind of oppositional potency of its own; the other by attempting to oppose God, to transgress the hierarchical distance separating the self from God in inevitably unsuccessful ways that italicize God's superiority. As Milton's God is able to turn the opposition of Satan to His own greater glory, so does Herbert's God turn the aggression of his servant into the occasion for his own praise.

The astute comments of Jeffrey Hart on Herbert's best-known poem of opposition, "The Collar," are pertinent here:

Part of the brilliance of the poem lies in the fact that it expresses rebellion and atonement in the same vocabulary, and by so doing epitomizes its central idea: that rebellion necessarily entails, because of God's justice and mercy, atonement.[31]

I would argue that another aspect of the brilliance of Herbert's poetry is its concern with an analogous but opposite procedure—how submission inevitably includes, because of the corruption of mortal faculties, the rebellious energies it attempts to deny. By utilizing the terminology of secular submission to disclose his own demands, Herbert demonstrates how frequently gestures of submission are contingent upon acts of assertion, and how easily attempts at petitioning God become mired in persuasive, even manipulative, tactics.

In "The Church-porch," a work that bridges the apparent gap between the devotional world inside "The Church" and the social world outside, Herbert advises a mode of oxymoronic behavior toward superiors:

> Towards great persons use respective boldnesse:
> That temper gives them theirs, and yet doth take
> Nothing from thine. (253–55)

Herbert's "Dedication" works in precisely this way, fusing respect and boldness in a single utterance, submerging the demands of self in a discourse declaring obeisance to superior power. Yet in doing so, "Dedication" reveals the impossibility of sustaining a posture of pure respect toward God. In the social world, it is important to preserve a demeanor that "doth take / Nothing from thine"; self-esteem is a virtue.[32] But in relation to God, such behavior is impertinent. It does not give to God what is his, because everything is his. It creates the illusion of autonomy, as if the self did not owe its very existence and abilities to God. By bending toward God the social strategy of "respective boldnesse," Herbert reveals the presumption percolating through his attempts to salute God.

"Supplication of man to man may diffuse itself through many topics of persuasion," remarks Samuel Johnson in his famous critique of devotional poetry, "but supplication to God can only cry for mercy."[33] "Dedication" calls our attention to Herbert's brilliant solution to this predicament. By employing the language of supplication between mortals in his lyric supplication to God, Herbert manages to expand the limited range of expression that Dr. Johnson found to be the principal shortcoming of the devotional lyric. Rather than the inarticulate cry for mercy posited by Dr. Johnson, Herbert's lyrics diffuse themselves through the many "topics of persuasion" available to the secular poet. By figuring God through the Bible's metaphors of social superiority— specifically those depicting God as a king, a master, a lord, and a father— and assuming for himself the corresponding inferior status of a subject, a servant, a tenant, and a son, Herbert is able to employ in his lyrical addresses to God the deferential, precatory, encomiastic lexicon humans direct toward figures of authority. Herbert's extended use of the situation of a subordinate addressing a superior provides him with a supple language able to register simultaneously the extremes of self-assertion and self-abnegation, aggression and submission. *The Temple* is valuable not as a portrait of perfect piety but as a ledger of what T. S. Eliot terms "the cost at which [Herbert] acquired godliness."[34] The arts of secular supplication allow Herbert to depict not only the dedication of his poetic labors to God but also his dedication to excavating and analyzing the compound of obedience and insurgence at the core of all acts of submission.

Notes

An earlier and shorter version of this essay appeared as "Submission and Assertion: The 'Double Motion' of Herbert's 'Dedication,'" *John Donne Journal* 2 (1983): 39–49. Permission to reprint material from this article is gratefully acknowledged.

1. John R. Roberts's exhaustive *George Herbert: An Annotated Bibliography of Modern Criticism 1905–1974* (Columbia: University of Missouri Press, 1978), for example, lists no discussions of "Dedication." Recently, however, the poem has begun to garner the attention it both discourages and deserves; see A. D. Nuttall, *Overheard by God: Fiction and Prayer in Herbert, Milton, Dante and St. John* (London: Methuen, 1980), 63–64; Barbara Harman, *Costly Monuments: Representations of the Self in George Herbert's Poetry* (Cambridge, Mass.: Harvard University Press, 1982), 62–63, 203–4 n. 14; and Ilona Bell, "Circular Strategies and Structures in Jonson and Herbert," in *Classic and Cavalier: Essays on Jonson and the Sons of Ben*, ed. Claude J. Summers and Ted-Larry Pebworth (Pittsburgh: University of Pittsburgh Press, 1982), 158–62.

2. Baldassare Castiglione, *The Book of the Courtier*, trans. Thomas Hoby (London: Dent, 1929), 46. Castiglione is defining sprezzatura, the studied nonchalance that should grace all courtly performances.

3. In *Self-Consuming Artifacts: The Experience of Seventeenth-Century Literature* (Berkeley: University of California Press, 1972), 157, Stanley Fish cites the first two-and-a-half lines of "Dedication" as an example of the characteristic process of "letting go" in Herbert's poetry.

4. All citations of Herbert are from *The Works of George Herbert*, ed. F. E. Hutchinson (1941; corrected repr., Oxford: Clarendon Press, 1945).

5. Eleanor Rosenberg, *Leicester: Patron of Letters* (New York: Columbia University Press, 1955), 92–93.

6. Denys de Refuges, *A Treatise of the Court*, trans. John Reynolds (London, 1622), A4r.

7. *The Riverside Shakespeare*, ed. G. Blakemore Evans et al. (Boston: Houghton Mifflin, 1974), 1722.

8. George Puttenham, *The Arte of English Poesie*, ed. Gladys Willcock and Alice Walker (Cambridge: Cambridge University Press, 1936), 215. On *metanoia* in Herbert, see Harman, *Costly Monuments*, 63; and Helen Vendler, *The Poetry of George Herbert* (Cambridge, Mass.: Harvard University Press, 1975), Chap. 2, "Alternatives: The Reinvented Poem."

9. Rosenberg, 6. In a brilliant essay on the patronage network surrounding Ralegh's *History of the World*, Leonard Tennenhouse observes:

> It was not the efficacy of the author's language, then, so much as the social realities of the patronage system that governed both the production and the reception of Ralegh's literary work.

"Sir Walter Ralegh and the Literature of Clientage," *Patronage in the Renaissance*, ed. Guy Fitch Lytle and Stephen Orgel (Princeton: Princeton University Press, 1981), 258.

10. Edmund Spenser, *The Faerie Queene*, ed. Thomas P. Roche (Harmondsworth: Penguin, 1978), 26.

11. The fact that "Dedication" is in the Williams Manuscript, an early version of the poems that were to become *The Temple*, suggests that Herbert intended to make public his poetic devotions from near the beginning of the project.

12. Significantly, Herbert's revisions of "The Elixir" (originally entitled "Perfection") enact just this process, replacing the claim that "He that does ought for thee, / Marketh y^t deed for thine" ("Perfection," 12–13) with the more modest hope: "And what I do in any thing, / To do it *as for* thee" ("Elixir," 3–4; italics mine).

13. Barbara Lewalski, *Protestant Poetics and the Seventeenth-Century Religious Lyric* (Princeton: Princeton University Press, 1979), 302.

14. Rosenberg, 33–34n.

15. Exodus 23:19. See also Exodus 22:29, 34:26; Leviticus 23:10, 17; Deuteronomy 14:22. All citations of the Bible are from the 1611 King James Version.

16. John Wing, *Abels Offering* (Flushing, 1621), 13.

17. Ilona Bell suggests a different interpretation of the word-play in these lines:

Herbert seems to think that each reader makes the poems anew, for better or

worse, for he puns on the final rhymes of the poem: "make a gain" and "refrain."
To profit, to make a gain, we must "make" the poem "again," afresh.

"Circular Strategies and Structures on Jonson and Herbert," 159.

18. Sir Philip Sidney, *The Defense of Poesy*, ed. Lewis Soens (Lincoln: University
of Nebraska Press, 1970), 8. Puttenham suggestively compares the poet's act of mak-
ing with God's act of creation:

A Poet is as much to say as a maker . . . Such as (by way of resemblance and
reverently) we may say of God: who without any travell to his divine imagina-
tion, made all the world of nought . . . Even so the very Poet makes and con-
trives out of his owne braine, both the verse and matter of his poem. (3)

C. A. Patrides explores the analogy between Creator and poet in " 'A Crown of Praise':
The Poetry of Herbert," in *The English Poems of George Herbert* (Totowa: Rowman
and Littlefield, 1974), 15–16. In "Master W. H., R.I.P.," *PMLA* 102 (1987): 42–54,
Donald W. Foster analyzes the topos of God as maker in dedicatory language.

19. Castiglione, 51.

20. I examine more fully the relationship between Herbert's performances before
political authority as University Orator and his lyric performances before God in "'Sub-
ject to Ev'ry Mounters Bended Knee': Herbert and Authority," in *The Historical Renais-
sance: New Essays on Tudor and Stuart Literature and Culture*, ed. Heather Dubrow and
Richard Strier (forthcoming, University of Chicago Press).

21. Puttenham, 299. On the relationship between tactics of dissimulation and poetic
performance, see Daniel Javitch, *Poetry and Courtliness in Renaissance England* (Prince-
ton: Princeton University Press, 1978).

22. Louis Montrose, "Celebration and Insinuation: Sir Philip Sidney and the Mo-
tives of Elizabethan Courtship," *Renaissance Drama*, n.s., 7 (1977): 28–29.

23. Francis Bacon, "Of Vainglory," *A Selection of His Works*, ed. Sidney Warhaft
(New York: Odyssey Press, 1965), 181. In "Bacon and Herbert and an Image of Chalk,"
William A. Sessions explores the close relationship between Herbert and Bacon (*"Too
Rich to Clothe the Sunne": Essays on George Herbert*, ed. Claude J. Summers and Ted-
Larry Pebworth [Pittsburgh: University of Pittsburgh Press, 1980], 165–78).

24. Daniel Featley, *Ancilla Pietatis, or, The Hand-Maid to Private Devotion* (London,
1626), 20. All citations of Featley are from this edition. Lewalski, *Protestant Poetics*,
222–23, quotes Featley as an example of the "centrist position" on the relationship
of art to the sacred subject. Although he does criticize both extreme positions, Feat-
ley seems to be equally uncomfortable with a theological and aesthetic *via media*.

25. Featley, 24. At the end of "Jordan (II)," Herbert exprsses a desire to "save
expense" by copying out "a sweetnesse readie penn'd," but never in his volume of
poems does he succumb to the temptation of a devotion whose sincerity is achieved
by a conscious lack of effort.

26. When Herbert explains to the reader his motives for composing *The Country
Parson*, his manual of conduct for rural clergy, he likewise traces his own beneficent

intentions back to their divine origin: "Being desirous (thorow the Mercy of God) to please Him, for whom I am and live, and who giveth mee my Desires and Performances" (224).

27. In *Love Known: Theology and Experience in George Herbert's Poetry* (Chicago: University of Chicago Press, 1983), 164, Richard Strier argues that "The whole dynamic of ['Love Unknown'] lies in the shift . . . from tendering sacrifices to God to being made tender by Him."

28. *The Divine Poems of John Donne*, ed. Helen Gardner (Oxford: Clarendon Press, 1978), 23.

29. Vendler, 54.

30. William V. Nestrick, "'Mine and Thine' in *The Temple*," in *Too Rich to Clothe the Sunne*, ed. Summers and Pebworth, 121–27, offers a trenchant reading of Herbert's linguistic duelling with God in "Artillerie."

31. Jeffrey Hart, "Herbert's 'The Collar' Re-Read," *Boston University Studies in English* 5 (1961): 66, reprinted in *Essential Articles for the Study of George Herbert's Poetry*, ed. John R. Roberts (Hamden: Archon, 1979), 454.

32. As Herbert remarks in a letter of behavioral advice to his younger brother Henry: "have a good conceit of your wit; that is, be proud, not with a foolish vanting of yourself when there is no caus, but by setting a just price of your qualities: and it is the part of a poor spirit to undervalue himself and blush" (366).

33. Samuel Johnson, *Lives of the English Poets*, 2 vols. (London: Dent, 1925), I:174.

34. *George Herbert*, Writers and Their Works, no. 152 (London: Longmans, 1962), 13.

Altering the Text of the Self:
The Shapes of "The Altar"

M. THOMAS HESTER

In Chapter 10 of *De civitate dei*, in the passage that Bishop John Williams identifies as the classic definition of "the true, proper, and literall *Altar* of all spiritual Sacrifices,"[1] St. Augustine explains that since "we are all His temple, ... to Him we offer on the altar of our heart the sacrifice of humility and praise." "If therefore," he continues, "the body being but servant and instrument unto the soul, being rightly used in God's service be a sacrifice, how much more is the soul one, when it relieth upon God, and being inflamed with His love losseth all form of temporal concupiscence, as is *framed according to His most excellent figure*."[2] The "true sacrifice of man," then, is when we "reformemur in novitate mentis nostrae,"[3] when we undergo a process of reformation. Herbert's "The Altar" offers a visual and verbal dramatization of such an exemplary process: a re-forming, re-framing, or re-creating of the self (or the various "parts" of the self) in order to "frame" the speaker's poem and self as a mirror of the divine "figure" that continually and ultimately re-makes fallen man. As an act of meditative re-creation in which visual and verbal, spoken and unspoken words "meet" in order to "frame" and "To praise," "The Altar" presents a dramatic re-writing of the speaker's self, "cut" out of the materials of Herbert's literary, personal, and spiritual "parts" and "held" together in a "piece" by his faith in the gracious (re)creativity of The Word of Peace. In these ways the poem is not just the *place* where Herbert dedicates[4] his collection to God's glory but the image (or *topos*) by which he introduces the paradoxical poetics of *The Temple*.

"The pattern poem," Joseph Summers points out, "is a dangerous form."[5] It presents dangers, I would suggest, for the reader as well as for the poet. One danger or problem of hieroglyphic forms lies in the temptation to treat the visual and verbal elements of the poem as either separate or complementary. If, for instance, we accept the shape of "The Altar" *as an altar* once we turn to this page in *The Temple*, then there is the tendency to read the poem as merely a reflection of that shape — rather than as a dynamic unfolding of that shape. Too often, in other words, readings explain every line in terms of the poem's *final* shape, therein treating the poem as a created or spoken artifact. The language of the poem suggests, however, that the significances of the final shape of the poem are a result of the process that the poem unfolds. From this perspective, each of the unfolding shapes (or verbal sections) of the poem is a "word," a hieroglyphic image of that "part" of the medita-tive speaker's consciousness — or an emblem of his self at that particular time. Seen in this light, "The Altar" is an unfolding series of verbal and visual "parts" of speech that serve as images of the speaker's self.

Immediately, of course, such a reading is complicated by the fact that the words of the poem are themselves only "images" of the Word, bib-lical allusions or paraphrases embedded in the speaker's meditation and applied to his condition as he understands it. But the "double motion"[6] of the language of the poem only indicates the complicated nature of the speaker's attempt to re-create himself *in imagine dei*. That is, as the speaker attempts to "frame" his "parts" *according to His most excellent figure*, the words and shapes of his poem/heart/self are "noth-ing but" images of the Word he seeks "to praise." As Augustine ex-plains, "I am not able to praise thee without thee."[7] How "mine" and "thine" ("may") "Meet," then, is both the subject and the method of "The Altar," which presents a metaphoric process, or the process of metaphorizing, that *shows* how and why man can and should "frame" himself in the image of God in order to praise his Maker. The poem is a process of re-formation in which Herbert's speaker re-makes his texts/self.

Thus, one of the major concerns of recent readings of the poem — with the identity of the creator of the poem (Herbert the poet? Her-bert the priest? Herbert's persona? God? the reader?) — should be amplified so as to focus attention on the central concern of the poem: the self as a *topos*. That is, "The Altar" is an image of an image created by a Form man can only imagine "through a mirror." The poem is concerned with its self as a "meeting" place where signification takes place: the text, the self, the workings of Grace "meet" in the heart of man. How signification takes place, or, in the language of the poem, "Wherefore" signification takes place is the continuing conversation of God and man — how, why, when, and to what ends meaning unfolds — is what "takes place" in "The Altar." *In principio erat sermo.* My concern in what follows, then, is with the search for signification by Herbert's speaker; specifically, with the unfolding levels of re-creation by which man comes to understand that he is most his own self when he is entirely His.

One text that is re-made in "The Altar" is Herbert's first altar poem, "Λογικὴ Θυσία", a four-line syllogism which itself, Philip Dust points out, is a re-working of pagan texts describing pagan sacrifices:[8]

Ararumque Hominumque ortum si mente pererres,
    Cespes viuus, Homo; mortuus, Ara fuit:
Quae diuisa nocent, Christi per foedus, in vnum
    Conueniunt; & Homo viua fit Ara Dei.

It is difficult to capture the allusive resonance of the poem in an English linear translation; but here, with some attempts to convey the suggestiveness of the words noted, is one possible rendition of the poem:

Reasonable[1] Sacrifice

If one considers the rise[2] of men and altars,

Man was living earth,[3] dead earth an altar:

These which, separated, are harmful,[4] through Christ's covenant
into unity[5]

Were brought;[6] and so man becomes the living altar of God.

[Notes: [1]or: Logical (with the play on *Logos*); [2]or: the source, origin; [3]or: an altar of turf; [4]or: are guilty, unlawful; [5]or: in one place; [6]or: meet.]

This short, discursive poem, which offers a skeletal thematic outline of the central argument of "The Altar," is an unemotional syllogism which explains that Christ's covenant (*Christi per foedus*) transforms the pagan altars (alluded to in the poem's classical echoes) into "The living altar of God" that is the man of faith (*& Homo viua fit Ara Dei*). Many of the same words used in the English poem, or at least their Latin roots, appear here: the Latin quatrain considers the rise of man and altars (*ortum*)—which is recalled in "rears" of "The Altar"; it explains how the ascent of men and altars to heavenly sanctification (*pererres*) was achieved by the restorative powers of Christ's Incarnation (*Conueniunt*: which means both "puts together" and "meeting together," and is thus recalled in "made" and "Meets"); and it affirms that Christ's actions overcame the divisiveness of man's mortality (*diuisa*), which is recalled in later view of the speaker's heart/altar/self as "broken" and in "parts." But the changes Herbert makes in "The Altar" are more significant than the "parts" he retains of this early *disputatio*. The revision alters the shape and content of the earlier exercise, transforming the scholastic tenet into a meditative drama in which the hieroglyphic shapes of the sections of the later poem figure forth the argument of "Reasonable Sacrifice." In many significant ways, then, "The Altar" interiorizes, fleshes out, or incarnates the argument present in the Latin poem. The idea of the first poem becomes the action of the second,[9] just as the second poem attempts to appeal to the Incarnate Word it meditatively strives to "image."

There are other literary texts that are revised in "The Altar," as Summers, Mary Ellen Rickey, and John Hollander have illustrated.[10] To these should be added the initial dedicatory sonnet of Sidney's *Astrophil and Stella*.[11] Like Herbert's speaker, Sidney's lover attempts "in verse to show" the effects of his beloved on him and his verse—or to show that his verse is one "*effectus passionis.*" Seeking "fit words to paint" his situation—just as Herbert's speaker turns to the words of others (the Bible)—Astrophel finally realizes that he has to "'look in thy heart and write.'" "The Altar" offers a sacred parody of this playful *apologia*. Both poems dramatize the fore-conceit of the ensuing collections: to frame/to praise in the hope of "grace [to] obtain." A pastiche of biblical phrases, the first fourteen lines of Herbert's poem re-trace Astrophil's experience ("Loving in truth," his words too "come halting forth"), until he follows the advice of the love sonnet in lines 15–16 and allows "his heart" to speak its own words. (In a sense, the suggestion that the last two lines of the poem are spoken by God[12] overlooks the fact that they are the only lines in the poem not biblical allusions "previously" spoken by God.) But how the speaker of "The Altar" achieves the "heart" to speak those last lines (the only "plain" speaking in the poem) and the significances of this couplet which is attached to his parodic, allusive love sonnet which completes the altar-format of the poem and which offers the most personal, heart-felt lines of the poem, are clarified by a closer look at the unfolding speaking picture of "The Altar."

Verbally and formally, the poem assumes three parts, each of which presents in shape and language the unfolding drama of the speaker's attempt to create and to understand (to "frame") a personal unification that reflects, understands, and admits its status as an image of the divine Word. The first section (1–4), the *compositio* of the meditation which presents the speaker's self in terms of the divine scheme, is a dramatic, imaginative re-writing of the first couplet of "Reasonable Sacrifice." As Philip Dust points out, in the Latin poem the classical sentences of Horace and Vergil are embedded in order to present the hopeless position of man without a redeemer who can unify him; forbidden by Christian injunctions from submitting the sacrifices necessary to appease his Maker, he is precariously separated (*diuisa*) from the oblations which alone can bring him integrity and re-union with his Lord (*in vnum*). Thus, the Latin poem opens by distinguishing between the pagan insufficiency of altar-sacrifices and the Christian interpretation of God's gracious sacrifice *for man*. In the English poem, the *compositio* borrows Old Testament words to suggest not a separation but a similarity, not a displacement but a fulfillment. However, even though Christian "law" replaces pagan example in "The Altar," the opening four lines present a rather problematic picture of the speaker's fulfilling the letter of the Law concerning sacrifice. As recent readers have observed, even though the speaker fulfills the Law, the most he can offer "is not perfect and whole, but something flawed and broken";[13] a "broken and purged heart"[14] is the best he can offer *sub lege*.

The *compositio* "significantly allegorizes"[15] several biblical injunctions (Psalm 51, Exodus 20:22 ff., Deut. 27, Hosea 8:6) in order to present the speaker in conformity with Mosaic covenants. He has *literally* fulfilled the law, for the language of the first couplet insists not that his heart is an antitype of the Hebrew altar but that he is literally raising an altar which only happens to be "Made of a heart." What is problematic in this section, in other words, is not the New Testament antitypes that the lines may shadow but the condition and actions of the speaker *as he describes them*. In this sense, these lines present problems, problems verbally that are reflected by the shape of this section of the poem. The characteristics of the speaker *given* in the first lines are that he is "broken," "Made," "cemented," and in servitude; that he sees himself as a literal fulfillment of the Old Testament type; and that his present action is one of "rearing." On one level of evocation, then, he is presented as a sacred parody of Sidney's Astrophil, who also finds himself to be the creation of his beloved, "framed" by his beloved's actions, a product of his "Lord's" prescriptions. Indeed, the startling oxymorons here (broken/altar, servant/rears, heart/cemented, broken/untouched, construction/unconstructed) evoke the fragmented self who addresses many love sonnets: hard-hearted but penitent, angry but loving, independent but dependent, pure but broken. However, since most sonnet sequences are themselves but secular parodies of sacred appeals, perhaps such a similarity should not surprise us here. Nevertheless, such a similarity does indicate the problematic condition of the speaker brought about by his fulfillment of the letter of his Lord's Law, *regant Scripturae canones sacrae*.[16]

That these lines present a problematic self is reiterated by the ambiguity and troublesome syntax. For instance, the opening clause can be read an an appositive, modifying "the servant": the servant who is a *broken* altar now "reares." Stanley Fish raises such a problematic possibility in these lines, but dismisses it when he reads "reares" as "constructs." However, the multiple (troubling) connotations of the verb should also be taken into consideration. In one sense the speaker offers his "altar" as an obligatory payment to his judicious Lord. But "rear" also means "to rise up, to arise, [even] to arise from the dead," and "to lift upright," "to rebel." These interpretations of the initial action of the speaker suggest that he is indeed "broken," in a sense of being a rebellious "servant"/lover who reacts defiantly to the "broken" condition brought about by the "hand" of his beloved/"Lord." In this sense, the initial picture of the speaker contains echoes of the conventional courtly lover, angry and rebellious, who raises his poem in reaction to the treatment he has received from his beloved; and, in this sense, the Old Testament passages provide "a type of the heart of man"[17] as we are to see it in many of the following poems in *The Temple*. Furthermore, the fact that the "parts" of the speaker are only "as" they were "framed," that is, only *alike* to their original state—fallen, "broken," not re-touched—reiterates the possibility of problems with the speaker's condition. Indeed, the ambiguous referent for "the same" concludes the quatrain with additional troublesome possibilities. If the speaker's altar has not been "touch'd" by any "workmans tool" (human or divine), then it is unsanctified and/or badly in need of repair; if the "servant" is only "as" he was created and untouched since then, then he is dangerously "broken" also; and if the speaker's heart has not been "touched" by its Creator and his tears are not the result of love, then his initial action can be seen as a cold-hearted and "broken" attempt to fulfill *literally* the oblation due his "Lord." Even if he has been "broken," and thus "touched," by God's actions, the speaker's present action yet can be seen as both a proud and self-consciously troubled reaction to God's "frame."

One solution to such a problematic reading of these lines, of course, is to read them typologically. As in "The Collar," where the speaker's diction implies the answer to his doubts, fears, and rebellious objections, so here we can hear how the speaker's broken heart/altar/self has already been re-framed by the *kenosis* of Christ (He "emptied himself, taking the form of a servant"— Phil. 2:4) and how "the message of salvation [is] engraved on [his] heart (2 Cor. iii.3)."[18] In this sense, the speaker's action can be read as a response to Christ's sacrifice, an imitation of Christ's fulfillment of the Law and of man's oblation upon "the altar of the Cross."[19] Such, in fact, was the basis of Augustine's definition of the "true sacrifice of man" in *De civitate Dei*, where he refers to Phil. 2 in order to insist that man must "reformemur in novitate mentis nostrae ad probandum quae sit voluntas Dei . . . hinc ei placens quod ex eius pulchritudine acceperit."[20] In this sense, we might see the speaker as responding to the example of Christ, "reared" or educated by His example.

However, even if we except this typological *promise* as operative in these lines, the problem remains that the speaker is not yet "reformed" ("reformetur . . . incommutabili formae subdita"); as the shape of this section of his poem attests, he is not yet "framed according to His most excellent figure." His altar, his poem, his self is "broken." Whether he "rears" his altar as a type of rebellious or angry response to that condition or as a type of *imitatio christi* is not made clear by his *literalized* conformity to the rules of love/Love. Either way, the opening lines present him as "broken" *sub lege*.

The hieroglyph formed by this section of the poem supports such a troubling view of the speaker's piety at this stage of his "creation." Regardless of what we see when we turn to this poem in *The Temple* and regardless of the title of the poem,[21] what we see in the opening section of "The Altar" and hear in these staccato lines is an utterance "broken" into ambiguous phrases that are further broken into words with several levels of connotation. At the most, we see a fluctuating, uneven, vague sentence, a broken rectilinear line, symbolic of man at his lowest. We see pieces of a sentence, disordered and syntactically "broken," "cemented" together as poetry only by the unwritten laws of rhyme—but no peace, and certainly not the Peace that is supposed to be seen metaphorically on the *mensa* of the altar. We can edit the lines into an altar, of course, if we follow the directions of the caesuras, with the uninterrupted third and fourth lines serving as the *mensa* and the base of the altar and the broken phrases of the first couplet forming the pillar itself. But even so, we can see only a *"broken* ALTAR," which suggests that the speaker has not yet been re-created "according to His most excellent figure." In re-writing his earlier Latin argument about altars, then, Herbert implicitly undercuts the efficacy of his own words to describe or create the necessary oblation. The large number of questions that his words "rear" and the paradoxes and ambiguity created by his attempt to use the words of his Lord suggest that his literal fulfillment of the Law only shows how unfit and incapable he is of re-creating himself. What we hear in the opening lines is what we see: *Miserere Mei.*

This poetically "broken" presentation of his frailty is at least transformed into a form of *poetic* regularity in the second section of the poem.

But this stage of the speaker's meditation, which activates his memory (5–8) and his reason (9–12) in order to recollect *how* and *why* his present condition arose, is yet troublesome in its cryptic sententiae and gnomic expression. The consistency of the iambic dimeter in these lines intimates that a pattern is now discernible in the textualized creation of his self. In other words, if the patterns of the lines mirror the condition of his mental self, then the recollection and the understanding of his mortal condition figured forth by these two quatrains suggest that he has moved beyond the contradictory and troublesome position mirrored by the irregular, syntactically disordered shape of the *compositio*.

On one level of evocation lines 5–8 support the pejorative connotations of the opening section. His description of himself as "A Heart alone," "such a stone," and "nothing but" confesses his individual insufficiency and its deadly consequences. "Alone," "stone" and "nothing" intimate the absence of rectitude of which he is capable on his own (*absentia recti*) and the hellish separation from God such mortal obduracy merits. Even the final clause here—with its possible implication that his heart is like nothing that God's power can "cut"—suggests his limited recreative powers, which are depicted by the poetically sparse repetitiveness of his short lines—as heaps of stones, the same length as the opening phrases, piled on top of each other. Rather than "rearing" or raising himself by his attempts, the speaker has only descended; as one reader phrases it, "As we move into the pillar we descend into hell" through the speaker's recollection that a heart as his is as stone—"hard, impenetrable, cold—which nothing can cut . . . nothing can make it in contrition that which God means it to be." [22] Thus, both visually and vocally, this section elaborates the consequences flatly presented in the earlier Latin poem—*Quae diuisa nocent*. In that version the vague referents of *Quae*—it could refer to earthly man and earthly altars being separated from each other or to both being separated from the source of their life, the "breathe" of God (*viuus*)—suggest that both men and altars return to their lifelessness before Creation (*Cespus* = sod, *mortuus* = belonging to the dead) when separated from the Breathe of the Word. In the English revision, this assumption is transformed into a fearful confession that recalls visually and verbally the helplessness, obduracy, and eternal consequences of man's mortality. The section of the poem, then, shows *why* the first section, why man *sub lege*, is a broken altar.

Nevertheless, at the same time the shape and words of this quatrain explain how that mortal insufficiency has already been overcome by the "pow'r" of God. Not only do the lines form a square "stone," but it is already "cut" into small pieces, the sentence ordered into four equal "pieces." Unlike the ambiguous and irregular heap of the first section, this section has already been re-created. The harmful *diuisa* of the Latin poem, then, has been re-created as a form of divine recreativity, for the tribulations of mortal man in a providential universe are "nothing but" God's continuing efforts to help him conform to the letter of the Law; "Thy power *doth* cut." The application of the memory to the speaker's situation, then, relates his condition to His Creator.[23] An enigmatic image of the Father, Augustine explains in *De trinitate*, the memory "recollects" both present and past events, and in the faithful acts to "piece together again" the past and present actions of God in one's life so as "to receive, and by marking to take heed [of] benefits received" from him.[24] In this vein, Herbert's speaker "recalls" the creative and "cutting" Power of the Father, returning therein to the creative Source that empowers and has already re-created his own memory. His recollections re-write in the poem the divine source that they now imitate. As he visually "cuts" his poem into pieces in order to recollect his mortal frailty and his fortunate tribulations, he visually and verbally recreates his memory into an image of the Father's creative power.

The analysis of his meditation (9–12) is introduced aptly with the word "Wherefore" ("for what *reason*"). "We attribute to the Understanding, all which we finde to be true in *thinking*," says St. Bernard;[25] and in this section the speaker analyzes the truth of his situation—*sub lege* and *sub gratia*. As Philip McGuire says, "the critical phrase [in this section] is 'this frame,' which refers not only to the altar of the speaker's heart but also to the poem itself . . ."[26] But the fact that "Wherefore" means also "as a result of what went before" and "because of what was said and happened before" intimates that this "frame" is not just a creation but a re-creation; that is, the speaker's poem is not only a response to and a result of the actions of God but also the place ("where") wherein His actions occur. "*This* frame" is the place where "*thy* Name" and "*my* hard heart" "Meet." Each "part" of the cosmic drama must be understood before the poet can successfully "frame" "Thy Name." This is still action *contemplated*, after all, as "to praise" suggests. He understands the reasons *why* he should "praise thy Name," but his heart/poem/self is still in "parts." It is still, if you wish, only parts of speech, only human words that cannot fully or sufficiently praise the name of God. The "Name" that has re-united those "parts," in fact, the Name that reunites man with his Creator, saves him from nothingness, and "Meets" him in the Incarnation has not been *named* in the poem.

In this sense, the analysis section of "The Altar" presents Herbert's most radical revision of his earlier, Latin poem. There he clearly announces how man as an altar can be reformed into an instrument capable of praising his Lord: "Quae diuisa nocent, *Christi per foedus*, in vnum / Conueniunt." "Through Christ's covenant" man has been re-made, reunited with his Creator, and reformed into a self that images his creator — *viua fit Ara Dei*, "The living altar of God." Herbert's meditator, however, is still only "parts." That is, from a meditative point of view, through the second section of his meditation he has only re-formed his memory and understanding. He has only recalled and understood his relation to his Lord. Until he submits his will, redirecting his entire rational soul to God, until his faith has issued in "good works," he has not fulfilled his obligation or his selfhood. Thus, it is not until the submission of his will to that of God in the last section of the poem that the speaker literally becomes "I" (in line 13). This does not mean, of course, that his good works, his submission, will prove a worthy sacrifice, that it will be either accepted or acknowledged by his Lord — as the careful provisionals *if* and *may* and the three infinitives in the last lines illustrate. But until the contemplative becomes the active, until the will responds to the promptings of the memory and reason, the speaker has not totally recreated himself — or finished his poem.

But before moving to that final section of the poem it is important to look more closely at the second "part" of his meditation. Why did Herbert omit *Christi per foedum* from his revision? A closer look at the "parts" of the poem reveals that he did not. In addition to the traditional association of Christ with "thy name" (the Word-made-Flesh), other "parts" of the poem frame "thy name." Crucial here is the phrase

"Meets in this frame." Given the seventeenth-century meaning of "meets" as "submits," the speaker's memory and understanding "meet" in order *to submit* his will to God through poetic praise. But, at the same time, since "frame" refers to his poem also, it is significant that the "meeting" of the first and second "parts" of his poem resembles a cross. In a poem of contrition, a confession in which he strives to understand the tribulations that have "cut" his hard heart into "parts," a cross is an appropriate emblem of his condition.[27] In this sense, the changing, progressive shapes of the poem gauge the speaker's unfolding understanding of himself in relation to the covenants of Law and Grace. Man as a "broken Altar" incapable of praise is a deadly heap of stony nothingness without the "touch" of God that brings about contrition; but those tribulations and that contrition are only the cross he merits under the Law—but, more importantly, the merciful means by which he is made capable of imitating his Savior. In the Latin altar poem, Herbert said that "men and altars," man and God, were "put together" through Christ's covenant—*"in vnum / Conueniunt"*; in "The Altar" the speaker's understanding of the cruciform of his life creates an emblem of the divine form that explains why he should "praise thy name."

Certainly such a shape is appropriate to the analysis section of his meditation, the reason re-created being the image of Christ. And such a visual frame was central to the Anglican interpretation of "altars." In his explanation of the New Testament passage that was the source of many debates about altars in the Renaissance (Hebrews 13:10), for example, Bishop Becon says, "The sacrifice of Christ's body, which he himself, that everlasting Priest, offered on *the altar of the cross* to God the Father, is a plentous, full, perfect, and sufficient satisfaction for the sins of the whole world."[28] Archdeacon Philpot uses the same words to explain Anglican Eucharist theology: "it is the sacrament of the sacrifice which Christ offered upon *the altar of the cross*, the which sacrifice all the altars and sacrifices done upon the altars in the old law did prefigure and shadow."[29] And Herbert's friend, John Cosin, while submitting that the earlier Reformers were too fastidious in their attempts to eradicate the word "altar" from all forms of the liturgy, urges that Communion Table where the Cross is recalled may be termed an altar: "The names themselves may, I hope, be retained without sin, (as St. Paul retained it in *ad Hebr.*) in respect of that proportion of things established By our Saviour have unto them which by Him are abrogated . . . the only difference is, that whereas before they had a literal, they now have a metaphorical, use, and are so many notes of remembrance unto us, that what they did signify in the letter is accomplished in the truth . . . , by way of analogy and allusion"[30] — or, in the case of "The Altar," by way of emblematic shape. Once again, then, the poem aims to be "framed according to His most excellent figure," its visual and verbal parts mirroring the meditator's attempt to know, understand, and participate in the re-writing of human history by the divine Word.

The transformation of the shape of the poem from a broken altar to a cross by the second section is complemented by the alteration of the speaker's mode of discourse, from a literal to a metaphorical level of address. His literal application of the Old Testament sentences in the first two couplets is replaced by the admission that that opening figure cannot be taken literally, as signaled by the shift to metaphor in "A Heart alone / Is such a stone." His metaphorical altar — his heart — is "meet" for his "frame" (appropriate for his metaphorical sacrifice). Thus, while admitting that even his heart is inadequate — only God's power can effect the required "cutting" — the speaker ceases his attempt to fulfill the Law literally and admits the *merely* metaphorical character of his actions: the poem is not an altar nor a heart but "this frame" — a metaphor, an image. As Hooker explains in Book 4 of the *Laws*, "the words which were, do continue; the only difference is, that whereas before they had a literal, they now have a metaphorical use, . . . what they did signify in the letter is accomplished in the truth" (4.9.10).[31] Meditatively re-creating himself in God's image, Herbert's speaker transforms his poem into a metaphoric image of the Cross, alters his poem from a literal to a metaphoric mode of praise, therein transforming the poem of his self into an image of the active Word it imitates and seeks to praise. Such, of course, is the understanding that is central to the poem and to Anglican doctrine — the literal altars of the Hebrews and the Catholics are to be understood metaphorically, to be interiorized. The altar of the Cross is "framed" in the heart of man.

In the analysis section of the poem, then, the speaker's "broken" heart is transformed into an image of the Cross (or, if one wishes, Herbert accommodates the words of his poem to the cruciform shape of the *mensa* and pillar of an altar) through his realization of his pitiful condition "alone" and his acknowledgment that God's Mercy "alone" is capable of re-creating him—has already transfigured him, in fact, through his "Meet[ing]" man on the Cross. By itself, "alone," this section of the poem, the verbalization of his "Heart alone," by itself, on its own, assumes the shape of a rectangular stone; allowed to assume its own shape, to shape itself, the heart is "nothing but" "such a stone." However, when this "part" of the poem "Meets" with the earlier "pieces," and with the earlier "Peace" of God's Grace, it is changed into the shape of a cross, just as the union of the meditator's memory and understanding *shows* the answer to his dilemma: made, cut, and framed by the Word, man offers praise to God when he "frames" himself as an image of "His most excellent figure." The idolatry of altar-worship forbidden under the Law is reshaped by Christ's Cross into an interior experience by the Law of Grace.

The last section of the poem, the base of the altar and the colloquy of the mediation, presents the re-integrated, whole man, as intimated by the shape and texture of his unbroken lines and the use of the pronoun I. The point of this closing, allusive variation on the courtly convention of claiming immortality for his verse is not that the poet has disappeared from the poem until now, but that he is now integrated mentally for the first time, "reformemur in novitate mentis nostrae" (transformed by the renovation of our heart), in Augustine's terms. And rather than admitting that God wrote his poem, the speaker carefully qualifies the import of the biblical phrases he applies in order to specify his own limited creativity as an enigmatic image of God. These lines, that is, still present problems, slightly revising the matter-of-fact conclusion of the earlier Latin version, "so man becomes the living altar of God." The finality (and confidence) of that conclusion is re-written here into qualifying, provisional infinitives, reinforced by "if," "may," and "let," as Herbert shifts the focus of the discursive Latin poem's article of faith to a dramatization of the difficulty of relating the ultimate mysteriousness of the Word. Man, Augustine explains, can never actually attain his original status as God's image: even when the rational faculties "shall be cured of every infirmity and shall be mutually equal, even then that thing, which through grace shall not be changed, will not be made equal to the thing that is unchangeable in its nature . . . Whatever ideas are in the mind of a believing man from this faith and from such a life when they are contained in the memory, examined in the recollection, and accepted by the will, form a trinity of its own kind. But the image of God [even] with His help, . . . is not yet in it."[32] In this vein, lines 13–14 of "The Altar" present the speaker's final instructions to his will, and lines 15–16 enact that submission of his will to His Maker, thus completing the meditative re-creation—but his claims about the significances of his re-formed actions are carefully qualified. Poised at the threshold of "The Church," the poem, after all, is only the first of the speaker's many "calls" to God made in response to His Words, the first of his many attempts to bridge the gap "betwixt God and [his] Soul." The tentativeness of these lines, then, evokes the insufficiency of his response alone, the impossibility of poetic closure without the sanctification by "thy name," and, therein, the necessity for the *response* from Christ in the next poem of the collection.

The first couplet of this section continues the accommodation of biblical wisdom, identifying the speaker as a member of the Christian community of disciples: the "stones" of his poem affirm the eternality of Christ's Peace (Luke 19:40). However, the conditionals in his affirmation indicate his understanding of the freedom of his will. He *can* "hold [his] peace," deny that his re-creation is totally the product of God's Grace, or simply remain silent. He can continue to "hold" to himself, to rely on himself—and thus remain a fragment of "stones." Regardless of how "good it is for [him] to hold fast by God" (Psalm 73:27), he may not even be able to continue to praise God—he may die, and he certainly will yet be guilty of sins. But if he decides to "die" in another sense, to accept the life of faith, regardless of whether he dies or not these "stones" (either as a "funerary monument"[33] or a figurative altar upon which he has sacrificed his moral independence) will continue "to praise thee." He chooses, of course, the Peace that passes all understanding. But even that does not ensure that he himself will "not cease." He most assuredly will die; he most assuredly will continue to "seize" his Lord by his sins, crucifying Him again and again. ("Every sin," preached Dean Donne, "is a crucifying of Christ."[34]) And even if he is able to and does follow all the ameliorative possibilities before him he cannot be sure that his acts of praise will prove sufficient, for man is justified by faith alone. Thus, like his courtly image in *Astrophel and Stella*, the speaker is yet "helpless in my throes, / Biting my truant pen, beating myself for spite," and more conscious than ever of his need and desire "to speak." Even in its fullest presentation of the speaker as "a man of true and lively faith,"[35] the poem privileges the problematic character of human freedom even for the renovated man.

Thus, the final couplet, which in one way completes the meditator's re-creation of his self and submission of his will to God, also insists on the limited nature of the speaker's achievement. Having meditatively "tune[d] the Instrument"[36] of his rational soul, reformed it into an image of God's Word, having created a text that is literally a metaphoric re-writing of the Scriptural Words of God, the speaker submits freely that his self, his poem—"this ALTAR"—is inadequate and incomplete and unfinished without the sanctifying Grace of God. "Mine" and "thine" are still brought together only by the artificial rules of rhyme, still appearing on separate lines.[37]

This is not to suggest, of course, that Herbert's poem does not confirm his faith in the continuing efficacy of Christ's Sacrifice. The Book of Homilies points out, for instance, that "In the supper of the Lord ... is a marvelous *incorporation*, which by the operation of the Holy Ghost (the very bond of our *conjunction* with Christ) is through faith wrought in the soules of the faithful" (197). Submitting his will to God, giving his own words to God in these last lines, subjecting the image of the Holy Ghost in his rational soul to the "operation of the Holy Ghost," indicates the faith of Herbert's speaker in and praise for such an "incorporation." In fact, a marvelous "conjunction" and "incorporation" *is* framed by his submission: his poem now assumes the shape of an altar. It is, of course, only a metaphoric altar, an image on a page, an arrangement of images intended to mirror the speaker's dedication of self and poem to his Maker. In this sense, the final shape of the poem becomes that "good work" which acknowledges its own origin in God's gift of faith—that "sign" of which Augustine speaks, "framed according to His most excellent figure." And as an image of the speaker's self, it attests to his faith and hope in a time "to be" when, through Christ's sacrifice, he shall see "face to face." As Augustine explains, that vision yet "to be" shall come to those "who look upon their mind as an image, so that they are able, in some way or other, to refer what they see to Him, whose image it is, and also to see by conjecturing that which they now see through the image by beholding, since they cannot yet see face to face. For the Apostle did not say that we now see a mirror, but that 'we now see through a mirror.'"[38] "The Altar" is that process of "seeing through"—a poetic "conjecturing" which insists on its own status as an enigmatic image but which "refers" the final significance of its poetics to Him.

The final lines of the poem, then, present visually and verbally the paradox of the human condition. The questioning, hesitant provisionals of lines 13–14 intimate "the inept comprehension of mere humanity"[39] at the height of rational powers—at least as far as his ultimate understanding of the fate ("chance") of his own efforts is concerned. This tentative couplet conveys not only his humility but also his cognizance of the limitations of his powers—limitations that have gradually unfolded through the changing verbs of the poem: it moves from the speaker's active "reares," to his contemplation of action ("To praise"), to the contemplation of non-action ("if I chance to hold"), a pattern completed by the submission that it is God's action that he wishes to participate in (You "let") if he is to "receive a new form, a new essence, a new nature."[40] In one sense, of course, he acknowledges that his poem and his self have been re-shaped all along by the actions of Christ—but such an assent does not efface the *exemplary* character of his own actions (*imitatio christi*); acknowledging that God provides the *energeia* and form of his imitation *is* a response, a participation in the recreation He allows "to be." His words, his "parts," his faculties are still "stones," but by submitting them as a sacrifice to the Word that "Made" them, the speaker creates an image of God's power to transform them into "living stones" (2 Peter 2:5).

The poem, then, is as much self-creating as self-consuming. It is a re-writing and a re-uniting of the "parts" of the broken self of the type incarnated in The Word-made-Flesh. The union of the shape and the heart of the poem imitates generally and particularly the Incarnation it celebrates. In this sense, the poem does not plead for an annihilation of the self but for a continuous, continued re-creation. Just as the speaker's self has been re-created through this gift of Grace (in the Passion and in his own contrition), so he appeals for an eternal re-writing of the self and sanctification of his poem, for renewal and fulfillment. Moving from declamation to prayer, in the final couplet Herbert's speaker looks in his heart and writes. The only lines in the poem that are not a biblical accommodation, the only lines spoken *by* and not *about* his heart in the poem, these lines "yield [his] final, deepest thought, which is a prayer and a song of praise, leading us to the next poem"[41] (appropriately, "The Sacrifice," since "thy name" still remains unvoiced in this poem, rendering terminal closure impossible). But as the *words of the speaker* these last lines still leave us with an important paradox central to Herbert's poetics. In one way, the speaker's personal response, the words of praise from his heart, invoke his response to, participation in, and poetic sacrifice to his Lord—his words, his response, his submission at the threshold of *The Temple* "frames" his poem into the shape of an altar. But, at the same time, the final shape of the poem is an *I* as well as an altar—an image of his limited self as well and of his Lord's plenitude. As Stanley Fish suggests, the impetus of the entire poem is for the speaker to "let go," to give himself and his words entirely to God; but this does not predicate an annihilation of the self but, rather, in Robert B. Shaw's words, "a transfiguration of the self"[42] in which, as in the sacrament performed at the eucharistic altar table, the self is renewed, re-made, and re-formed so that man is able to speak aright the words of praise. The final shape of "The Altar," is *both* an *altar* and an *I*—an image of the speaker's self and his Christ. To urge that it is not both is to dissolve the enigma of the human condition, to see the poem as an affirmation of *either* free will *or* predestination. The final couplet carefully retains the paradox of man's shape; for until the final transfigurative re-writing of God, all poets and readers must "see through a glass darkly," or in Augustine's terms, "see through a mirror enigmatically." Until then, man can do no more than "frame" himself as an enigmatic image of Christ. The furniture, sacraments, covenants, and instruments of God's Temple provide the forms he should imitate. But his imitations of those forms are yet *his* fictions, his enigmatic attempts "to praise." And they are only entirely his when he admits they are entirely His.

Thus, the dynamic altering of the self "framed" by God's presence that is meditatively dramatized in "The Altar" is complemented and clarified by the unfolding shapes of the poem. How and why the "broken Altar" of man's heart can be transfigured into an instrument of praise that mirrors (however enigmatically) God's continuing conversation with His creation—from the time of Hebraic altars and the altar of the Cross to the remembrance of His sacrifice in Anglican worship—is both verbally and visually framed by the speaking picture of Herbert's emblematic meditation. The poem stands finally, then, in marvelous verbal and visual tension—as an altar and an I, an imitation of the Word and an image of the Word, a re-created re-creation and an altered altar—a unified reformation that stands poised, in Herbert's own description of *The Temple*, "betwixt" God and man. As such, "The Altar" serves not only as an appropriate introduction to and dedication of the poems of praise that follow it in *The Temple* but equally well as the *place* where Herbert unfolds the poetics-of-the-self central to those subsequent re-creations. How the heart of man, "a broken Altar," is by God's Grace re-formed into an altar "framed according to His most excellent figure" is the central visual and verbal drama of Herbert's unfolding emblem. The dynamic fulfillment of the covenant by Grace in the heart of man is at the heart of Herbert's altered altar.

Notes

1. *The Holy Table* (London, 1637), 111.
2. I have used the English translation by John Healey (London, 1610, 1620). Citations of the Latin are from the Loeb Classical Library text, edited by David S. Weisen (Cambridge: Harvard University Press, 1968). Augustine's definition of "the true sacrifice" occupies chapters 5–6 of Book 10.
3. Healey, 276. Weisen's translation reads: "to be transformed by the renovation of our heart" (277).
4. As Joseph Summers points out, the poem "*is* the altar upon which the following poems . . . are offered, and it is an explanation of the reason for their composi-

tion": *George Herbert: His Religion and Art* (Cambridge: Harvard University Press, 1954), 142.

    5. Summers, 145.

    6. Herbert, "Coloss. 3:3." All citations of Herbert are to the F. E. Hutchinson edition (Oxford: Clarendon Press, 1953).

    7. Soliloquy 10, in *A Heavenly Treasure* (London, 1624), 201.

    8. "George Herbert's Two Altar Poems," *Humanistica Louvaniensia* 24 (1975): 278–87. Citations of Herbert's Latin poetry are to the edition of Mark McCloskey and Paul R. Murphy, *The Latin Poetry of George Herbert* (Athens: Ohio University Press, 1965). See also Thomas B. Stroup, " 'A Reasonable, Holy, and Living Sacrifice': Herbert's 'The Altar,'" *Essays in Literature* 2 (1975): 149–63.

    9. This distinction is based on my understanding of the Sidneyan poetic, as explained by A. Leigh DeNeef, "Rereading Sidney's *Apology*," *Journal of Medieval and Renaissance Studies* 10 (1980): 155–91. That is, Sidney distinguished between Idea, foreconceit, and text: the text is a metaphoric imitation of the Idea of a poem. In these terms, "The Altar," as the language of the poem suggests, is an act of *framing*, an imitation of *Frame*, that teaches the reader "how and why" *to frame* the text of his self.

    10. Summers, 140–43; Mary Ellen Rickey, *Utmost Art: Complexity in the Verse of George Herbert* (Lexington: University of Kentucky Press, 1966), 9–16; and John Hollander, *Vision and Resonance: Two Senses of Poetic Form* (Oxford: Oxford University Press, 1975), 263–64.

    11. Citations of *Astrophil and Stella* are to the edition of William A. Ringler, Jr. (Oxford: Clarendon Press, 1962).

    12. Stanley Fish, *Self-Consuming Artifacts* (Los Angeles: University of California Press, 1972), 207–15.

    13. Booty, "Contrition in Anglican Spirituality: Hooker, Donne and Herbert," in *Anglican Spirituality*, ed. William J. Wolf (Wilton, CT: Morehouse-Barlow, 1982), 37–38.

    14. Summers, 142.

    15. Rosemund Tuve, *A Reading of George Herbert* (Chicago: University of Chicago Press, 1952), 183.

    16. Herbert, "De Rituum vsu," in *Latin Poetry*, 38.

    17. Summers, 141.

    18. Summers, 141–42.

    19. On the description of the altar as the Cross, see 128–32 following and notes 26–28.

    20. *De civitate dei*, 10.6, p. 276: "to be transformed by the renovation of our heart, that we may have judgment to know what is the will of God, . . . becoming in his sight by the reflections of his beauty that it has received" (277, 275).

    21. The puns on "collar," "choler," and "caller" in the title of "The Collar," to choose only one example from *The Temple*, should alert us to the playfulness of Herbert's titles.

    22. Booty, 37.

23. The memory, says Dean Donne, should "comprehend God for benefits received": *Sermons*, edited by George R. Potter and Evelyn M. Simpson (Los Angeles: University of California Press, 1953–62), 5:149.

24. St. Bonaventura, for example, points out that "the function of the memory is to retain and to re-present . . . This actual retention on the part of the memory [is] of time, past, present, and future": *Itinerarium Mentis in Deum*, trans. Father James (London: Burns Oates and Washbourne, 1937), 36–37.

25. *Saint Bernard His Meditation*, pt. 2, p. 6, cited in Louis Martz, *The Poetry of Meditation*, rev. ed. (New Haven: Yale Univ. Press, 1962), 36.

26. "Private Prayer and English Poetry in the Early Seventeenth Century," *Studies in English Literature, 1500–1900* 14 (1974): 76.

27. "The end of the Lord," explained Donne, "was the crosse; So that to follow him to the end, is not onely to beare afflictions, . . . but it is to bring our crosses to the Crosse of Christ. . . . You see foure stages, foure resting, baiting places in this progresse. . . . The afflictions of the wicked exasperate them, enrage them, stone and pave them, obdurate and petrifie them, but they doe not crucifie them. The afflictions of the godly crucifie them. And when I am coming to that conformity with my Saviour, as to *fulfill his sufferings in my flesh*, . . . then I am crucified with him, carried up to his Crosse. . . . Thus my afflictions are truly a crosse, when those afflictions doe truly crucifie me, and souple me, and mellow me, and knead me, and roll me out, to a conformity with Christ. It must be this *Crosse*, and then it must be *my crosse* that I must take up, *Tollat suam*": *Sermons*, 2:300.

28. "The Sick Man's Salve," in *Works* (Cambridge, 1844), 1:138; see also "The Displaying of the Popish Mass," 1:258 ff.

29. "Eleventh Examination," in *Works* (Cambridge, 1842), 119.

30. "Notes on the Book of Common Prayer," in *Works* (Oxford, 1855), 5:89.

31. Richard Hooker, *Of the Laws of Ecclesiastical Polity*, intro. Christopher Morris (1907; New York: E. P. Dutton, 1969), 1:402.

32. *The Trinity*, trans. Stephen McKenna (Washington, DC: Catholic University of America Press, 1963), 510–11, 409.

33. Charles V. Nestrick, " 'Mine and Thine' in *The Temple*," in *"Too Riche To Clothe the Sunne": Essays on George Herbert*, ed. Summers and Pebworth (Pittsburgh: University of Pittsburgh Press, 1980), 116.

34. *Sermons*, 1:196.

35. *Book of Homilies* (London, 1623), 30.

36. Donne's description of meditation in "Hymn to God my God, in my sicknesse," line 4: *The Divine Poems*, ed. Helen Gardner (Oxford: Oxford University Press, 1952), 113.

37. As William V. Nestrick points out, "By coupling 'mine' and 'thine' as rhymes, Herbert discovers the separation that is the basis for the Christian's sense of God, and the attempt to overcome these words, to bring them into a union is a poetic and religious desideratum": " 'Mine and Thine' in *The Temple*," in *Too Riche to Clothe the Sunne*, 115. See also the incisive reading of this idea by A. L. Clements, "Theme,

Tone and Tradition in George Herbert's Poetry," *English Literary Renaissance* 3 (1973): 264–83, especially on the way these two crucial words voice "the idea of the two selves in each man."

38. *The Trinity*, 510–11.

39. A. D. Nuttall, *Overheard by God* (London: 1980), 3.

40. This is Donne's description of Holy Communion, *Sermons*, 7:295.

41. Booty, "Contrition," 37–38.

42. *The Call of God* (Cambridge, Mass.: Cowley, 1981), 104.

The Poem as Hierophon:
Musical Configurations in George Herbert's "The Church"

DIANE McCOLLEY

In a note to his chapter on music in *George Herbert: His Religion and Art*, Joseph H. Summers observed that "The study of the interrelations between poetry and music in the English Renaissance has only been begun."[1] Since then much has been published that illuminates Herbert's use of musical images, metaphors, puns, and prosody. Taking a clue from Summers's key essay on "The Poem as Hieroglyph," or sacred carving, I wish to consider some of Herbert's poems as hierophons, or sacred "composures," having sonic properties analogous to the glyphic forms that Summers has taught us to enjoy.[2] These poems display configurations of "concent" comparable to kinds of music Herbert heard, played, and sang at Westminster, Cambridge, and Salisbury, and in whose company he traveled "to heavens doore."[3]

Readers often think of Herbert's as a solo voice, "playing and singing," as John Hollander says, "in secluded retirement."[4] But in many of his poems the voicing is polyphonic, and these add resonance to *The Temple* as a work that combines meditation with corporate celebration as one does, not in seclusion, but in church. In *The Country Parson* Herbert stresses public worship. In "Providence" he admonishes that anyone who fails to praise God "Doth not refrain unto himself alone, / But robs a thousand" (18–19), and in "The Church-Porch" urges, "though private prayer be a brave designe, / Yet publick hath more promises, more love: / ... let us move / Where is it warmest. Leave thy six and seven; / Pray with the most: for where most pray, is heaven" (397–398, 400–402).

Heaven is not a solitary place. The church, its model on earth, not only raises a multitude of voices but does so "with Angels and Archangels, and with all the company of heaven."[5] Though poems are written in seclusion, the voice of the self is not the only voice in them, especially for a poet who asks God to "let thy blessed Spirit bear a part" and who, when most alone, begs for one strain so that he may join God's consort. Humankind, as secretary of God's praise, sings for the whole creation; and praise, however private, is the joining of one's voice to the voices of everything that hath breath.[6] The more one listens to the kind of music Herbert heard and performed, the more one hears these voices in his poems.

Although the solo "ayre" was popular in Herbert's time, most of the music sung in collegiate and cathedral churches (and, of course, that played at "Music-meetings")[7] was part-music. The language of liturgy—psalms, canticles, collects, and the ordinary of the communion service—is full of the imagery of cosmic diversity in harmony. Renaissance and early Baroque choral music was peculiarly suited to express this "concent" in a multitude of ways: by its use of both contrapuntal and chordal textures; by its "word-painting"; by its command of modes and keys understood to "set the affections in right tune";[8] by its ways of "twisting a song" that give each singer a distinct, equal, individual strand to wreathe into the whole, keeping serenely in tune with heaven by means of exact pitch and pulse, while flexibly responsive in phrasing to the text, the musical line, and the other singers. For the singer, such music provides exercise in mutual and multiple responsiveness, "That all together may accord in thee, / And prove one God, one harmonie" (41–42). For the listener, it provides an echo of "delights on high" (1).[9] For both, it is a mimetic model of Love's banquet, the Eucharistic feast that figures Heaven.

One of the edicts of the Reformation was that liturgical singing should "not be full of notes, but, as near as may be, for every syllable a note."[10] But by Herbert's time—often called the golden age of English church music—composers honored this intention more in the spirit than in the letter, using moderate polyphony to represent words in such apt musical lines and textures that the by then familiar words of the English liturgy and psalter set to expressive music could be better understood than words alone. Moreover, once one has learned aptly set texts, the notes alone will bring the words to mind; and, conversely, certain often-set words alone acquire the grace of song. Herbert's poems, begotten in liturgy, are borne on wings of music.

William Byrd, known to his contemporaries as "the father of music" and a friend of the Herbert family,[11] composed service music that Herbert is highly likely to have heard. For Byrd, as for Herbert, the Holy Spirit bore a part:

> to sacred words in which the praises of God and of Heavenly host are sung, none but some celestial harmony (so far as our powers avail) will be proper. Moreover, in these words, as I have learned by trial, there is such a profound and hidden power that to one thinking upon things divine, and diligently and earnestly pondering them, all the fittest numbers occur as if of themselves.[12]

In a setting of the *Te Deum Laudamus*,[13] Byrd "twist[s] a song / Pleasant and long" in which the many voices gathered in the canticle are represented in vocal textures consonant with the words. The humble beginning by trebles and tenors increases, at "all the earth doth worship thee," to full choir. For the verses that follow, Byrd alternates counterpoint with chordal harmonies, the heavenly voices getting most of the polyphony and earthly ones most of the chords. When all the angels cry aloud "Holy, holy, holy," cherubim and seraphim first sing antiphonally, then join together, in chords of airy clarity, then diversify in polyphony. The words *Heaven* and *earth* are contrapuntal and antiphonal; the apostles and martyrs enter separately, in chords: "the holy Church throughout all the world" is full choir. As is characteristic of the music of this period, the musical rhythms alter freely, over a steady pulse, between duple and triple rhythms, either to give long notes to accented syllables or—as at "the Father everlasting"—to cast words about God into triple or "perfect" time. Although most syllables do get a note apiece, Byrd allows a modest melisma when a word invites him to increase and multiply his numbers: *everlasting, Sabaoth, glory, armie* and *Comforter*. Such voicing and word-painting, familiar to Herbert through liturgy, make their way into the forms and diction of his poems.

Herbert's two *Antiphons* are explicitly composed in choral form. The first (which, like many of Herbert's poems, is less simple than it looks) is a verse anthem[14] with choral refrain:

> *Cho.* Let all the world in ev'ry corner sing,
> *My God and King.*
> *Vers.* The heav'ns are not too high,
> His praise may thither flie:
> The earth is not too low,
> His praises there may grow.
>
> *Cho.* Let all the world in ev'ry corner sing,
> *My God and King.*
> *Vers.* The church with psalms must shout,
> No doore can keep them out:
> But above all the heart
> Must bear the longest part.
>
> *Cho.* Let all the world in ev'ry corner sing,
> *My God and King.*

Herbert's title refers both to antiphonal singing by two or more choirs and to refrains sung in response to liturgical texts. In English cathedral and collegiate churches and in some parish churches, including the one Herbert re-designed at Leighton Bromswold (and perhaps called "a place where I might sing"),[15] two complete choirs face each other across the chancel aisle. Seventeenth-century verse anthems make full use of the diverse voicing this arrangement affords, with voices coming literally from "ev'ry corner," a pattern Herbert applies to "all the world." At the same time, the poem is a private response to the Venite, or invitatory canticle sung at Matins, which begins "O come let us sing unto the Lord" and includes the verse "In his hands are all the corners of the earth." By casting his invitatory poem as a verse anthem, Herbert chooses a choral form that evokes the multiple voices—both individual and united—it invokes.

The poem's diction would offer a composer numerous opportunities for word-painting by means of pitch, vocal textures, rhythmic and harmonic changes, suspension, and melisma. The words *high, low, flies, grow, above all,* and *longest part* obviously suggest such treatment. *Shout* implies many voices, not necessarily loud ones; Renaissance composers wrote what we call "dynamics" into the music by adding or reducing the number of voices, so that each voice could retain the reticent clarity by which the music of Herbert's time produces supernal serenity. The church's psalms will penetrate every door and beget singing within; but the heart "above all"— that is, most important, but also descanting over the voices of "all the world"— must go on singing after the psalms are done, and indeed forever.

Herbert may have set the poem, or intended it to be set, in ways the words suggest. But even when we read it silently in our chairs, these musical expectations add resonances and a sense of infinite voices.

Herbert's second *Antiphon* formally represents two choirs, one of men and one of angels, dividing antiphonally and reuniting in full choir.

> *Chor.* Praised be the God of love,
>   *Men.* Here below,
>   *Angels.* And here above:
> *Cho.* Who hath dealt his mercies so,
>   *Ang.* To his friend,
>   *Men.* And to his foe;
>
> *Cho.* That both grace and glorie tend
>   *Ang.* Us of old,
>   *Men.* And us in th'end.
> *Cho.* The greatest Shepherd of the fold
>   *Ang.* Us did make,
>   *Men.* For us was sold.
>
> *Cho.* He our foes in pieces brake;
>   *Ang.* Him we touch;
>   *Men.* And him we take.
> *Cho.* Wherefore since that he is such,
>   *Ang.* We adore,
>   *Men.* And we do crouch.

> *Cho.* Lord, thy praises should be more.
> *Men.* We have none,
> *Ang.* And we no store.
> *Cho.* Praised be the God alone,
> Who hath made of two folds one.

Angelic and human voices are often joined in anthems and in the liturgy—the *Sanctus*, the *Te Deum*, and the *Gloria* contain angelic utterances—and early seventeenth-century composers, like painters and poets, drew humankind and angelkind close together in works that gave them distinct but unified parts. In a verse anthem called "Lord, Grant Grace," Orlando Gibbons, Byrd's successor as organist of the Chapel Royal, composed musical patterns that illuminate both Herbert's *Antiphons*. Like many of Herbert's poems, the anthem is a sort of miniature liturgy. The text is a free rendering of the angelic choruses in Revelation, opening with a brief collect and preface and ending with the last line of the last Psalm:

> Lord, grant grace we humbly beseech thee, that we with thine angels and saints may sing to thee continually: Holy, holy, holy, Lord God of hosts. Glory, honour and power be unto thee, O God the Creator, O Lord Jesus the Redeemer, O Holy Spirit the Comforter. And let every thing that hath breath praise and magnify the same Lord.[16]

Beginning with a duet and reticent viols, Gibbons sets the words "Lord, grant grace, we humbly beseech thee" in quadruple or "common" time, with a dissonance on "beseech." "That we with thine angels and saints may sing continually" is in triple or "perfect" rhythm (as are the words). The song they sing together, the *Sanctus*, syncopates to conjoin the two kinds of time. Then, in full choir, this integration of heaven and earth is achieved by fluid alternation of four-pulse and three-pulse phrases. Next, the choirs divide, but not into cantoris and decani parts. Instead, each phrase is sung by two voices from one side of the chancel and one from the other: simultaneously alternating two high voices and one low voice with two low and one high, troping the antiphony of humans and angels without wholly separating them. "Glory, honour, and power" is strongly in threes. The names of the persons of the Trinity start with three voices in triple time, with actively moving parts on "God the Creator," and move, on "the Redeemer," to quadruple time. By means of moderate polyphony, the three names of God are perfectly distinct, yet overlapped: a musical expression of three-in-one. For the final verse, "Let everything that hath breath praise and magnify the same Lord," the choir in five parts sings first in homophonic chords, representing unanimity, then repeats in polyphony, representing diversity. The rhythms provide fit numbers that correspond with both the verbal phrases and the verbal concepts, altering so freely that the modern editor has supplied five new time signatures in this one sentence; yet the whole anthem flows with serene simplicity.

Herbert's first *Antiphon* contains three choruses in common time (dividing his fourteeners differently, however, from the 8.6 "common meter" of most of the authorized metrical psalms) and two quatrains in triple time. His second *Antiphon* firmly integrates earthly and heavenly numbers—being about men and angels as fellow worshippers—by disposing quatrains, as Helen Vendler has pointed out, in *terza rima*.[17] Moreover, the heavenly threes and earthly fours of musical and numerological convention are combined in an octave of choruses: full diapason.[18]

In her expert account of its "fierce principles of construction," Vendler remarks that this poem is strangely toneless, that "the meter is peculiarly heavy-footed in its trochaic insistence," and that "for once Herbert's euphony and gracefulness have deserted him, especially in lines like 'Wherefore since that he is such, / We adore, / And we do crouch.'"[19] I think that the poem's tones are supplied partly by the ways composers treated the voicing of human and angelic antiphony, of which Gibbons' anthem is an elaborate example, and by their usual word-painting of the diction Herbert chooses. *Praise* and *glorie* suggest melisma and soaring descants; *none* reduced voicing and *store* multiple notes; *grace* an embellishment; *mercy* warm harmony; *break* and *crouch*, dissonance. "Crouch" is an especially interesting instance of Herbert's phonic decorum, having roots in both "crook" (fitting the metaphor of shepherd and fold) and "cross." Musically, words having to do with the cross, or with supplication or holiness, were often expressed by the dissonance of close intervals. Gibbons uses such dissonance on "beseech" and "holy." [20] Herbert's uneuphonious "crouch" acknowledges not only the bodily form and the humility of the kneeling worshippers but also the crucifixion by which Christ broke not only "our foes" but himself, and the breaking of bread by which, kneeling, "him we take." Formally, the passing dissonance makes way for a resolution in which form and thought are again perfectly conjoined. The voicing literally crosses, so that after the humble access represented by "crouch" the last come first: men and angels reverse their order (as they had at the beginning) and thus return formally to the beginning of this octave of choruses. Moreover, after the mutual renunciation of "we have none" and "we no store" the two choirs are united "in one fold." "Fold" hearkens back to "shepherd" and even "tend." Musically it invites instrumental "doubling" of the vocal parts for a richly textured conclusion. [21] Throughout, the divided choirs suggest polyphonic imitation, and the choruses, especially the last one—and more especially the last word "one"—cry for the union of voices in sonorous homophonic chords. Again, we do not have to hear actual settings to let the words be enriched, the trochees lightened and aerated, by these connotations.

In both *Antiphon* I and "The 23rd Psalm" Herbert acknowledges the Psalm-singing movement in which his own family participated. [22] The singing of Psalms by men, women, and children in churches, homes, and public gatherings was a characteristic Reformation activity. Nicholas Temperley describes it as beginning with a great burst of enthusiasm which had diminished as a congregational practice in Herbert's time but diversified in printed editions at various levels of musical interest meant for gatherings of family and friends. [23] The singing of the Sternhold and Hopkins psalms—which much improves their pedestrian verse—"in every corner" of the land had lasting effects on both music and poetry, Temperley and his sources show, marshalling the march of English verse toward iambic regularity and establishing ballad or "common" meter and other simple strophic forms as the norm for participatory psalm- and hymn-singing. Meanwhile, poets continued to versify psalms and composers to set them in varied stanzas. [24] Forty years after Herbert's death, Thomas Mace was still urging that there should "not be too great a variety of Poetical *forms* or *shapes* in the *Staves*" so that all the Psalms could be set to a few known tunes; "And doubtless he is to be looked upon as the most *exquisite Poet*, who is *thus* able to command his *Fancy*."[25]

Herbert, a Pierian flood of fresh stanza forms, produced one common-meter psalm, the twenty-third, modeled on Sternhold's translation. This most pastoral of psalms, in which the shepherd-psalmist becomes God's lamb, is perhaps the one most suited to this act of artistic humility, the conforming of his measure to another's staves. Yet, the singer says to God, it is "thy staffe" that bears the burden of his song; "thy rod" guides and measures his (prosodic) feet. He rhymes both the eight-syllable and the six-syllable lines, in the manner practiced by Hopkins but not Sternhold and deplored by George Puttenham as "trifling";[26] but, being Herbert, who does not leave English lines unrhymed except to express disjunction and who never trifles, he recasts the psalm into full rhyme while freeing the rhythms within their measure and weaving the syntax more connectedly, and so making the verse more musical. As is usual with Herbert, effects that may at first seem weak or jarring prove on further inspection to be particularly apt. If "shadie black abode" sounds unwontedly Spenserian, it does so suitably in a pastoral poem. The uninspired-sounding "frame," which is Sternhold's word to start with, alludes both to the frame of mind God supplies and to the process Herbert's mind is engaged in of "framing" words to fit known tunes: reversing Thomas Morley's advice that "whatsoever matter it be which you have in hand such kind of music you must frame to it."[27] Since metrical versions do little for Hebrew poetry apart from making it singable in strophes, his purpose seems to have been to sweeten and deepen lines that could still be sung to the familiar melodies bound into the prayer book and abounding in four-part settings for domestic gatherings. The "measure" in Herbert's well-loved closing stanza assents to the enterprise of metrical order. If Herbert can "measure" the psalm so sweetly with a mind God has brought in frame, "surely thy sweet and wondrous love" can compose his days in even meeter form.

Herbert's consciousness of the relations between words and musical genres is further revealed in "A Dialogue-Antheme" and "A true Hymne," whose titles are chosen with a musician's precision.

"A Dialogue-Antheme" shows Herbert's recognition of the etymological root of *anthem* in *antiphon*. In the first antiphonal exchanges, *Christian* and *Death* answer each other in parallel points of imitation. But at the end the counterpoint is interrupted by a musical *stretto: Death* is cut off by *Christian*—rather than the other way around.

In "A true Hymne," as in *Antiphon* I, Herbert responds to St. Paul's exhortations in Ephesians 5:19 and Colossians 3:16 to encourage one another in "psalms and hymns and spiritual songs, singing and making melody . . . with grace in your hearts to the Lord." A hymn is generally a song of praise that unlike the psalms is not an exact Scriptural text but a free composition, something the heart "fain would say." The Greeks, Warren Anderson notes, "connected the term 'hymnos' with *hyphainein*, meaning 'to weave' or 'to combine words artfully,'"²⁸ a process Herbert's poem both abnegates and performs. From the late Middle Ages on, two trends applicable to Herbert's lines emerged: toward through-composition and toward the "accord of particular texts with particular tunes."²⁹ In all these ways (counting Herbert's prosody as "music") Herbert's is "a hymne in kinde." And it provides a "kind" rare in Herbert's time. Congregational singing of non-liturgical hymns was not yet approved in the English church, apart from the few non-Scriptural poems included in *The Whole Book of Psalms*, which were not for the most part hymns of praise.³⁰ Since the sacred texts most often set for secular use were the psalms, vernacular hymns to Christ and renderings of New Testament texts were rare. Herbert must have welcomed John Amner's *Sacred Hymns* of 1615,³¹ a collection of part-books of the through-composed meditations on New Testament passages, including many of Herbert's favorite themes; it is conceivable that Herbert hoped to provide better texts (or "weavings") for Amner and his contemporaries, since for the most part the music is more interesting than the verse. For all these reasons, "a hymne in kinde" is exactly the right genre in which to express a desire to sing praise truly and immediately, from the heart, and the need and difficulty of doing so in perfect lines. But Herbert takes the idea of through-composition to its ultimate end: not only must the "soul" or message accord with the "lines" or verse-music, but the heart and soul of the singer must be in tune with both: "The fineness which a hymne or psalme affords, / Is, when the soul unto the lines accords." This accord will not occur if the words *only* rhyme (but are not the aptest ones for the sense), or if the words only *rhyme* (but do not express or stir the heart), or if the *words* only rhyme (but the music does not fit the meaning or the heart resonate with both). "A true hymne" (a song of praise) must be a repayment "in kinde" of these gifts to him who gave them. But the heart's "rhyming" is so much more important than all the rest that, given that alone, God will mend the song.

The versification, though strophic, suggests through-composition by its varied phrase and line lengths, its fluidly changing rhythms, and its word-coloring, some lines going rapidly ("And still it runneth mut-t'ring up and down"), others slowing ("Yet slight not these few words") or coming to full stops (as at "stops"). The use of rhyme—the node of the theme—is itself mimetic. The identical rhyme of "crown" mimes the heart's poverty of words, while the circular stanza mimes "crown." The off-rhyme of "behinde" with "time" (though with a regular stan-za) suggests "musically out of step" as well as ungenerously withheld; and the God who mends the rhyme "writeth" *Loved* to call attention to the eye-rhyme, reply to the direct address ("My joy, my life, my crown") and perfect (literally complete) the poem. The three voices— the heart, whose words are few but fine; the "I" who meditates on the heart's part in a true hymn; and God, for whom one word suffices— are tonally distinct, yet interwoven, like part-singing (Sacred hymns were never written for solo voice in Herbert's time). In all these ways, the poem's verbal music formally presents "a true hymne" in the very process of subordinating art to the fineness of the accord between art and heart, and that accord to the heart's impulse of love, and that impulse to God's love; and this humility exalts, of course, when God supplies what wants.

Herbert's "Easter" is a meditation in two parts[32] upon the Proper of the Feast alluding to the lessons, psalms, collect, and prayer book "anthems" of the Easter liturgy. The first part is a poem about heart-tuning and art-tuning, beginning with a *sursum corda*, the call to "lift up your hearts" in preparation for the central mystery of the Eucharist.[33]

> Rise heart; thy Lord is risen. Sing his praise
>   Without delayes,

> Who takes thee by the hand, that thou likewise
> 　　　　　　　　With him mayst rise:
> That, as his death calcined thee to dust,
> His life may make thee gold, and much more, Just.
>
> Awake, my lute, and struggle for thy part
> 　　　　　　　　With all thy art.
> The crosse taught all wood to resound his name
> 　　　　　　　　Who bore the same.
> His stretched sinews taught all strings, what key
> Is best to celebrate this most high day.
>
> Consort both heart and lute, and twist a song
> 　　　　　　　　Pleasant and long:
> Or, since all musick is but three parts vied
> 　　　　　　　　And multiplied,
> O let thy blessed Spirit bear a part,
> And make up our defects with his sweet art.

The poem's root metaphor is the Latin pun on *chordae*, strings, and *corda*, hearts. Zarlino notes that Aurelius Cassadorius thought strings so named because they move our hearts.[34] Easter anthems were often composed, in honor of the Trinity, in either three voice parts, or three structural parts, or both. Herbert's has both. And it specifically alludes to the Psalms appointed for Easter Matins, which include the verse "My heart is fixed, O God, my heart is fixed: I will sing and give prayse. / Awake up my glory, awake Lute and harpe; I my selfe will awake right early." Orlando Gibbons set the latter verse by twisting a song, as Herbert does, of one voice, then two, then full consort.[35] Byrd's setting of the Latin verse "This is the day that the Lord hath made" has six (or three divided) antiphonal voice parts in three structural sections, the middle in triple time, alternating long and short phrases, as the poem does.[36] This alternation of long and short lines gives the poem a kinetic quickening mimetic of resurrection, alacrity, and jubilant response, enriched by the fact that all the key words in the short lines—*delayes, rise, art, bore, same, pleasant, long,* and *multiplied*—would be "word-painted" with suspensions or melisma by Renaissance composers. "Without delayes" would offer a composer an especially pleasant challenge, since melisma would simultaneously delay and quicken the line. Further, the poem "twists a song" polyphonically by its flexible phrasing. Its three voices enter contrapuntally, its closely-spaced rhymes weave similar sounds like closely-woven points of imitation, and its many enjambments carry the sense in varied, arching phrases.

The second part, in contrast, is made of tetrameter quatrains, the lines (with one appropriate exception) end-stopped, like the regular strophes of metrical psalm-singing.

> I got me flowers to straw thy way;
> I got me boughs off many a tree:
> But thou wast up by break of day,
> And brought'st thy sweets along with thee.
>
> The Sunne arising in the East,
> Though he give light, & th'East perfume;
> If they should offer to contest
> With thy arising, they presume.
>
> Can there be any day but this,
> Though many sunnes to shine endeavour?
> We count three hundred, but we misse:
> There is but one, and that one ever.

These poems are verbal examples of what Peter Le Huray calls the fundamental change in Renaissance composition "from a primarily horizontal method of working, in which the separate parts were composed one after the other, to a vertical method in which all parts were developed simultaneously."[37] They are not only linear songs, but vertical verbal harmonies. Most good poets write with such attention to verbal connections that words in different lines answer to each other in various ways. But Herbert carries this art to a perfection that suggests the richly layered sonorities of Renaissance music. "Rise," "awake," and "consort," for example, are linked to each other and to the daybreak imagery of the second poem both by logical, linear progression and by a common tie, their echoes of the Song of Songs. "Consort" lightly puns on that connection, and it is abundantly figured in the imagery of flowers, trees, perfumes, and "sweets." "Consort" in its secondary meaning links to "takes three by the hand," and its primary one to "twist a song" and "bear a part" (which also connects with "bore the same"), and "twist," more obscurely, lines up with "key," which is etymologically connected with the "clue" that Herbert calls a "silk twist let down from heav'n" in "The Pearl." The word *contest* connects vertically with "struggle" and "vie." "our defects" links to "we misse," and that word is mimed in the obviously (if Biblically) inaccurate "we count three hundred." The "three" of the first poem links to the "three" and the "one" of the second, as well as to the three-in-one stanzaic form of each poem. "The Sunne arising" plays by a familiar pun on "thy Lord is risen" in ways that Rosalie Colie has taught us to recognize as the re-literalization of metaphor;[38] and the whole second poem may be seen as what Rosemond Tuve has taught us to recognize as Herbert's use of "parody" in the musical sense, the importation of a secular melody as a *cantus firmus* for sacred singing,[39] since its imagery commonly appears in love poems complimenting the beloved whose beauty outshines the sun and outspices the perfumes of the East. One thinks of Donne's "The Sunne Rising," for example. Through the "Son" who comes forth as a bridegroom, Herbert re-sacralizes this imagery, returns it to the Song of Songs from whence it came, and applies it typologically to the Easter Gospel, in which the three Marys bring sweet spices to the tomb of Christ, only to find him already risen.[40]

The poem adds to the language of the Easter liturgy the quality that music adds to the liturgy itself; that is, sweetness: a term the Renaissance associated with pure consonances, in tune with the cosmos and the divine archetypes, giving pleasure to the ear that Kepler and Galileo compare with the pleasure of "the business of generation,"[41] and which Herbert, in keeping with his promise to make sonnets of God rather than Venus, attributes to the Holy Spirit.

However, two lines from the first part may strike us as reductive, and so a little off-key: "His life may make thee gold, and much more, Just," and "all Musick is but three parts vied / And multiplied." Why is the ethical "just" much more than the God-transmuted "gold"?[42] Why is *all* music "but three parts"? And why, on Easter morning, his heart rising with his risen Lord, must Herbert be so mathematical?

Herbert's "just," though it may fall flat on the unprepared ear, is — in addition to its theological propriety — the perfect figure for tuning both heart and lute. It resonates with Plato's teaching that the "just man" is one who tunes "in the proportion of a musical scale" the three parts of his soul: reason, appetite, and a mediating spirit we might call "heart."[43] "Just" is therefore consonant with both "key" in the second stanza and "three parts" in the third. "Proportion," as Orlando Gibbons argued in defense of church music, "beautifies everything, this whole Universe consists of it, and Musick is measured by it"; thus music can, in Thomas Morley's words, "draw the hearer . . . in chains of gold by the ears to the consideration of holy things."[44] Musical proportions, of which the universe is made, can set the soul in tune with God. The word "just" was regularly used in music, astronomy, and mathematics to mean "exact." Morley speaks of "just Diatonicum," Peacham of "just Diapason," and Milton of "just concent."[45] Herbert's "Just" is therefore le mot juste for a poem about heart-tuning. And the word receives musical treatment that reinforces its significance. The fact that "gold" is a noun in relation to "dust," but an adjective in relation to "just," and is held over the phrase "and much more," provides a suspension that strengthens the resolution on "Just." Christopher Tye gives a musical equivalent in his setting of the words "I lift my heart to thee, O God most just," working up through long polyphonic phrases to near homophony on the last three words.[46]

The scribe of the Williams manuscript has been careful to make the poem a hieroglyph of the word: the short lines are justified on both sides — that is, the lines are all the same length, written in perfect parallel, as can be done in manuscript — giving the pleasure of what musicians call "eye-music," in which the notation visibly represents the verbal figure. Following the Bodleian and 1633 versions, some editors omit the comma before "just." But Herbert or his scribe takes special pains to have it noticed. It is the largest comma on the page. It is important because "much more Just" is not compact enough to be good poetic diction, and because "Just" is not properly comparative. It means "exact," as musical pitches have to be, and as scales of justice have to be. Christ's rising, Herbert suggests, not only transmutes the heart to a golden instrument, but tunes it.

Herbert's concern for tuning and for "what key is best," as both a singer and a lutenist whose lute is a figure for his poesie, touches on fresh permutations in musical and astronomical thought. In the early seventeenth century, the church modes were giving way to keys based on thirds, which required a different kind of tuning from the Greek modes and their medieval successors. Ancient and medieval monody use Pythagorean tuning based on simple arithmetical ratios, in which the smallest consonance is a fourth. As polyphony developed, a scale providing more consonances was needed. Since the time of Dunstable, English music had used thirds as consonant intervals. Many Renaissance music theorists preferred "pure" or "natural" tuning (which is now called "just intonation" and known to conform to the overtone series) for part-singing and meantone temperament for instruments with fixed tuning because they produced the greatest number for pure consonances.[47] As D. P. Walker explains, for monody "Pythagorean intonation [in which thirds are dissonant] is more suitable than just, . . . For polyphonic music, . . . in which the major triad occupies a dominating and central position, just intonation has the advantage of making this chord as sweet as possible and in general of making all chords, both major and minor, more consonant." Kepler's music of the spheres, he points out, unlike Pythagoras's, is polyphonic and is in just intonation, having consonant thirds and sixths. But he was not able empirically to "find these ratios in the heavens" until "he placed himself in the sun and looked at the angular speeds of the planets from there."[48] For Herbert there is "but one" sun to teach "what key / is best." Kepler, incidentally, finds the major and minor third to be derived from the golden section.[49] If one's heart is "gold," and much more, "Just," it is presumably in tune with a triune Creator and a sun- and Son-centered creation.

Renaissance singing is itself an ethical experience. One must sing sweetly and "suavely," making "one body" of all the parts, as Giovanni de' Bardi teaches;[50] and in order to intone justly, one must sing reticently and purely, without display and without vibrato, so as to hear and be in right relation to all the other singers. Theoretically, one is then in tune with the proportions of the cosmos, the triune triplicities of angels, and a creation in which, Herbert says, even stones concent with song:[51] and so with God—at least, for Herbert, if one takes the risen Son as the center, "whose stretched sinews taught all strings what key / Is best."

A remarkably consonant musical analogue for this poem is Thomas Weelkes's *Gloria in Excelsis Deo*,[52] an anthem in three sections vied in six antiphonal voice parts (high, middle, and low, each divided) and multiplied both in the polyphonic imitations of the angelic *gloria* that begin and end it and in the multiple modulations of the central English verse. Like Herbert's poem, Weelkes's anthem is a mimesis of heart-tuning. The poem Weelkes sets is almost a précis of Herbert's, without its grace and complexity:

> Sing, my soul, to God thy Lord,
> All in glory's highest key;
> Lay the Angels' choir abroad,
> In their highest holy day.
> Crave thy God to tune thy heart
> Unto praise's highest part.

The similarities of diction and the six-line stanza tie the verse to Herbert's, as well as its theme; but the music Weelkes supplies in setting it, Herbert incorporates into the poem itself, in ways that familiarity with the anthem can help us hear. At "Crave thy God to tune thy heart" Weelkes takes the choristers through a difficult pattern of harmonic changes that provides a mimetic experience of the tuning of the breast: from C minor to G major to C major, and then, on the word *tune*, to intervals so unexpected that each singer, looking at his separate part-book, must feel that he is about to sing an utterly discordant note. Instead, they all wind up in the brilliant key of A major. They have had to make a leap of faith; it has felt all wrong; and they have arrived at a new and higher harmony: a mimetic conversion experience. On "heart" they return to G major, the chord on which "God" was sung, so that the heart is now literally in tune with God. The chord progression fits the word-coloring of Herbert's second stanza, in which the process of tuning—which is taught by Christ's "streched sinews"—is painful, yet issues in joy. Each section of the anthem, moreover, begins in what Plato might have thought the "slack" key of C minor and ends in C major. The third section returns to the polyphonic *gloria* of the first, but—as in Herbert's *Antiphon* II—cantoris and decani parts are reversed. The *Amen* recapitulates the movement from minor to major, from passion to affirmation.

Why—given the wonderful variety of harmonic expression Herbert knew—does he say that "all musick is but three parts vied / And multiplied"?

All consonances, as music theorists repeatedly pointed out, can be produced by three voices. But Herbert's phrase is characteristic in its multiple relations. Writers have vied since antiquity to multiply variations on the three parts of music. For Plato they were "words, musical mode, and rhythm."[53] For Boethius they were universal music, human music, and instrumental music, or the concord of the cosmos, the concord of human faculties, and the music that can actually be heard.[54] Herbert's "heart," "lute," and "Spirit" varies and christens these. In the Middle Ages, the three mathematically simple consonances of octaves, fourths, and fifths, were thought necessities of a cosmos created by a three-personed God. In the *Ars novae musicae* of 1319, Jean de Muris says that "all perfection is implicit in the ternary number,"[55] and Mersenne's compendious *Harmonie Universelle*, printed in 1636, collects masses of such numerology. But in the spirit of empiricism and Reformation thought, Kepler detaches the three parts of music from these iconic applications and gives a pristinely mathematical account of the fact that "all harmonies can be accomplished by three notes," concluding, "The cause of this fact different people seek vainly in different ways. . . . For . . . this threefold number . . . does not give form to the harmonies, but is a splendour of their form. . . . But since the Threefold is common to divine and worldly things, whenever it occurs the human mind intervenes and knowing nothing of the causes marvels at this coincidence."[56] The statement corresponds with the disciplined musical freedom of Renaissance composers and the disciplined verbal freedom of Herbert's poems.

According to Johannes Lippius, defining the triad in 1612, "this harmonic Trinity is . . . twofold. One [the major triad] is perfect, noble, and suave. . . . The other [the minor triad] is imperfect and soft. Each has its 'species' through chromatic notes."[57] Lippius's wording suggests traditional descriptions of the sexes, as musical ratios did for Galileo and Kepler: and so to the business of increasing and multiplying. Mersenne seems to echo the same source (probably Kepler) as Herbert when he says "One of the principle reasons why three parts suffice in music" is that "they can make all the variety of consonances," so that further voices "only redouble and multiply the same harmony."[58] But Herbert's "vye" is more inclusive than Mersenne's "redouble" because it suggests dissonance as well as consonance among its connotations. And since "vying" means matching "by way of return, rivalry, or comparison,"[59] it may refer to musical counterpoint and to matched and countered antiphonal choirs. The word resonates with both "likewise" and "contest." Considering Lippius's twofold trinity multiplied in chromatic notes, for the religious poet or composer, vying and multiplying must seem the right way of creating, since the triune Maker of that maker, having created "the three parts of the soul" in his image, vied it in counterparts, male and female (one noble, one soft, some say) and told them to multiply. All creation is thus vied and multiplied, and for Herbert all creation is God's music.

For Herbert, language is not only a means of expression, but also a way of finding out what is true. For the music theorists whose works were probably circulating among musicians and students of the quadrivium at Cambridge, music is a way of finding out what is true. The way of discovery is the way of concinnity. The more ways our perceptions of things fit together, according to this habit of mind, the surer we may be that we are freely in tune with the heavenly source of both mind and matter. To scientists intent on showing that empirical observation and revealed religion accord together, music offered proof that the human intellect can know the intelligible world—those invisible forms of which the perceptible world gives evidence—because of the correspondences between the soul of man, made in God's image, and the cosmos, which is in some ways a hieroglyph of its creator. For, as D. P. Walker has explained, the harmonies of music were empirically discovered. Men first noticed that certain musical intervals please the ear and move the soul. Only later did they measure their harpstrings and discover that these consonances could be mathematically expressed by simple and commensurate ratios. *Ratio* in Latin and *Logos* in Greek both mean, among other things, "relation" and "reason."[60] The reasonable order is the work of the God who produced the reasoning soul, which could be described as having three parts corresponding to musical ratios. And this design, empirically confirmed by the ear, is the work of a triune God who has beautified his cosmos in multiple corresponding proportions: not as a necessity, but as a "splendour."

As scientists and musicians found in music empirical and psychic links between heaven and earth, so for Herbert the resonances of words were means of discovery. Although the physics of harmonic overtones had not yet been formulated, I think we may speak of Herbert's use of language as musical in this sense: the secondary suggestions, allusive echoes, metaphoric bonds, puns, rhymes, and other conjunctions of sound and sense make real—not just adventitiously felicitous—connections. Human languages, with their chains of associations, are "clues," let down from heaven, which, like musical consonances, reveal their source when put in right relation. And the fact that so many connections felicitously and even unexpectedly occur in the process of composing or interpreting a poem and resonate together, adding insight on insight and forming link on link, shows that language is more than an autonymous system constructed by a precarious consensus. Like mathematics and music, it springs from the Logos. It means more than we can plan for. It unlocks truth, if we can find "what key is best." When Herbert says to God, "My musick shall find thee, and ev'ry string / Shall have his attribute to sing,"[61] I think he means that his poems, as prayers, will get where they are going but also that his language-music will discover God; each string will sing the attribute of God that God has given it, if it is justly tuned.

Herbert's simplicity is like the simplicity of Copernicus, Galileo, and Kepler, whose descriptions of the universe are more economical than those of their predecessors because they pack more information into fewer terms. As for Kepler the concords of music display the design of the cosmos to the marveling mind, for Herbert the art of God and the uprisen hearts and arts of his creatures entwine in mutual and responsive song. The discipline of exact tuning in language, as in music, leads to greater simplicity and plenitude. Herbert newly configures the three parts of music by joining the voice of the risen heart, the lute retuned with all creation, and the "sweet art" of the Spirit. It is a bold yet orthodox suggestion that the voice of the Spirit should complete the song, and the poem's through-composed concinnities offer literal concent to that process. To join God's consort, Herbert composes words that resonate together and with the heavens. And this matching of multiple meanings, justly tuned, clearly understood, and sweetly sung, makes these poems "gold, and much more, Just."

Notes

1. Summers, *George Herbert: His Religion and Art* (Cambridge, Mass.: Harvard University Press, 1954), 232, n. 16. Other studies that consider Herbert's use of musical metaphor and form are Arnold Stein, *George Herbert's Lyrics* (Baltimore: Johns Hopkins Press, 1968); Albert McHarg Hayes, "Counterpoint in Herbert," *Studies in Philology* 35 (1938): 43–60; Alicia Ostriker, "Song and Speech in the Metrics of George Herbert," *PMLA* 80 (1965): 62–68; and Amy M. Charles, "George Herbert: Priest, Poet, Musician," *Journal of the Viola da Gamba Society of America* 4 (1967): 27–36. The last three essays are reprinted in John R. Roberts, *Essential Articles for the Study of George Herbert's Poetry* (Hamden, Conn.: Archon Books, 1979). Anthony Low discusses ways the singing of hymns and psalms enters seventeenth-century devotional poetry, with special attention to Herbert's poems for the liturgical year, in *Love's Architecture: Devotional Modes in Seventeenth-Century English Poetry* (New York: New York University Press, 1978), especially chapters 2 and 4. Louise Schleiner, in *The Living Lyre in English Verse* (Columbia: University of Missouri Press, 1984) has recently supplied an expert study of ways Herbert incorporates the musical patterns of secular solo song into his verse and ways composers interpreted his poems (chap. 2).

I have coined the word "hierophon" by analogy with Summers's use of "hieroglyph" in *George Herbert: His Religion and Art*, chap. 6. Summers makes the point that Herbert does not write emblem poems, or poems about visual symbolism, but makes the poem itself a hieroglyph, "so that its form imaged the subject . . . to reinforce the message for those who could 'spell'" (135). A similar incorporation happens in Herbert's aural forms, I think, for those who could sing: an embodiment that goes beyond the natural music and onomatopoesis of language to include specific structures and performance practices from Renaissance part-music. Research for this essay was aided by a leave and a Research Council travel grant from Rutgers, the State University of New Jersey.

2. I am grateful to members of the School of Music at the University of Illinois for the experience of singing early choral music: especially Louise Halsey, whose seminar

in English Choral Music and summer choruses provided several of the musical concepts and examples used here; Harold Decker; Nicholas Temperley; and Larry Brandenberg. Professors Halsey and Temperley kindly read and helpfully commented on versions of this essay.

3. George Herbert, "Church-musick," *Works of George Herbert*, ed. F. E. Hutchinson (1941; repr., Oxford: Clarendon Press, 1953), 66. All quotations from Herbert's poems are taken from this edition unless otherwise noted.

4. Hollander, *The Untuning of the Sky: Ideas of Music in English Poetry, 1500–1700* (Princeton: Princeton University Press, 1961), 288.

5. Quotations from the Book of Common Prayer are from the 1625 edition, with orthography modernized.

6. Compare *Paradise Lost* 5.137–208 and 9.192–99; and see Psalms 148 and 150.

7. Izaak Walton, *Lives* (New York: Scott-Thaw, 1903), 290–91:

His chiefest recreation was music, in which heavenly art he was a most excellent master, and did himself compose many divine hymns and anthems, which he set and sung to his lute or viol: and though he was a lover of retiredness, yet his love to music was such, that he went usually twice every week on certain appointed days, to the Cathedral Church in Salisbury; and at his return would say, "That his time spent in prayer, and Cathedral music, elevated his soul, and was his Heaven upon earth." But before his return thence to Bemerton, he would usually sing and play his part at an appointed private music-meeting; and, to justify this practice, he would often say, "Religion does not banish mirth, but only moderates and sets rules to it."

(The word *composures* is also taken from Walton.)

8. John Milton, *The Works of John Milton*, ed. Frank Allen Patterson et al., 18 vols. and two index vols. (New York: Columbia University Press, 1931–40), 3:238.

9. Herbert, "The Thanksgiving," 35; "Heaven," 188 (an echo-song, using a technique familiar from madrigal and catch-singing).

10. Thomas Cranmer, in a letter to Henry VIII dated October 7, 1544; quoted in F. E. Brightman, *The English Rite, being a synopsis of the sources and revisions of the Book of Common Prayer* (London, 1921): I:lxi.

11. Byrd was among the dinner guests recorded in "Mrs. Herbert's Kitchen Booke"; see Amy Charles's article of that name in *ELR* 4 (Winter 1974): 164–73.

12. Byrd, dedicatory letter to the *Gradualia* (1605–07), translated by Oliver Strunk, *Source Readings in Music History: The Renaissance* (New York: W. W. Norton, 1965), 138.

13. Edited by Craig Monson in *The Byrd Edition*, gen. ed. Philip Brett, vol. 10 (London: Stainer and Bell, 1982). "The Great Service," from which this setting of the *Te Deum* comes, has been recorded by The Saint Thomas Choir, Gerre Hancock, Organist and Master of the Choristers (Saint Thomas Church: N. Y., 1981), and by the Tallis Scholars, dir. Peter Phillips (1987).

14. That is, an anthem alternating choral sections with "verse" sections for solo voice or voices. Peter Le Huray notes that Elizabethan verse anthems and services

"differ from all earlier solo-chorus forms . . . in the use of obligato instrumental accompaniments": *Music and the Reformation in England, 1549–1660* (Cambridge: Cambridge University Press, 1978), 217.

15. On the possible relation of Herbert's "The Crosse" to his re-building of Leighton Ecclesia, see Amy Charles, *A Life of George Herbert* (Ithaca, N. Y.: Cornell University Press, 1977).

16. Gibbons, ed. David Wulstan, in *Early English Church*, gen. ed. Bernard Rose (London, 1962-), 3:100–110 (henceforth *EECM*).

17. Vendler, *The Poetry of George Herbert* (Cambridge, Mass.: Harvard University Press, 1975), 210–11.

18. *Diapason* can mean both the concord of a perfect octave and the concords through all the notes of a musical scale. Milton uses "perfect diapason" for the harmony of all creatures in "At a Solemn Musick."

19. Vendler, 212.

20. Gibbons sets D against C (twice) and G against F on "we humbly beseech thee" by means of suspensions and combines E-flat and E-natural in the same chord on "holy, Lord God": measures 4–7 and 17 in Wulstan's edition. In pure intonation such close harmonies are not unpleasant but provide intensity and expectancy of resolution.

21. Heather Ross Asals says of "crouch" that "it is this gesture which finally *makes one* of the heaven and earth which the poem echoes between: 'Praised be the God alone, / Who hath made *two folds one*' ": in *Equivocal Predications: George Herbert's Way to God* (Toronto: University of Toronto Press, 1981), 31. Asals suggests, I think, that the literal "two folds" of the crouching bodies are an emblem of the union.

22. A full-length study of Herbert's knowledge and use of the Psalms may be found in Coburn Freer, *Music for a King: George Herbert's Style and the Metrical Psalms* (Baltimore: Johns Hopkins Press, 1972).

23. Temperley, *The Music of the English Parish Church* (Cambridge: Cambridge University Press, 1979), 1: chapters 2–4. Temperley supplies examples of early harmonized versions in volume 2. Among the many part-settings of the Sternhold and Hopkins metrical psalms (the words of which were often bound into Bibles and Prayer Books with their approved tunes) are Thomas East's (or Este's) *Whole Booke of psalmes: with their wonted tunes, as they are song in churches, composed into foure partes: all of which are so placed that foure may sing ech one a several part* (1592), and Thomas Ravencroft's *Whole booke of psalms: with the hymns evangelicall, and songs spirituall, Composed into 4. parts by sundry authors* (1621), which Ravenscroft calls "so composed, for the most part, that the unskilful may with little practice, be enabled to sing them in parts, after a plausible manner."

24. See for example Matthew Parker, *The whole psalter translated into English metre*, which includes settings by Thomas Tallis, and George Wither's three books of paraphrases, some set by Orlando Gibbons.

25. Mace, *Musick's Monument: or, a remembrancer of the best practical musick, both divine and civile, that has ever been known, to have been in the world* (London, 1676), 2;

in the facsimile reproduction by Editions du Centre National de la Recherché Scientifique (Paris, 1977).

26. Puttenham, *The arte of English poesie* (London, 1589), 96; in the facsimile reproduction of the Kent State University Press of the 1906 reprint (1970), intro. Baxter Hathaway.

27. Morley, *A Plain & easy introduction to practical music* (London, 1597), in the facsimile reproduction, ed. Alec Harman (New York: W. W. Norton, 1973), 290.

28. Anderson, "Hymn" (1), in Stanley Sadie, ed., *The New Grove Dictionary of Music and Musicians* (London: Macmillan, 1980), 8:836.

29. Tom R. Ward, "Hymn" (3) and Nicholas Temperley, "Hymn" (4) in *Grove*, 8:845–88.

30. The title page of the authorized metrical Psalms reads "*The Whole Book of Psalms*. Collected into English meeter by Thomas Sternhold, John Hopkins and others, conferred with the Hebrew with apt notes to sing them with all. Set forth and allowed to be sung in all Churches of all the people together, before and after Morning and Evening Prayer, and also before and after Sermons: and moreover in private houses for their godly solace, & comfort laying apart all ungodly songs and ballads which tend onely to the nourishing of vice and corrupting of youth." In addition to the Psalms and versified versions of portions of liturgy, the book includes eight somewhat original works: the "Veni Creator," "The humble suit of a sinner," "The Lamentation of a sinner," "The complaint of a sinner," "A Prayer to the holy Ghost to be sung before the Sermon," "Da Pacem Domine," "The Lamentation," and "A thanksgiving after the receiving of the Lords Supper." (These standard titles are taken from the 1640 Company of Stationers' edition.)

31. Amner was an organist of Ely Cathedral, near Cambridge, during Herbert's Cambridge years.

32. The two poems called "Easter" have separate titles in the Williams manuscript but are printed as one poem in subsequent editions. I am treating them as a poem in two "parts" in the sense of through-composed hymns or anthems, which were often divided into "prima pars," "secunda pars," and so on with quite different musical treatments.

33. I have retained the capital J of "Just" from the Williams manuscipt (in the facsimile edition by Amy M. Charles) and added accent marks on "calcined" and "streched."

34. Gioseffe Zarlino, *Istituzione armoniche* (1558), in Strunk, 60.

35. Gibbons, "Psalm to the First Precs," *Orlando Gibbons*, vol. 4 of *Tudor Church Music*, ed. P. C. Buck, E. H. Fellowes, A. Ramsbotham, and S. Townsend Warner (London, 1925), 13–19. After the central section for full choir, partly antiphonal and largely homophonic, the psalm concludes with the verse "This is the day which the Lord hath made: we will rejoice and be glad in it" for three polyphonic voice parts. The Proper Psalms for Easter Day are Psalms 2, 57, 111, 113, 114, and 118.

36. Byrd, "Haec Dies," ed. Alan Brown, in *The Byrd Edition*, gen. ed. Philip Brett, (London: Stainer and Bell, 1981), 3:251–59.

37. Le Huray, *Music and the Reformation in England*, 135.

38. Colie, *"My Ecchoing Song": Andrew Marvell's Poetry of Criticism* (Princeton: Princeton University Press, 1970), part 3.i: "The Garden."

39. Tuve, *Essays by Rosamond Tuve*, ed. Thomas P. Roche (Princeton: Princeton University Press, 1970), 207–51.

40. Mark 16:1: "And when the sabbath was past, Mary Magdalene, and Mary Jacobye, and Salome, had brought swete odours, that they myghte come, and anoynt him" (quoted from Brightman, 400). This passage was used "for the second communion" in the Sarum Rite and the 1549 Book of Common Prayer, but not in subsequent editions. Composers setting this text could make use of sensuous rich and floating harmonies on "sweet odoures" (Latin *aromata*), as John Taverner does in "Dum Transisset Sabbatum" (ed. Philip Brett, Oxford, 1975). If Herbert was aware of such settings or of the former inclusion of this verse in the liturgy, he may be acknowledging the omission in his aromatic meditation on the needlessness of burial spices.

41. D. P. Walker, *Studies in Musical Science in the Late Renaissance*, vol. 37 of *Studies of the Warburg Institute*, gen. ed. J. B. Trapp (London: University of London; Leiden: Warburg Institute, 1978), 32 and 53–54. I am much indebted to this study, especially chapter 4, "Kepler's Celestial Music."

42. I allude to Herbert's "The Elixir."

43. *The Republic of Plato*, trans. Francis MacDonald Cornford (London: Oxford University Press, 1945), 142.

44. Gibbons, *The First Set of Madrigals and Mottets of 5. Parts: apt for Viols and Voyces* (London, 1612); Morley, *A Plain & Easy introduction*, 293.

45. Morley, 103; Peacham, *The Compleat Gentleman* (1622), quoted in Strunk, 147; Milton, "At a Solemn Musick."

46. Tye, ed. John Morehen (London: Stainer and Bell, 1977), EECM 19:99–124. Here the word "just" is intensified by suspension and resolution (measures 10–11). In Sir William Leighton's *The Tears or Lamentations of a Sorrowful Soul* (1614; ed. Cecil Hill, EECM 11:115–17) Gibbons sets the verse, "O Lord I lift my heart to thee / My soul in Thee doth ever trust: / O let me not confounded be, / but make me righteous with the just" so that the final word, "just," is the only word sung by all voices at once. In Byrd's "Justorum Animae" the words "justorum animae" are set homophonically, the rest mainly polyphonically, in part 1 of *Gradualia* (1605), in vol. 4 of *The Collected Vocal Works of William Byrd*, ed. Edmund H. Fellowes, (London: Oxford University Press, 1938), 195–98. These composers treat the word "just" mimetically, as Herbert does by his prosody.

47. The differences among kinds of tuning may be heard on J. Murray Barbour and Fritz A. Kuttner, *The Theory and Practice of Just Intonation*, on Musurgia Records, Theory Series A, no. 3 (Jackson Heights, N.Y.). A clear explanation of these kinds of tuning and temperament may be found in chapter 3 of William Duckworth and Edward Brown, *Theoretical Foundations of Music* (Belmont, California: Wadsworth, 1978), which includes this suggestive comment on meantone tuning:

The enharmonic intervals produced by this system ($A_\flat$-$G_\sharp$) result in a pitch discrepancy of almost a quarter-tone, and require that a choice be made between the $A_\flat$ and the $G_\sharp$.

As an alternative to previous tuning systems, meantone temperament offered distinct advantages. Since it was generally tuned from C, it made available a group of keys through three sharps and three flats, assuming both the $A_\flat$ and $G_\sharp$ would be used at one time or another. This greater range of keys for fixed-pitch instruments made possible greater explorations of key relationships and modulation. In addition, because in meantone temperament the pattern of just and tempered intervals is different for each key, each key possesses its own distinctive coloration (19).

Herbert's concern with "what key is best" is further illuminated by his brother Edward's lute book, in which the pieces are arranged by keys. In the description of this book in *Cambridge Music Manuscripts, 900–1700*, ed. Iain Fenlon (Cambridge: Cambridge University Press, 1982), we read:

> This unusual arrangement seems designed to serve a practical purpose. The music in Cherbury's book is for six-course lute with several diapasons, additional bass strings which (with the exception of the seventh course) were not usually stopped but rather were tuned to the key of the piece to be attempted. Since retuning the diapasons was a tedious process which must often have required retuning all the courses — since their pitches would be affected by the change of tension on the lower strings — Cherbury's arrangement clearly facilitates performance (159).

It is tempting to speculate whether the much-discussed arrangement of *The Temple* is affected by the keys in which Herbert set his poems or intended them to be sung. It is also tempting to speculate whether the first "Easter" triad is a hieroglyph of a nine-course lute (having eighteen lines, or strings, tuned in octaves as represented by the half-lines).

48. Walker, 35–37.

49. Walker, 53.

50. De' Bardi, in Strunk, 108–11.

51. Herbert, "On Sacred Music," trans. Edmund Blunden, in "Some Seventeenth-Century Latin Poems by English Writers," *UTQ* 25:12.

52. Weelkes, ed. Walter S. Collins (London: Oxford University Press, 1960); also in Peter Le Huray's edition in his *The Treasury of English Church Music, 1545–1650* (Cambridge: Cambridge University Press, 1982).

53. Plato, *The Republic*.

54. Boethius, *De Institutione Musica* in Strunk, *Source Readings in Music History: Antiquity and the Middle Ages* (New York and London: W. W. Norton, 1965), 84–85. See also Gretchen Finney, *Musical Backgrounds for English Literature, 1580–1650* (New Brunswick, N.J.: Rutgers University Press, [1962]), chap. 1.

55. Jean de Muris, Strunk, *Middle Ages*, 173.

56. Kepler, *Harmonice Mundi*, chap. 3: "On the Harmonic means, and the Trinity of Consonant Sounds," section 37. I am grateful to A. M. Duncan of the Department of History of Loughborough University, Loughborough, Leicestershire, for permission to use his translation-in-progress.

D. P. Walker explains that Kepler rejected number symbolism in favor of geometric analogies that correspond to "archetypes in the soul of man [and the] mind of God" (44).

57. Lippius, *Synopsis Musicae Novae* (1612), chapter 8; quoted in *Grove*, "Polyphony," 12:417.

58. Marin Mersenne, *Harmonie Vniverselle, contenant la theorie et la pratiqve de la mvsiqve* (Paris, 1636), IV:213. This treatise was of course published too late for Herbert to have seen it in print.

59. *Oxford English Dictionary*, "vie," 5.

60. Walker, 7.

61. Herbert, "The Thanksgiving," lines 40–41.

An Augustinian Reading
of George Herbert's "The Pulley"

CHAUNCEY WOOD

More than 160 years ago an anonymous writer for *The Retrospective Review* said that "The quaintness and oddity of *The Pulley* are compensated for by some excellent lines."[1] In the intervening years we have made substantial advances in our understanding of George Herbert generally and of "The Pulley" specifically, but the admitted oddity and intriguing quaintness of the device of the pulley, heading a poem that never talks about pulleys at all, has perhaps deflected criticism away from the meaning of the poem as a whole to a concentration on the mechanics of pulleys, or the meaning of the word play, or the poem's recollection of the Pandora story.[2] Moreover, in a surprising number of instances something or other about the poem has deflected criticism away entirely, for although "The Pulley" is one of Herbert's more frequently collected and anthologized poems, nevertheless very few essays are devoted to its interpretation. Of the books on Herbert one regularly looks to only Helen Vendler's has a full-scale analysis of the poem, and it is scarcely "Augustinian."[3]

What I propose to do in my own "Augustinian" interpretation of the poem is to begin with Herbert's idea that man is restless until he finds rest in God, putting off any discussion of the physics of pulleys until we have a clearer understanding of the metaphysics of man's longing for God. But let me begin by rehearsing the text:

The Pulley

When God at first made man,
Having a glasse of blessings standing by;
Let us (said he) poure on him all we can:
Let the worlds riches, which dispersed lie,
Contract into a span.

So strength first made a way;
Then beautie flow'd, then wisdome, honour, pleasure:
When almost all was out, God made a stay,
Perceiving that alone of all his treasure
Rest in the bottome lay.

For if I should (said he)
Bestow this jewell also on my creature,
He would adore my gifts in stead of me,
And rest in Nature, not the God of Nature:
So both should losers be.

Yet let him keep the rest,
But keep them with repining restlesnesse:
Let him be rich and wearie, that at least,
If goodnesse leade him not, yet wearinesse
May tosse him to my breast.

There are a variety of sources whence Herbert might have gotten the idea that man is restless when separated from God. Louis L. Martz has suggested a source in Thomas à Kempis, *The Imitation of Christ*, while C. Stuart Hunter has advanced Psalm 95, and C. A. Patrides has called attention to the expression of the idea in John Hayward's *David Teares*.[4] Girolamo Savonarola is another promising source, for we know that Herbert had read Savonarola's *De simplicitate vitae Christianae*. Arthur Woodnoth, writing about George Herbert in a letter to Nicholas Ferrar, says "Sauonorola in Latine he hath of the Simplicity of Chr: Religion and is of great esteme with him."[5] Therein Herbert would have read, and probably esteemed, the following:

In sola ergo Dei contemplatione & fruitione, quiescit desiderium hominis, & eius beatitudo consistit. Ideo egregie dixit Augustinius:

Fecisiti nos Domine ad te; & inquietum est cor nostrum, donec requiescat in te. The desire of man rests only in the contemplation and enjoyment of God, which constitutes his blessing. Thus excellently says Augustine: Thou hast made us, Lord, for Thyself, and our heart is restless until it finds rest in Thee.[6]

This Augustinian idea about restlessness and rest is prominently featured at the very opening of Augustine's *Confessions*. Since we know Herbert had read Savonarola's *De simplicitate vitae Christianae*, we know he could have learned of this Augustinian passage there. There is, however, good reason to think that he had read the *Confessions* itself. The works of St. Augustine feature prominently in Herbert's will, for he leaves them to his curate, Nathaniell Bostocke. As Joseph Summers has emphasized, Augustine is the only church father mentioned in the will, to which one may add that along with the commentary on scripture by Lucas Brugensis, the works of Augustine are the only writings by *anyone* mentioned in the will.[7] Beyond this one can only speculate, but it is worth noting that Helen White has remarked on Augustine's popularity in the sixteenth and seventeenth centuries; and, according to White, the most popular works from his long canon were the *Prayers* and the *Meditations*.[8] The latter is comprised mainly of selections from the *Confessions*, and it is reasonable to assume that what was popular reading for other pious folk of the age would have appealed to Herbert as well. Certainly Augustine's account of his own stormy life shares a great deal tonally with the spiritual tempests rehearsed in *The Temple*. We shall never know whether or not George Herbert actually read the *Confessions*, but if he did so he, like Savonarola, would have noted the importance that Augustine gives to rest and restlessness, an importance we shall do well to reflect upon.

That the *Confessions* are a likely source for Herbert's idea of man's restlessness in "The Pulley" has received so little attention from students of the poem that for a measurable period of time I thought I had, through reading Savonarola, discovered it myself. I was, however, 175 years behind George Herbert Palmer, who annotated his 1805 edition of the poem with a reference to the *Confessions*—an annotation usually ignored by modern critics, although glanced at by Helen Vendler and Richard Strier.[9]

In order to understand what Augustine means by man's restlessness, and why he begins a story of his life with reference to it, we must look at the series of statements that open the work:

Great art Thou, O Lord, and greatly to be praised; great is Thy power, and of Thy wisdom there is no end. And man, being a part of Thy creation, desires to praise Thee—man, who bears about with him his mortality, the witness of his sin . . . yet man, this part of Thy creation, desires to praise Thee. Thou movest us to delight in praising Thee: for Thou hast formed us for Thyself, and our hearts are restless till they find rest in Thee.[10]

God is great, God deserves to be praised, God creates man, man desires to praise God, and in spite of man's insignificance— lacking God's power, God's wisdom, and bearing the shame of mortality—God nevertheless has created man for Himself, and moves man to delight when man praises Him. Our hearts are restless, but our discomfort may be eased a little through the delight we receive when praising God during this life, prior to the complete peace we may find with rest in God.

Augustine opens the *Confessions*, then, with a series of declarative statements about the nature of God and man. But he goes on to do more than merely tell us about God's creation of restless mankind. He gives us an example of one such man in his account of himself: born into an infancy of anger and greed, growing through adolescent delight in sin for its own sake—we remember the pears that were stolen only to be thrown away—and entering a manhood in which lust vied with intellectual pride for dominance in his soul. It is a case history, presented not as an end in itself, but to illustrate a point: that we are created with restless hearts. In the case of St. Augustine, a very restless heart. The autobiographical books of the *Confessions* follow inevitably from Augustine's view of the nature of man's psychology, but comprise only a little more than half of the *Confessions* as a whole. For Augustine's goal is not merely to tell what he was in restlessness, but to show us also what he became. In so doing he does not praise himself, as the author of only an autobiography might be thought to do, but praises God. Augustine shows his own progression from restlessness to delight, and gives us, his readers, the promise of final rest. Moreover, he can, through the mixture of example and precept, teach others how they may accompany him on the earthly pilgrimage. Having told us about God's creation and man's restlessness, he gives us an example. Having given us the example, he tells us why:

This is the fruit of my confessions, not of what I was, but of what I am, that I may confess this not before Thee only, in a secret exultation with trembling, and a secret sorrow with hope, but in the ears also of the believing sons of men—partakers of my joy, and sharers of my mortality, my fellow-citizens and the companions of my pilgrimage, those who are gone before, and those that are to follow after, and the comrades of my way. (149)

Having established the purpose of his confessions, Augustine turns to his desires in his new life and how he may attain them. Rejecting all the things of the world, he seeks God through his books of scripture, and starts with the story of creation:

Lord, have mercy on me and hear my desire. For I think that it is not of the earth, nor of gold and silver, and precious stones, nor gorgeous apparel, nor honors and powers, nor the pleasures of the flesh, nor necessaries for the body, and this life of our pilgrimage; all which are added to those that seek Thy kingdom and Thy righteousness. Behold, O Lord my God, whence is my desire. . . . let it be pleasing in the sight of Thy mercy, that I may find grace before Thee, that the secret things of Thy Word may be opened unto me when I knock. . . . These do I seek in Thy books. . . . Let me hear and understand how in the beginning Thou didst make the heaven and the earth. (184–85)

The story of creation leads Augustine to a commentary on the first book of Genesis—something unexpected in a confessional tome unless we remember that man's restlessness is because of man's creation. Created for God he is restless away from Him. Thus the *Confessions* opens with an image of the creation and man's consequent restlessness, and closes with an examination of that creation through a study of the first book of Genesis. Not surprisingly, Augustine follows the story of creation to the seventh day, the day of God's rest, which is symbolic of the rest awaiting man. " . . . the seventh day . . . Thou hast sanctified . . . that that which Thou didst after Thy works, which were very good, resting on the seventh day, . . . that the voice of Thy Book may speak beforehand unto us, that we also after our works (therefore very good, because Thou hast given them unto us) may repose in Thee also in the Sabbath of eternal life" (255). In the *Confessions*, then, God may be seen to create man, to endow him with certain mutable and therefore unsatisfactory goods, and finally to promise man eternal rest with Him. In Augustine's closing words, " . . . we also have certain good works, of Thy gift, but not eternal; after these we hope to rest in Thy great hallowing" (256). There are other references throughout the *Confessions* to man's restless state, but the opening and closing ones are the most significant.

It is easy enough to see that Herbert's "Pulley" has a great deal in common with Augustine's idea of man's restlessness. "The Pulley" begins with reference to the time "When God at first made man," which is just where the *Confessions* begins. The poem then tells of God's outpouring of "blessings" and "the worlds riches" which are very reminiscent of Augustine's "certain good works of Thy gift." Rest only is withheld in the poem, lest man, God's creature, seek comfort in nature rather than in God:

> For if I should (said he)
> Bestow this jewell also on my creature,
> He would adore my gifts in stead of me,
> And rest in Nature, not the God of Nature:
> So both should losers be.

Paul's letter to the Romans (1:25) warned against those who "worshipped and served the creature more than the Creator," and in the *Confessions* St. Augustine twice warns against "that intoxication wherein the world so often forgets Thee, its Creator, and falls in love with Thy creature instead of Thee . . ." (22) the second time quoting Romans 1:25 directly (101).

In addition to the idea of man's restlessness on earth, one can find in the *Confessions* some language and ideas that may have suggested to Herbert the image of the pulley as a help in raising things. If we concentrate for the moment on only this aspect of the pulley, and bear in mind the usual idea that one arises from earth to heaven, then St. Augustine's concept of the soul's love for God is quite pertinent:

In Thy gift [of the Holy Spirit] we rest; there we enjoy Thee. Our rest is our place. Love lifts us up thither, and Thy good Spirit lifteth our lowliness from the gates of death. In Thy good pleasure lies our peace. The body by its own weight gravitates towards its own place. Weight goes not downward only, but to its own place. Fire tends upwards, a stone downwards. . . . Out of order, they are restless; restored to order, they are at rest. My weight is my love; by it am I borne withersoever I am borne. By Thy Gift we are inflamed, and are borne upwards. . . . We ascend Thy ways that be in our heart, and sing a song of degrees; we glow inwardly with Thy fire, with Thy good fire, and we go, because we go upwards to the peace of Jerusalem. . . . (232–33)

In Augustine's metaphysics, the natural direction of the heart is upward toward God, with love as the efficient cause. The heart is restless until it finds rest in God. If the love or desire of the heart is improperly ordered, its "weight" may, like a stone, drag it downward towards earth rather than upward like a flame. The period of time from the creation to the seventh day may be construed as a direct reference to Genesis and may also be taken allegorically (St. Augustine's term) as the story of all mankind. Furthermore, there is a sense in which Augustine's own life is told over the period of time from his own creation to his own rest in God. The *Confessions* is not a story of Everyman, for its does not recount a series of events that happens to every person, but, to borrow Charles Singleton's felicitous phrase, it is an allegory of "whicheverman," for what happened in Augustine's life *could* happen to any man.[11] Herbert's "The Pulley" is similar, in that he tells the story of the creation of man with both "certain good works" and an innate restlessness of the heart, here phrased as "the worlds riches" and the "jewel" of "rest." Herbert then advances two possible motivations for man's being led or tossed to God's breast:

> Let him be rich and wearie, that at least,
> If goodnesse leade him not, yet wearinesse
> May tosse him to my breast.

The two motivations, "goodnesse" and "wearinesse," are presumably both prompted by man's restlessness, but "goodnesse" has not always been construed that way.

Augustine divided love into a weight that would bear a man "whithersoever" he was to be borne, and Herbert similarly divides man's love for God into two forms, both somewhat passive. Richard Strier, in a very searching examination of "The Pulley," has argued against Helen Vendler's reading of "goodnesse" as pertaining to man's own good works. Strier contends that good works could not, for Herbert, lead man to Heaven.[12] Strier is, in my view, right about this. "Goodnesse" in the poem must refer to God's goodness, as though, in Strier's words, "within the myth of the poem, God seems to consider it an actual possibility that appreciation of his generosity could lead man to a proper adoration."[13] Because we live in a fallen world, Strier sees this possibility of man's being led by goodness to be "unlikely or impossible" (43–44); yet while finding this idea to be presented as "a piercing irony," he nevertheless does not read the poem as "finally a dark one" (44). This view of the poem is very balanced, yet perhaps needs a little more detailed reconciling than Strier gives us. A consideration of some of Augustine's language in the *Confessions* can help in this regard, especially if we bear in mind that "The Pulley" is set at the time of the Creation.

In a passage already cited, St. Augustine said that the love that permits man to be borne upward is not something of man's own making, but rather comes from God: "By Thy Gift we are inflamed" (233). Similarly he writes a little earlier, "Love lifts us up thither, and Thy good Spirit lifteth our lowliness from the gates of death" (232). There is, we may see, a certain passivity in man's love for God, since man cannot be a self-starter after the Fall. The passages from St. Augustine that have been cited here are all, it should be remembered, from what is in fact a commentary on the first chapter of Genesis, but for Augustine it is not possible to think of the creation of man without also recalling man's subsequent transgression. Thus at the beginning of Book Thirteen of the *Confessions* Augustine writes:

> I call upon Thee, my God, my mercy, who madest me, and who didst not forget me, though forgetful of Thee. I call Thee into my soul, which by the desire which Thou inspirest in it Thou preparest for Thy reception. . . . For Thou, O Lord, *hast blotted out all my evil deserts, that Thou mightest not repay into my hands wherewith I have fallen from Thee*, and Thou hast anticipated all my good deserts, that Thou mightest repay into Thy hands wherewith Thou madest me. . . . (228) (Emphasis added.)

When George Herbert sets "The Pulley" at the time of Creation, he indeed creates what Strier has called a "piercing irony" in laying out the alternatives of wearinesse or God's goodness as motivations for man's being led or tossed to God. However, the irony is not, as Strier would have it, in that love of goodness is "unlikely" or "impossible." Rather, at the time of the creation there is something more like a dramatic irony in the suggestion that man's love of God's goodness could lead him to God, for without that real possibility, without Adam's freedom to choose wrongly, there would not have been a Fall. Yet God, through his foreknowledge, and the reader of the poem, through his historical awareness, both know that man will, after Adam, have only one possibility open, that of being tossed by weariness to God. Indeed, there may be a further irony here, in that at the moment of creation there is still the possibility that "goodnesse" in the sense of man's capacity for rectitude could lead to God, but that, too, is ended by the Fall. Since "The Pulley" as a whole is concerned with God's bounty, there is little doubt that the primary meaning of "goodnesse" late in the poem refers to God's goodness. Still, it would be hard to rule out a kind of secondary meaning in which the general drift of the poem gives way to momentary consideration of the possibilities for man's goodness, which must have existed at the moment of creation. However, as St. Augustine wrote in his account of Genesis in the *Confessions*, "The angels fell, the soul of man fell . . ." (232).

In "The Pulley" Herbert is at pains to emphasize that there are — or rather *were* — two possibilities for man's ascent to God. One, whether it is thought of as man's love for God's goodness to him or man's capacity for doing good, is, after the Fall, more of a theoretical than a practical possibility. The other, the desire for an Augustinian rest with God, persists beyond the creation and pertains to potential readers of Herbert's poem in his own time. The differences, therefore, are in part temporal; the similarity is that both are inspired by God. As Augustine wrote in the passage already cited, it is God who inspires "desire" in the soul (228). Herbert himself addressed the concept in "The Holdfast," in which the speaker is led to realize that observing God's decrees, trusting in God, and even confessing that God is his succor is nevertheless not truly his own: "But to have nought is ours, not to confesse / That we have nought." This troubling thought stays with the poet until the "friend" reassures him about the superiority of the postlapsarian situation: "What Adam had, and forfeited for all, / Christ keepeth now, who cannot fail or fall." Something like this idea lies behind the tone of "The Pulley," for at the moment of creation the possibilities for man's return to God are rich indeed. "What Adam had," was quite a lot, but forfeited it was, and "for all." Hence the emphasis in "The Pulley" on conditionality and possibility: "*If* goodnesse leade him not, yet wearinesse / *May* tosse him to my breast."

Insofar as "The Pulley" has to do with pulleys, we are not concerned merely with a device to pull something upwards, as I earlier suggested, but with a device that can raise either of two things, or, in the present case, one thing by two means. The commonest use of such a pulley in the seventeenth century was to facilitate the raising of well-buckets on the opposite ends of a rope. This two-bucket well, of course, is not to be confused with the one-bucket variety, which normally used a kind of crank. Herbert's pulley is widely conceded to be a kind of emblem, and it is in the emblem books that we should look for an explanation of how pulleys work, bearing in mind the caution of Rosemary Freeman that Herbert's relationship with emblem books is "hard to define," and Barbara Lewalski's emphasis on the "shaping influence" of some general types of emblems rather than on particular figures.[14]

In Thomas Jenner's *The Soules Solace* (1631), there is an emblem of a two-bucket well with a prominent pulley. The well and its buckets Jenner explains as an emblem for the opposition of sin and grace:

In great and common *Wells* for every man,
Such as is neere the *Burse* in *Amsterdam*,
There are two *Buckets* fastened to a chaine,
The easier downe to sway, and vp againe.
One being aloft, the tother then is vnder,
Necessitie doth force them thus asunder,
When one is emptie'tother straight doth fill;
They ne're are both aboue; one's vnder still.
Like to these *Buckets*, hanging thus apart,
Is *grace* and *sinne*, in every good mans heart.
. . . .
Consider this, who lou'st in sinne to liue,
Yet hop'st in heaven thy portion *God* will giue.
The Iron chaine compells one Bucket low,
And forceth still the other vp to goe.
So *sinne* and *grace* (Gods justice doth command)
Nor in *one heaven*, nor in *one heart* may stand.[15]

Fig. 1

Jenner does not mention the pulley at all, but it features prominently in the emblem—indeed it almost dominates it—and its function in relation to the two buckets and the chain is clear enough. (See fig. 1.) Insofar as one might say that Herbert's poem is about the salvational possibilities of goodness and weariness, one might wonder why he did not entitle it "The Buckets" instead of "The Pulley." The answer, of course, is that whereas Jenner's buckets were representative of the opposites of sin and grace, Herbert's goodness and weariness are not opposite forces that cannot co-exist but are rather opposite—or at least different—means of going in the same direction: upwards. Thus Jenner is concerned to stress the necessary polarity of the buckets. When one is up the other must be down. But Herbert stresses the evenly symmetrical dynamism of the pulley. Both buckets will or can arise. In the two-bucket well, the bucket filled with water is drawn up by three things: the weight of the other, empty and lighter bucket going downwards, the strength of the person pulling the rope, and the mechanical advantage of the pulley. But in Herbert's spiritual concept, there is nothing man can do to bring about his own salvation. What he needs is something that will do the work for him, and that, of course, is why the poem is called "The Pulley" and not "The Buckets." Herbert stresses God's providential order, his creation, and his generosity in opening two avenues to man: God's own goodness and man's weariness, by which man may arise to God. If he does arise, it will be because a pulley was there, not because he managed it himself. Herbert would agree with Augustine that love, the "weight" of the soul, properly ascends, and he imagined that man's love needed help from God to arise, just as Augustine observed that "by Thy Gift we are inflamed."

Herbert's idea of the role of God's providence in man's affairs is well set out in *A Priest to the Temple, or The Country Parson*. There Herbert says that God

> exerciseth a threefold power in every thing which concernes man. The first is a sustaining power; the second is a governing power; the third a spirituall power. By his sustaining power he preserves and actuates every thing in his being. . . . By Gods governing power he preserves and orders the references of things one to the other. . . .

The third power is spirituall, by which God turnes all outward blessings to inward advantages. . . . And it is observable in this, how Gods goodnesse strives with man's refractoriness; Man would sit down at this world, God bids him sell it, and purchase a better. (270–72)

In "The Pulley" Herbert shows God creating the world and endowing his creature with certain gifts. But God also withholds rest so that man will not "sit down at this world." God's spiritual power causes man to seek him through God's goodness or man's own weariness. His governing power causes man to "depend" on him, and his sustaining power "actuates every thing in his being." Although "The Pulley" has often been likened to the Pandora story, it must be emphasized that in Herbert's version it is God who pours out the blessings, God who engineers both man's restless nature and his possible final rest. Man, in this sense, is passive in the poem, for he is either led or tossed. For some, this might be seen as a flaw in the poem, but for Herbert man's weakness was not a source of embarrassment, rather God's willing strength was the source of joy. To cite "The Holdfast" again, "all things [are] more ours by being his." Herbert expressed man's weakness in terms of being led or tossed by means of God's pulley in the poem under discussion, and even the language seems Augustinian. "Thou alone [art] rest. And behold, Thou art near, and deliverest us from our wretched wanderings, and stablishest us in Thy way, and dost comfort us, and say, 'Run; I will carry you, yea, I will lead you, and there also will I carry you'" (90). As St. Augustine saw God carrying man on the earthly pilgrimage, so George Herbert saw God lifting man to him, as though with the mechanical advantage of a pulley. Thus, in a paradox not often emphasized, man's weariness does not lead to stasis as we would expect, but by means of God's loving force to movement, to tossing man to God's breast.

Notes

1. Cited in *The Works of George Herbert*, ed. F. E. Hutchinson (1941; corrected repr., Oxford: Clarendon Press, 1945), xlviii. All quotations of Herbert's writings will be from this edition.

2. On the mechanics of pulleys see *inter alia*, D. S. Mead, "Herbert's 'The Pulley,'" *The Explicator* 4 (1945): 17, *Exploring Poetry*, ed. M. L. Rosenthal and A. J. M. Smith (New York, 1955), 545, and C. Stuart Hunter, "Herbert's 'The Pulley,'" *The Explicator* 34 (1976): 43. For a very different interpretation of the significance of the pulley, which imagines it as an instrument of torture, see Raymond B. Waddington, "The Title Image of Herbert's 'The Pulley,'" *George Herbert Journal* 9 (1986): 49–53. On word play see Janet Grayson, "Bernadine Paronomasia in Herbert's 'The Pulley,'" *American Notes and Queries* 15 (1976): 52–53, and Michael Routh, "A Crux of 'The Pulley,'" *Seventeenth-Century News* 40 (1982): 44–45. Hutchinson cites Alice Meynell, who regretted that Herbert did not avoid "this rather distressing ambiguity" (533). Many critics allude in passing to the echoes in "The Pulley" of the Pandora myth. However, there are variations in the Pandora story that make comparison with Herbert problematical, and one should also bear in mind that Herbert's emphasis on blessings and weariness is very different from the portrayal of evil borne through hope in the Pandora legend.

3. Helen Vendler, *The Poetry of George Herbert* (Cambridge, Mass.: Harvard University Press, 1975), 32–37.

4. Louis L. Martz, *The Poetry of Meditation*, rev. ed. (New Haven: Yale University Press, 1962), 281, n. 14; Hunter, 43; *The English Poems of George Herbert*, ed. C. A. Patrides (Totowa, N.J.: Rowman and Littlefield, 1975), 12.

5. *The Ferrar Papers*, ed. B. Blackstone (Cambridge: Cambridge University Press, 1938), 268.

6. Hieronymus Savonarola, *De Simplicitate Vitae Christianae* (N. P. Lazarus Zetznerus, 1615), 111. Translation mine. Mrs. Betty Robertson was kind enough to point out to me the precise Augustinian location for Savonarola's vague reference.

7. Joseph H. Summers, *George Herbert: His Religion and Art* (1954; repr., Binghamton, N.Y.: Medieval & Renaissance Texts & Studies, 1981), 76. At the risk of oversimplification, one may say that in the past few years there has been a movement to promote a "Protestant," seventeenth-century George Herbert, influenced by Calvin and Luther, at the expense of a "Catholic," medieval George Herbert, influenced by St. Augustine. The former position is represented by Lewalski and Strier, in opposition to the more traditional position of Summers, Martz, and Tuve. It is clear from my argument that I believe St. Augustine's works to be influential on "The Pulley," and I take Herbert's ownership of St. Augustine's writings—important enough to him to prompt him to leave them in a bequest—to be a powerful piece of evidence for St. Augustine's influence on all of Herbert's thought and work. The crucial, and very difficult issue, is to determine how Augustine would have been understood by someone like George Herbert. For a challenge to the revisionist view of Herbert,

arguing from the 'medieval' emphasis of Nicholas Ferrar at Little Gidding, see Stanley Stewart, "Herbert and the 'Harmonies' of *Little Gidding*," *Cithara* 24 (1984): 3–26. The other documents referred to are: Barbara Lewalski, *Protestant Poetics and the Seventeenth-Century Religious Lyric* (Princeton: Princeton University Press, 1979); Richard Strier, *Love Known: Theology and Experience in George Herbert's Poetry* (Chicago: University of Chicago Press, 1983); Rosemond Tuve, *A Reading of George Herbert* (Chicago: University of Chicago Press, 1952). For the work of Martz see note 4.

    8. Helen C. White, *The Tudor Books of Private Devotion* (Madison, Wis.: The University of Wisconsin Press, 1950), 27.

    9. Vendler, *Poetry of George Herbert*, 33; Strier, *Love Known*, 11.

    10. *Basic Writings of St. Augustine*, trans. Whitney J. Oates (New York: Random House, 1948), I:3. Subsequent references will be to this edition.

    11. Charles S. Singleton, *Dante Studies 2: Journey to Beatrice* (Cambridge, Mass.: Harvard University Press, 1985), 5. For Singleton the journey of the *Commedia* is in fact the journey of "the unquiet heart" (4), which phrase he takes from the opening of the *Confessions*.

    12. Richard Strier, "Ironic Humanism in *The Temple*," in *"Too Rich to Clothe the Sunne": Essays on George Herbert*, ed. Claude J. Summers and Ted-Larry Pebworth (Pittsburgh: University of Pittsburgh Press, 1980), 51–52, nn. 19–20; Vendler, 35–36.

    13. Strier, "Ironic Humanism," 43. Herbert's earliest published critic, George Ryley, interpreted "goodnesse" the same way. "The goodness in the Divine Nature is a powerfull Attractive. . . ." See John Martin Heissler, "Mr. Herbert's Temple & Church Militant Explained & Improved By A Discourse Upon Each Poem Critical & Practical by George Ryley: A Critical Edition" (Ph.D. diss., University of Illinois, 1960), 545.

    14. Rosemary Freeman, *English Emblem Books* (London: Chatto & Windus, 1948), 156; Barbara K. Lewalski, "Emblems and the Religious Lyric: George Herbert and Protestant Emblematics," *Hebrew University Studies in Literature* 6 (1978): 48.

    15. Thomas Jenner, *The Soules Solace or Thirtie and One Spirituall Emblems* (London, 1631), C_4^{r-v}.

Milton

In *Paradise Lost* the poet was to imitate as well as to relate the largest of God's actions.

The Muse's Method

Gul. Faithorne ad Vivum · Delin. et sculpsit ·

Joannis Miltoni Effigies Ætat: 62.
1670.

John Milton at the age of 62.
By permission of the National Portrait Gallery, London.

Generic Multiplicity
and Milton's Literary God[1]

BARBARA K. LEWALSKI

It is a commonplace of criticism that the most difficult problem Milton faced in *Paradise Lost* involved the portrayal of God. Milton indeed undertook to "justify the ways of God to men," but the problem for many readers—from his day to ours—has been to justify Milton's ways with God. Early to late, readers have questioned the theological appropriateness and literary success of Milton's anthropomorphic presentation of God as epic character. For Addison he is simply dull, a "school divine" delivering long sermons; for Shelley and Empson a cruel torturer and tyrant; for A. J. A. Waldock a divine egotist; for Douglas Bush an "almighty cat watching a human mouse."[2]

Recent theological approaches offer somewhat more positive interpretations: C. A. Patrides' examination of Milton's theology of Accommodation; Michael Lieb's focus upon the poem's evocation of the numinous; Georgia Christopher's description of Milton's God in Reformation terms, as a powerful dramatic and noetic voice, whose decrees challenge characters and readers alike.[3] And newer critical methods have redefined the problem in other terms. Stanley Fish emphasizes the fallen reader's inappropriate responses to a "determinedly non-affective" God; William Kerrigan analyzes the God of the poem in terms of the Oedipal psychic history of the poet; and Andrew Milner's Marxist analysis finds in *Paradise Lost* an unfortunate hybrid of the anthropomorphic God of Genesis and the God of Milton's true belief—the abstract principle of Reason.[4]

In my view, interpretation should start from the fact that God and the Son in *Paradise Lost* are literary portraits. As Bard, Milton had to attain an imaginative apprehension of the Divine himself and also to accommodate that vision to his readers in literary terms that would serve his poetic and educative purposes. I suggest that he employed a special strategy of generic multiplicity to address those needs.

In portraying God and the Son Milton called upon an even wider range of literary forms than he employed in presenting Satan. They include generic paradigms, conventions, and topoi from epic, romance, drama, dialogue, judicial oratory, and more; as well as models and analogues from Homer and Virgil, from Hesiod and Ovid, from Plato and Lucretius, from Genesis and Exodus, and many other texts. These reference points are made to serve as interpretative frames for particular scenes and episodes in which specific aspects of God are presented. Such complex layering and fusion of many generic elements in individual scenes provide multiple perspectives upon God, suggesting the Divine totality and transcendence but at the same time pointing up how partial, inadequate, and incomplete is any single frame — even the biblical one. An analysis of the literary means by which both Bard and reader imagine the God of the poem may not dispel all our resistance to that figure, but it should indicate that Milton finds a more daring and more satisfactory resolution to his poetic problem than we have realized. And that Milton's God deserves, on balance, a better press than he has had.

This poetic strategy is entirely consonant with the theological principles Milton outlined in his theological treatise, *De Doctrina Christiana*, as guidelines for all conceptions of or imaginations of God — and so by definition those of a poet intending to write a great and true epic of the human condition. The first principle, wholly commonplace, is that God "as he really is" is utterly beyond human conception or imagination.[5] The second principle, also a commonplace among Protestants but potentially radical in its forthright repudiation of metaphysics, is that our idea or image of God should correspond precisely to the way he is presented in the Bible — not because the biblical image is literally true (it cannot be) but because that is how God wishes to be understood by us, the way in which he has "accommodated" himself to our capacities:

It is safest for us to form an image of God in our minds which corresponds to his representation and description of himself in the sacred writings. Admittedly, God is always described or outlined not as he really is but in such a way as will make him conceivable to us. Nevertheless, we ought to form just such a mental image of him as he, in bringing himself within the level of our understanding, wishes us to form. Indeed he has brought himself down to our level expressly to prevent our being carried beyond the range of human comprehension, and outside the written authority of scripture, into vague subtleties of speculation. . . . We should form our ideas with scripture as a model, for that is the way in which he has offered himself to our understanding.[6]

The third principle, yet more radical as Milton interprets it, is that *all aspects* of the biblical portrayal of God are intended by him to figure in our conception, so that we should not try to explain away passages which seem to us "unworthy" of God, or which present him anthropomorphically:

On the question of what is or what is not suitable for God, let us ask no more dependable authority than God himself. If *Jehovah repented that he had created man*, Gen. vi.6, *and repented because of their groanings*, Judges ii.18, let us believe that he did repent. . . . If it is said that God, after working for six days, *rested and was refreshed*, Exod. xxxi.17, and if he *feared his enemy's displeasure*, Deut. xxxii.27, let us believe that it is not beneath God to feel what grief he does feel, to be refreshed by what refreshes him, to fear what he does fear. . . . In short, God either is or is not really like he says he is. If he really is like this, why should we think otherwise? If he is not really like this, on what authority do we contradict God? If, at any rate, he wants us to imagine him in this way, why does our imagination go off on some other tack?[7]

One implication of this radically metaphoric but yet insistently biblical imagination of God is that it gives Milton full warrant as poet to portray God as an epic character who can and does feel a range of emotions (fear, wrath, scorn, dismay, love), who makes himself visible and audible to his creatures in various ways, who engages in dialogue with his Son, with the angels, and (through the Son) with man and woman. Moreover, though the portrayal of God and the Son in *Paradise Lost* draws heavily upon biblical language and imagery,[8] the fact that, for Milton, the Bible itself offers only accommodated images of God evidently sanctions for him the use of other literary accommodations, so long as they accord with and help to expand the biblical images. In addition, since Milton sees that the biblical portrayal is by no means univocal, that God is variously conceived and represented by the various biblical writers through a panoply of literary forms—folk tale, history, law, prophecy, epic story, drama, psalm, and more—he has warrant for his similar generic strategy in *Paradise Lost*.

For such reasons, I think, Milton does not attempt to make the incomprehensible God a unified, fully realized character in *Paradise Lost*, or, always, an attractive one by human standards. I think he would have considered the attempt to do so presumptuous and absurd. Rather, following the biblical model, he employs a mix of generic patterns and references to suggest the manifold qualities and aspects we are to associate with God (subsuming thereby much that has been imagined about the Divine in literature). The Son is presented often but by no means exclusively in terms of heroic patterns transformed. And the Father is at times presented with reference to various Old Testament theophanies, but also with reference to the activities of Zeus in Homer and Hesiod, and of Jove in Ovid. This method accommodates God and the Son to us as figures in a kaleidoscope, presenting different images as the generic perspective shifts and requiring from us a strenuous process of comparison, contrast, and judgment. The analogues in themselves help us to image the divine attributes and acts, but also lead us to refine our conceptions as we recognize that these analogues are exceeded in an infinite scale by the nature and deeds of God and the Son.[9] The final effect is to suggest God's transcendence of any and all biblical or literary accommodations—including that offered in *Paradise Lost*.

In illustration of this thesis, I want to look especially at the Dialogue in Heaven scene (3.56–348), which offers the most complex layering and mixture of genres in the entire poem. The Bard's introduction to that scene provides some guide to interpretation. He portrays God "High Thron'd above all highth," with his Eye encompassing all time, past, present and future, and viewing "His own works and their works at once." He enumerates these works as the "Sanctities of Heaven," the "radiant image of his Glory," "Our two first Parents," "Hell and the Gulf between, and Satan." This striking description identifies God as the origin and final cause of all these creatures and their actions, while at the same time indicating that his creatures also shape themselves by their own choices and actions. Also, the inclusion of the Son among the "works" of God prepares us for the presentation of him in the Dialogue and throughout the poem in a manner consistent with the antitrinitarianism of Milton's De Doctrina. That tract portrays the Father as the supreme and only self-existent God, who generated the Son "within the bounds of time" as the "firstborn of the creatures" by an act of will (not natural necessity), and who imparted to him only "as much as he wished of the divine nature and attributes."[10] As we will see, the poem also accords with the theology of the tract in portraying the Son as the Father's Image; as the agent or instrument of the Father's creation, vengeance, judgment, regeneration, and providential government; and as an independent moral agent, taking on these roles freely, in obedience and by choice.[11]

The Dialogue in Heaven itself is intended to emphasize the aspect of Divine Love. The Father indicates the centrality of this issue when he couches his challenge to the heavenly assembly in such terms:

> Say Heav'nly Powers, where shall we find such love,
> Which of ye will be mortal to redeem
> Man's mortal crime, and just th'unjust to save,
> Dwells in all Heaven charity so dear?
>
> (3.213–16)

Later, the Father declares that the Son's voluntary offer to die for humankind proves him "By Merit more than Birthright Son of God, / . . . because in thee / Love hath abounded more than Glory abounds" (3.309–12). The suggestion is that heroic love, freely tendered, is the core of the Son's goodness and merit, and the quality wherein he most resembles the Father as Image of God's divine love.

The Bard imagines and presents the Dialogue through many generic frames and with reference to several specific models, holding forth true and transcendent norms to supplant Satan's debased or perverted ones.

First of all, it is a species of epic *Concilia Deorum.*[12] The Father's self-justification is intended to remind us of the Council of the Gods in the *Odyssey,* in which Zeus and Athena discuss Zeus's ways toward Odysseus, and Zeus defends himself by pointing to humankind's own responsibility for the evils they suffer:

> O for shame, how the mortals put the blame upon us
> gods, for they say evils come from us, but it is they, rather,
> who by their own recklessness win sorrow beyond what
> is given.[13]

Zeus applies this precept to the punishment of Aigisthous, who despite the gods' warnings persisted in his design to kill Agamemnon, and now has paid for it. Milton's God offers a more elaborate theological defense, but in much the same aggrieved tones and terms:

> They therefore as to right belong'd,
> So were created, nor can justly accuse
> Thir maker, or thir making, or thir Fate;
> As if Predestination over-rul'd
> Thir will, dispos'd by absolute Decree
> Or high foreknowledge; they themselves decreed
> Thir own revolt, not I.
>
> (3.111–17)

This analogue intimates that the problem of God's justice is perennial and the particular solutions always partial. But further comparison underscores the profound difference in the two epics in the relation of God and man. In the Council of the Gods in the *Odyssey,* Athena, Goddess of Wisdom, plays the suasory role, appealing on the same grounds of justice which rightly condemned Aigisthous, for pity and aid to beleagured Odysseus who is agreed to be wise and worthy. By contrast, the Son's pleas for fallen man (hardly wise and worthy) are appeals for mercy not justice; and Athena's advice and assistance to Odysseus pales before the aid the Son provides to humankind at the cost of his own life.

The Son's offer to die for fallen man is also placed in relation to another generic topic from epic and romance—deeds of bravery and self-sacrifice inspired by erotic love or noble friendship.[14] The specific frame is Nisus's offer (*Aeneid* 9.427–28) to exchange his life for that of his captured friend, Euryalus: "Me, me adsum, qui feci, in me convertite ferrum / O Rutuli! mea fraus omnis." ("On me—on me—here am I who did the deed—on me turn your steel, O Rutulians! Mine is all the guilt").[15] The Son directly echoes Nisus: "Behold mee then, mee for him, life for life / I offer, on mee let thine anger fall" (3.236–37). Pursuing the indicated comparison, we are to recognize that, unlike Nisus, the Son had no share whatever in the guilt for which he offers to die, and that his love extends beyond the individual friend or beloved to all humankind.

This comparison points up how the Son's heroic love transcends and transvalues the heroic virtues and actions central to epic and romance. His willing embrace of suffering and death in love provides the true pattern of that "better fortitude / Of Patience and heroic Martyrdom" which the Bard defines as more heroic than the battle courage honored in ancient epic—the pattern Satan perverted by his magnificent but prideful endurance of loss and pain in Hell. Also, the Son utterly transforms the concept of epic action by saving, not a tribe or a country, but an entire creation. Moreover, he revises the quest pattern fundamental to romance, as he here undertakes the salvation of mankind in something like the manner of a knight undertaking a quest at Arthur's Court. But he predicts that he will achieve through that quest a final, fully satisfactory closure foreign to romance: the return of all creation to union with the Father, so that "God shall be All in All" (3.335–341).

Yet another literary analogue and frame, indicated by broad structural patterns and specific allusions, is the dialogue between Apollo and his son Phaethon in Ovid's *Metamorphoses* (2.1–152). In both scenes a Son undertakes, in colloquy with his Father, an enterprise which causes his death. Milton's description of God on his throne echoes Ovid's description of Apollo on his radiant throne in the Palace of the Sun.[16] Also, God's proclamation that the Son has shown himself "By Merit more than Birthright Son of God" (3.309) is a rather surprising echo of Apollo's declaration that Phaethon is indeed his son and worthy of the name: "nec tu meus esse negari / dignus es, et Clymene veros," rendered in Sandys' 1632 version as follows: "By merit, as by birth, to thee is due / That name."[17]

Such allusions point up how entirely the Father-Son dialogue in Milton reverses that in Ovid. In the *Metamorphoses* Phaethon initiates the dialogue with Apollo to seek confirmation of his sonship, and Apollo immediately testifies to that sonship and to Phaethon's merit. In *Paradise Lost* the Son's relation to the Father is never in doubt, but God testifies to the Son's merit only after that merit has been demonstrated in the dialogue itself. In Ovid Apollo rashly offers Phaethon any boon he wishes, and Phaethon (still seeking to prove his sonship) rashly asks to drive Apollo's chariot despite Apollo's lengthy and urgent efforts to dissuade him. In *Paradise Lost* the Son undertakes his passion and death after full and reasoned discussion, and with the high praise of the Father. Phaethon, a mortal who takes on through hubris a divine role he cannot perform, wreaks fiery havoc upon heaven, earth, and mankind and is himself destroyed. The Son, a God humbling himself to human estate to save mankind, succeeds and makes possible a re-creation after apocalyptic fire: "The World shall burn, and from her ashes spring / New Heav'n and Earth, wherein the just shall dwell" (3.334–35). By such reversals, and by the incarnation which links his divine nature with human nature, the Son transforms the Ovidian metamorphic patterns, and their Satanic perversions, into a divine, transcendent metamorphosis in which human nature itself will be exalted to the throne of God:

> Therefore thy Humiliation shall exalt
> With thee thy Manhood also to this Throne;
> Here shall thou sit incarnate, here shalt Reign
> Both God and Man, Son both of God and Man.
> (3.313–16)

The Bard also imagines and presents this scene in relation to a dramatic model and frame, the allegorical "Parliament of Heaven" scene which figured prominently in medieval Mystery and Morality plays and in Milton's own outline for a drama on the topic of the Fall.[18] The basis of the episode was Psalm 85:10, a text prominent in the Christmas liturgy: "Mercy and truth are met together; righteousness and peace have kissed each other." As Hope Traver showed, the "parliament" usually took the form of a debate between these four qualities (called daughters) of God over the issue of Adam's or mankind's sin and its punishment, with Truth and Righteousness ranged against Mercy and Peace. The issue was ultimately resolved—often after a thorough search of heaven and earth for volunteers to substitute for man—by the offer of the Son of God (sometimes called Heavenly Love or Sapience).

Milton's Dialogue in Heaven alludes to this dramatic tradition by the issues raised in the theological discourse, by the Son's response to a call throughout heaven for a volunteer, and quite specifically by language in the four speeches focusing, in turn, upon the four qualities. Here, however, instead of allegorical personifications setting forth fixed and apparently exclusive positions, the speakers are dramatic characters, each of whom responds to and incorporates the position of the other.

God's first speech (3.80–134) sets forth the *truth* of things—Satan's escape, his impending success in the temptation, man's Fall, the doctrines of free will, sufficient grace, and personal responsibility for choice—but concludes with an affirmation of the other qualities: "In Mercy and Justice both, / Through Heav'n and Earth, so shall my glory excel, / But Mercy first and last shall brightest shine." [19] Responding to that statement, the Son (3.144–66) pleads the case for *mercy* to mankind, but appeals also to God's justice to prevent the triumph of Satanic evil: "That far be from thee, Father, who art Judge / Of all things made, and judgest only right." The Father's next speech (3.168–216) pronounces the stern demands of *justice*—"Die hee or Justice must"—but it begins with a restatement of his purpose to renew and save mankind, and it ends with a call to all the heavenly powers for "charity." The Son's response (3.227–65) emphasizes the "*peace* assured, / And reconcilement" he will achieve for man, but affirms as well that he will satisfy God's justice by his death and so allow the divine mercy to flow to man. The Father's concluding speech (3.274–343) celebrates the Son for reconciling all these elements in love: "So Heav'nly Love shall outdo Hellish Hate."

In itself, this scene is tragicomic: it begins in wrath, strife, and loss, and we are made aware throughout of the potential for a tragic outcome, but it ends in joyful resolution and celebration. God's words seem to proclaim the Fall an irreversible tragic event—until the Son elicits God's plan for redemptive grace. And the dilemma God poses in regard to man's guilt—"Die hee or Justice must"—seems an insoluble tragic dilemma until the Son breaks through that impasse by agreeing to "pay / The rigid satisfaction, death for death." That undertaking—the willing and patient endurance of suffering and death, out of love, to fulfill divine justice—provides the fundamental paradigm and norm for Christian tragedy in the poem.[20] It transcends the Promethean norm of defiant endurance of a Divine tyrant's unjust tortures, and comments on the debased, Satanic parody of Promethean tragedy we encounter in Book I. In this scene we see the Son embrace the tragedy of the human fallen condition, even as the scene's conclusion provides an emblem of the final resolution of that human tragedy within God's all-embracing Divine Comedy.

Several discursive genres, chiefly varieties of dialogue, also provide frames of reference for this scene. At times throughout the poem, the Father sets forth formal, solemn decrees, as when he proclaims his Son Viceregent (5.600–615),[21] but his speech most often permits or invites an auditor to make a genuine verbal contribution to the interpretation or implementation of the Divine purposes. We see this in God's commission to Raphael, which allowed that angel wide scope in determining how to convey the warning to Adam and Eve. In this scene the Father's speech is designed to promote a dialogue that engages the Son to share in and assume responsibility for the full elaboration and realization of God's will.

God's first speech is not couched in the unrhetorical, passionless style of his proclamations. Rather, it begins as informal dialogue—"Only begotten Son, seest thou what rage / Transports our adversary" (3.80–81)—and then takes on the character of a forensic or judicial oration before the heavenly court, accusing Satan and the human pair for the crime about to occur. It conforms closely to the norms laid down by Cicero and others for a prosecutor's speech of the equitable kind, concerned, as Cicero said such speeches should be, with "the nature of justice and the right or the reasonableness of reward and punishment"; and it presumes a defense based upon a *remotio criminis* issue, that is, an attempt to shift the guilt or responsibility from the accused to another.[22] Remarkably, Milton presents God arguing his own case publically and submitting it, as it were, to the bar of angelic and human judgment.

The opening lines serve as exordium, inviting abhorrence of Satan by showing him "transported" by rage and bent on desperate revenge. Then a brief narration describes the crime, and the motives and attitudes of those involved:[23] Satan's "false guile" and "glozing lies"; man's faithless transgression of God's sole command. The *confirmatio*, or argument proving the guilt of the accused, follows Cicero's recommendation to begin this kind of case by defending the one to whom the responsibility might be shifted.[24] Accordingly, God offers a long and passionately reasoned defense of his ways—"ingrate, he had of mee / All he could have; I made him just and right, / Sufficient to have stood, though free to fall"—concluding that fallen men and fallen angels alike must take full responsibility for their actions: "they themselves ordain'd thir fall" (3.96–128). At this point, however, God distinguishes between the accused parties: the angels fell "self-deprav'd," but Adam and Eve were deceived by Satan and so have some basis for a *remotio criminis* plea against him. The Father delivers his conclusion not as a prosecutor but as a judge taking all this into account, and pronouncing sentence in decisive if somewhat ambiguous terms: "Man therefore shall find grace, / The other none: in Mercy and Justice both . . . shall my glory excel, / But Mercy first and last shall brightest shine" (3.131–34).

The Son's plea for mercy breaks through and transforms the rigid structure of judicial debate. As sentence has already been passed, this is not a speech of defense, intended as such speeches were, to answer charges, or mitigate guilt, or stir up pathos. Rather, the Son challenges the Father to explain the ambiguities of his sentence, calling attention to his own continued vulnerability before the court of opinion if his enemy should wreck his creation: "So should thy goodness and thy greatness both / Be question'd and blasphem'd without defense" (3.165–66). The exchange between God and the Son transforms the judicial debate of adversaries into a dialogue, during which the Divine litigants agree to a unique *remotio criminis*, assigning full responsibility and guilt to Satan and humankind but shifting the punishment from man to his Divine Advocate.

Another frame is provided by several Old Testament dialogues of mediation, in which a prophet strives with God on behalf of his erring people. Specific verbal echoes recall Moses pleading with God to spare the rebellious Israelites who seek to return to bondage in Egypt, and especially recall Abraham pleading with God to save Sodom and Gomorrah for the sake of even ten righteous who might be found in those cities (Gen. 18:25): "That be far from thee to do after this manner, to slay the righteous with the wicked: and that the righteous should be as the wicked, that be far from thee: Shall not the Judge of all the earth do right?"[25] The echo in the Son's speech is clear:

> For should Man finally be lost, should Man
> Thy creature late so lov'd, thy youngest Son
> Fall circumvented thus by fraud, though join'd
> With his own folly? that be from thee far,
> That far be from thee, Father, who art Judge
> Of all things made, and judgest only right.
>
> (3.150–55)

The Son cannot ground his claim for mankind on righteousness, but only on mitigating circumstances — until he himself agrees to become the one just man for whom humankind (unlike Sodom and Gomorrah) will be spared. By such associations we are led to recognize the Son as the original and archetype of the Old Testament mediators, and the Dialogue in Heaven as paradigm for all subsequent biblical dialogues of mediation.

Again, and especially in retrospect, we are led to view the exchanges between God and the Son as a species of Socratic dialogue. In them the Father deliberately refrains from revealing his providential plan for man's salvation, so as to challenge the Son to discover, through dialogue, how the Divine goodness can overcome the evils of the Fall, how God's design for man can yet be realized, and just what a heroic love embracing both justice and mercy must be — and do. Like Socrates at his trial, incorporating in his judicial oration the very dialectical method his enemies denounced as dangerous,[26] Milton's God justifies his ways in part by his use of dialogue, since that genre calls upon the Son to display the freedom of choice which is the very ground of the Divine justification.

The later dialogue between God and Adam (8.357–450) also has a Socratic dimension. There, Adam asks to be given a mate and God seems to oppose his request, forcing Adam through dialogue to achieve and manifest self-knowledge. As he meets God's counter-arguments, Adam is led to define for himself what it is to be human: that it is not to find company with beasts, or to be perfect in himself as God, but to seek completion, help, and solace in human companionship and human love.

On both occasions God uses dialogue to achieve the essential Socratic purpose, education in self-knowledge. However, he departs from Socrates' structured dialectical method of leading his interlocutors by a chain of successive questions to affirm or deny a series of propositions, or to choose between alternative statements. Instead, he promotes the growth of his Divine and his human Son by a somewhat more open—and more gracious—method: he challenges them with an apparent dilemma, casts full responsibility upon them to work out its terms in dialogue with him, and then honors them highly for doing so. He commends Adam for knowing himself rightly and reasoning well, rewarding him with the mate he desires; and he commends the Son here for having realized his own nature, showing himself in his abounding love to be "By Merit more than Birthright Son of God."

Later scenes in the epic also present God and the Son through a layering of genres and generic frames, albeit somewhat less dense than in the Dialogue in Heaven episode. In the space remaining, I can only indicate, without elaborating upon, the presence and function of some of them.

Milton's emphasis in presenting the Battle in Heaven and the Creation is on the Divine Power. To render the Battle in Heaven he transforms the Homeric epic of wrath and strife into a "brief epic" of divine power exercising divine vengeance, employing several generic frames, of which the *Iliad* is primary. Through that frame we see that the Son's heroic role is defined by, but wholly transcends, the Homeric ethos. He exhibits martial prowess and attains battle glory beyond anything imaginable in Achilles. The Son does not, however, ascribe value to or seek glory from his martial deeds, observing ironically that he will engage the rebels on these terms "since by strength / They measure all, of other excellence / Not emulous, nor care who them excels" (6.820–22).[27] In the Battle in Heaven the Son bears God's power, exercises God's vengeance, and seeks God's glory, not his own, as hero of a transcendent epic of wrath.[28]

Other generic frames for this episode draw our attention beyond the Son to the Father as the source of the power and vengeance he images. When the angels turn to hill-hurling and the battle reaches an impasse in which heaven's destruction is threatened, the frame is clearly Hesiod's *Theogony*.[29] But by his transformations of Hesiod, the Bard emphasizes the incalculable distance between Zeus, strongest of the Gods, and Divine Omnipotence.[30] Again, the Exodus "epic" of the Lord's destruction of Pharaoh and his forces[31] is established as frame for the final rout of the rebel angels through allusions to Moses' words to the Israelites on the shores of the Red Sea—"Fear ye not, stand still, and see the salvation of the Lord which he will shew to you to day" (Exod. 14:13). The Mosaic charge echoes in the Son's command to the angels: "Stand still in bright array ye Saints, here stand / . . . stand only and behold / God's indignation on these Godless pour'd" (6.801–11).[32] Still other allusions frame this episode in terms of the "epic" visions of apocalyptic wrath and terror in the Book of Revelation.[33] By such means, Milton suggests as fully as literary accommodation can, the nature of God's awesome power in the dimension of wrath and vengeance.[34]

In a very different vein, the Creation account (Book 7) is designed to emphasize Divine Creativity as the primary manifestation of God's power.[35] Milton here transforms classical and hexaemeral creation poems (such as Lucretius's *De rerum natura* and Du Bartas's *Semaine*) into a second "brief epic" celebrating the power of God as exuberant vitality and creativity.[36] The actual creation decrees remain very close indeed to Genesis.[37] Each day's work is introduced by a close paraphrase of the creating words ascribed to God, but the Bard renders the creatures's responses very freely, highlighting by vibrant descriptive terms and dynamic verbs the vitality evoked from all things by the source of that vitality, God.[38]

To that end he employs another generic frame, Lucretius's *De rerum natura*.[39] We are directed to Lucretius by the terms of Adam's near-presumptuous query to Raphael broaching the creation topic: "what cause / Mov'd the Creator in his holy Rest / Through all Eternity so late to build / In *Chaos*" (7.90–94). Lucretius asks an analogous question, but ironically, intimating that the gods could have had nothing to do with creation: "What novelty could so long after entice those [Immortal Gods] who were tranquil before to desire a change in their former Life?"[40]

Milton lays Lucretius under contribution especially in presenting the work of the third, fifth, and sixth days, to develop the implications of the phrase in Genesis 1:12, "And the earth brought forth." Lucretius portrays the earth as a marvelously prolific *magna mater* who gives birth to and nurtures all creatures: she is "our fostering mother earth" who receives liquid drops of water from heaven, "and then teeming brings forth bright corn and luxuriant trees and the races of mankind, . . . [and] all the generations of wild beasts."[41] Milton heightens the metaphor, presenting earth first as an embryo brought to birth in cosmic waters (7.276–82), and then herself the fertile womb within which the seeds of all life were conceived, and danced forth into vibrant life:

> He scarce had said, when the bare Earth, till then
> Desert and bare, unsightly, unadorn'd,
> Brought forth the tender Grass, whose verdure clad
> Her Universal Face with pleasant green,
> Then Herbs of every leaf, that sudden flow'r'd
> Op'ning thir various colors, and made gay
> Her bosom smelling sweet: and these scarce blown,
> Forth flourish'd thick the clust'ring Vine, forth crept
> The smelling Gourd, up stood the corny Reed
> Enbattl'd in her field; and th'humble Shrub
> And Bush with frizzl'd hair implicit: last
> Rose as in Dance the stately Trees.
>
> (7.313–24)[42]

And while Lucretius's portrayal of the earth generating creatures and pouring them forth from several wombs[43] probably stands behind Milton's striking description of the animals emerging from the earth as at a birth, Milton's lines are more graphic and sensuous:

The Earth obey'd and straight
Op'ning her fertile Womb teem'd at a Birth
Innumerous living Creatures, perfet forms,
Limb'd and full grown: out of the ground up rose
As from his Lair the wild Beast . . .
. . . .
The grassy Clods now Calv'd, now half appear'd
The Tawny Lion, pawing to get free
His hinder parts, then springs as broke from Bonds,
And Rampant shakes his Brinded mane; the Ounce,
Rising, the crumbl'd Earth above them threw
In Hillocks; the swift Stag from under ground
Bore up his branching head.
(7.453–70)

From such comparisons we are intended to see that the marvelous processes of creation which Lucretius ascribed to the random motion of atoms are far surpassed by the prodigious vitality of the Divine Father, who makes his creatures vigorous, active, and potent, and sustains them in continuous processes of growth and generation. By his several generic frames and brilliantly evocative imagery, Milton presents the creation as the epic act of God himself, the ground of all other action,[44] evoking from us the quintessential epic response, wonder.

In Books 10 and 11 three scenes are presented in which God dispenses judgments upon fallen mankind and the fallen world. All are public assemblies — or synods, as the third and most formal of them is called — appropriately suggesting an ecclesiastical court.[45] Language in them is often close to biblical paraphrase. It is sometimes formal proclamation, sometimes harsh invective, and at times dialogic as the Son enacts the roles, first of appointed judge, then of mediatorial priest.

For these scenes the chief generic frames are biblical paraphrase and hexaemeral epic, which supply many of the topics though few formal elements. And for the sequence as a whole, the primary literary paradigm and reference point is Ovid's account of the universal flood in the *Metamorphoses*,[46] to which we are directed by an explicit comparison of Adam and Eve's repentant prayer at the beginning of Book 11, to the petitions of Deucalion and Phyrra. By thus recalling Ovid's account of Jove's sweeping condemnations and furious punishments, the Bard highlights the justice and mercy of God's judgments, and their consonance with the very nature of things.[47]

I have been arguing that Milton's method in presenting God and the Son involves the complex layering of genres, generic paradigms and specific texts, and their use as frames for the scenes in which the divine characters appear. Such literary accommodations lead us to make constant comparisons and contrasts, and thereby to apprehend something of Milton's literary God in the aspects of his justice and mercy, his omnipotence and creativity, his judgments and his love. By design we are presented with multiple reflections—at times uncongenial as well as attractive—of a God who cannot be seen whole. Indeed, were I to invoke here the vocabulary of contemporary theory, I might suggest that Milton's God is a supreme example of textuality, a text to which all these echoes and subtexts accrue, challenging interpretations which must always be inconclusive and undecidable. But those terms do not quite fit the present case. Even though, as I have been arguing, Milton meets the special challenge of representing Deity by a strategy of generic multiplicity which prevents our attaining a unified conception of the infinite God, he nonetheless intends to guide our attitudes by foregrounding certain of the divine qualities rather than others.

By generic strategies involving the density of the generic layering in some scenes, some surprising departures from identified models in others, and at times (as in the creation scene) the special brilliance of poetic language, Milton emphasizes certain aspects of the God he portrays. These dominant and peculiarly Miltonic aspects are, I suggest, the heroic love the Son manifests in the Dialogue in Heaven; the vibrant, exuberant creativity which the Father infuses into and nurtures in all his creatures; and especially the dialogic processes by which God as Socratic educator promotes reason, self-knowledge, and freedom of choice in all his sons. These last are preeminently the human values which Milton's poem endeavors to foster in its fit reader, by engaging that reader continuously and strenuously, but always delightfully, with its rhetoric of literary forms.

Notes

1. An expanded version of this paper appears as Chapter 5 in my book, *"Paradise Lost" and the Rhetoric of Literary Forms* (Princeton: Princeton University Press, 1985).

2. Joseph Addison, *Spectator* #315, in *Criticisms on "Paradise Lost"*, ed. Albert S. Cook (Boston: Ginn & Co., 1982), 61–62; Shelley, "On the Devil, and Devils," in *The Romantics on Milton: Formal Essays and Critical Asides*, ed. Joseph A. Wittreich, Jr. (Cleveland and London: Case Western Reserve University Press, 1970), 534–35; William Empson, *Milton's God* (London: Chatto & Windus, 1961); A. J. A. Waldock, *"Paradise Lost" and Its Critics* (Cambridge: Cambridge University Press, 1947; repr. 1967), 103; Douglas Bush, *English Literature in the Earlier Seventeenth Century, 1600–1660* (Oxford: Clarendon Press, 1945), 381.

3. See, e.g., C. A. Patrides, "*Paradise Lost* and the Theory of Accommodation," *Texas Studies in Literature and Language* 5 (1963): 58–63, reprinted in *Bright Essence: Studies in Milton's Theology*, by W. B. Hunter, C. A. Patrides, and J. H. Adamson (Salt Lake City: University of Utah Press, 1971), 159–63; Charles G. Shirley, Jr., "The Four Phases of the Creation: Milton's Use of Accommodation in *Paradise Lost* VII," *South Atlantic Bulletin* 45 (1980): 51–61; Michael Lieb, *Poetics of the Holy: A Reading of "Paradise Lost"* (Chapel Hill: University of North Carolina Press, 1981); Dennis R. Danielson, *Milton's Good God: A Study in Literary Theodicy* (Cambridge: Cambridge University Press, 1982); Georgia B. Christopher, *Milton and the Science of the Saints* (Princeton: Princeton University Press, 1982), 3–29, 89–133.

4. Stanley Fish, *Surprised by Sin: The Reader in "Paradise Lost"* (London: Macmillan; New York: St. Martin's, 1967), 62–87; William Kerrigan, *The Sacred Complex: On the Psychogenesis of "Paradise Lost"* (Cambridge: Harvard University Press, 1983); Andrew Milner, *John Milton and the English Revolution* (London: Macmillan, 1981).

5. *De Doctrina Christiana* 1.2, trans. John Carey, in *Complete Prose Works of John Milton*, ed. Don M. Wolfe et al., 8 vols (New Haven: Yale University Press, 1953–1982), 6:133.

6. *De Doctrina*, 133–34.

7. *De Doctrina*, 134–35. For a review of the literature on Milton's anthropomorphic (or anthropopathic) God, see Sister Hilda Bonham, "The Anthropomorphic God of *Paradise Lost*," *Papers of the Michigan Academy of Science, Arts and Letters* 53 (1968): 329–35.

8. See James H. Sims, *The Bible in Milton's Epics* (Gainesville: University of Florida Press, 1962), 17–20, and his index of Bible references, 259–78.

9. Michael Murrin in "The Language of Milton's Heaven," *Modern Philology* 74 (1977): 350–65 points to Milton's fusion of biblical prophetic images in such a way as to prevent distinct visualization of God or Heaven—ascribing this to Milton's iconoclasm. I suggest that the mix of genres performs a somewhat similar function, by preventing reductive or presumptuously comprehensive conceptions of God. But the generic patterns and paradigms also assist our understanding of God by directing us to clarify our perceptions through comparisons, contrasts, and emphases.

10. *De Doctrina* 1.5, *CPW*, 6:205–11, 227, 261–64.

11. *De Doctrina*, 236–39, 267–70. This is substantially the position of Maurice Kelley in *This Great Argument: A Study of Milton's "De Doctrina Christiana" as a gloss upon "Paradise Lost"* (Princeton: Princeton University Press, 1941), and "Milton's Arianism Again Considered" *Harvard Theological Review* 54 (1961), 195–205; also, Christopher Hill in *Milton and the English Revolution* (London: Faber & Faber, 1977), 285–305. For further consideration of Milton's antitrinitarianism with special application to *Paradise Regained*, see Lewalski, *Milton's Brief Epic: The Genre, Meaning, and Art of "Paradise Regained"* (Providence: Brown University Press; London: Methuen, 1966), 133–63. For the counterargument see essays by W. B. Hunter, C. A. Patrides, and J. H. Adamson in *Bright Essence: Studies in Milton's Theology*.

12. For a study of this epic motif in reference to the Council in Hell, see Mason Hammond, "Concilia Deorum from Homer through Virgil," *Studies in Philology* 30 (1933): 1–16; and O. H. Moore, "The Infernal Council," *Modern Philology* 16 (1918): 169–93. For an argument that both councils are transformed by Milton's prophetic impulse, see Joseph Wittreich, "'All Angelic Natures Joined in One': Epic Convention and Prophetic Interiority in the Council Scenes of *Paradise Lost*," in *Composite Orders: The Genres of Milton's Last Poems*, Milton Studies 17 (Pittsburgh: University of Pittsburgh Press, 1983), 43–74.

13. *Odyssey* 1.32–34, trans. Richard Lattimore (Chicago: University of Chicago Press, 1965), 28.

14. In the Romances erotic love is central and occasionally heroic, as when Edward and Gildippes fight and die side by side in battle (Tasso, *Gerusalemme Liberata*, trans. Edmund Fairfax, [London, 1600], 20.32–43, 94–100), or Britomart rescues her spouse-to-be Artigall from enslavement by Radigund (*FQ* 5.5–8). For a discussion of Milton's revalution of several heroic virtues, see John Steadman, *Milton and the Renaissance Hero* (Oxford: Clarendon Press, 1967).

15. *Aeneid* 9.32–34, trans. H. R. Fairclough, 2 vols. (Loeb, Cambridge: Harvard University Press; London: William Heinemann, 1960), 2:141. Several of Milton's editors, including Newton and Todd, have noted this allusion.

16. Cf. *PL* 3.56–71, and Ovid, *Metamorphoses* 2.31–32, trans. Frank J. Miller, 2 vols. (Loeb, Cambridge: Harvard University Press; London: William Heinemann, 1977): "Ipse loco medius rerum novitate paventem / Sol oculis juvenem, quibus adspicit omnes."

17. Ovid, *Metamorphoses* 2.42–3; George Sandys, *Ovid's Metamorphosis Englished, Mythologized, and Represented in Figures*, ed. K. K. Hulley and S. H. Vandersall (Lincoln: University of Nebraska Press, 1970), 80–81.

18. Milton's sketch in the Trinity College manuscript for a drama on "Paradise Lost" (*John Milton: Poems*, facsim. [Menston: Scolar Press, 1972], 35), has a version of the Parliament of Heaven, with Justice and Mercy "debating what should become of man if he fall." The debate was evidently to be resolved by the next listed character, Wisdom. For a review of this motif in drama and in allegorical narratives, see Hope Traver, *The Four Daughters of God. A Study of the Versions of this Allegory* (Philadelphia: J. C. Winston, 1907). Studies of Milton's Dialogue in Heaven with some reference

to this tradition include Merritt Y. Hughes, "The Filiations of Milton's Celestial Dialogue," *Ten Perspectives on Milton* (New Haven and London: Yale University Press, 1965), 104–35; and Irene Samuel, "The Dialogue in Heaven: A Reconsideration of *Paradise Lost* III.1–417," *PMLA* 72 (1957): 601–11.

19. The thematic development of the speeches in Milton's Dialogue resembles most closely the Coventry Cycle *Salutatio and Conception*, and the morality, *The Castell of Perseverence*, in which Truth (rather than Mercy as is more usual) opens the debate. See Traver, *Four Daughters of God*, 138–40.

20. As Milton did in his "Preface" to *Samson Agonistes*, Renaissance critics found ancient precedent for Christian tragedy based on the Passion in the *Christus Patiens*, commonly though perhaps erroneously attributed to the fourth century bishop Gregory Nazianzen. Hugo Grotius's neo-Latin play, *Tragoedia Christus patiens* (Monachii, 1627) provides a contemporary example.

21. On this point see also Anthony Low, "Milton's God: Authority in *Paradise Lost*," *Milton Studies* 4 (1972): 19–38.

22. Cicero, *De Inventione* 1.11.14–15, 2.28.86–87, trans. H. M. Hubbell (Loeb, Cambridge: Harvard University Press; London: William Heinemann, 1949), 31, 253; [pseudo-Cicero], *Rhetorica ad Herennium* 1.14.24–26, 2.17.26, trans. Harry Caplan, (Loeb, Cambridge: Harvard University Press; London: William Heinemann, 1948), 43–49, 105.

23. Cicero, *De Inventione* 1.16.22, 1.19.27, Hubbell, 45, 55; *Ad Herennium* 1.6.9–1.8.13, Caplan, 17–25.

24. Cicero, *De Inventione* 2.29.88, Hubbell, 255; *Ad Herennium* 1.15.25, Caplan, 47–9.

25. See also Moses' plea to God for the backsliding Israelites in Numbers 14:15–16:

Now if thou shalt kill all this people as one man, then the nations which have heard the fame of thee will speak, saying,
Because the Lord was not able to bring this people into the land which he sware unto them, therefore he hath slain them in the wilderness.

Compare *PL* 3.162–65:

or wilt thou thyself
Abolish thy Creation, and unmake
For him, what for thy glory thou hast made?
So should thy goodness and thy greatness both
Be question'd and blasphem'd without defence.

26. Plato, *Apology*, trans. Henry North Fowler (Loeb, Cambridge: Harvard University Press; London: William Heinemann, 1953), 69–145. At his trial, Socrates held forth his speech of defense as a model for forensic rhetoric. For discussion of some adaptations of Socratic dialectic in the Councils of Hell and Heaven, and in the Abdiel-Satan debate, see Elaine B. Safer, "The Use of Contraries: Milton's Adaptation of Dialectic in *Paradise Lost*," *Ariel* 2 (1981): 55–69.

27. Cf. Zeus's claim to rule the gods on the basis of his superior strength, *Iliad* 8.5–27, trans. Richard Lattimore (Chicago: University of Chicago Press, 1951), 182:

> Hear me, all you gods and all you goddesses: hear me
> while I speak forth what the heart within my breast urges.
> Now let no female divinity, nor male god either,
> presume to cut across the way of my word, but consent to it
> all of you, so that I can make an end in speed of these matters.
> Any one I perceive against the gods' will attempting
> to go among the Trojans and help them, or among the Danaans,
> he shall go whipped against his dignity back to Olympos;
> . . . .
> Then he will see how far I am strongest of all the immortals.

Also, see Achilles' relish of the idea of universal slaughter as glorious, *Iliad* 16.49–100: "if only / not one of all the Trojans could escape destruction, not one / of the Argives, but you and I could emerge from the slaughter / so that we two alone could break Troy's hallowed coronal," Lattimore, 332–33.

Yet we are not to conclude from Milton's critique of war in *Paradise Lost* that he has repudiated the Civil War, or the Lord's battles in the Old Testament, or the very idea of war itself. What he had repudiated is the notion that war is in itself glorious— however necessary it may sometimes be as an instrument of God's judgment or providential design. For various views on the issue, see Jackie Di Salvo, "The Lord's Battles: *Samson Agonistes* and the Puritan Revolution," *Milton Studies* 4 (1972): 39–62. See also Boyd M. Berry, *Process of Speech: Puritan Religious Writing and "Paradise Lost"* (Baltimore and London: Johns Hopkins Press, 1976).

28. The scene of investiture is presented as an infusion of the divine power of the Father to the Son: The Father "on his Son with Rays direct / Shone full; hee all his Father full exprest / Ineffably into his face receiv'd" (6.720–22).

29. Hesiod, *Theogony* 11.674–81, 687–712, *Hesiod, The Homeric Hymns and Homerica*, trans. Hugh G. Evelyn-White (Loeb, Cambridge: Harvard University Press; London: William Heinemann, 1977), 128–31. For discussion of these and other Hesiodic elements, see Merritt Y. Hughes, "Milton's Celestial Battle and the Theogonies," *Ten Perspectives*, 196–219. See also Philip J. Gallagher, "*Paradise Lost* and the Greek Theogony," *English Literary Renaissance* (1979): 121–48, for the questionable argument that Milton intends by these allusions to ridicule Hesiod's poem as a Satanic epic.

30. In Hesiod it takes all Zeus's strength and that of the Giants to defeat the Titans, but the Son of God needed no aid, and withheld half the divine power bestowed on him. The Miltonic God's omnipotence is further emphasized by the fact that in other Christian epics treating the Battle in Heaven, Michael and the loyal angels are able to defeat and cast out the Satanic forces. See, e.g., Erasmo di Valvasone, *Angeleida* (Venice, 1590). And see Stella Purce Revard, *The War in Heaven: "Paradise Lost" and the Tradition of Satan's Rebellion* (Ithaca and London: Cornell University Press, 1980), 235–63.

31. Ps. 24:81. For a discussion of Hebrew exegetical tradition treating the Exodus as an epic-like event, see Harold Fisch, "Hebraic Style and Motifs in *Paradise Lost*," in *Language and Style in Milton*, ed. Ronald D. Emma and John T. Shawcross (New York: Frederick Ungar, 1967), 37–39; and Jason P. Rosenblatt, "Structural Unity and Temporal Concordance: The War in Heaven in *Paradise Lost*," *PMLA* 87 (1972): 31–41. For discussion of Exodus motifs in other parts of the poem, see Shawcross, "*Paradise Lost* and the Theme of Exodus," *Milton Studies* 2 (1970): 3–26. For the theory of the epic-like meter in Exodus 15, see Philo, *De vita contemplativa*, in *Philo*, 11, trans. F. H. Colson (Loeb, Cambridge: Harvard University Press; London: William Heinemann, 1929–62); and Andrew Willet, *Hexapla in Exordium: that is, a Sixfold Commentary upon the Second Book of Moses Called Exodus* (London, 1608), 210–11.

32. Cf. also Exod. 19:16, 18, and *PL* 6.56–60; the analogue is noted by Murrin, "Language of Milton's Heaven," 352–53.

33. We are directed to the great epic battle and cataclysm at the Apocalypse by the rebel angels' wish that "The Mountains now might be again / Thrown on them as a shelter from his ire" (6.843–44), echoing the cry of the wicked at the Last Judgment "to the mountains and rocks, Fall on us, and hide us from the face of him that sitteth upon the throne" (Rev. 6:16). For the argument that the three-day Battle in Heaven is primarily typological, looking forward to the Apocalyptic warfare of Christ and Anti-Christ, see William Madsen, *From Shadowy Types to Truth: Studies in Milton's Symbolism* (New Haven: Yale University Press, 1968), 99–111; and for the argument that it foreshadows Christ's Death and Resurrection, see W. H. Hunter, "Milton on the Exaltation of the Son: The War in Heaven in *Paradise Lost*," *ELH* 36 (1969): 215–31. While the first victory of the Son clearly foreshadows those to come, I think we are intended to focus on this battle primarily as literal event, accommodated to us by reference to all other accounts of the Son's warfare against Satan throughout all time.

34. Kitty Cohen, *The Throne and the Chariot: Studies in Milton's Hebraism* (The Hague: Mouton, 1975), 103–32, emphasizes Milton's strategies for portraying the Divine power as essentially spiritual. The Chariot of Paternal Deity as a war chariot may also owe something to Isaiah 66:15: "For behold, the Lord will come with fire, and with his chariots like a whirlwind, to render his anger with fury, and his rebuke with flames of fire."

35. The language of mission makes clear that the Creation is the distinctive act of the Father: "This I perform, speak thou, and be it done" (6.164).

36. For specific parallels with Du Bartas and Joshuah Sylvester's translation, see George C. Taylor, *Milton's Use of Du Bartas* (1934; repr., New York: Octagon Books, 1967), and Susan Snyder's introduction to her edition of Sylvester's *The Divine Weeks and Works of Guillaume De Saluste Sieur Du Bartas*, 2 vols. (Oxford: Clarendon Press, 1979), I:72–95.

37. See Sims, *The Bible in Milton's Epics*, 33–35, 266–67; Ernst Haublein, "Milton's Paraphase of Genesis: A Stylistic Reading of *Paradise Lost*, Book VII," *Milton Studies* 7 (1975): 101–25.

38. See, e.g., *PL* 7.243–49:

Let there be Light, said God, and forthwith Light
Ethereal, first of things, quintessence pure
Sprung from the Deep, and from her Native East
To journey through the airy gloom began,
Spher'd in a radiant Cloud, for yet the Sun
Was not; shee in a cloudy Tabernacle
Sojourn'd the while. God saw the Light was good.

39. See Lucretius, *De rerum natura* 5.1–854, trans. W. H. D. Rouse (Loeb, Cambridge, Mass.: Harvard University Press; London: William Heinemann, 1975), 378–445. Milton also lays under contribution Ovid's stories of Creation and Flood, *Metamorphoses* 1.1–437.

40. *De rerum natura* 5.168–69, Rouse, 390–91:

quidve novi potuit tanto post ante quietos
inclicere, ut cuperent vitam mutare priorem?

For discussion of Adam's question and its significance, see Lewalski, "Innocence and Experience in Milton's Eden," in *New Essays on "Paradise Lost,"* ed. Thomas Kranidas (Berkeley: University of California Press, 1969), 86–117.

41. *De rerum natura* 2.992–95, Rouse, 172–73:

omnibus ille idem pater est, unde alma liquentis
umoris guttas mater cum terra recepit,
feta parit nitidas fruges arbustaqua laeta
et genus humanum, parit omnia saecla ferarum.

See also Ovid, *Metamorphoses* 1.417–21, trans. Frank J. Miller, 2 vols. (Loeb, Cambridge, Mass.: Harvard University Press; London: William Heinemann, 1977) 1:30–33:

postquam vetus umor ab igne
percaluit solis, caenumque udaeque paludes
intumuere aestu, fecundaeque semina rerum
vivaci nutrita solo ceu matris in alvo
creverunt faciemque aliquam cepere morando.

42. *De rerum natura* 5.781–91, Rouse, 438–41:

novo fetu . . .
. . . .
Principio genus herbarum viridemque nitorem
terra dedit circum collis camposque per omnis,
florida fulserunt viridanti prata colore,
arboribusque datumst variis exinde per auras
crescendi magnum inmissis certamen habenis.

> et pluma atque pili primum saetaeque creantur
> quadripedum membris et corpore pennipotentum,
> sic nova tum tellus herbas virgultaeque primum
> sustulit.

43. *De rerum natura* 5.795–924, Rouse, 440–42, 450–51, esp. 11. 806–13, 916–17:

> multus enim calor atque umor superabat in arvis.
> hoc ubi quaeque loci regio opportuna dabatur,
> crescebant uteri terram radicibus apti;
> quos ubi tempore maturo patefecerat aetas
> infantum, fugiens umorem aurasque petessens,
> convertebat ibi natura foramina terrae
> et sucum venis cogebat fundere apertis
> consimilem lactis.
>
> . . . .
>
> nam quod multa fuere in terris semina rerum
> tempore quo primum tellus animalia fudit.

44. The structural centrality of the Creation was first argued by Arthur Barker, "Structural Pattern in *Paradise Lost*," *Philological Quarterly* 23 (1949): 16–30.

45. The term is also used in Sandys' *Ovid*, ed. Hulley and Vandersall, 30: "Just anger, worthy *Jove*, inflam'd his breast. / A Synod call'd." Cf. *Metamorphoses* 1.166–67: "ingentes animo et dignas Iove concipit iras / conciliumque vocat."

46. *Metamorphoses* 1.160–416, Miller, 1:12–31.

47. For discussion of the major exegetical traditions regarding the curse on nature and Milton's distinctive conception of it in *Paradise Lost*, see Ellen Goodman, "The Design of Milton's World," (Ph.D. diss., Brown University, 1966).

Doctrine as Deep Structure in Milton's Early Poetry

WILLIAM SHULLENBERGER

Since its resurrection and publication in 1825, *De Doctrina Christiana* has been treated, more or less respectfully, as a learned, but somewhat poor and curmudgeonly cousin to Milton's poetry. The title of what remains the seminal modern treatment of the relationship between theology and poetry in Milton indicates the critical limitation and impoverishment of the treatise. I refer to Maurice Kelley's *This Great Argument: A Study of Milton's "De Doctrina Christiana" as a Gloss Upon "Paradise Lost."*[1] Theology as gloss: such an investigation is bound to diminish the theology to the status of prosaic supplement, "gloss" or footnote to the poetry. At its most respectful, this thematic approach will yield the thorough and fertile cross-referencing of Kelley's text; at its most insensitive, it will yield C. A. Patrides' assessment of the treatise as the withered fruits of a Puritan Gerontion: "thoughts of a dry brain in a dry season."[2]

What if we were to take Milton's cue in calling the treatise "my dearest and best possession,"[3] and read *De Doctrina Christiana* as an inspired and integrated text in its own right? Milton conceived of his project as a systematic exposition of the deep structure of scripture, an imaginative unification "in unum corpus"[4] of doctrine scattered through the light and dark places of the holy books. "In unum corpus": in a single body: Milton suggests that his document is a textual projection of the mystic body of Christ. And as the Son is the Word — which Milton renders as *Sermo*, to stress the linguistic dynamism and substantiality of the second person of the godhead — so in *De Doctrina*

Milton poses the doctrines of faith as ideas about the creative power of language. Looked at this way, *De Doctrina* reveals an implicit theory of language and poetics, a unique example of a poet rigorously investigating the sources of his own power as a poetic maker.[5] Perhaps the only equivalent explication of the sources of poetic instruction available to us in English literature is Yeats's eccentric commentary, *A Vision.* The analogy to Yeats shows us that a new approach to *De Doctrina* will not simplify matters when we try to read Milton's poems with his theology in mind, but it may permit us to ask new questions, and thus to break through the impasses of thematic criticism. The new questions will not be "was Milton or was he not an Arian," or "how does Milton's Arianism or Arminianism or thnetopsychism find thematic or dramatic expression in the epics," but how does the theological idea entertained in a given poem affect that poem formally? How does the theological idea function as deep structure, or what Milton would call "formal cause," of a poem?

We can turn to a pair of Milton's early poems, "On the Morning of Christ's Nativity" and "The Passion," for evidence of how doctrine determines linguistic form in the poetry. These poems not only take for their themes the conventional topics for Christian meditation and invention, the Incarnation and the Passion; they disclose the structural power of the theological concepts in the ways that they unfold as language events. In *De Doctrina Christiana* the Incarnation and the Passion are critical— the orthodox would say heretical—moments in Milton's articulation of a Christology which is the creative center of his treatise. For Milton, the great mystery of Christian faith is the Incarnation. Railing against the wild and unfounded analyses of the Trinity by the scholastic Fathers, Milton poses the impenetrable identity of Christ as both God and Man as the only mystery offered us by Scripture:

> There is then in Christ a mutual hypostatic union of two natures, that is to say, of two essences, of two substances, and consequently of two persons; nor does this union prevent the respective properties of each from remaining individually distinct. (Columbia *Milton*, 15:271)

This explanation of the Incarnational structure of Christ is characteristically Miltonic; it does not exactly fit any of the conventional Christologies. Yet whether we type Milton in consequence as a Nestorian, as W. B. Hunter suggests, or as a Monophysite, as does Barbara Lewalski,[6] seems beside the point that can be made by substituting the word "metaphor" for the word "Christ" in Milton's description:

There is then in metaphor a mutual hypostatic union of two na-tures, that is to say, of two essences, of two substances, and conse-quently of two persons; nor does this union prevent the respective properties of each from remaining individually distinct.

In describing Christ, Milton is also describing the structure of figurative language, and confirming that figurative thinking, in-structed by Christ, is the only way in which existence in relation to God can be truthfully conceived. That the mysteries of God coincide with the mysteries of figura-tive language is the recognition which Milton celebrates in the Nativity *Ode*, whose language registers Milton's own Incarnation as poet, his ac-cession to mature creative power. In the *Ode*, the infant Christ is the master trope, the very power of metaphor to speak truly; his birth trans-figures the fallen language of creation, and we can see how the stages of poetic exposition turn upon the stages of that transfiguration.[7]

"The Passion," intended as a companion poem to the Nativity *Ode*, is a fragment and an admitted failure. "This subject," Milton appended to the fragment, "the Author finding to be above the years he had, when he wrote it, and nothing satisfi'd with what was begun, left it un-finisht."[8] It is surprising to find little critical acknowledgment of or reflection on the subject of the poem—Christ's death—and its disfigur-ing implications for a poet of the Word.[9] For one of Milton's heresies in *De Doctrina Christiana* is mortalism, and the Renaissance mortalist stressed the finality of death for both body and soul.[10] There is no com-forting severing of heaven-bound soul from the dregs of the body: "the whole man dies," Milton declares (Columbia *Milton*, 15:219), and body and soul must endure the silence and the absence of the grave until God reveals his saving power to the faithful in the day of resurrection. Milton compounds the heresy by insisting that Christ, "who was the sacrificial lamb, must be considered as slain in the whole of his nature" (Columbia *Milton*, 15:309). Milton puts it in perhaps the most beautiful, because least evasive, lines of "The Passion," "Yet more; the stroke of death he must abide, / Then lies him meekly down fast by his Brethren's side" (20–21). Imaginatively stationing himself in the moment of linguistic incertitude between the death and the Resurrection of Christ, Milton in this poem attempts a subject which must destroy the very possibility of poetry: the loss of the Word. The fragment provides evidence of what happens when a poem loses its formal cause, when the metaphoric structure which permits poetic creativity is itself broken, and language is cast into a moment of self-doubt so profound as to undermine all poetic structure. By its very loss of form, "The Passion" indicates as clearly as the Nativity *Ode* that Milton's early poetry was already being shaped by the poetics of faith which would receive full and systematic articulation in *De Doctrina Christiana*.

In each of these early poems, then, the surface structure of the verse is less the figurative illustration of a theological idea than the poetic speech which issues from that idea as a formative principle — or, in the case of "The Passion," a principle of disfiguration. To refer the poems to *De Doctrina Christiana* seems to be anachronistic because the treatise was composed at least twenty years after the composition of the poems in question, and Milton continued his revisions of the treatise until his death. However, in the Preface to *De Doctrina Christiana*, Milton testifies to an intellectual engagement with biblical exegesis and theological controversy beginning in his early school days (*CPW* 6:119–20). It seems likely that by his early twenties, when the poems in question were composed, Milton was engaged in matters of theological controversy even if he had not arrived at a formal articulation of his position on these matters. Although they do not seek the doctrinal exactitude or the polemical intentions of *De Doctrina Christiana*, the poems anticipate the kind of knowledge of God which the treatise would be written to explicate. Kenneth Burke explains the paradoxical relation of poetry to poetics:

> Insofar as a poet's practices involve decisions, and decisions imply principles, the principles implicitly guiding his procedures are "logically prior" to the poems in which they are embodied. In this sense the principles of a poetics could be treated as *logically* prior to the poems that exemplify them, *though they are formulated after-*

wards in time, as with Aristotle's reduction of Greek tragedy to Poetics, or the codifying of the grammar implicit in a language.[11]

The poems are deeply instructed theologically. Even if the Christological principles systematized as Christian Doctrine had not yet been consciously articulated by the young Milton, they were already making themselves felt in the poetry.

2

One of the remarkable features of the Nativity *Ode* is its exclusion of direct reference to the Johannine figure of the Word made flesh. The silence here speaks as loudly as the words, for the missing figure presides over the poem, which demonstrates the Word's passage into the body of inspired human speech, claiming the poet as its witness, instructing the prophetic rewriting of history, and banishing the perverse orders of religious imagination. The effect of Christ, as the structuring power which redeems the imagination, can be measured by reference to the generally accepted map of the poem laid out by Arthur E. Barker. Barker traces three movements, each controlled by a major theme, and a coda. Stanzas 1 to 8 describe the striking of a "universal Peace" which creates a setting of preternatural stillness and expectation. Stanzas 9 to 17 describe the incursion and the effects of the "angel choir" whose heavenly music expands the temporal range of the poem to the beginning and the end of time. Stanzas 18 to 26 describe the banishment of the pagan gods by the advent of the "Infant God." Stanza 27 is the poetic coda, which closes the poem in a mood of heightened peace, in the presence of the newborn Christ.[12] Each of these sections corresponds to a phrase in the renovation of signs—human language and the language of creation—achieved in the poem.

In the first movement of the poem, things are stopped in their tracks. Whatever mythic reference they might once have had, the stars of stanza 6 are characteristic of all created signs as they "stand fixt" (70), their connotative potential frozen. The first note of the strange new peace is thus a sudden uncertainty as to what things mean, what they stand for as signs. That the stars "bend one way their precious influence" (71) suggests that this limitation of natural function is also a concentration of energy, a kind of laser effect which gives them focus, freeing them from the random and conflicting patterns of force which Milton was to imagine as one of the destructive results of the Fall. For now, all the "precious influence" is beamed upon the infant, yet they wait for him to instruct them in their dispersal, as signs of a renewed natural language, whose energy is fully recharged.

The interruption of Lucifer's activity as shepherd of the stars by the "Lord himself" raises the question of how "Lucifer" is to be read. The editors of the *Variorum* are anxious to expunge in advance the satanic potential of the term, and they quote the anonymous reviewer of Brooks and Hardy's book on Milton in order to dismiss the suggestion that the passage may imply the trouble stirred up by the interim lord of the middle air:

> It detracts from the charmed air of peace the poet is in the act of creating. And it is hard on a poet if critics, in their eagerness for an ambiguity at all costs, thrust on him a secondary meaning which, though possible theoretically, he never intended.[13]

The question, however, is not so much of Milton's intention, but of the presence and the function of "Lucifer" as a sign at this moment in the poem. Is it possible, in the phase of the poem which calls up all the conventional implications of signs in order to cast them in doubt, that the satanic implication of "Lucifer" can be eliminated beforehand as a potential reading? It is the incarnational strategy of the poem to introduce the term "Lucifer" at this point, in order to remind the reader of the sign's demonic possibilities, to halt the operation of the sign as a force counter to the organizing and concentrating power of Christ, and to empty it of its fallen connotations in order to appropriate it as a sign for the true Light-bearer who is Christ. By cancelling out the satanic potential of "Lucifer," the editors of the *Variorum* pre-empt the incarnational strategy, and deny the reader's participation in the renovation by which signs are first halted and then emptied of their conventional significance, then rewritten as the terms by which God represents himself to humanity.

This strategy informs stanza 7 as well. The Sun appeared in stanza 1 as the "lusty Paramour" of Nature (35), yet the disengagement of the image from the routine of merely natural generation had begun even here. In stanza 7, a personified Sun is displayed in a crisis of identity, in which he doubts not only his own natural function as light-bringer, but his capacity as a sign to "bear" the greater Sun which is Christ. This moment, in which the image calls into doubt its own signifying potential, is a paradigm of the limitation of ordinary or habitual meaning enacted in the Ode's first movement. The appearance of the "greater Sun" in this stanza indicates the prevenient grace by which the sign has already been claimed and reconstituted as the means of divine accommodation. Yet the sun's self-doubts, his questioning of the sufficiency of his metonymic attributes (throne and axle-tree) to serve as the vehicle for the transcendental tenor which is Christ, shows the delay involved in working out through process of speech what are the immediate acts of God.

Striking a music as "never was by mortal finger struck," the angel choir of the Ode's second movement stills the mundane chatter of the last creatures on earth to note the impending change, the Shepherds on the lawn. Love and sheep, the bonds of affection and labor which bind the shepherds, like us, to the earth, acquire new imaginative implication through the dwelling of the sacrificial lamb with his brethren, reminding them that the labor of love is the way in which the human perfects itself as an image of God. This is, like the image of the "greater Sun," foreshadowing, but in the sudden incursion of the sublime music, it is upon us now, requiring us — shepherds, poets, readers — to shift our attention from the stalled operations of the fallen world familiar to us to a contemplation of the limits of created time. In that shift of attention, we lay aside for a time the signs of the earth we inhabit in order to imagine the eschatological events which were the origin and will be the consummation of all created signs. The rapid temporal and imaginative expansion of this section inaugurates the next phase in the poem's renovation of language. It performs what the kabbalists call the "breaking of the vessels" of ordinary, or fallen, speech, by imposing a set of Scriptural images which rupture our habits of thinking.[14] The circling of extrasensory sound toward the music of Creation and the world-shaking thunder of Judgment, the voice from the whirlwind which challenges Job, and the ominous yet promissory fireworks of Sinai break open our sense of literal time and literal space, and the created forms by which we have assured ourselves of certain certainties:

> The aged Earth aghast
> With terror of that blast,
>> Shall from the surface to the center shake,
> When at the world's last session,
> The dreadful Judge in middle Air shall spread
>> his throne.
>
> (160–64)

Earth here stands metonymically for all the vessels to be broken, all the signs of the created order which must be ruptured, shaken from surface to center, and then judged as to their adequacy to serve as signs in an imaginative order which cannot be conceived by means of even the signs which Christ was born to transfigure.

The thresholds of Creation and Judgment approached in the second movement of the poem provide the imaginative framework within which we can properly understand the acts by which God has made our world and makes it meaningful. But until the final imageless bliss which exceeds even the apocalyptic imagination—"And then at last our bliss / Full and perfect is" (165–66)—we can conceive of God and his acts only by means of figures, and these figures can be provided only by the world we inhabit. Thus the third movement of the *Ode* returns its readers to a Nature whose reign does not yet have its last fulfilling, in order to complete the "breaking of the vessels," to purge the body of the world of demonic infestation, and thereby to claim its signs for the renovated language in which God can be imagined properly. This part of the *Ode* is an act of imaginative purification; it eradicates the claims of other mythic speech, and salvages the signs of that speech in the name of the indwelling Word.

At every level of imaginative failure documented in the third movement of the Nativity *Ode*, the key word for the displacement and rout of the pagan gods is the preposition "in." We recall from the first two stanzas that Nature sought a covering for her "foul deformities," symptoms of the infection which the Fall had occasioned and a history of error had aggravated. Stanzas 19 to 25 diagnose that infection as an infestation, for the gods are repeatedly displayed as having occupied inner spaces of earth and its landscapes, and inner shrines established for them by their vain believers. In shrine and cell and twilight shade of thickets, in consecrated earth and temple, in Memphian grove and green and in "worshipt Ark" (220), the gods have burrowed into interior spaces which correspond to the interiority of the imaginative thought which engendered them. The violent proleptic vision of the second movement of the *Ode*, forecasting that the earth will from "surface to the center shake" (162), generates the anticipatory tremors which drive out all the pagan figures from the sites they have usurped, and in so doing purge interiority itself, the human breast where all false deities were conceived. "In" is the linguistic marker of these tremors, functioning as part of the negative formula "in vain," which along with the negatives "not" and "nor" sounds through the passage as a kind of incantatory beat which penetrates the wonted seats of the false deities to drive them out. "In" is claimed twice by the poet to represent the mighty act of binding which frames the sequence: the Old Dragon is "In straiter limits bound" (169); and "Our Babe, to show his Godhead true, / Can in his swaddling bands control the damned crew" (227–28). Possessed by the false deities as a term to represent the particular realm of their usurped sway, "in" is itself thus penetrated and claimed through the Incarnation to purify not only the body of the world, but the interiority of thought, and to limit the imaginative scope of the displaced gods.

The figure of the Sun is latent in this passage. Lawrence Kingsley has demonstrated that the chief gods routed in the third movement have all claimed to be sun gods, and that Christ's displacement of them involves an appropriation of their privileged symbolism.[15] Halted in its signifying capacity in stanza 7, the sun is divested of pagan connotation here: broken as a vessel for other myths, it can now function as a master sign in the new imaginative order of the Incarnation.

Thus the penultimate stanza restores the Sun as an image adequate to bear the new-born "greater Sun." The stanza rewrites the dark undertones of the third movement into a gorgeous and fanciful description of the emergence of dawn. The lyric is not primarily naturalistic, nor merely descriptive; it serves as an exemplum of the imaginative possibilities redeemed through the Incarnation. For it places the reader in a perfect interpretative poise, disclosing what Woodhouse has called the order of nature and the order of grace simultaneously in the same figure.[16] The Sun returns to his place in the stable diurnal round of the cosmos, and sets in motion the regular operations of the created world, which the first movement of the *Ode* had stalled. It also proposes, for the first time in the poem, the Christian commonplace of the Sun as a sign for the "greater Sun," the Son of God. The poem thus allows its readers to witness, as if for the first time, the emergence of one of the primary metaphors of Christian thinking. The final stanza is a perfected hieratic emblem of the Incarnation: it represents the orderly and completed integration of the natural and the supernatural, a world whose signs have been claimed, emptied, and restructured by the indwelling of the paradoxically silent word.

3

In "The Passion," Milton attempts an antithetical completion of the Nativity *Ode* by taking for his subject the matter of the "bitter cross" about which the earlier poem displayed considerable reticence. But for Milton, the Passion could be no topic for sacramental meditation or copious invention because of the linguistic emptiness it opens. The eight stanzas of the fragment chronicle a series of failed beginnings, in which Milton resorts to virtually every strategy in the poetic repertoire in order to broach his subject. He abandons each strategy, for Christ's passion is a death-blow to the passion which is poetry, and its consequences are the often recited forms of failure in the poem: obsessive self-consciousness, "literary" rather than genuine emotion (whatever this can mean in a poem),[17] gratuitous and even grotesque conceits, obligatory and obviously feigned inspiration. The poem founders on its own pathetic fallacy, yearning to transform the world according to the poet's apocalyptic desire, yet persistently confessing that its subject undermines all poetic form and its pretense to power. The poem is thus a self-consuming artifact which issues not in the silence of beatitude but in the silence of the tomb.

If we can speak at all of form in a poem whose subject entails its disfiguration, we could suggest that the first four stanzas attempt a cautious disclosure of the subject, and the next four try to imagine a *mise en scene* for that subject, in which the poet may position himself as a witness to the suffering Christ. These stages of poetic structure seem to be at odds with each other. The first four stanzas entertain the idea of the poem as elegaic music, "Of Lute, or Viol still, more apt for mournful things" (28). The "latest scenes" of Christ's life would be represented in the form of a tragic masque, replete with music, a stage, and royalty in disguise. Yet each possible mode of figural or formal organization disintegrates nearly as soon as it is proposed. The movement from stanza 2 to stanza 3 is typical. "Most perfect *Hero*, tried in heaviest plight / Of labors huge and hard, too hard for human wight" (13–14) climaxes the second stanza with a Herculean typology. The third stanza immediately drops this typology in favor of the figure of the "sovereign Priest" (15), which is developed for four lines, then ruptured by the exclamation, "O what a Mask was there, what a disguise!" (19) The exclamation renders uncertain the extent to which the poet can count on any metaphoric or narrative strategy to represent the now absent Christ or the paradoxically heroic action of his Passion. Yet in the wake of exposing metaphor itself as disguise, the poet can at last speak with a bare simplicity of the event upon which his poem turns and founders: "Yet more; the stroke of death he must abide, / Then lies him meekly down fast by his Brethren's side" (20–21). Death is the triumph of the literal, and the "stroke of death" marks the end of the metaphoric potential opened by the Incarnation. Yet Christ's brotherly relation to men is the last metaphor to survive, and in submitting to death, Christ proves the truth of metaphor, even as its power against death is temporarily suspended: "Death," Brooks and Hardy write, "will complete the humanization of Christ."[18]

The renewed figural possibilities of resurrection will underwrite the power of poetry again; yet Milton chooses to situate "The Passion" in the figural intermission between the Crucifixion and Easter, so that the horizon of the poem delimits a field of signs whose reliability, in the absence of the Logos, is open to doubt. The fifth stanza, with its invocation to Night, seems to be a new beginning. Music and masquelike ritual are abandoned for the attempt to compose an imaginative space in which the poet can witness the Passion. Yet in summoning Night, "best Patroness of grief" (29), the poet exposes in advance the illusoriness of any scene composed by what he calls his "flatter'd fancy" (31). He does not call for inspiration, but for a conspiratorial response to his emotional state which will write that emotional state out upon the larger world. Night, the "dark and long outliving" agent of engulfment figured forth at the close of the first stanza (7), is summoned to an apocalypse which will envelop heaven and earth in a monotony of darkness corresponding to the poet's woe. Indicating the disjuncture between human demand and material reality when both are bereft of the Logos, the stanza poses the pathetic fallacy as a self-exposed longing for imaginative extension, pitched to an extreme which wishes nothing less than the extirpation of a world resistant to transfiguration.

This apocalyptic impulse wells up in each of the remaining three stanzas to disrupt the poet's uneasy struggle to compose a setting in which the Passion might be imaginatively re-enacted. The poet calls on the chariot of Ezekiel to taxi him to the "glorious towers" of Salem, the literary landscape of Scripture. Yet this site, which Milton will imagine successfully at the climax of *Paradise Regained*, is already deluged with the blood of Christ. Literary transport leaves the poet still in a position of retrospective contemplation, as if the only approach to the Passion could be after the fact. In Milton's inability, or tacit refusal, to envision the broken body of Christ, we can recognize his humility or embarrassment before his chosen subject.[19] Where indeed does the poet sit, if the towers to which he has been borne have been "sunk in guiltless blood" (40)? He reports a visionary condition which cannot be situated in the imagined landscape: "There doth my soul in holy vision sit, / In pensive trance, and anguish, and ecstatic fit" (41–42). The discrepancies between these multiple states of consciousness indicate a kind of nervous paralysis which cannot settle upon an attitude appropriate for the occasion of the poem. Thus the poem shows the dissolution of a coherent *persona*, and the flood of feelings in which the poet welters is a microcosmic version of the apocalyptic engulfment of the landscape he has imagined.

By this point the poem has entered a surreal condition in which land-scape and consciousness are dissolved into each other by the very language which attempts to compose them. This language without ontological security or orientation accounts for the figural excesses and violence of the final two stanzas. Each is a violent attempt to mark the imagination's claims on an unresponsive world; each poses its wish in the conditional or optative ("would," "would," "should," "would," "Might") as though fully aware of the wish's absurdity. The longing for a magic writing emerges here, to make the world over into a text sufficient to what imagination desires: a writing whose miraculous typography will display its power over death itself. The "sad Sepulchral rock" is a sign of the poem's inviolable subject, an impenetrable surface and a depthless depth (for how can one describe the depth of stone?) which permits the poem to exist only as a graffito, a wishful memory scrawled on its surface. Yet the poem, in entertaining the idea of its unrealizable negative, a magic writing, demands more than this: in scoring its characters on that stone, it would not merely leave a mark of consciousness, but would alter the condition against which it protests. The first sign of this change is the rock's becoming "soft'ned Quarry," perhaps turning to flesh as the Logos it contained hardened into metaphor ("Heav'n's richest store"). Read literally, the conceit developed here is easy to deride, as Brooks and Hardy have demonstrated.[20] Yet the poet expresses here the desire for a poem which "The Passion" cannot be, in which a miraculous, purely expressive writing makes the world over into its text. Such a writing would breach materiality, create an opening in the universe of death for imagination to fecundate, and compose time and space according to its own periodicity.

The poem makes a brief and self-censored attempt at such an imaginary potency in the eighth stanza, before it leaves off. The calling of Echo in the final stanza is a latent reminder of the poet's doomed self-involvement in his writing, which, in the absence of the inward structure provided by Christ, can only be a form of narcissism. Thus he renders the imagined replication of his grief upon the echoing landscape as "infection": "And I (for grief is easily beguil'd) / Might think th'infection of my sorrows loud, / Had got a race of mourners on some pregnant cloud" (54–56). His sorrow is a prolific disease with no cure and a trouble to an otherwise untroubled world. Yet that the world would be untroubled, but for the troubled human voice which haunts it, is what troubles Milton most. It is the loss of the Logos, in his own language and in the unanswering world, which he laments. Although Milton never broached the topic of the death of Christ so directly again, the implications of the subject were to shadow all his major poetry. If the immediate consequence of the Passion was the dissolution of poetic form, its ultimate consequence was the enlargement of poetic form in the great poems of Milton's maturity, which comprehend death not as a material limit, but as a final phase of an imaginative passage into an existence which is neither temporally nor spatially bound. *Lycidas* broaches the subject of "The Passion" yet once more, as if Milton had never disengaged himself from it. "The Passion" founders because its subject subverts the rhetorical and elegiac conventions which traditionally contained the problem of death. *Lycidas* triumphs because it enlarges those conventions in such a way that their very insufficiency, their status as "false surmises," reveals the grandeur of the imagination which invents them, and thereby liberates imagination for a more sublime calling. And *Lycidas* in turn seems a rehearsal for the great epics, where Adam will confess the hard won knowledge, "to the faithful Death [is] the Gate of Life" (*Paradise Lost* 12.571), and where Christ himself will achieve the imaginative triumph Milton seeks for in "The Passion."

Notes

1. Maurice Kelley, *This Great Argument: A Study of Milton's "De Doctrina Christiana" as a Gloss upon "Paradise Lost"* (Princeton: Princeton University Press, 1941).

2. C. A. Patrides, "*Paradise Lost* and the Language of Theology," in *Bright Essence: Studies in Milton's Theology*, ed. C. A. Patrides, W. B. Hunter, and J. H. Adamson (Salt Lake City: University of Utah Press, 1971), 168.

3. *Complete Prose Works of John Milton*, ed. Maurice Kelley (New Haven: Yale University Press, 1973), 6:121. All references to this edition will be indicated parenthetically by reference to *CPW* in the text of the essay.

4. *The Works of John Milton*, ed. Frank Allen Patterson et al. (New York: Columbia University Press, 1933), 15:271. All references to this edition will be indicated parenthetically by reference to Columbia *Milton* in the text of the essay.

5. A fuller treatment of these ideas may be found in my essay, "Linguistic and Poetic Theory in Milton's *De Doctrina Christiana*," *English Language Notes* 19 (March 1982): 262–78.

6. W. B. Hunter, "Milton on the Incarnation," in *Bright Essence*, 132; Barbara Lewalski, *Milton's Brief Epic: The Genre, Meaning, and Art of "Paradise Regained"* (Providence: Brown University Press, 1971), 156.

7. My essay, "Christ as Metaphor: Figural Instruction in Milton's Nativity Ode," *Notre Dame English Journal* 14 (Winter 1981): 41–58, studies incarnational theory as metaphoric structure, and its effects in the *Ode*.

8. John Milton, *Complete Poems and Major Prose*, ed. Merritt Y. Hughes (New York: The Odyssey Press, 1957), 57. All references to Milton's poetry, cited by line in the text of the essay, will be to this edition.

9. Interesting speculations on the reasons for Milton's publication of the fragment have been ventured by John A. Via, "Milton's 'The Passion': A Successful Failure," *Milton Quarterly* 5 (May 1971): 35–58, and Philip J. Gallagher, "Milton's 'The Passion': Inspired Mediocrity," *Milton Quarterly* 11 (1977): 44–50. Via proposes that "The Passion" serves as a kind of moral exemplum: "I suggest that 'The Passion' is retained because, in its failure on the aesthetic level, it shows the normal fluctuation which the regenerate man may anticipate as a real and significant part of his religious life" (36). Gallagher, who has given the fragment perhaps the closest attention it has yet received, reads it as a prologue equivalent to the Nativity *Ode's* prologue, but the prologue here yields no poem, because "The poet is concerned to depict not the Passion, but the psychological state of a speaker who is attempting—without success—to become inspired about that event" (45). Brooks and Hardy have made what is perhaps the most accurate diagnosis of the problem in the poem: "With Christ's death, the poet is left with God present only in his mind and emotions, disembodied, and no longer visible in effects upon external nature. How is the poet to find appropriate forms for the presentation in terms of the sense of what is now a spiritual reality?" Cleanth Brooks and John Edward Hardy, *Poems of Mr. John Milton: The 1645 Edition with Essays in Analysis* (New York: Harcourt, Brace, 1951), 107. This diagnosis is limited by the authors' failure to attend to the theological depth of the problem for Milton: the absoluteness of Christ's death places "spiritual reality" itself in question.

10. To read the poem as entertaining the theory of thnetopsychism is to go against the grain of critical investigation which regards Milton's theological "heresies" as the product of the maturity which also produced the late epics and *Samson Agonistes*. However, Milton indicates that he began his scriptural compilations in his youth (Columbia *Milton*, 14:5), and it seems likely that his theological speculations may have been extending beyond orthodoxy at that time as well. Sir Thomas Browne confesses the "Arabian heresy" as an error of his youth, and if Milton had not yet formu-

lated his "mortalism" as doctrine, it might have represented a problem which tested his imagination and poetic ambition.

The most thorough study of Milton's mortalism is by William Kerrigan, *English Literary Renaissance* 5 (Winter 1975): 125–66. He claims that in the period of Milton's youth, Milton was drawn to the typology of immediate assumption as a way of resisting the affront to imaginative integrity represented by the orthodox split of the soul from the body in death. Kerrigan's neglect of both the Nativity *Ode* and "The Passion" suggests that both poems resist his thesis. The Nativity *Ode* refers to the Last Judgment as the occasion when "to those ychain'd in sleep, / The wakeful trump of doom must thunder through the deep" (155–56). Kerrigan notes that "Mortalists were called 'soul sleepers' in Renaissance jargon" (146), and it is hard to avoid reading these lines from the Nativity *Ode* as evidence of Milton's appropriation of the thnetopsychist/psychosomnolescent theory at least for imaginative exploitation, if not for doctrine. "The Passion" takes for its subject the event of Christ's death which Milton seems reluctant to approach in the Nativity *Ode*, and when the subject is finally stated, it is done so with finality, identifying Christ in death with mortal men: "Yet more; the stroke of death he must abide, / Then lies him meekly down fast by his Brethren's side" (20–21).

11. Kenneth Burke, "Poetics in Particular, Language in General," *Language as Symbolic Action* (Berkeley and Los Angeles: University of California Press, 1966), 34.

12. Arthur E. Barker, "The Pattern of Milton's Nativity Ode," *University of Toronto Quarterly* 10 (1941): 167–81.

13. *A Variorum Commentary on the Poems of John Milton*, vol. 2, pt. 1: *The Minor English Poems* (New York: Columbia University Press, 1957), 76–77.

14. See Harold Bloom, *Kabbalah and Criticism* (New York: Seabury Press, 1975), for an exposition of the kabbalistic approach underwriting this analysis.

15. See Lawrence W. Kingsley, "Mythic Dialectic in the Nativity Ode," *Milton Studies* 4 (1972): 163–75.

16. See A. S. P. Woodhouse, "The Argument of Milton's *Comus*," *University of Toronto Quarterly* 11 (1941–42): 46–71.

17. William R. Parker, *Milton: A Biography* (Oxford, Clarendon Press, 1968), 1:71–72: "His delight in the implication and details of the Christmas story had been genuine, but his professed grief at the thoughts of the Crucifixion turned out to be literary." This seems a curious distinction: how can the profession of emotion in a poem be anything but "literary"?

18. Brooks and Hardy, 107.

19. One might usefully compare the sacramental approach to the crucifixion in Crashaw's "On our Crucified Lord, Naked and Bloody," and "On the Bleeding Wounds of our Crucified Lord," or Herbert's "The Agonie." Both poets can make the blood of Christ the source of the conceit of the poems because the blood means redemption rather than death to them.

20. It is hard to resist quoting this delicious and indisputable (on its own terms) remark: "Yet here the poet would have us believe that, in the grip of an emotional

frenzy so long sustained and so intense that it binds his hands, he could be sufficiently at ease to master a trick as difficult as that of wagging his head to make his falling tears form letters. On the other hand, if line 48 is to be taken literally, the idea is even more difficult to entertain. A self-animated tear is inconceivable; and a rational tear, capable of being instructed, is—if the term will admit a comparative—even less conceivable" (Brooks and Hardy, 110).

"In Pensive trance, and anguish, and ecstatic fit": Milton on the Passion

MARSHALL GROSSMAN

Critics have noticed the absence of a sustained and direct treatment of the crucifixion from Milton's work.[1] Milton's early attempt at a poem commemorating the Passion breaks off with a confession of failure; the crucifixion is alluded to but not portrayed in *Paradise Lost* and is not, as one would expect it to be, the central episode of *Paradise Regained*.[2] Nevertheless, the Passion does have a presence in Milton's poetry through its typological equivalents. For example, Edward Tayler suggests that the temptation portrayed in *Paradise Regained* is a displaced presentation of the Passion in which Milton elects "as usual to treat the figure rather than the fulfillment,"[3] and Joseph Summers looks to *Samson Agonistes* for a displaced portrait of the Passion.[4]

I should like to attempt an explanation of the absence of direct depiction of the Passion from Milton's work and of his practice of treating the figure rather than the fulfillment, the shadowy type but not the true. The explanation proceeds through three steps: 1) a brief review of some aspects of Milton's Christology and Soteriology as given in *De Doctrina Christiana*, 2) a consideration of the specific problems Milton may have encountered in trying to put his Christological notions into a narrative form, and 3) a reading of Milton's early fragment on the Passion to suggest the way in which Milton's theological ideas were already interacting with his poetry in the early 1630s and to relate Milton's difficulties in his sole attempt to treat the crucifixion directly to his treatment of the Passion in his mature poetry.

The peculiarities of Milton's Christology have been much discussed and, on some points, hotly debated. I am concerned here only with Milton's, apparently unique, understanding of the union of man and God in the incarnate Christ.[5] Milton's Christological argument is fundamentally philological. As Barbara Lewalski has noted, Milton believes the terms *essentia, subsistentia,* and *persona* are "virtually identical" or "at any rate interchangeable when predicated of any one intelligent being."[6] Milton, therefore, understands the Son's assumption of manhood as complete—essential, substantial and personal:

> For human nature, that is, the form of man contained in flesh, must, at the very moment when it comes into existence, bring a man into existence too, and a whole man, with no part of his essence or his subsistence (if that word signifies anything) or his personality missing.[7]

Milton goes on to summarize his view of the incarnation in this way:

> The union of two natures in Christ was the mutual hypostatic union of two essences. Because where a perfect substantial essence exists, there must also be an hypostasis or subsistence, since they are quite evidently the same thing. So one Christ, one ens, and one person is formed from this mutual hypostatic union of two natures. There is no need to be afraid that two persons will result from the union of two hypostases, any more than from the union of two natures, that is, of two essences. But supposing Christ's human nature never had its own separate subsistence, or supposing the Son did not take the subsistence upon himself: it would follow that he could not have been a real man, and that he could not have taken upon himself the true and perfect substance or essence of man. . . . There is, then, in Christ a mutual hypostatic union of two natures or, in other words, of two essences, of two substances and consequently of two persons. And there is nothing to stop the properties of each from remaining individually distinct. It is quite certain that this is so. We do not know how it is so, and it is best for us to be ignorant of things which God wishes to remain secret. (423–24)

Despite Milton's contrary assertion, more orthodox (or more logical theologians) did fear that two persons would result from the union of two hypostases. Milton himself acknowledges the difficulty in defining the unity of a single person comprising two distinct hypostases by asserting the ineffability of the union. His retreat into silent respect for God's mysteries at the conclusion of his argument has its counterpart in his poetic silence with respect to Christ's Passion.[8]

The poetic question that is raised and that Milton forebears to answer is how one person possessed of two distinct natures may be depicted as a coherent character. The usual solution to this problem is stated in the *Westminster Confession*:

Christ, in the work of Mediation, acteth according to both Natures, by each Nature doing that which is proper to itself: yet by reason of the unity of the Person, that which is proper to one Nature, is sometimes in Scripture attributed to the Person denominated by the other Nature.[9]

The portrayal of Christ in Scripture is understood as compound. His divine nature and his human nature are known when each is shown *doing* what is proper to itself. Scripture dramatizes the "unity of the Person" by naming the human nature when the act is proper to the *Logos* or naming the *Logos* when the act is proper to the human nature. The indistinguishability of the two natures is, in fact, the ultimate goal of the narration, since Christ is come to show men how to live according to what is divine in them and to be exemplary to them.[10]

We may see in this method of achieving unity of the Person by cross-denominating the acts or "doings" of Christ's two distinct natures the familiar rhetorical device of metaphor. The identity or unity of the Person is grounded in the interchangeable predication of the attributes of its two natures. With respect to these acts, the natures are assimilable. Milton's rejection of the union of two natures in favor of the union of two complete subsistences is, in effect, a rejection of this metaphor. This rejection logically extends to a rejection of language itself as a vehicle for the transmission of the Passion.

It will be useful at this point to consider the way in which character is depicted in language. We all remember Aristotle's discrimination in the *Poetics* of plot and character as two elements of a *mimesis*. *Mythos* and *ethos*, Aristotle tells us, must be compatible. A character's acts must be consistent with his nature and his nature consistent with his acts. It is significant, however, that *mythos* is the privileged term in this set of interrelated aspects of *mimesis*. Aristotle tells us *mythos* is logically prior to *ethos*; one can have plot without character but not character without plot.[11] In other words, we, as readers, understand a character's nature from the sorts of things the character does. The demand of decorum is that all the things a character does be compatible on some level. A characterization that fails to maintain this self-consistency is rejected as either incoherent or unbelievable. The predication of divine and human attributes of Christ in Scripture uses metaphor to establish a sense of compatibility between the "doings" of Christ's divine and human natures. In this way it suggests that the *imitatio Christi* consists in making one's corporal actions compatible with a divine *ethos*.

There is an affinity here between grammatical and logical categories. When one makes Christ the subject of a sentence one necessarily predicates various actions or attributes of him. His nature or natures inhere in these predications.[12] Metaphor, as Aristotle understands it, is a device *of language* that allows us to suggest the shared characteristics of two subjects by selectively transferring their predicates.

Milton's philological assimilation of essence, subsistence and person speaks directly to this issue. For, as Aristotle says, metaphors transfer attributes and are, in effect, condensed similes or comparisons.[13] Milton's insistence on a union of complete subsistences asserts in the strongest possible terms that there is no transfer, that the union takes place *in fact* and not in language, which can imitate but not reproduce it. The attributes of both natures are essential to Christ. The union *necessarily* transcends both logic and language. The union is ineffable, and the Scriptural mode of suggesting it through metaphor must be understood as accommodated speech. The reason for this is that all human language is temporal. Language can depict the "doings" of each of Christ's natures, but only one at a time. The metaphor discloses its internal discontinuity as soon as we realize that either one or the other nature is the subject of each verb.[14] The submerged simile is perceived and the identity of man and God becomes a mere comparison. Milton's Christ is not a blend of the human and divine distributed according to the temporal context but a God-man, wholly human and wholly divine at all times.

Milton's ambivalence about one Person comprising two *personae* and his decision to abandon the subject to respectful silence turn on the problem of translating an interior, immanent duality to an external, and therefore speakable, unity, without decomposing it into a series of discrete, alternating moments:

> After all, if it were legitimate to be definite and dogmatic about mysteries of this kind, why should we not play the philosopher and start asking questions about the external form common to these two natures? Because if the divine nature and the human nature coalesced in one person, that is to say, as my opponents themselves admit, in a rational being numerically one, then they must have coalesced in one external form as well. As a result the divine form, if it were not previously identical with the human, must have been either destroyed or blended with the human, both of which seem absurd. Or else the human form, if it did not precisely resemble the divine, must have been either destroyed or blended with the divine. Or else Christ must have had two forms. How much better for us, then, to know only that the Son of God, our Mediator, was made flesh and that he is called and is in fact both God and man.[15]

As soon as one tries to make external the interior dual nature of the God-man, the problem of external form comes into play. In language this problem becomes a question of how to portray *in time* a unitary and self-consistent character possessed of, and resolving *in his actions*, two wills, two natures, two subsistences.[16] Any representation *in time* will tend to disclose one or the other of Christ's natures. But, for Milton, this would threaten the unity of the Person.

How then is Milton able to portray Christ in *Paradise Regained*, and why does the problem here outlined arise specifically with respect to the Passion?

As Barbara Lewalski has shown, "Milton's comments on the hypostatic union provide for the endurance of the properties appropriate to the two natures, but . . . he persistently refrains from distinguishing among the functions, the words, and the actions of the incarnate Christ so as to ascribe some to one, some to the other, nature." [17] In *Paradise Regained*, Milton utilizes the traditional notion of Christ's *kenosis*, derived from Phil. 2:6–8, to fashion a character who, possessed of perfect faith, relies on human understanding and will.[18] However, Milton's view of the Passion would require the depiction of both natures in a distinct, and, if my argument is correct, an impossible way.

Milton believed that man's salvation required the suffering and death of Christ in both his human and divine aspects:

A lot of passages in the Bible make his divine nature succumb to death along with his human nature, and they seem to do so too clearly for it to be explained away as mere idiomatic parallelism, Rom. x.9: *if you will confess the Lord Jesus with your mouth, and will believe in your heart that God has raised him from the dead, you will be saved.* The man whom we ought to confess with our mouths is the same as the man whom God has raised from the dead. But we ought to confess *the Lord Jesus*, that is, the whole person of Jesus: therefore God raised the whole person of the Lord Jesus from the dead . . . . God, therefore raised not only Christ as man but the whole Christ, and it was through Christ not as man but as θεάνθρωπος that Paul was sent.[19]

The death of Christ as God-man is a necessary antecedent to the resurrection, which is, according to Milton, the first degree of exaltation. Exaltation includes "resurrection, ascension into heaven, and a seat at God's right hand."[20] "Christ's exaltation . . . applies to both his natures."[21] In the words of the Father in *Paradise Lost*:

> because in thee
> Love hath abounded more than Glory abounds,
> Therefore thy Humiliation shall exalt
> With thee thy Manhood also to this Throne;
> Here shalt thou sit incarnate, here shalt Reign
> Both God and Man, Son both of God and Man,
> Anointed universal King.[22]

At this pivotal point, in which the temporal world of mortal man and the eternal world of God are joined, language necessarily implies the temporality of both natures. When Christ is resurrected both natures are exalted, but the "external form" of the incarnation is removed from earth: "But although Christ's human nature is in supreme glory, it nevertheless exists in one definite place and not, as some people would like to think, everywhere."[23] Once the death and resurrection of the God-Man have fulfilled and satisfied the law, the incarnate Word is replaced by the indwelling spirit as the old law is superseded by the internalized law of love, now written in the regenerate heart.

A depiction of the Passion would mean, for Milton, a depiction of Christ suffering and dying in both natures and of the transition from the external to the internal presence of God's word. The humiliation, culminating in the Passion and the exaltation which it purchases, would have to be rendered in language, when, paradoxically, Milton understood this transition as eclipsing time and with it the temporal situation of human speech.

To treat the Passion as it had been treated within the meditative tradition, to depict and partake of Christ's suffering, would be to miss the point at which humiliation becomes exaltation, the point at which the divine nature partakes of mortality so that its manhood may achieve immortality. Insofar as death defines fallen, that is, mortal, man, and immortality is the shared attribute of God and restored man, the death and resurrection of Christ as God-man makes literal the exchange of attributes suggested by a metaphoric representation. Thus Milton escapes the tendency of language toward metaphor by positing the exchange as a historical event the literal truth of which language inadequately suggests.

A brief consideration of Milton's early fragment on the Passion will illustrate more specifically the way in which these Christological and Soteriological beliefs may have affected his poetry.

The eight, modified Spenserian stanzas of "The Passion" might stand as just a youthful fragment of an unsuccessful poem, but the addition of that famous and peculiar note which the author appended when he printed and proclaimed his failure in the 1645 edition of his poems and again when he reprinted it in 1673 invites attention. The printing of the fragment and its accompanying note both announces the place of the Passion in the Miltonic canon and refuses to fill that place.[24]

When, in 1630, the young Milton attempted to commemorate the Passion, he found that he could not situate himself adequately in the poem or in relation to the God at its center. Unlike the meditative poems of Crashaw and Herbert, which contemplate the intensity of Christ's suffering so as to appreciate the depth of his gift to man and man's need of that gift, Milton's poem dwells on the poet's choice of a place to stand, a vantage point from which to witness the events at Calvary.[25]

The poet's attempt to situate himself as a witness to the crucifixion involves curious displacements in both space and time: His spirit is borne in the chariot Ezekiel saw at "*Chebar* flood." The allusion puts us in mind of the exiles among whom Ezekiel prophesied, but it misses the Passion and gives us only a prefiguration. More surprising still, the poet's spirit, transported to Jerusalem, arrives too late, "where the Towers of *Salem* stood, / Once glorious Towers, now sunk in guiltless blood" (39–40).[26] Transported to the right place at the wrong time, the poet's eye sees not Christ's suffering but "that sad Sepulchral rock / That was the Casket of Heav'n's richest store" (43–44). Further, the sight of the tomb, "up-lock[s]" the poet's hands with grief. His pen thus disabled, he wishes for another mode of discourse:

> Yet on that soft'ned Quarry would I score
> My plaining verse as lively as before;
> For sure so well instructed are my tears,
> That they would fitly fall in order'd Characters.
>
> (46–49)

"Quarry" here refers to the stone tomb on which the poet's tears might carve an epitaph. But recalling the preceding allusion to Ezekiel, the phrase "softened stone" also refers us to Ezekiel 36:26: "A heart also will I give you, and a new spirit will I put within you: and I will take away the stonie heart out of your bodye, and I will give you a heart of flesh."[27] If this verse was in Milton's mind, as other verses from Ezekiel certainly were, we may associate the scored rock of the empty sepulchre with the heart written upon by the indwelling Spirit. The poet finding that language fails him, his hands "up-locked by grief," calls for "ordered characters," inscribed, on the place where the incarnate word had been, not by a pen but with tears. The exaltation of manhood is manifest in the regeneration of the heart transformed by Christ's act and the physical absence of Christ's external form.[28] The explicit reference to scoring the tomb with tears and the implicit allusion to the spirit-softened heart reveal a dichotomy of outward expression and inward experience. Within this dichotomy the silence of the voice reserves as unspeakable the moment when the soul attends the Word, now sounding within.

When Christ dies on the cross, he assumes the personal end of an individual man and thus shows man how to transcend mortality by accepting it, not as annihilation but as a passage to the apocalyptic eschatology of heaven. It is already clear in "The Passion" that, for Milton, the exchange of humiliation and glorification is achieved specifically by and through Christ's death as man and God:

> He sovereign Priest, stooping his regal head
> That dropt with odorous oil down his fair eyes,
> Poor fleshly Tabernacle entered,
> His starry front low-rooft beneath the skies;
> O what a Mask was there, what a disguise!
> Yet more; the stroke of death he must abide,
> Then lies him meekly down fast by his Brethren's side.
>
> (15–21)

William Hunter notes that Milton's use of "mask" in this passage in reference to the Incarnation anticipates his argument in *De Doctrina* that "*Person* is a theatrical term which has been adopted by scholastic theologians to mean any one individual being, as the logicians put it: any intelligent ens, numerically one, whether it be one God or one angel or one man."[29] The ambiguity of "mask" as signifying both the complete subsistence of the Incarnation and, in its etymological meaning, the mask donned by an actor when he assumes a role, is removed by "the stroke of death." The joining of God and man and the purchase of man's glorification by the humiliation of Christ is realized in the exchange of immortality for mortality. "The stroke of death" felt by the whole Christ as God-man finally resolves any ambiguity about the unification of two natures in one external form. The single temporal moment of death enables the resurrection that effects the eternal restoration of the link of manhood to divinity.

At the moment of Christ's acceptance and transcendence of mortality, history and eternity coincide. This temporal equivocation, this moment which is both within and outside of historical time, is reflected in the spatial and temporal instability of Milton's attempted poem on the Passion.

The temporal instability of a single, historical moment, realized as a diffuse transfiguration of history itself, is not only a theological fact but also, as I suggested earlier, a linguistic one. Whereas a poem like Herbert's "The Sacrifice" remains lyric through an elaboration of what Christ might have felt during the humiliation and torture that led up to his death, Milton's poem is betrayed by his emphasis on the moment of death as the central and determining event of the Passion and of human history. This moment, the still point at which history and eternity are joined, eludes the necessarily temporalizing process of linguistic predication: "Immediate are the Acts of God, more swift / Than time or motion, but to human ears / Cannot without process of speech be told" (*Paradise Lost* 7.176–78). Milton thus discovers that his vision of the Passion must be understood in the silence of the Word. Eschewing a lyric concentration on the suffering of Christ, which would, in effect, understand the Passion in wholly human terms, Milton sets himself the impossible task of simultaneously predicating two distinct natures of one subject and disclosing both in a single action. At this moment, at least in linguistic terms, divinity and manhood are indistinguishable, and the poet finds himself continually banished to the spatial and temporal periphery of the scene he wishes to describe.[30]

The significance of the Passion, as Milton understood it, could only be written inwardly on the softened stone of the heart. Milton later has Michael teach Adam this important lesson. When Adam inquires as to the fate of the faithful during the long period of persecution between the resurrection and the second coming, Michael assures him that the Father will send a "Comforter":

> The promise of the Father, who shall dwell
> His Spirit within them, and the Law of Faith

Working through love, upon thir hearts shall write,
To guide them in all truth, and also arm
With spiritual Armor, able to resist
Satan's assaults . . .

(*Paradise Lost* 12.487–92)

To translate this heart-writing to external speech would temporalize
the external and raise the question of an anomalous external form. Thus
the one moment of true pathos in "The Passion" depicts not the suffer-
ing of Christ, but the frustration of the poet, his soul "In pensive trance,
and anguish and ecstatic fit" (42), confronting his inability to speak
outwardly a necessarily inward grief:

Befriend me night, best Patroness of grief,
Over the Pole thy thickest mantle throw,
And work my flatter'd fancy to belief,
That Heav'n and Earth are color'd with my woe;
My sorrows are too dark for day to know.

(29–33)

To treat the Passion, as opposed to its figures, would be to substitute
words for an act of atonement, of identification with Christ in the ac-
ceptance and transcendence of death. In Milton's rigorous view, such
lamentation would not reproduce a necessary but ineffable inward state,
but would rather echo the mundane griefs that state is to redress. Thus
it is with this realization of the distinction between doing and saying
that he comes to reject his early attempt to speak the unspeakable:

Or should I thence hurried on viewless wing,
Take up a weeping on the Mountain wild,
The gentle neighborhood of grove and spring
Would soon unbosom all thir Echoes mild,
And I (for grief is easily beguil'd)
Might think th'infection of my sorrows loud
Had got a race of mourners on some pregnant cloud.

(50–56)

Unlike Ixion, to whom he here alludes, Milton, even at age twenty-
one, could distinguish between inward transformation brought about

by a historically transcendent event and the representations of that event, made insubstantial by his inability to include the transformation in the representation. He forbears to get a race of mourners on a cloud as he will later forbear discussion of the hypostatic union and its external form.

"The Passion" was above the author's years in 1630, and he saw fit to record this fact in 1645 and again in 1673. The one variant between the 1645 and 1673 texts is worth noting. The 1645 edition has "latter" in the lines "These latter scenes confine my roving verse, / To this Horizon is my Phoebus bound" (22–23). The word is "latest" in the 1673 text. Given the reading of the poem I have proposed, we can say that the 1673 reading is an improvement. Milton recognized in the enactment of the Passion the fulfillment of the last things; he saw, as early as 1630, that a rigorous understanding of Christ's death on the cross would require an unmediated connection of that historical event and the events that would end history. The long expanse of time between the two could be understood as containing the image in history of Christ's sacrifice, but the sacrifice remains unique until it is fulfilled. Thus, in the same lines, "bound" may be taken as both "confined" and "headed toward." The poet's verse is confined to the scenes of the Passion but headed toward the transcendent revelations of the "latest" scenes, those of the last days. The scene of the Passion is a "horizon" that divides, yet joins, time and eternity, death and life, humiliation and exaltation.

In his later work Milton never surrenders his conception of the crucifixion as a transforming moment which exists in time but cannot be represented in language. But he does learn to solve the specifically poetic problems that attend his theological conceptions. In his mature work we find the crucifixion evoked but not portrayed. It is an event always present beyond the borders of the narrative, permeating temporal life through its shadowy types. In *Paradise Lost* it is a promise whose fulfillment is at once anticipated and remembered. In *Paradise Regained*, the Passion is anticipated by Christ's renunciation of outward action and his triumph over Satan through the perfection of an inward grace and, in *Samson Agonistes*, the dialectic of humiliation and exaltation is ambiguously played out in Samson's prefiguring interpretation of Christ's submission and triumph. The absence of a direct depiction of the Passion from Milton's major works is the mark of the transcendent historicality he ascribes to it. On this episode in the career of Christ, he seems to have attended to the advice of Ignatius of Antioch:

It is better to be silent and be real, than to talk and to be unreal. Teaching is good, if the teacher does what he says. There is then one teacher "who spoke and it came to pass," and what he has done even in silence is worthy of the Father. He who has the word of Jesus for a true possession can also hear his silence, that he may be perfect, that he may act through his speech, and be understood through his silence.[31]

Notes

1. See for example, Denis Saurat, *Milton: Man and Thinker* (London: J. M. Dent & Sons, 1944), 149. E. L. Marilla's response to Saurat, "Milton on the Crucifixion," *Etudes Anglaises* 22 (1969): 7–10, notes that 238 lines of *Paradise Lost* are devoted to the Passion, but the fact remains that this event is kept beyond the limits of the narrative and that Milton nowhere provides a sustained description of Christ's sufferings on the cross. Milton's use of the temptation in the wilderness rather than the Passion as the central event of *Paradise Regained* has drawn considerable comment and provided the specific issue around which discussion of Milton's relationship to the Passion has occurred. See Charles H. Huttar's extremely useful summary and analysis of these debates in "The Passion of Christ in *Paradise Regained,*" *English Language Notes* 19 (1982): 236–61.

2. Huttar traces the medieval tradition of the Triumphant Crucifixion as an alternative to the dominant seventeenth-century, devotional mode of depicting the Passion. He argues that Milton found the devotional mode "unsuited to his personality" (245) and that in *PR* he came to see that "the Cross is itself the Exaltation, from which the Resurrection and Ascension follow as (so to speak) appendages" (258). According to this conception the temptation portrayed in *PR* reveals the triumphant Christ who proleptically defeats sin and already points toward the exaltation. I agree with Huttar that the coterminality of the crucifixion and exaltation are of central importance in understanding Milton's avoidance of direct depiction of the Passion, but I think we can say more on the subject than that the contemporary mode of handling the Crucifixion was unsuited to Milton's personality. While Huttar is right that Milton finds a way around the Passion, more needs to be said about why he found it necessary to do so.

218 □   *Marshall Grossman*

3. *Milton's Poetry: Its Development In Time* (Pittsburgh: Duquesne University Press, 1979), 33.

4. "Response to Anthony Low's Address on *Samson Agonistes* (Le Moyne College, May 4, 1979)," *Milton Quarterly* 14 (1979): 104.

5. William B. Hunter, Jr., in "Milton on the Incarnation: Some More Heresies," *Journal of the History of Ideas* 21 (1960): 349–69, reprinted in *Bright Essence: Studies in Milton's Theology*, ed. Hunter, C. A. Patrides and J. H. Adamson (Salt Lake City: University of Utah Press, 1971), 131–48, locates Milton's views in relation to the various Christological traditions. Also useful are Barbara K. Lewalski, *Milton's Brief Epic: The Genre, Meaning and Art of "Paradise Regained"* (Providence, R.I.: Brown; London: Methuen, 1966), 133–63 and *passim*, C. A. Patrides, *Milton and the Christian Tradition* (Oxford: Clarendon Press, 1966), 130–42.

6. *Milton's Brief Epic*, 138. See also, William B. Hunter, Jr. "Some Problems in Milton's Theological Vocabulary," *Harvard Theological Review* 57 (1964): 364–65.

7. *Christian Doctrine* in *Complete Prose Works of John Milton*, ed. Don M. Wolfe et al. (New Haven and London: Yale University Press, 1953–1982), 6:422. All citations of Milton's prose refer to the Yale edition.

8. See Lewalski, 155, Hunter, "Milton on the Incarnation," 144; Cf. A. P. Fiore, "The Problem of 17th Century Soteriology in Reference to Milton," *Franciscan Studies* 15 (1955): 48–59, 257–82. Fiore's claims for Milton's relative orthodoxy sometimes miss the details of Milton's position, especially with reference to the unity of personality and subsistence (259).

9. London, 1658, viii.vii. See also, Lewalski, 153.

10. See for example, William Ames, *The Marrow of Sacred Divinity, Drawne Out of the holy Scriptures, and the Interpreters thereof, and brought into Method* (London, 1642), 8: "Therefore Divinity is better defined by that good life whereby we live to God, then by a blessed life whereby we live to ourselves."

11. *Poetics* 1448b, 1450a, b.

12. For a detailed discussion of the relationship of character to predication in narrative, see Marshall Grossman, "The Subject of Narrative and the Rhetoric of the Self," *Papers on Language & Literature* 18 (1982): 398–415.

13. *Rhetoric* 1406b, 1407a.

14. Aquinas comments on Aristotle, *Peri Hermeneias*, 16 ab8, note 7, "to signify with time is to signify something measured in time. Hence it is one thing to signify time principally, as a thing, which is appropriate to the name; however, it is another thing to signify with time, which is not proper to the name but to the verb." *Aristotle: On Interpretation, Commentary by St. Thomas and Cajetan (Peri Hermeneias)*, trans. Jean T. Oesterle (Milwaukee: Marquette University Press, 1966). As soon as we express the "doings" of Christ, we express Christ with time and the question of which nature *now* arises.

15. *Christian Doctrine*, 424. Cf. *Paradise Lost* 3.315–16.

16. A similar ambivalence, I believe, leads to the doubled plots that Stanley Fish notes in *Paradise Regained*: "On the dramatic level the definition of the relationship

between man and God takes the form of a progressive narrowing of the area in which the self is preeminent or even, in a causal sense, active. On the verbal level there is a progressive diminishing, first of the complexity of language and then of its volubility, until finally, as the relationship between the self and God is specified, there is only silence. In other words, there is a perfect and inevitable correspondence between the conceptual thrust of the poem and the progress (or anti-progress) of its language." "Inaction and Silence: The Reader in *Paradise Regained*," in *Calm of Mind: Tercentenary Essays on "Paradise Regained" and "Samson Agonistes" in Honor of John S. Diekhoff*, ed. Joseph Anthony Wittreich, Jr. (Cleveland and London: Case Western Reserve, 1971), 27. Depicting the unity of man and God means, for Milton, withdrawal from action and ultimately from speech into a non- temporal and unspeakable identity with an eternal will. The same transcendence of external form (language) by an interior junction of divine and human appears in Milton's, typically Protestant, hermeneutics: "We have, particularly under the gospel, a double scripture. There is the external scripture of the written word and the internal scripture of the Holy Spirit which he, according to God's promise, has engraved upon the hearts of believers, and which is certainly not to be neglected." *Christian Doctrine*, 587.

17. *Milton's Brief Epic*, 155.
18. *Milton's Brief Epic*, 157–58.
19. *Christian Doctrine*, 439–40. See also p. 438: "Luke xxii.43: *an angel from heaven appeared to him, strengthening him.* What need would there be of an angel unless both Christ's natures were suffering? A similar argument may be applied to Matt. xxvii.46: *my God, my God, why have you forsaken me*? If his divine nature was not suffering too, why was it not there to help him when he cried out? And if it could have helped, but was unwilling to do so, what point was there in calling to the Father, since its will and the Father's were one and the same?"
20. *Christian Doctrine*, 442.
21. *Chirstian Doctrine*, 443.
22. 3.311–17. All citations of Milton's poetry refer to: John Milton, *Complete Poems and Major Prose*, ed. Merritt Y. Hughes (Indianapolis: Odyssey, 1957).
23. *Christian Doctrine*, 442.
24. There is a general agreement that the occasion for "The Passion" was a cycle of poems commemorating the Christian Calendar. For a useful summary of the literature on "The Passion" see A. S. P. Woodhouse and Douglas Bush, *A Variorum Commentary on the Poems of John Milton* (New York: Columbia University Press, 1972), vol. 2, pt. 1, 151–61. Philip J. Gallagher sees the fragment as a complete prologue used to represent the impossibility of writing divine poems without divine inspiration. "Milton's 'The Passion': Inspired Mediocrity," *Milton Quarterly* 11 (1977): 44–50. Although I join Gallagher in arguing that the printing of the poem serves to signify emphatically the impossibility of its completion, I see no need to posit a persona who speaks the stanzas and from whom Milton is distanced, as Gallagher does, nor do I believe inspiration to be the poem's central issue. Other treatments of "The Passion" include John A. Via's reading of the poem as "an ironic comment on religious and

poetic experience" (37) in "Milton's 'The Passion'; A Successful Failure," *Milton Quarterly* 5 (1971): 35–38, and Frederic B. Tromly's excellent reading of the fragment as "a vivid cautionary example of the 'plucking of untimely fruit'" (282) in "Milton's 'Preposterous Exaction': The Significance of 'The Passion,'" *ELH* 47 (1980): 276–86.

25. Tayler points out that the fragment attempts the standard *compositio loci* of the meditative poem (33). See also Louis Martz, *The Poetry of Meditation*, 2nd ed. (New Haven and London: Yale University Press, 1962), 167–68.

26. Gallagher notes the disjunction in stanza 6 between the poet who is "here" reporting on the visions of his soul "there" in Jerusalem (46). See also Tromly, 279. Lewalski notes in her discussion of the Tower scene in *Paradise Regained* that "Perkins and Diodati recalled that the scene of this episode, Jerusalem, was the center of the Old Law which Christ's priesthood would supplant, and the place where his death would found the new dispensation" (309). On the use of the pinnacle temptation to prefigure the Passion, see Huttar, 255–56.

27. I quote the Geneva Bible, 1560.

28. Stanley Fish comments in his discussion of *Paradise Regained* 4.560–61, "The voice we hear is not the voice we have come to know, but the impersonal voice suggested by the 'it' of 'it is written.' Christ does nothing less here than find a way to assert selflessness. It is a linguistic miracle in which language, the primary sign of personality, becomes the means by which personality is extinguished. The Son performs the impossible feat of saying silence and makes himself disappear." "Inaction and Silence: The Reader in *Paradise Regained*," 43. As the climax of the temptation prefigures the Passion, Milton prefigures the silence of the bodily word and the transcendence of language.

29. "Milton on the Incarnation," 147. The quotation is from *Christian Doctrine*, 423.

30. Cf. the systematic devaluation of specifiable time and place in the opening invocation of *Paradise Lost*. The fact that "The Passion" is a poem about writing a poem is noted by Gallagher, by W. R. Parker, *Milton: A Biography* (Oxford: Clarendon Press, 1968), 1:71–72 and by Northrop Frye, "Literature as Context: Milton's *Lycidas*," in *Lycidas: The Tradition and the Poem*, ed. C. A. Patrides (New York: Holt, Rinehart and Winston, 1961), 208.

31. Ignatius Martyr, *Epistle to the Ephesians*, XV in the *Apostolic Fathers*, with an English translation by Kirsopp Lake, in two volumes, the Loeb Classical Library (London: William Heinemann; New York: G. P. Putnam's Sons, 1925), I, k89.

Milton's "Umpire Conscience," the "Two-Handed Engine," and the English Protestant Tradition of the Divine Similitude

ALINDA SUMERS

I n *Lycidas*, Milton may draw upon the early tradition of English Protestant casuistry to suggest in his passage on the clergy (108–31) that the speaker's closing words— "But that two-handed engine at the door / Stands ready to smite once and smite no more"[1]—refer to the two potential actions his contemporaries attribute to the human conscience itself. Scholars have suggested that the terrible vision in *Lycidas* represents an enigmatic passage in the pastoral elegy; when the "two-handed engine" is glossed, however, in William Perkins's words, as the human conscience, or as the "little God" at the door of the heart who stands ready either to accuse or to excuse the soul to God, and to render judgment accordingly,[2] the famous crux[3] of *Lycidas* takes on artistic unity in terms of the whole.

My point is that Milton's passage on the clergy is a true "divine similitude," not a set of biblical typologies *per se*.[4] This passage glances at many scriptural texts and, certainly, suggests all the metaphors for divine justice that other scholars have mentioned.[5] Nevertheless, Milton's poetic tropes and figures often detour through the tradition of Protestant, especially Puritan, preaching. The "two-handed engine" metaphor is both unique in that it suggests biblical imagery without, perhaps, directly imitating any specific biblical text, and wholly conventional, in that Milton's seventeenth-century reader would easily have deciphered it because the image of the human conscience is a common Renaissance trope, or similitude, that in the writings of English theologians and poets reflects the mental iconography associated with the

Word. As interpreted by numerous Protestant casuists, from the begin-
ning of the Puritan era to well after the Restoration, the conscience
is, as Jeremy Taylor phrases it, that "great Instrument" in the souls of
those through whom "the holy Jesus sets upon this great reformation
of the world."[6]

The primary objective of this essay, then, is to support the trend in
Milton studies that, since Ralph Hone's 1959 article, has identified the
speaker of the passage as Christ, and to offer new evidence as appropri-
ate initiation into what has been termed the "fellowship of Miltonists
in the Quest of the Mysterious Engine."[7] The secondary objective of
this essay is to trace a poetic figure through the tradition of English
Protestant casuistry.

Because modern readers disagree over the fundamental meaning of
the engine, we need, as Professor Claes Schaar might say, to establish
not only a scholarly but also a literary "vertical context system" for the
"two-handed engine."[8] I emphasize the need for a literary context sys-
tem primarily because those critics who believe Milton's speaker is St.
Peter often respond to biblical exegesis that is supported by the con-
tinental tradition of pictorial iconography in England. This tradition
allows us to entertain, as Mother Mary Christopher Pecheux suggests,
a poetic "ambivalence" in the figure of the speaker who may then
represent simultaneously Christ-Peter-Moses; or to accept, as Karl E.
Felson does, the otherwise incongruous image of the Angel Michael
smiting the sinner with the scales of justice.[9] Even Turner, who has
called for a return to visual simplicity in interpretation, and who urges
Miltonists to look "for a single, concrete, instrument, appropriate to
the purpose, and one which Milton would have expected his readers
to identify immediately and without doubt," believes that the speaker
of the passage in question must be St. Peter, since in Milton's day "every-
one knew that St. Peter was the keeper of the door of Heaven."[10]

On the contrary, that Christ has given St. Peter the keys to the king-
dom of heaven is, I would argue, a major source of embarrassment for
sixteenth- and seventeenth-century Protestant theologians, from the
proto-Puritan William Perkins to the high churchman Jeremy Taylor.
By accessing for the modern reader the cultural tradition associated with
the human conscience, we may be able to say what a young student

at Cambridge during Milton's day would have made of the "two-handed engine." We may also be able to predict what Milton's contemporaries in the later seventeenth century would still understand as the appropriate frame of reference for *Lycidas*.[11]

A reading of the "two-handed engine" as one and the same figure as Milton's "Umpire *Conscience*" of *Paradise Lost* 3.194–97, the divinely appointed guide or light of the mind, is supported especially by William Perkins's late sixteenth-century treatise *A Discovrse of Conscience*.[12] There, Perkins develops numerous imagistic similitudes illustrating the conscience as God's mechanism for condemning the princely man whose chief desire is for the goods of this world. In one place, for example, Perkins asks his readers to imagine a man sitting in a "chaire of estate" at a great feast, and to "withall suppose one standing by, with a naked sword to cut his throat, or a wild be[a]st readie euer and anon to pull him in peeces." This terrible creature standing by is, Perkins tells his reader, the man's own "euill conscience, which is as a sword to slay the soule" (chap. 4, p. 552, col. 2c–d).

The divine similitude elaborated above is matched in Perkins's works by countless others drawn primarily from the tradition of the sermon exemplum. As the first of the English Protestant casuists, however, Perkins also follows St. Thomas Aquinas in locating the seat of conscience in the practical understanding and in describing its operation as being "by a kinde of reasoning or disputing," called a "practicall syllogisme." Perkins chooses as his biblical proof text Rom. 2:15, which he translates as "*Their reasoning . . . accusing or excusing each other*" (chap. 2, p. 535, col. 2b-c) and glosses by an example drawn from the judgmental action taking place in the conscience of a murderer:

Eury murtherer is cursed, saith the minde:
*Thou art a murthere*r, saith conscience assisted by memorie:
Ergo, *Thou art cursed*, saith conscience, and so giueth her sentence.
(chap. 2, p. 535, col. 2d)

Still following Rom. 2:15, Perkins insists that the conscience renders judgment "either by accusing and condemning, or by excusing and absolving" (chap. 2, p. 535, col. 2d). Following Acts 2:37, he observes that the first two of these actions are "very forcible & terrible: for they are the *compunctions* and prickings that bee in the heart" (chap. 2, p. 536, col. 1a). Following 2 Sam. 24:10, Perkins compares the two acts of accusing and condemning to "the stripes as it were, of an yron rod, wherewith the heart of a man smiteth it selfe" (chap. 2, p. 536, col. 1a).

Perkins uses scholastic logic and legalistic argument as far as he can, but he appropriates Hebrew organ psychology when he seats conscience in the heart.[13] In one of his finest similitudes, Perkins again interrelates the two traditions:

> Herein conscience is like to a iudge that holdeth an assise, & takes notice of inditements, and causeth the most notorious malefactor that is, to hold vp his hand at the barre of his iudgement. Nay it is (as it were) a little God sitting in the middle of mens hearts, arraigning them in this life as they shal be arraigned for their offences at the Tribunal seat of the euerliuing God in the day of iudgement. Wherefore the temporarie iudgment that is giuen by the conscience is nothing els but a beginning, or a fore-runner of the last iudgement. (chap. 2, p. 519, col. 1a–b)

Perkins thinks of the conscience as the "little God" in the human breast. On judgment day, the conscience is God's vicegerent in the court of man's sentient faculties (cf. Milton's "Vicegerent Son" in *Paradise Lost* 10.55); on a daily basis, too, this spirit, or being, is either the bad man's "greatest enemie" or the good man's "best friend" (chap. 4, p. 552, col. 2d–p. 553, col. 1a).

Perkins frequently alludes to many classical texts in order to create what becomes the stock English metaphor for the anthropomorphized conscience. On the one hand, the evil conscience is the "Lords sergeant" (ch. 4, p. 552, col. 2d); it is the "Iaylor to keepe man in prison in bolts and irons"; the "witnesse to accuse him, the Iudge to condemne him, the hangman to execute him, & the flashings of the fire of hell to torment him." The conscience can cause a man to "lay violent handes vpon himselfe," or to become his "owne cut-throat." On the other hand, the good conscience provides a "continuall feast, & a paradise vpon earth." At the "terrible day of iudgement," Perkins concludes, "euery man must receiue according to his doings"; if our own evil consciences "condemne vs in this life, God will much more condemne vs" (chap. 4, p. 552, col. 2d-p. 553, col. 1b).

As early as 1600, then, students at Christ's College, Cambridge, would learn the rhetoric and theology of conscience from the tradition of Augustine, Aquinas, Calvin, and Beza as interpreted by their own William Perkins.[14] By the mid 1630s, Perkins's disciple William Ames echoes that tradition, firmly locating the dual operations of the human conscience in the understanding and identifying the operations of conscience, according to Isa. 5:3, as "a mans judgement of himselfe, according to Gods judgement of him."[15] Ames does not accept, however, Perkins's analysis of the conscience as only a natural power or faculty, arguing that because "thoughts themselues" are also "acts" (Rom. 2:15) the conscience is most properly a supernatural light and law implanted by God and intimately connected with the powers of human choice (see bk. 1, chap. 1, nn. 4–9, 2–3). Instead, Ames takes up where Perkins had left off. Ames forms a syllogism asserting that in its major premise conscience knows the moral law; in its minor premise, conscience functions as an "Index," or "Booke," cataloguing a person's acts; in its conclusion, conscience becomes a witness and a judge. To support his argument, Ames refers to Rom. 2:14–15, the same passages that Perkins uses, and adds to them allusions to Rev. 20:12 and 1 John 5:10 (summary, bk. 1, position 8, 50). From the conclusions of conscience, Ames argues, certain effects follow: either acts of conscience—such as knowing and approving, or knowing and disapproving—or acts of will that arise from the former. Then the will translates these cognitive "acts" into volitional terms, into the realm of human choice (see bk. 1, chap. 10, nn. 1–3, 30).

Certainly, as a student at Christ's College between 1625 and 1632 Milton would have been exposed to Perkins's works on casuistry and to the original Hebrew, Greek, and Latin texts from which the famous English Calvinist draws his examples. It is also possible that by the mid 1630s Milton is aware of Ames's radical revision of the logical basis for Puritan casuistry. By the time Milton composes *De Doctrina Christiana*, his theory of the conscience is obviously influenced by Ames:

The standard of judgment will be the individual conscience itself, and so each man will be judged according to the light which he has received. (bk. 1, chap. 33, 623)[16]

Milton immediately supports this statement by citing, along with other passages, the same biblical proof texts that Perkins and Ames before him use: Rom. 2:14–15. Milton, like Ames, elaborates his proof by adding commentary based upon Rev. 22:12:

Rom. ii.12: those who have sinned . . . will perish . . . and ii.14: when the Gentiles, who have . . . not the law, do by nature the things contained in the law, then although they have no law, they are their own law: for they show the work of the law written in their hearts. Their conscience supplies evidence too, and their own thoughts will mutually accuse or excuse each other, on the day when the Lord will judge the secrets of men, according to my gospel, through Jesus Christ; . . . Rev. xx.12: and the books were opened; . . . And the dead were judged in accordance with the things which had been written in these books, in accordance with the things that they had done. (bk. 1, chap. 33, 623)[17]

At this later point in his theological development, Milton defines the individual conscience as the accusing and excusing faculty representing the standard of God's judgment both in this life and for the life to come. Could the young Milton, however, the orthodox Puritan who developed the divine similitude of the last judgment in *Lycidas* have as early as 1637 meant the "two-handed engine" to reflect the same powers attributed to the conscience in *Christian Doctrine* and to his "Umpire Conscience" in *Paradise Lost*? The answer is a qualified "yes."

The "yes" is qualified by the work Ames (and other Puritans) did to free conscience from being a passive tool of God's judgment through Christ and to proclaim it as simply the ability to interpret the "Scriptures, or a judgement to discern Gods will for a mans selfe" (*Conscience*, corollaries to summary, bk. 1, corollary 3, 55). In Milton's later poetry, and in *Christian Doctrine*, the conscience is for Milton the divinely appointed guide and light of the mind. It is the illuminated spiritual faculty whereby Milton's characters are assured, beyond doubt, of God's will.

Their own wills, however, are left free to choose, not inclined from
without; they are not the shackled wills of the Augustinian and Cal-
vinistic tradition as Perkins interpreted it. For Milton, as for Ames, the
conscience is still the knowing and accusing faculty; but the will is free.
For this reason, Milton argues, the "seat of faith is not really the in-
tellect but the will" (see *CD*, bk. 1, chap. 20, 476).

In Milton's mature poetry and prose, then, we seem to have evidence
that the conscience participates in the volitional as well as in the know-
ing faculties of the mind.[18] For the youthful Milton, however, for the
poet of *Comus, Arcades,* and *Lycidas,* the idea of the conscience was not
so theologically clarified because his idea of faith was not as yet separate,
perhaps, from his idea of the operation of human reason. We may im-
agine Milton's early orthodox understanding of Christ's efficacy as related
to his simple acceptance of early Puritan casuistry; for this reason, we
need not trace the development of the conscience further into radical
Puritan documents; instead, we may back up, theologically speaking,
to study what happens to similitudes of conscience in the works of Mil-
ton's orthodox Protestant contemporaries. Here we find that the con-
science is always thought of as it is in Perkins's works, as Christ's own
instrument, the double action in the heart which knows and acts, judges
and smites, reflecting the control of evil human acts by God through
Christ. Later in the century, the orthodox Jeremy Taylor can still write
that the "conscience does accuse or excuse a man before God, which
the will cannot. If it could, we should all stand upright at doomesday"
(*DD*, bk. 1, chap. 1, rule 1, n. 12, 6).

In order to illustrate this, we must return, first of all, to Perkins him-
self. The Milton of *Lycidas* is still very close to the works of the Ehud
of Christ's College.[19] Indeed, *Lycidas* reads like a manifesto in tribute
to the early English reformer. In the theme of the corrupt clergy as
in the theme of the conscience as the instrument whereby Christ will
judge them, Milton and Perkins are as one. In Perkins's early diatribes
against the unreformed populace and clergy, he warns that "not to
preserue the conscience without spot is the way to desperation" (*Dis-
covrse*, chap. 4, p. 554, col. 2b). Like Perkins's picture of false ministers,
the reprobate clergymen of *Lycidas* have not preserved their consciences
without spot. Rather, these evil pastors resemble those in whom the

conscience has been "benummed" or silenced by avarice and vice (*Discovrse*, chap. 3, p. 550, col. 1b). Thomas Taylor, in *Christs Combate*, points out that such a conscience, perverted by Satan, will "stiffen it selfe in errour euen to the death."[20] Even a wounded conscience would be "sometimes talking" to the sinner and was therefore not to be feared, according to one Puritan divine.[21] But a dead, or sleeping, conscience, Perkins insists, is "most daungerous":

> It is like a wild beast, which so long as he lies a sleepe seemes verie tame and gentle, and hurts no man: . . . And so it is the manner of a dead conscience, to lie still and quiet euen through the course of a mans life: . . . but when . . . death approcheth, it beeing awaked by the hand of God, beginnes to stand vpon his legges, and shewes his fierce eies, & offers to rend out euen the very throat of the soule. (*Discovrse*, chap. 3, p. 550, col. 1c)

Milton's contemporary readers would surely recognize the conscience as a terrible instrument of God's justice. They would not have been at all surprised to think of that creature as a bestial other-self possessing "eies," "legges," and hands. This image of the conscience as a psychological projection of the human mind, or as a creature with the upraised sword of justice, is very likely what Milton's contemporaries would instantly have associated with the "two-handed engine" that in *Lycidas* stands ready to smite the false princes of the English church.

I suggest that we turn now for more supporting evidence not to Ames's treatise on conscience but, again, to Jeremy Taylor's magnificent compendium entitled *Dvctor Dvbitantivm*. Although this work appears for the first time in 1660, obviously long after *Lycidas* appeared, and although it was written by an Anglican bishop, not by a Puritan divine, it collects together countless references from numerous Greek and Latin authors and from the writings of the early church fathers, sources that Milton, as Jeremy Taylor's contemporary at Cambridge, also would have read. Further, like all English Protestant casuists, Taylor acknowledges a tremendous debt to Perkins's idea of how conscience operates, allowing us to continue our gloss on the early Milton of the "two-handed engine."

On one level, Milton's "two-handed engine" could refer to the human conscience in the same way that Jeremy Taylor's term "Rule of Conscience" obviously refers to the "great Instrument" that, he says, is "nothing but the certain expectation and fear of the Divine vengeance" (*DD*, bk. 1, chap. 1, rule 2, n. 20, 21). By the end of the eighteenth century, in fact, the term two-handed as given in *Burley's Universal Dictionary* (1782) means only "bulky, enormous in magnitude."[22] And this is the meaning it retains, for example, in Fielding's *Tom Jones*.[23] This simple meaning is sufficient for *Lycidas*, too, if we consider that the rule or standard of conscience is that great instrument—"that two-handed engine"—whereby God through Christ disciplines the hearts of men and women and ushers in the reformation of the ancient world and of the English clergy.

When we trace seventeenth-century usage of the term "engine," we find that English authors nearly always use it to mean either mechanism or method. Satan's engines are his military arsenal of carnal weaponry, while mankind's "onley engine" is, as Perkins says, the simple words of "Scripture truely vnderstood and wel applied."[24] Thus, when during the celestial battle in *Paradise Lost* Milton compares Satan's engines to military cannons belching death, the poet can expect his audience to recall sermons and tracts comparing the saint's weaponry to the sword of scripture: Raphael tells us that with a divinely powered sword Michael smites "with huge two-handed sway" the squadrons of the devil (6.250–51). Milton's comparisons are not lost on modern scholars who in their search for the "two-handed engine" of *Lycidas* have suggested biblical modes of justice ranging from concrete implements such as Michael's sword or Christ's sword, rod, or staff to more abstract spiritual weapons such as the voice of God or Bunyan's power of prayer.[25]

Among modern critical interpretations, however, I like best Professor Harry Robins's argument that Milton uses the term engine in its Latin sense of agent, or intelligence, that the "two-handed engine is an engine with two hands—a man."[26] Perkins's theory of the conscience as the little deity in the heart reinforces Robins's perception. We must not forget that comparisons to various human-like spirits provided plausible interpretations of the human conscience even down to the end of the century. Jeremy Taylor's treatment of the Greek and

Latin etymologies for conscience in *Dvctor Dvbitantivm*, for example, simply collects together the proof texts that were available to all educated persons of the day. Taylor defines the conscience as God's "Substitute" and refers to conscience as *"oikeios phylax, enoikos theos, epitopos daimon* [Greek transliterated],[27] *The Household Guardian, The Domestick God, The Spirit or Angel of the place."* This little household deity, Taylor feels, is really "Gods Vickar" in our hearts (bk. 1, chap. 1, rule 1, n. 2, 2). Thus, Origen calls the conscience the *"Spiritum correctorem, & paedagogum animae"* or *"the instructor of the soul, the spirit, the corrector"*; Basil believes the conscience to represent the *"Naturale judicatorium,"* or the *"natural power of judging"*; "Damascen," according to Taylor, refers to conscience as the *"Lucem intellectus nostri,* the light of our understanding" (bk. 1, chap. 1, rule 1, n. 12, 6). Taylor agrees with Hierocles who identifies the conscience as the *"Watchman* and *Intelligencer* of the soul" (bk. 1, chap. 1, rule 1, n. 3, 2).

Taylor elaborates his catalogue by remarking that "so long as we beleeve a God, so long our conscience will at least teach us, if it does not also smite us." Sometimes, he says, God will allow a man to go unpunished, but "unless the man be smitten and awakened before he dies, both God & the conscience reserve their wrath to be inflicted in hell." Taylor concludes, "It is one and the same thing; *God's wrath, and an evil guilty conscience*: For by the same hand by which God gives his law, by the same he punishes them that transgress the law" (bk. 1, chap. 1, rule 1, n. 7, 3).

In the paraphrases above we notice that for Milton's contemporary Jeremy Taylor the conscience carries out two spiritual functions corresponding to two potential roles: one role is enacted in the private domain of human ethics and personal morality; the other role is enacted at the bar of God's divine justice. Yet both courts are internal, paradoxically representing the player, conscience, as natural faculty and as supernatural judge.

We notice, too, that Taylor's similitudes for the conscience are far from original, depending upon ancient authorities and the standard legalistic idiom of the age to convey the sense of double judgmental powers. In another place, Taylor cites St. Paul and St. Bernard in order to interpret the concept of judgment in the book of Revelation. At the

last day, he writes, a "great Scene or Theatre" will display the private
drama of "our actions good and bad." Then "Gods Book, the Book
of life or death," will be opened, and the conscience will be brought
forth as witness to reflect, as in a "Looking-glass," the condition of the
soul (see bk. 1, chap. 1, rule 2, nn. 4–6, 13–14). In the private judg-
ment seat of conscience, the drama of the Last Assize is ultimately enacted:
"In the Court of Conscience," Taylor assserts, "every man is his own
accuser, and his own executioner" (bk. 3, chap. 2, rule 2, n. 12, point
5, 63).

In *Dvctor Dvbitantivm* Tayor's similitudes and discussions of the pow-
ers of conscience closely follow the pioneering work of Perkins. In one
passage, though, Taylor departs from his written authorities and fol-
lows, possibly, contemporary parlance — or, possibly, Calvin's reference
to conscience as the eye of faith looking out of the watch tower of reli-
gious duty[28] — when he compares the functioning of conscience to the
striking of a clock:

> conscience does the work of a Monitor and a Judge. . . . conscience
> is a Clock, which in one man strikes aloud and gives warning,
> and in another the hand points silently to the figure, but strikes
> not; but by this he may surely see what the other hears, *viz.* that
> his hours pass away, and death hastens, and after death comes judge-
> ment. (bk. 1, chap. 1, rule 2, n. 23, 23)

The conscience is God's clock, the monitor or engine measuring out
the moments of eternity. In the reprobate, the hand moves silently; in
the saved, the hand strikes aloud, warning of the fleeting hours and
signaling the heart to prepare for the time of judgment.

Given the comparison above, Milton's "two-handed engine" may well
refer to God's clock. It is unlikely that Milton intends a literal clock,
however, since in the seventeenth century, as Claud Adelbert Thomp-
son points out, clock faces on London watch towers had only one hand.
Thompson thinks it possible, however, that Milton intends his audience
to compare the "two-handed engine" to the jack of the clock house
automatons, the mechanical figures that did indeed have two hands in
order to sound the clocks, or bells, announcing prayers. Thompson ar-
gues that Donne's famous words "never send to know for whom the

bell tolls; it tolls for thee" refer to the sounding of the passing bell by a jack of the clock.[29] Thompson's comparison of Donne's bell and Milton's "two-handed engine" to a mechanical Jack calls to mind June Winter's suggestion that the "two-handed engine" may refer to the porter at the gate in *Macbeth*.[30] Both literary figures, though, are merely similitudes for symbolic processes that Milton's contemporaries attribute to the power of conscience. Donne, for example, in what is purported to be his last hymn on death, writes: "I tune the Instrument here at the dore, / And what I must doe then, thinke here before."[31] Here Donne may well refer to his own conscience as it prepares to stand at the last judgment, either to smite the soul or to walk through the "new wicket or doore" of death into paradise.[32]

Like the seventeenth-century bell or clock, and like the trope of the bellman or watchman, Milton's "two-handed engine" represents the great instrument of the conscience. It is God's "ingenious device"[33] to convert the sense of time passing into the moral awareness of doom. As an internalized sense of time as mortality, the conscience makes us "remember our end." Milton's enigmatic figure symbolizes God's watchman, monitor, and intelligencer in daily life and may serve as the Lord's sergeant, judge, and executioner at the Great Assize. If so, the two hands of God's clock stand, as Jeremy Taylor might say, for the "direct act" of self-knowledge, and for the "reflex act of judgement" (see *DD*, bk. 1, chap. 2, rule 2, n. 2, 39).

Seventeenth-century Protestant casuistry does allow us to interpret the "two-handed engine" as the human conscience, and it reinforces nearly all modern scholarly readings of the engine as some biblical instrument of God's justice. The English tradition of religious commentary does not support, however, modern scholarly theories that equate the "two-handed engine" with Christ. While the conscience is "our Guide and our Lawgiver, our Judge and our Rule," Jeremy Taylor remarks, it is not "our Lord" (*DD*, bk. 1, chap. 3, rule 2, n. 6, point 4, 103). Rather, the "spirit" of our conscience functions as God's agent in the heart. Because the conscience is the voice of God in the soul, it is Christ's instrument, not Christ himself. Indeed, the conscience is "affirmed" by St. Paul to be "*The word of God sharper then a two edged Sword*" (*DD*, bk. 1, chap. 1, rule, 1, n. 8, 4).

Neither does seventeenth-century English casuistry support the modern trend to identify Milton's "Pilot of the *Galilean* Lake" (109) with St. Peter. In Protestant theology, Christ is not only equipped with that "great Instrument," the "Rule of Conscience"; but he is also understood as the keeper of the keys. Perkins tells us that these keys belong to Christ alone because the "soueraigne power of binding & loosing, is not belonging to any creature, but is proper to Christ, who hath the keies of heauen and hell: he openeth and no man shutteth, he shutteth & no man openeth, Reu. 3.5" (*Discovrse*, chap. 2, p. 525, col. 2c).

Then, too, in seventeenth-century documents commentators frequently identify the keys to the kingdom as one and the same as Christ's keys in Rev. 1:18, the keys of hell and death. Richard Sibbes, for example, in a series of sermons entitled *The Gloriovs Feast of the Gospel*[34] writes that the identification of Christ with the "Key of Hell and Death" looks back to the ancient custom of "Governours that carryed the Key." As the Lord of mankind, Christ "hath the Government and Command of Hell and Death." While the bodies of the elect are "safe in the grave," Sibbes believes, their "dust" is being "fitted" for their heavenly bodies, and "Christ that hath the Key will let them out againe" (sermon 4, on Isa. 25:7–8, 69). The reprobate, we may assume, will not be so fortunate. In Sibbes's works, death symbolizes the entrance, the "doore and passage to life" (sermon 4, 62). The elect welcome the day when they will stand at this door, and Christ will unlock it. At the hour of death, Sibbes believes, "then conscience standeth our friend" (sermon 2, on Isa. 25:6, 2627).

Christ, not St. Peter, guards the doors of the kingdom of heaven, then, and Christ has the key of the soul, as Protestant theologians believed. When reading *Lycidas*, the seventeenth-century English theologian might also have remembered that in *Morals on the Book of Job*, St. Gregory comments upon Job 38:17, identifying the gates of death as wicked thoughts and the "gloomy doors" as the "lurking evils of the mind, which can both exist within, and yet not be observed by another." The Lord, St. Gregory says, does behold evil thoughts and "destroys them by the secret look of grace."[35] Not surprisingly, then, Milton's contemporary Richard Baxter defines the conscience of a hypocrite as next to

Christ a man's greatest enemy, as the "secret Judge" that delivers the "smart" of a self-inflicted wound.[36]

When in *Lycidas* Milton gives the speaker of his similitude of judgment "Two massy Keyes . . . of metals twain / (The Golden opes, the Iron shuts amain)" (110–11), he surely refers, as modern scholars have thought, to the figure of Christ in judgment of Rev. 1:18 and 3:7–8, and he merges references to these passages with echoes of Matt. 16:19. In this respect, at least, modern interpretations are supported in both Perkins's and in Jeremy Taylor's commentaries when they consider the legalistic or judicial role the minister plays in advising sinners on personal ethics. Both writers stress particularly that the pastor does not act under his own power, or even under St. Peter's symbolic power. Thus, we may agree with critics such as Thomas Kranidas that the keys in *Lycidas* stand for "instruments of retributive justice," but we need not attribute them to St. Peter since in seventeenth-century theology they did not have special reference to St. Peter as head of the temporal church.[37] Even when Jeremy Taylor writes that the "power of the Keyes is by a Metaphor chang'd into a sword," he refers not to St. Peter's power to excommunicate or to smite sinners but to St. Paul's "wish" that "evil persons" should be "cut off from the congregation of the Lord" (*DD*, bk. 3, chap. 4, rule 1, n. 14, 218).

I know of no single Protestant theologian who would not have agreed with Milton when in *Christian Doctrine* he comments that the keys of the kingdom of heaven are not "entrusted to Peter alone" because Peter has "been tried and found wanting" (bk. 1, chap. 33, 567). Perkins likewise had urged English pastors to remember that they are not directly mandated as judges, or as keepers of the keys, but that they are, on the contrary, only "Messengers and Embassadors."[38] Jeremy Taylor, too, admonishes the ideal minister to remember that Christ as head of the church keeps the "spiritual regality and the jurisdiction in his own hands." The power to "smite" sinners is not in the hands of any temporal minister, but in God's, he chides (*DD*, bk. 3, chap. 4, rule 1, n. 17, 220). It is unlikely, therefore, that Milton's contemporaries would have associated Milton's "Pilot" in *Lycidas* with St. Peter, since for them Peter was no different than any other minister of the gospel.

In *Lycidas*, Milton's theme is that the English clergy must feed the sheep, and not (as Perkins often remarks) feed on them. That the English clergy have lost their way and have arrogated to themselves the powers to bind and loose the conscience of their flocks is a dominant idea in the works of Perkins, Sibbes, and Goodwin, Milton's spiritual mentors before 1640.[39] The "dread voice" of the "Pilot of the Galilean lake" belongs to none other than to that "dreadful Judge" who like the Son in Paradise Regained, and like the "dreadful Judge" in "On the Morning of Christ's Nativity," shall shortly overspread Satan's throne in middle air, rendering the false ministers entirely powerless.[40] In Lycidas, however, the prophetic voice of doom is spoken by Christ in his role as bridegroom, as head of the church militant, and as the pilot of what Perkins had called the "ship" of conscience (Discovrse, chap. 4, p. 554, col. 2d).

To support this reading of Milton's similitude, we may profitably turn to Perkins's popular little treatise entitled Deaths Knell, Or, the sicke mans Passing-Bell: Summoning all sicke Consciences to prepare themselues for the comming of the great Day of Doome, lest mercies Gate be shut against them.[41] I quote the title at length because all its rhetorical members are illustrated by highly visual metaphors and tropes that are telling for Lycidas. First, we notice the commonplace maritime application to the ship of passage that carries man to judgment day:

> . . . whilest Worme-like, thou crawlest heere below, fasten all thy faculties vpon the Commandements of thy Creator; for those in thy finall passage, must be the Pylot to steere thee into the Hauen of Heauen; Thinke euery moment thou art in the waning, that the date of thy Pilgrimage is wel-nigh expired, and that the lampe of thy life lyeth twinckling vpon the snuffe; and that now it stands thee vpon to looke toward thy Celestiall home. (Deaths Knell, 1628, sig. A2r)

In this similitude Perkins compares the Word of God as creator to the pilot who steers the ship of conscience by looking homeward to heaven as to the safe shore of death. The familiar expression of this image in Lycidas as "Look homeward Angel" (163) may well have brought tears to the eyes of the seventeenth-century reader, even as in our century these words still have power to move. What we experience as poetic emotion, however, the Puritan reader knew also as theological conviction. Milton's first readers may have remembered, as Milton perhaps does when he admonishes the "woeful Shepherds" to "weep no more" (165), the sermons of such a preacher as Sibbes. Below, for example, Sibbes preaches on Isa. 5:8: "And all teares shall be wiped away from all faces":

> If he [Christ] brings us to heaven through a valley of teares; its no matter, for in heaven all teares shall be wiped from our eyes. And therefore Christianity is called wisdome. . . . What is the chiefest point of wisdome? To looke home to the end, . . . for God will wipe away all teares from their eyes. (*Feast*, sermon 5, on Isa. 25.8, 83)

Even as God shall wipe the tears from the eyes of the saved, so may the figures in *Lycidas* expect their tears to be dried when they consider (as does Master John Dod) that death is a "safe harbour" from the world, from the sea of sin.[42]

Milton's readers may have remembered the sermons of Sibbes, or they may have heard a sermon preached in eulogy upon the death of a Puritan saint. In a compendium of such sermons entitled *The House of Mourning*, a Puritan divine compares "Sathans engines" to the sins of the flesh, and the flesh itself to a "treacherous Pilot" whereby the devil makes "shipwracke" of us all.[43] Of course, Perkins tells us that when conscience is our pilot Satan's methods to ensure shipwreck come to naught:

> And as in the gouerning the ship on the sea, the Pilot holding the helme in his hand, hath alwaies an eie to the compasse; so we likewise, in the ordering of our liues and conuersations, must alwaies haue a speciall regard to conscience. (chap. 4, p. 553, col. 1c)

The similitude Perkins develops above and the one that Milton develops in *Lycidas* suggest to the seventeenth-century reader the image of Christ, the pilot of the conscience, as he admonishes, guides, and governs his apostolic crew of English clergy.

One impediment that the modern reader may raise to such an interpretation is that Milton's speaker has "Mitred locks" (112). The seventeenth-century reader, however, might understand "Mitred" as reflecting its Greek and Latin origins.[44] Milton's captain on the sea of this world may be wearing a simple garland, bonnet, or headress, not a bishop's cap. Or, based upon his knowledge of Gregory the Great's exegesis of Isaiah in *Morals on the Book of Job*, Milton's contemporary reader may think of Christ as head of the church, wearing "a mitre like unto a Bridegroom" (preface, vol. 1, pt. 1, point 14, 26). Or, Milton's early readers may have envisioned, as does Jeremy Taylor in *The Great Exemplar*, man's "Priest" and "Sacrifice" as wearing his own proper "Miter," his "Crown of Thorns."[45]

Milton's figure recalls the prophetic Christ of the Apocalypse, then, and may wear the bonnet or crown of Christ in Judgment. But most of all, Milton's treatment of Christ in *Lycidas* recalls the figure of the Good Shepherd. The false pastors in *Lycidas* have lost what Sibbes, like Perkins, calls the "continuall feast" of a good conscience because, as Perkins notes, they have "pierced" the "apple of the eye" or conscience by sin (Sibbes, *Feast*, sermon 2, 26; Perkins, *Discovrse*, chap. 4, p. 553, col. 1b; p. 554, col. 1d). They have become "Blind mouths" (119) incapable of nourishing themselves or of feeding the hungry sheep in their flocks. Milton portrays the sheep in this poem as rotting and "swoln with wind" (126); in this way, they become an emblem of the easily misguided common man and of the errant conscience itself.

Similarly, in Thomas Fuller's dialogue on Prov. 18:14 entitled *The Cause and Cure of a Wounded Conscience*, the speaker Philologus elaborates a similitude centering upon the image of the suffering conscience aimlessly wandering like a flock of sheep:

> Sheep are observed to flye without cause, scared, (as some say) with the *sound* of their own *feet*: Their feet knack, because they flye, and they fly, because their feet knack, an *emblem* of Gods Children in *a wounded conscience*, selfe-fearing, selfe-frighted.[46]

In *Lycidas* the sheep likewise symbolize the English church as God's children who are lost and hungry in the moral wilderness created by a lack of spiritual leadership. The clergy are not looking after either their own consciences or the conscience of their flock. As a result, they will render judgment upon themselves when at the final day their consciences will be "selfe-frighted," and, we may imagine, self-smitten.

Perkins in *Deaths Knell* brings into the realm of personal terror the image of the awakened, reprobate conscience when he discusses the "sting of a guilty crying conscience" one feels when the "force of death" begins "cracking thy heart-strings asunder." Then, he says, a sinner would give anything for but a "dayes contrition" or an "houres repentance" in order to clear the soul of its "duty to God promised, but not performed" ([sig. A5r]). The unrepentant clergy of *Lycidas* have not performed their duty either to God or to man; such fellows will tremble in fear when on their deathbeds their guilty consciences cry out against them.

When Milton composes his similitude of Christ in Judgment he has in mind, perhaps, a passage such as the following one from Perkins's *Deaths Knell*:

> What wouldst thou doe, when stripped and turned out of thy house of Clay, into the World of Wormes, . . . from thence to be conuented before a most seuere Judge, carrying in thy owne bosome, thy Inditement ready written and a perfect Register of all thy mis-deedes; when thou shouldest behold the glorious Maiestie of Jesus Christ, (clothed in white linnen, through which, his body shining like precious stones, his eyes like burning Lampes, his face like lightning, his Armes and Legs like flaming Brasse, and his Voice as the shout of a multitude) prepared to passe the sentence vpon thee; when thou shouldest see the great Judge offended aboue thee, hell open beneath thee; the Furnace flaming, the Deuils waiting, the World burning, thy conscience accusing, and thy selfe standing as a forlorne wretch, to receiue thy fearefull and irrecouerable sentence of condemnation? ([sig. A5r-A5v])

"Oh," Perkins remarks, "bethinke thy selfe, how these visions would affright thee" ([sig. A5v]). Such a powerful vision may be the theological, literary counterpart for Milton's passage on the clergy in *Lycidas*. There we may imagine the mitered Christ as a wrathful figure holding the keys of David, opening the graves of the English clergy, reading from the book of conscience, and cataloguing the duties not performed. The vision closes with a terrifying image of the individual conscience standing up and preparing, first, to accuse and, after, to smite.

The woeful voice of Christ in his role as Judge forecasts the doom of the fallen clergy who have neglected to follow the teaching of the Good Shepherd. Because an evil conscience is the greatest enemy a person can have, at the last day it will raise its hand to smite the soul for the last time. We will recall that for Perkins conscience is of "great force and beares a great stroke" (*Discovrse*, chap. 2, p. 537, col. 1a). Perhaps Milton's "two-handed engine" of the conscience becomes in *Lycidas* "as a sword to slay the soule" (see *Discovrse*, chap. 4, p. 552, col. 2d).

Whatever scholars may ultimately conclude about the "two-handed engine," no one could disagree that in *Lycidas* Milton sets the picture of the evil preacher against his portrait of Edward King as the true pastor who becomes the engine, the "Genius of the shore" (183). After his death, "Young Lycidas" (9) is enobled, perhaps, as the "Watchman" and "Intelligencer" (as Jeremy Taylor might say) of the place. It is no accident that the poetic construct "Genius of the shore" mirrors in syntax, stress, and rhyme the "engine at the door."[47] The shore here is the analogue for the door of the heart, and for the gate of death that "opes" (111) into the heavenly home. Milton also compares Lycidas to the spirit of Christ who retroactively guides "all that wander in that perilous flood" (185) of ancient philosophy prior to the revelation of the Word.[48] All this the young man receives in recompense for his lost potential role as spiritual guide and conscience to his English flock.

Milton mourns for Lycidas, then, because the drowned youth cannot take his place among the responsible clergy who, like William Perkins, had provided a steady hand to guide the ship of conscience for the English nation. In such a context, the image of Milton's engine may be understood as drawn first from that common fund of similitudes that were the stock-in-trade for the Cambridge-trained, Protestant divine.

I have argued that to discover a theological context system for Milton's similitude of the "two-handed engine" implies that the continental tradition of pictorial iconography may not prove entirely satisfactory. Even so, like other scholars, I am fascinated by the possibility of pictorial analogues for *Lycidas*. There are, in fact, two interesting illustrations by English artists that support my case for Milton's figure with the keys as Christ and for the trope of the "two-handed engine" as signifying the double powers of the human conscience to accuse and smite.

One of these illustrations Milton did not see, but the other illustration he may well have seen.

The first is a drawing of Christ holding the keys (fig. 1) by an English Franciscan monk, Brother William of the order of the Minors. It was executed as an illustration for a thirteenth-century English commentary on the apocalypse and may be found in facsimile in the Peter Brieger's *English Art 1216–1307*, pl. 55a.[49] Brieger explains that this illustration is a simple one executed with "only light yellow wash" for the "hair and the garments, with red for the flames of the candles and black for the pupils of the eyes" (161). He also says that the spiritual tradition of Joachim of Fiore accounts, possibly, for the relative peacefulness of the figure. What is useful for our purposes, though, is that Christ in this drawing obviously holds in his hand the keys to hell and death; the early English imaginative interest in the Christ of Revelation as the keeper of the keys is demonstrated in a pictorial way that was clearly not popular on the continent.

The second illustration, the one that Milton may have seen, is the title page woodcut to one of Perkins's numerous editions of *Deaths Knell* (fig. 2).[50] According to Peter W. M. Blayney, as an example of the English printmaker's art, this simple woodcut, a block print, is quite ordinary, although it may represent a "specific moment" illustration, one created from a drawing presented, possibly, along with the text.[51] This illustration may owe, too, to the tradition of English "tomb art favored by members of the highest secular and religious estates in fifteenth-century England" identified by Marjorie Malvern.[52] She notes, for example, that the medieval manuscript of "A Disputacion betwyx þe Body and Wormes" (1450) features drawings of worms that are intended to portray the "devourers of the Body's flesh" as well as to suggest the "Body's 'pricke of conscience'" (426). The skeleton in the *Deaths Knell* illustration clearly owes to the "tomb art" identified by Malvern. Then, too, one of Perkins's favorite images is also the "worme of conscience" (*Discovrse*, chap. 4, p. 553, col. 1d), although the illustrator may not have been aware it.

What seems plausible is that the artist attempts to accommodate Perkins's newfangled idea of an anthropormorphic conscience to the medieval English tradition of tomb art. What is not clear is whether or not the

Fig. 1

Deaths Knell,

Or, *The sicke Mans Paßing-Bell* :

Summoning all sick Consciences to pr

pare themselves for the comming of the grea
Day of Doome, lest mercies gate be shut
against them.
Fit for all those that desire to arrive at the
Heavenly Jerusalem.

Whereunto are added Prayers fit for Housholders.

The sixteenth Edition.

Written by *W. Perkins.*

Printed at London for *John Wright*, and are to be so
at his Shop without Newgate. 1637.

Fig. 2

artist knowingly met the conventions of the continental tradition calling for the painter to depict a miniature human being leaving the dead body, and to represent death as a skeleton or as father time.[53] Whatever the composition history behind the illustration, the soul of the sinner seems to appear as the darkened outline of a small circular form on the left shoulder of the dying man.[54] By the window (representing, possibly, the cross,[55] or the door to life) stands a Doppelgänger, a partially realized other-self.[56] The figure is also poised very much as were the jacks of the clock houses, with one hand ready to ring the passing bell and the other to strike the hour. Here, though, the figure readies itself to smite with death's dart.

The dart as the emblem of the guilty conscience is familiar from Spenser's House of Holiness in *The Faerie Queene* (1.10.18–29).[57] Likewise familiar to Milton's seventeenth-century audience may have been Timotheus in Thomas Fuller's *Cause and Cure of a Wounded Conscience* who asks, "*Why is a* wounded conscience *by* David resembled to Arrowes?*" (Dialogue 4, 28). In the woodcut on the title page to *Deaths Knell*, the skeletal figure may represent the standing conscience who prepares to ring the bell summoning the soul to judgment day.

Perkins writes at the end of *Deaths Knell* that at the moment of death no one will offer to go with the sinner—no one, that is, except his "bosome-friend, his Conscience" ([sig. B3r]). Perhaps the standing figure in the illustration is as close as we shall ever come to finding a picture of Milton's "two-handed engine" standing "at the door," ready to "smite once and smite no more."

Notes

1. The poetry of John Milton is quoted from *John Milton: Complete Poetry and Major Prose*, ed. Merritt Y. Hughes (New York: The Odyssey Press, 1957).

2. See William Perkins, *A Discovrse of Conscience. Wherein is set Down the nature, properties, and differences thereof: as also the way to get and keepe good Conscience*, 2nd

ed., vol. 1 of *The Workes of . . . William Perkins* (London: Printed by Iohn Legatt, Printer to the Vniuersitie of Cambridge, 1612), chap. 2, p. 519, col. 1a; and chap. 4, p. 552, col. 2b-p. 553, col. 1c. DFo call number STC 19650, vol. 1. Hereafter referred to as *Discovrse.*

3. Edward S. Le Comte, *A Milton Dictionary* (New York: Philosophical Library, 1961), s.v. "engine at the door, that two-handed," 114–15, refers to the problem of the "engine" as the "most celebrated (non-textual) crux in English literature" and reviews scholarly opinion prior to 1950. See, also, his "'That Two-Handed Engine' and Savonarola," *Studies in Philology* 47 (1950): 589–606. The genesis of my essay dates from a conversation with Professor Christopher Hill, Balliol College, Oxford, who encouraged me to pursue my interpretation of the "two-handed engine" as the human conscience. I am grateful to Professor Joseph Anthony Wittreich, Jr., The University of Maryland, and to Professor Mary A. Maleski, Le Moyne College, who read versions of the text. I wish, also, to thank the competent and kindly staffs of the Folger Shakespeare Library and the British Library.

4. William Haller explains the divine similitude as a preaching device, a poetic and imagistic elaboration of biblical texts. See *The Rise of Puritanism: Or, the Way to the New Jerusalem as Set Forth in Pulpit and Press from Thomas Cartwright to John Lilburne and John Milton, 1570–1643* (New York: Columbia University Press, 1938; Philadelphia: University of Pennsylvania Press, 1972), 147–48.

5. Exhaustive critical opinion on the "two-handed engine" may be found in the excellent note on *"Lycidas"*, lines 130–31, in *A Variorum Commentary on the Poems of John Milton*, vol. 2, *The Minor English Poems*, pt. 2, by A. S. P. Woodhouse and Douglas Bush (London: Routledge & Kegan Paul, 1972), 686–706. See, also, Balachandra Rajan's article on *Lycidas* in *A Milton Encyclopedia*, ed. William B. Hunter, Jr. (Lewisburg: Bucknell University Press, 1979), vol. 5, Le–N, 55–56. See, also, Louis Martz, *Poet of Exile: A Study of Milton's Poetry* (New Haven: Yale University Press, 1980), 71; Kathleen M. Swaim, "The Pilot of the Galilean Lake in *Lycidas*," *Milton Quarterly* 17 (May 1983): 42–45.

C. A. Patrides cites various "conjectures" of Milton's editors in *Milton's "Lycidas": The Tradition and the Poem* (Columbia: University of Missouri Press, 1983), 356–57. S. Viswanathan isolates "three major schools of interpretation" depending upon whether the engine is a sword, an axe, or the scales of St. Michael at the Last Judgment. See "'That Two-handed Engine,' Yet Once More," *Archiv für Das Studium Der Neueren Sprachen und Literaturen* 217 (1980): 108–11.

6. See Jeremy Taylor, *Dvctor Dvbitantivm, or the Rule of Conscience In all her generall measures; Serving as a great Instrument for the determination of Cases of Conscience.* In Four Books, 2nd ed. (London: Printed by James Flesher, for Richard Royston, 1660), title-page; bk. 1, chap. 4, rule 2, n. 22, 134. DFo call number 153329. Hereafter abbreviated *DD.*

7. Ralph E. Hone, "The Pilot of the Galilean Lake," *Studies in Philology* 56 (1959): 55–61; and W. Arthur Turner, "The Quest of the Mysterious Engine," *Milton Quarterly* 13 (1979): 19.

8. See Claes Schaar, *The Full Voic'd Quire Below: Vertical Context Systems in "Paradise Lost,"* Lund Studies in English 60 (Lund: C .W. K. Gleerup, 1982), 17–18. Schaar argues that in the poetry of Dante, Milton, and Eliot, "surface context is charged with significance by contact with the infracontext, the hidden word pattern." To the informed reader the "surface context" operates as a "signal" that "triggers a memory" of another literary similitude, or "infracontext." The reading process then coalesces the "surface and infracontexts" into a "sign." My argument is that modern criticism has created a sub-text for Milton's "two-handed engine" that is often only accidentally close to the seventeenth-century theological context. We can reconcile many critical disagreements by illustrating the way the term conscience functions as a sign for Milton's contemporaries. (I am grateful to Barbara Lewalski for pointing out the usefulness of Schaar's methodology for my work.)

9. See Mother Mary Christopher Pecheux, "The Dread Voice in *Lycidas,*" *Milton Studies* 9 (1976): 224, 234; and Karl Felsen, *Milton Quarterly* 9 (1975): 6–14; Philip Rollison, "The Traditional Contexts of Milton's 'Two-Handed Engine'," *English Language Notes* 9 (1971): 29.

10. Turner, 18, 19.

11. G. M. Young observes that a useful introduction to the recovery of nineteenth-century cultural history might be to follow a young man's intellectual development as he searches "for some creed by which to steer at such a time." *Victorian England: Portrait of an Age,* 2nd ed. (1953; repr., London: Oxford University Press, 1977), 1. Elizabeth Marie Pope suggests that Milton could count on a "common fund of knowledge he shared with his audience" and that it is necessary to "recover a lost frame of reference" in order to deal with the traditions of the past. *"Paradise Regained": The Tradition and the Poem* (Baltimore: Johns Hopkins Press, 1947), xiii.

12. See n. 2 above.

13. See *The Jewish Encyclopedia* (New York: Funk and Wagnalls, 1904), s.v. "conscience"; and *The New Schaff-Herzog Encyclopedia of Religious Knowledge* (New York: Funk and Wagnalls, 1909), s.v. "conscience."

14. For background reading see Ian Breward's introduction to *The Work of William Perkins,* vol. 3 of The Courtenay Library of Reformation Classics (Appleford, Abingdon, Berkshire, England: The Sutton Courtenay Press, 1970), 64, 85–87, 95.

15. William Ames, *Conscience with the Power and Cases Thereof,* Devided into V. bookes . . . Translated out of Latine into English . . . [n.p.] Imprinted 1639, facsimile of Bodleian Library, Oxford copy STC 552, The English Experience no. 708 (Norwood, New Jersey: Walter J. Johnson, 1975), summary of bk. 1, position 2, 49.

16. John Milton, *Christian Doctrine,* ed. Maurice Kelley and trans. John Carey, in *Complete Prose Works of John Milton,* vol. 6, ca. 1658–1660 (New Haven and London: Yale University Press, 1973), bk. 1, chap. 33, 623. Hereafter abbreviated *CD.* Cf. *De Doctrina Christiana,* ed. James Holly Hanford and Waldo Hilary Dunn and trans. Charles R. Sumner, in *The Works of John Milton,* vol. 16 (New York: Columbia University Press, 1934), 356: "Norma iudicii erit ipsa conscientia, ex illa luce quam quisque accepit."

17. Cf. *De Doctrina Christiana,* trans. Charles R. Sumner, *Works,* 16:356, 358.

Rom ii.12. quicunque absque lege peccaverunt, . . . per legem damnabuntur. et v. [sic] 14. nam quum gentes quae legem non habent natura quae legis sunt faciunt; . . . sibi ipsis sunt lex: ut qui ostendant opus legis scriptum in cordibus suis; una testimonium reddente ipsorum conscientia, et cogitationibus se mutuo accusantibus aut excusantibus; in die quo iudicabit Dominus de occultis hominum ex evangelio meo, per Iesum Christum. . . . Apoc. xx. 12. et libri aperti sunt: . . . iudicatique sunt mortui ex iis quae scripta erant in libris, secundum opera ipsorum.

18. For an illuminating speculation on this point, see Camille Wells Slights, *The Casuistical Tradition in Shakespeare, Donne, Herbert, and Milton* (Princeton: Princeton University Press, 1981), 295.

19. When Milton refers to writing prose with his left hand, he may well have alluded to Perkins whose right hand was "lame," yet who, like "Ehud, Jud. 3.15" defended the faith with his left hand. See Thomas Fuller's "Life and Death of William Perkins," *Abel Redevivus: Or, The dead yet speaking. The Lives and Deaths of the Moderne Divines* (London: Printed by Tho. Brudenell for John Stafford, 1651), 428 [actually 438: page numbers not consecutive]. DFo 2400. See, also, Thomas Merrill, ed. and intro., *William Perkins, 1558–1602: English Puritanist: His Pioneer Works on Casuistry: "A Discourse of Conscience" and "The Whole Treatise of Cases of Conscience"* (The Hague: Nieuwkoop and B. De Graaf, 1966), xvii.

20. Thomas Taylor, *Christs Combate and Conquest: Or, the Lyon of the tribe of Iudah, vanquishing the Roaring Lyon, assaulting him in three most fierce and hellish Temptations* ([Cambridge]: Printed by Cantrell Legge, Printer to the Vniuersitie of Cambridge, 1618), [commentary on Matt. 4:6, reason 1], 230. DFo STC 23822.

21. See Doctor Harris's comment in "The Life and Death of Mrs. Elizabeth Wilkinson, who dyed Anno Christi 1654," in Samuel Clarke, ed., *A General Martyrologie, containing A Collection of all the Greatest Persecutions which have Befallen the Church of Christ, From the Creation, to our Present Times; wherein is given an exact Account of the Protestants sufferings in Queen Maries Reign. Whereunto is Added the Lives of Thirty Two English Divines . . .* , 3rd ed. (London: William Birch, 1677), pt. 2, 424. Hereafter referred to as *General Martyrologie.*

22. Professor Christopher Hill, in a letter to the author, 29 Nov. 1982, sent this information from his acquaintance, Mr. Burden.

23. Oxford English Dictionary, s.v. "Two-handed."

24. William Perkins, *The Combate Betweene Christ and the Deuill displayed: Or A Commentarie vpon the Temptations of Christ*, 2nd ed. much enlarged (Printed for E. Edgar, 1613), in vol. 3 of *The Workes of . . . Mr. W. Perkins* ([Cambridge]: Printed by Cantrell Legge, Printer to the Vniuersitie of Cambridge, 1613), [commentary upon Matt. 4:6], p. 393, col. 1a. DFo STC 19650, vol. 3.

25. John Reesing notes that "images of rod and staff conspicuously recur, along with images of smiting," in the tenth chapter of Isaiah. The "multivalent image of the rod comes to symbolize a divine power that in a single act works vengeance upon

the wicked and deliverance for the faithful." *Milton's Poetic Art: A Mask, "Lycidas," and "Paradise Lost"* (Cambridge, Mass.: Harvard University Press, 1968), 31–32. Reesing's interpretation is substantiated by William Perkins when he writes that "it is a peculiar priuiledge" of Christ's "rodde" to "smite and wound the conscience" (*Discovrse*, chap. 2, argum. 7., 1. Cor. 4:21, p. 527, col. 2a). James F. Forrest argues that Bunyan's "'instrument'" of "prayer" conveys the "double potential of condemnation and commendation." See "Milton and the Divine Art of Weaponry: 'That Two-Handed Engine' and Bunyan's 'Nameless Terrible Instrument' at Mouthgate," *Milton Studies* 16 (1982): 132.

26. See Harry F. Robins, "Milton's 'Two-Handed Engine at the Door' and St. Matthew's Gospel," *Review of English Studies*, n.s., 5 (1954): 25–36. Robins concludes that the "two-handed engine" represents "the Son as God's instrument of judgement" (31).

27. For transliteration of the Greek, I am grateful to my colleague at Howard University, Professor Carrie Cowherd, Department of Classics.

28. See The *New Schaff-Herzog Encyclopedia of Religious Knowledge*, s.v. "conscience."

29. Claud Adelbert Thompson, "'That Two-Handed Engine' Will Smite: Time Will Have a Stop," *Studies in Philology* 59 (1962): 187 n. 7; 193.

30. June Winter, "The Two-Handed Engine and the Fatal Bellman: 'Lycidas' and 'Macbeth,'" *Notes & Queries*, n.s., 26 (1979): 126–28.

31. John Donne, "Hymn to God my God, in my sicknesse," lines 4–5, in *The Complete Poetry of John Donne*, ed. John T. Shawcross (Garden City, New York: Doubleday Anchor Books, 1967), 390. Donne's use of this phrase was called to mind by Joseph E. Duncan's article entitled "Donne's 'Hymne to God My God, in my sicknesse' and Iconographic Tradition," *John Donne Journal* 3 (1984): 157–80.

32. William Perkins, *A Salve For a Sicke Man. Or, A Treatise Containing the Natvre, Differences, and Kindes of Death, As also the right manner of dying well* (London: Iohn Legatt, 1612), in vol. 1 of *The Workes of . . . William Perkins* (London, 1612), 491, col. 1c.

33. I am indebted to Professor Victoria Arana Robinson, Howard University, for the term "ingenious device."

34. Richard Sibbcs, *The Gloriovs Feast of the Gospel. Or, Christ's gracious Invitation and royall Entertainment of Believers . . .* (London: Printed for John Rothwell, 1650). DFo S3736, copy 1, bd. w. STC 22491. Hereafter referred to as *Feast*.

35. *Morals on the Book of Job by St. Gregory the Great*, 3 vols., trans. John Henry Parker and J. Rivington, in *A Library of Fathers of the Holy Catholic Church, Anterior to the Division of the East and West* (London: Oxford University Press, 1844–1847), vol. 3, pt. 6, bk. 29, sec. 16, points 29–30, 321.

36. Richard Baxter, *A Christian Directory. The First Part, Christian Ethicks . . .* (London, 1677), in *A Christian Directory: Or, A Summ of Practical Theologie, and Cases of Conscience. . . . In Four Parts*, 2nd ed. (London: Printed, by Robert White, for Nevil Simmons, 1678), pt. 1, chap. 4, pt. 3, n. 29, dir. 24, 179. DFo B1220.

37. See Thomas Kranidas, "Milton's *Lycidas*," *The Explicator* 38 (Fall 1979): 29–30;

and Pecheux, "The Dread Voice in *Lycidas*," 234. Cf. William P. Shaw, *"Lycidas* 130–131: Christ as Judge and Protector," *Modern Language Studies* 7 (1977): 39, 41.

38. William Perkins, *The second Treatise of the Duties and Dignities of the Ministerie* (Printed for W. Welkie, Cantrell Legge, 1613), in vol. 3 of *The Workes of ... Mr. W. Perkins*, ([Cambridge], 1613), 462, col. 1c.

39. See William Haller, *The Rise of Puritanism*, 294.

40. See Milton's "On the Morning of Christ's Nativity," stanza 17, line 164; and "the dreaded Infant's hand," stanza 25, line 222.

41. William Perkins, *Deaths knell: or, The sicke mans Passing-Bell: Summoning all sicke Consciences to prepare themselues for the comming of the great Day of Doome, lest mercies Gate be shut against them . . .*, 9th ed. (London: Printed for M. Trundle, 1628). DFo call number STC U–19684. Subsequent references in the text are to this edition.

42. "The Life of Master John Dod, who died Anno Christi 1645," in *The Lives of Thirty-Two English Divines . . .* , *General Martyrologie*, 171. For a discussion of the wiping of tears as an "activity customarily associated with Christ's Pastoral function," with special reference to seventeenth-century exegesis of Hebrews and Isaiah, see Joseph Anthony Wittreich, Jr., *Visionary Poetics: Milton's Tradition and His Legacy* (San Marino, California: Henry E. Huntington Library and Art Gallery, 1979), 146–53.

43. "A Christians Victorie; or, Conqvest over Deaths Enmitie" (London: Printed by Iohn Dawson, for Ralph Mabbe, 1638), sermon 13 in *Threnoikos* [Greek Transliterated]: *The House of Movrning; . . . Delivered in XLVII Sermons, Preached at the Funeralls of divers faithfull Servants of Christ*, by Daniel Featly, and others (London: Printed by G. Dawson, for R. M., 1640), 271. DFo 24048.

44. *Oxford English Dictionary*, s.v. "mitre." See, also, Pecheux, "The Dread Voice in *Lycidas*," 228; 240 n. 22.

45. Jeremy Taylor, *The Great Exemplar of Sanctity and Holy Life according to the Christian Institution. Described In the History of the Life and Death of . . . Jesus Christ*. In three parts (London: Printed by R. N. for Francis Ash, 1649), pt. 3, ad. sect. 15, n. 6, 161. DFo 138200.

46. Thomas Fuller, *The Cause and Cure of a Wounded Conscience* (London: Printed for John Williams, 1647), Dialogue 4, 23. DFo F2414, bd. w. M2785.

47. On the etymology linking "engine" and "genius" with doorkeepers see Forrest, "Milton and the Divine Art of Weaponry," 137, 140 n.23.

48. On this topic see Jason Rosenblatt, "The Angel and the Shepherd in *Lycidas*," *Philological Quarterly* 62, no. 2 (Spring 1983): 253, 257 n. 3; and John C. Ulreich, Jr., "'And by Occasion Foretells': The Prophetic Voice in *Lycidas*," *Milton Studies* 18 (1983): 3.

49. See Peter Brieger, *English Art 1216–1307*, vol. 4 of *The Oxford History of English Art* ed. T. S. R. Boase (Clarendon: Oxford University Press, 1957), pl. 55a. I am grateful to Mr. David Hagen, photographer of the Audio Visual Learning Resource Center, Georgetown University, for a slide which I showed at the Le Moyne Conference in Honor of Professor Joseph H. Summers, Oct. 23, 1983. For the tradition illustrating Christ with the two-edged sword, see A. M. Gibbs, "'That Two-Handed

Engine' and Some Renaissance Emblems," *Review of English Studies*, n.s., 31 (1980): 178–83.

50. *Deaths Knell* was in its ninth edition by 1628, and in its sixteenth edition by 1637.

51. Dr. Peter W. M. Blayney, Scholar-in-Residence at the Folger Shakespeare Library, and expert on early British printing, graciously shared with me his opinion of the woodcut and title-page of the 1637 edition of *Deaths Knell*.

52. Marjorie M. Malvern, "An Earnest 'Monyscyon' and ! inge Delectabyll" Realized Verbally and Visually in "'A Disputacion betwyx ! e Body and Wormes,' A Middle English Poem Inspired by Tomb Art and Northern Spirituality," *Viator: Medieval and Renaissance Studies* 13 (1982): 419.

53. See Erwin Panofsky's chapter 3, "Father Time," in *Studies in Iconology: Humanistic Themes in the Art of the Renaissance* (London: Oxford University, 1939; repr., Harper & Row, 1972), 69–93. For artistic representations of Death with a spear, see Roland Mushat Frye, *Milton's Imagery and the Visual Arts: Iconographic Tradition in the Epic Poems* (Princeton: Princeton University Press, 1978), 117. Joseph H. Summers discusses Milton's figure of Death in *The Muse's Method: An Introduction to "Paradise Lost"* (Cambridge: Harvard University Press, 1962), 46–47, 49, 55.

54. I am indebted to helpful questions and hypotheses offered from the audience at the Le Moyne Conference in Honor of Professor Joseph H. Summers, Oct. 23, 1983, especially to Sister Mary Irma Corcoran and Professor Marjorie M. Malvern.

55. Cf. Duncan, "Donne's 'Hymne to God my God, in my sicknesse' and Iconographic Tradition," 157–58.

56. I borrow the term "Doppelgänger" from Carl E. Schorske's discussion of Freud's relationship to Arthur Schnitzler in *Fin-De-Siècle Vienna: Politics and Culture* (New York: Alfred A. Knopf, 1980), 11, 23 n. 7. Professor Schorske's comment that one of Schnitzler's typical characters is "paralyzed" by "hypertrophied sensibilities" (14) illustrates that the seventeenth-century concern with a deadened conscience is still of moral and intellectual interest.

57. For this reference, I am indebted to Dr. Kathleen Lesko, Consultant for Planning and Development, Georgetown University.

Milton on the Creation of Eve: Adam's Dream and the Hieroglyphic of the Rib

FANNIE PECZENIK

In Book 8 of *Paradise Lost* Adam, who has heard with wonder of the war in Heaven and how the world was created to fill the vacant space left by the Fall of the rebel angels, tells his own story. His awakening to consciousness culminates in his request for a mate, but his account of the actual creation of Eve is brief, somewhat less than thirty lines, and ostensibly little more than a slight fleshing out of the bare Genesis narrative. After the cosmic flight and the novelty of an epic battle fought by incorporeal spirits, it is easy to overlook the significance of an event which seems familiar and self-evident. Yet in the light of the hexameral speculations widespread in the seventeenth century, Adam's description of his dream-vision of the creation of Eve is perhaps no less full of strange, new wonders than the war in Heaven. As I shall show in the following study of the commentaries, Milton's version of Gen. 2:21–24 is a profound critique of the prevailing contemporary beliefs. His creation of Eve is remarkably secular and free of the harshness and embarrassment that is almost always present in the standard interpretations. The uniqueness of Adam's dream-vision, fragile even in the context of the prelapsarian world, becomes apparent when he tries to append traditional questions about Eve's creation to his narrative. Only the Archangel's appeal to Adam's still uncorrupted reason makes him see that his doubts are based on misapprehensions and that they have no place in the unfallen imagination. But when Eve offers him the forbidden fruit, Adam once again reinterprets his dream-vision, this time succumbing to the received popular opinions. Immediately after the Fall, the crudest interpretations of the origin of woman, baldly misogynous, find their place in his vituperation of Eve. Adam's exegeses of her creation, changing with the shift in consciousness from innocent to disobedient, chart the course of his Fall.

The Hebrew word for Adam's sleep in Gen. 2:21 is *tardemah*, which means a torpor or state of senselessness. Rabbinic commentary interprets the sleep as a device used by God to prevent Adam from knowing the truth about Eve's origin.[1] The Talmud says that the sleep prevented Adam from seeing God extract the rib because if he had seen it, he would have found the woman disgusting.[2] Rashi explains that Adam was cast into a sleep so that he would not see the piece of flesh from which Eve was created, whereby she would have been humiliated in his eyes.[3] Not only does the sleep hide the facts of Eve's bloody birth, but it also makes a secret of their close kinship. The rabbis believe that Adam would not have been moved to love Eve if he had known that she was taken out of his own body. As a gloss to Eve's creation, in *Midrash Rabbah* a woman tells how she was to marry a relative, but because they had been brought up in the same house, he found her unattractive and chose instead to marry another woman less beautiful than she.[4] The deep, unconscious sleep, therefore, serves the dual purpose of shielding Adam from disgust and Eve from his contempt.

Christian exegesis, however, transforms Adam's sleep into a mode of revelation. Since Adam awakes to recognize Eve as bone of his bone and flesh of his flesh, the exegetes argue that God must have revealed the truth of her origin to him while he slept. Adam's sleep is not like the natural sleep which arises from the vapors of the stomach in ordinary men, but like the visionary sleep of the Patriarchs.[5] As a result, the Hebrew *tardemah*, though rendered literally as a "deep sleep," becomes identical with the Greek *ecstatis* of the Septuagint. John Salkeld, in his exposition of the six days of creation, calls it "an extaticall sleepe or a sleepe extasis: a sleepe, because the text in rigor doth signifie a sleep; an extasis, or rapt, because hee had then his minde supernaturally illuminated and filled with a propheticall spirit."[6] Hieronymus Zanchius specifies the form of supernatural illumination: when God led Eve to Adam, he understood that she was his wife because in his ecstasy he had seen her formed from his rib.[7] Moreover, the deep sleep imparts

higher knowledge to Adam than the origin of his wife. In the typolog-
ical reading the birth of Eve from the side of the sleeping Adam fore-
shadows the birth of the Church from the side of the wounded Christ
on the Cross. Because Eph. 5:31 repeats Adam's words of recognition
to Eve in Gen. 2:24, St. Augustine concludes that Adam is transported
in a trance to the *curia*, the heavenly meeting place, where he is divinely
inspired and wakes to speak of the mystery of Christ and His Church.[8]
In the Christian tradition the deep sleep does not hide the truth of Eve's
creation from Adam, but instead it becomes the source of his specific
knowledge of her origin and awakens his mind to religious mystery.

Yet while the general belief among the Christian exegetes is that the
method of Eve's creation was revealed to Adam, the rabbinic belief that
the sleep served as a means of concealment survives. The focus of the
concealment is now, however, not the close kinship of the first two hu-
man beings nor Eve's perhaps humiliating origin, but only the physical
reality of extracting a rib from Adam's side. Thus while Calvin argues
that Adam must have been informed of the facts of Eve's creation or
else God's work would have been superfluous, he adds that the sleep
was sent upon Adam to "exempt him from pain and trouble."[9] Or, as
the expositor Andrew Willett explains in greater detail, when Adam's
soul was in an ecstasy, his body was bound in a deep sleep so "that
neither Adams sight might be offended in seeing his side opened and
a ribbe taken forthe, not yet his sense of feeling oppressed, with the
griefe thereof."[10] The full surgical implication of this literal-minded ex-
egesis is summed up in the description of the creation of Eve in Syl-
vester's Du Bartas where God casts a sleep over Adam to serve as a form
of general anaesthesia:

> Even as a Surgion, minding off to cut
> Some cure-lesse limbe; . . .
> Bringeth his Patient in a sense-less slumber,
> And grief-less then (guided by use and Art)
> To save the whole, sawes off th'infected part:
> So, God empal'd our Grandsires lively looke,
> Through all his bones a deadly chilnesse strooke,
> Siel'd-up his sparkling Eyes with iron bands,

Led downe his feet (almost) to *Lethe* sands;
In briefe, so numb'd his Soules and Bodies sence,
That (without paine) opening his side. . . .[11]

Although for the Christian exegetes there is no danger that Adam's knowledge of their close physical bond would cause him to reject Eve, the disgust with the extraction of the rib persists and the sleep remains, at least in part, a natural means of shielding Adam from an unpleasant truth.

This view of Adam's sleep is not, however, universal among the Christian exegetes. Luther frees the sleep from the harsh naturalism implicit in a creation that requires anaesthesia by arguing that Adam is spared violence because of the mystery and majesty of the divine work. He reads the *tardemah* as a heavy, dreamless sleep, a sleep so sound that Adam is unaware that God extracts a rib from his side, but Luther cautions that it is meaningless to speculate on the physical details of the work of God who creates by His Word: "We should not suppose that, like a surgeon, He did some cutting."[12] For Luther the sleep hides nothing; it is a benevolent vehicle of transformation such as, in place of death, would have transported Adam to the spiritual life had he remained obedient.

The sleep of Adam in *Paradise Lost* is a mode of revelation, but in other respects it does not fulfill the functions adduced by the exegetical tradition. Milton's Adam is cast into a sleep neither to learn of the highest spiritual mysteries nor to avoid unpalatable physical realities—neither to learn of the birth of the Church nor to be shielded from pain. Though his sleep is visionary, it is the natural fatigue of a man who has been conversing with Omnipotence:

> strain'd to the highth
> In that celestial Colloquy sublime,
> As with an object that excels the sense,
> Dazzl'd and spent, sunk down, and sought repair
> Of sleep, which instantly fell on me, call'd
> By Nature as in aid, and clos'd mine eyes.
> (8.454–59)[13]

His sleep does not draw him into a heavenly meeting place; the "celestial Colloquy" that proves too much for human sense takes place before he sleeps, and now he is brought back to earth. Yet though Adam returns to the realm of nature, his sleep is not anaesthetic, pain so far being peculiar only to the rebel angels. In Milton's version of the sleep of Adam nature and revelation converge. The physical act of extracting the rib is neither harmful nor loathsome. Adam is cast into an ecstatic sleep with his inner eye, "the Cell / Of Fancy" (8.460–61), opened to a dream.[14]

The terrestial dream of Adam in *Paradise Lost* brings him a vision of domestic life in the Garden, a vision which depends largely on his exegesis of the creation of Eve from the rib. Throughout the long history of hexameral interpretation, the rib is a potent and popular emblem of the character of woman and her status in marriage. From the rabbinic commentaries onward, it is assumed that woman derives all of her essential femaleness from the properties of the rib. According to *Midrash Rabbah*, because God intended to create a modest woman, he chose the rib which is the "modest part of man, for even when he stands naked, that part is covered."[15] The rabbis enumerate other parts of the human body, head, feet, hands, heart, etc., to show how each one would have caused the woman to be defective. For the Christian exegetes the rib not only defines the woman but, more significantly, it is a rationale for female subordination. Aquinas alters the scope of the rabbinic catalogue so that it becomes hierarchical and determines the status of woman vis-à-vis her husband:

The woman should neither have *authority over the man* — and therefore she was not formed from his head; nor should she be despised by the man, as though she were merely his slave — and so she was not formed from his feet.[16]

At the midpoint of the human body, the rib establishes the pre-eminence of the husband although it also sets limits on his authority and on the wife's subjection.

The very form of Eve's creation, that she is made after Adam and from a part of his body, contrives to make her seem derivative and is used as another powerful argument for female subjection. The *locus clas-*

254 □ *Fannie Peczenik*

sicus for this argument is St. Paul: "For the man is not of the woman, but the woman of the man" (1 Cor. 11:8). Calvin comments on this passage that "as the woman derives her origin from man, she is therefore inferior in rank."[17] More specifically, the expositor Daniel Rogers argues that since God could easily have created Eve contemporaneously with Adam and without his rib, by creating her as He did, He meant to ennoble the male sex and subject the female.[18] A corollary to Eve's subjection implied in the manner of her creation is that woman is less than man because she is made from only one of his twelve ribs. As Sir Thomas Browne says: "The whole woman was made for man, but only a twelfth part of the man for the woman."[19] Other commentators hasten to add, however, that while man is the greater part of the woman and is therefore to be honored by her, by the same token, the man must remember that he supplied only one rib and the rest came from God.[20] Eve's creation from the rib, if it prevents the authority of the husband from becoming absolute, is almost universally understood as a solid justification for his superiority.

Among the commentators the use of the rib as a rationale for the domestic hierarchy is not, of course, at variance with the popular exegesis that the rib is a visible sign of the close conjunction God intended between man and woman. Adam and Eve are made of the same substance, from one source, to bind their union more strongly. As Pareus comments, God created Eve from Adam's side so that he would recognize their kinship and therefore love her, as St. Paul (Eph. 5:28) later enjoins men to love their wives as their own bodies.[21] Since love is implicit in Eve's creation, Renaissance commentators widely speculate that Eve was created from a rib taken from the left side, close to Adam's heart.[22] Francis Quarles, in a detailed exegesis of the rib as a hieroglyphic of wifely obedience and conjugal love, neatly sums up the kindest of the common beliefs:

> Ribs coast the heart, and guard it round about,
> And like a trusty Watch keepe danger out;
> So tender Wives should loyally impart
> Their watchfull care to fence their Spouses' heart:
> . . . .

> If Ribs be over-bent, or handled rough,
> They breake: If let alone, they bend enough:
> Woman must (unconstrain'd) be plyent still,
> And gently bending to their Husband's will.[23]

No matter how delicate the sensibilities invoked are, the rib still proclaims female subjection.

It is not unusual for the exegetes and expositors to add that the defects of woman, at the very least, her weakness, can be deduced from that same rib near the heart. God filled the place from which the rib was taken with flesh because, Zanchius argues, flesh means weakness and woman is called the weaker vessel (1 Pet. 3:7).[24] Alexander Ross likewise explains that Eve is created from the left side of Adam because the left is weaker than the right.[25] Nicholas Gibbon, on the other hand, maintains that Eve is created from the rib to compensate for female defect. Since bone is nobler matter than the earth out of which Adam was created, the rib was used to form the baser female sex so that she would be less despised.[26]

If among the pious commentators the weakness manifested in the rib serves as a cause for condescension but never outright denunciation, the contemporary misogynists, taking the exegetical tradition a few steps further, use the rib to prove that woman is essentially despicable.[27] The bent shape of the rib demonstrates her contrary, twisted nature; accordingly, Sir Thomas Browne calls woman "the rib and crooked piece of man."[28] The anonymous *Scholehouse of Women* catalogues a series of vile female attributes that are directly traceable to Eve's origin from the rib. The rib is stiff, crooked, and unbendable, as all women are. The *Scholehouse* appends a fanciful misogynous exegesis to Eve's creation: the rib that God took from Adam was eaten by a dog, so God took one of the dog's ribs and created the woman.[29]

The Genesis account of the creation of woman is, nevertheless, cryptic enough to allow the Renaissance debates over the value of women to engender interpretations completely contrary both to the exegetes and misogynists.[30] The defenders of women invert the traditional prejudicial readings to find evidence for female superiority. Agrippa von Nettesheim, for instance, argues that the order of creation does not establish Adam's superiority because God would not end creation in imperfection. God's creation is circular: the last created is the first intended, the sum and best of all. With Eve's creation, "the erthe, and al the goodly ornament of the same were perfeyted and fully finished. . . . and in her al the wisdome and power of the creator came to conclusion and ende."[31] The rib also declares the excellence of woman because it is purified, living matter extracted from a god-like creature, not like the vile clay or dust used to make man.[32] Depending on the imaginative propensity of the interpreter, the creation of woman seems to provide as much ground for praise as blame.

While most commentators do not, of course, follow the excesses of the misogynists (and certainly not of the defenders of women), a literal exegesis must deal with grotesque possibilities. The removal of Adam's rib creates a logical problem. Did Adam lose a rib for Eve's sake or was he born with an extra rib? Was he born a monster or did he suffer a mutilation? Neither is an attractive alternative. Some Renaissance exegetes declare that Adam was created with an extra rib which was specifically destined to be the source of Eve and, consequently, of all mankind; therefore Adam was not a freak of nature for having more than the normal number of ribs. Salkeld summarizes this explanation:

> Wherefore, though in regard to the particular nature of *Adam*, as hee was but one particular man, this ribbe was superfluous, and so consequently in another person might be thought monstrous, yet in regard of him, of whom the rest of mankinde was to proceed, it was most naturall.[33]

But the matter was not so easily settled. Rivetus believes that the rib could not have been superfluous or else Adam could not have called Eve bone of his bone and flesh of his flesh.[34] Calvin tries to mitigate the difficulties by advocating that while Adam certainly suffered the loss of a rib, he received due recompense: "a far richer reward was granted him, since he obtained a faithful associate of life."[35] Luther, on the other hand, denounces the argument as entirely unfit for theological debate:

> These questions have their origin in philosophy and in the science of medicine, which discuss the works of God without the Word.

Moreover, the result of this procedure is that the glory of the Holy Scripture and the majesty of the Creator are lost.[36]

The question of the number of Adam's ribs is superfluous, a reduction of God's creation to the narrow, literal laws of nature, which, according to Luther, is nonsense.

The actual transformation of the rib into a woman leads to speculation on the purposes of the female sex. The Hebrew uses the verb, *wayyiben*, to build, to describe the formation of Eve from the rib. Rabbinic commentary offers two explanations why the woman was "built." Either the word "build" simply refers to God adorning Eve, braiding her hair, before He leads her to Adam, or it refers to the female shape which is built like a storehouse, wide below and narrow above, for bearing children.[37] For the Medieval Christian exegetes, the building of the rib, *aedificavit* reads the Vulgate, inevitably refers to Eve as a type of the Church which is established by the blood and water, the sacraments, that flowed from the side of Christ on the Cross. In fact, St. Augustine defends the typology on the grounds that the text reads *aedificavit*, not *formavit* or *finxit*, that is, formed and fashioned.[38] Luther adamantly denies both Eve's analogy to the Church and the rabbinic exegesis, which he mistakenly believes concerns itself only with the form of the female shape and not its childbearing function. He argues that in Scripture women are commonly referred to as buildings, not for the sake of allegory, but for the sake of history, because they bear and bring up children.[39] Most commentators, however, are content to include both the historical and typological exegesis. Zanchius, for one, reads that Eve can be said to be "built" as the Mother of All Living in the sense that she is both the source of all future generations and a type of the Church.[40] Milton's version of the creation of Eve follows Luther's exegesis in rejecting both typology and naturalism. On the one hand, Adam describes the transformation of the rib with the words "formed and fashioned" (8.450), the same words which St. Augustine declares antithetical to his typological reading. On the other hand, while the physical details of the opening of Adam's side are prominent in his short narrative ("Who stooping op'n'd my left side, and took / From thence a Rib, with cordial spirits warm, / And Life-blood streaming fresh; wide was the wound,

/ But suddenly with flesh fill'd up and heal'd" [8.465–68]), the wound does not perforce indicate surgery. Yet Milton's solution to the problem engendered by a literal reading is radically different from Luther's. In the first place, the dream renders the rib completely emblematic and thus circumvents naturalistic questions: because Eve's creation occurs in a dream, it would be meaningless to inquire whether Adam lost a rib or had an extra one supplied expressly for that purpose. More significantly, instead of invoking the majesty of God's work, which is a miraculous creation by the Word, Milton thoroughly dispenses with naturalism by using the conventions of Renaissance poetry. The opening of Adam's side belongs to the secular tradition of erotic verse where the arrows of Cupid have made, as Spenser says, "many harts to bleed / Of mighty Victors, with wyde wound embrewed."[41] In the strictest sense, Eve's creation causes a wide wound in Adam's heart, not his side. The sleep sent by nature to aid Adam brings him a dream-vision that is more appropriate for a lover than a patriarch.[42] His dream is the Edenic version of Milton's own Sonnet 23, free of the pitiable condition of fallen man that turns the bright vision into darkness. In his trance, Adam perceives the extraction of the rib, an event read throughout the history of exegesis more or less overtly with horror and disgust as the mutilation of the man for the sake of the woman, as a metaphor for the piercing of his heart by love.

Milton resolves the difficulties of the awkward and perplexing manner in which God creates Eve by fusing it with the contemporary beliefs about the physiology of erotic love. Adam dreams of a mutual exchange of spirits in which the eyes act as passageways for the spirits travelling between heart and heart.[43] Adam's side is opened as though it were wounded by the blind god Eros and the "cordial spirits warm," the distillations of blood neither quite corporeal nor incorporeal, are carried to Eve whose spirits in return pass through Adam's eyes to his heart:

> And in her looks, which from that time infus'd
> Sweetness into my heart, unfelt before,
> And into all things from her Air inspir'd
> The spirit of love and amorous delight.
> (8.474–77)

By the seventeenth century the rib of Adam taken from the side nearest his heart signifies the love God intended between man and woman; in *Paradise Lost* it becomes an instrument in the genesis of erotic love as it is subsumed in an extra-biblical metamorphosis that alters Adam's relation to the Garden so that for the first time he perceives beauty with desire.

In the second half of his dream-vision, Adam perceives the creation of Eve as the first transformation in a cycle of giving and receiving that, as we later learn from Raphael, will end in man's achieving angelic nature. The central movement in Eve's creation is reciprocity: she receives the vital spirits not from God, but from Adam's "Life-blood streaming fresh" (8.467) and in return she guides him to Paradise, opening his eyes as she infuses sweetness into his heart. In effect, she replaces the creating God who brought Adam into the Garden in the first dream-vision. Twice before Adam narrates his vision, Eve's special relation to the Garden is emphasized. When Adam enters into the conversation with Raphael on abstruse astronomy, Eve leaves to tend her plants:

> With lowliness Majestic from her seat,
> And Grace that won who saw to wish her stay,
> Rose, and went forth among her Fruits and Flow'rs,
> To visit how they prosper'd, bud and bloom,
> Her Nursery; they at her coming sprung
> And toucht by her fair tendance gladlier grew.
>
> (8.42–47)

The flowers apparently delight in Eve's presence. Then the poet repeats his praise of Eve, making her beauty the focal point of the Garden:

> for on her as Queen
> A pomp of winning Graces waited still,
> And from about her shot Darts of desire
> Into all Eyes to wish her still in sight.
>
> (8.61–64)

We do not know whose eyes are charmed here; perhaps the animals delight in her as much as the flowers, or perhaps Adam and Raphael are watching her go. In any case, the narrator's invocation of Eve as

Venus verifies Adam's dream of Eve as the source and center of all beauty and love in Eden: "That what seem'd fair in all the World, seem'd now / Mean, or in her summ'd up, in her contain'd" (8.472–73). Eve is the mediatrix to the pleasures of the earthly Garden and, through the promised transmutation of love, she may become the mediatrix to the pleasures of the angels who see and love without the human limitations of localized sense and "restrain'd conveyance" (8.628). Eve returns the blood and bone taken from Adam's heart inspired with new meaning and new life.

The complex metamorphosis that Adam witnesses in his dream is contrary to the basic tenet of the exegetical tradition that Eve's creation from the rib is a valid justification for the domestic hierarchy. The nature of human marriage that is delineated in the dream is analogous to the model of the universe that Raphael outlines for Adam in answer to his question about the economy of the cosmos. The blood and bone taken from Adam's side are like the sunlight that is barren until it finds its purpose in the earth: "there first receiv'd / His beams, unactive else, thir vigor find" (8.96–97). It does not matter whether the sun revolves around the earth or the earth around the sun or whether the woman is made from only a part of the man. The true relation of sun and earth, and of man and woman, is defined by exchange and transformation, not hierarchy.[44]

But no sooner has Adam related his extraordinary dream-vision to Raphael than, looking for an explanation for the power of Eve's beauty, he attempts to impose a more traditional reading on it. He tries to read his dream as an actual, physical event which might be subject to scientific scrutiny and almost founders on the absurdity of wondering if God was perhaps overzealous and incautious when he created Eve:

> Or Nature fail'd in mee, and left some part
> Not proof enough such Object to sustain,
> Or from my side subducting, took perhaps
> More than enough.
>
> (8.534–37)

This is not a valid explication of his vision, unless it is true that divine creation is a bit haphazard. Adam is flirting with the popular exegetical

notion that he is a man mutilated for the sake of the woman. His sense
that he may be defective is humorously literal and reductive when com-
pared with his previous sense of imperfection. When he first saw Eve
and exclaimed "This turn hath made amends" (8.491), he was then not
referring to Calvin's notion of a just compensation for the loss of his
rib, but to the emendation of his condition, "in unity defective" (8.425).
That Adam finds himself defective again and attributes it to Eve's crea-
tion is a sign of his momentarily faulty reasoning which mirrors the
exegesis of his fallen descendants.

As he continues in his attempt to understand the place of Eve in the
Garden, Adam hesitates between Agrippa's argument that Eve is the
end of creation, but the first in God's intent and therefore best, and
the more common belief, originally derived from Aristotle, that wom-
an is an occasional animal created not for herself but for man and there-
fore less than he: "Authority and Reason on her wait / As one intended
first, not after made / Occasionally" (8.554–56). In Paradise both Agrippa
and Aristotle are wrong. Adam can deduce neither his superiority nor
Eve's from the order of creation. Whether Eve is created first or last
means nothing unless one shares the confused Satanic belief that God's
creative powers must be limited by an immutable physical law of progress
and decay. At first, Satan argues that earth is better than heaven be-
cause it is a more recent creation, "built / With second thoughts, reform-
ing what was old! / For what God after better worse would build?"
(9.100–102). Shortly thereafter, he wonders if God created man instead
of angels to replace the fallen crew because His powers had declined
through overuse: "Whether such virtue, spent of old now fail'd / More
Angels to Create" (9.145–46). Satan's errors should make the reader wary
of using the order of creation as a basis for hierarchy.[45] But it is not
even necessary to wait until Book 9 to see that Adam is wrong in presum-
ing that Eve's secondary creation means that she was made only as an
afterthought. Both Adam and the reader know that God assented to
his request for a mate by saying, "I, ere thou spak'st / Knew it not
good for Man to be alone" (8.444–45). It is obvious that God's decision
to create Eve is contemporaneous with his decision to create Adam and
that he did not first notice the need for two human beings only after
the man made a convincing case for a wife. Raphael's rebuke to Adam,

"Accuse not Nature, she hath done her part" (8.561), warns him that his literal, naturalistic exegesis is unfit for the prelapsarian world where a failure of imagination is not excused by lending it physical substance.

At the Fall, Adam again reinterprets Eve's creation, reverting to the literal reading he dismissed with Raphael's help, and his new exegesis becomes a crucial element in his temptation. As we have seen, the Christian commentators believe that the knowledge of a link of flesh between Adam and Eve is essential to ensure love between them, but Milton recognizes and explores the dangers of such a connection. When Adam wakes to find Eve as he dreamt her, he applauds the link of flesh between man and woman because it identifies them as members of the same species. After having seen the paired animals and finding no mate for himself, he knows now that he has found one who is "Manlike but different sex" (8.471). But when Eve returns with the Forbidden Fruit, Adam reasons that he must join her because the rib establishes not only the identity of species but also the identity of fate:

> How can I live without thee, how forgo
> Thy sweet Converse and Love so dearly join'd,
> To live again in these wild Woods forlorn?
> Should God create another *Eve*, and I
> Another Rib afford, yet loss of thee
> Would never from my heart; no no, I feel
> The Link of Nature draw me: Flesh of Flesh,
> Bone of my Bone thou art, and from thy State
> Mine never shall be parted, bliss or woe.
> (9.908–16)

Adam telescopes his union with Eve so that beginning with the sweet conversation he fears to lose, he ends with her origin from his side, which he cannot lose. His first thought of Eve's companionship leads him to his heart and there he abandons love for his rib. He moves from a general concept of love which spares him solitude to a particular union of flesh, reversing the progressive generalization of a union of "one Flesh, one Heart, one Soul" (8. 499) that he proclaimed when she was created. This new exegesis of Eve's creation, designed to relieve Adam of responsibility for his choice, transforms the dream image into an irrefutable physical fact. This is the kind of reduction in meaning found consistently in Satanic rhetoric; it is the same literal-mindedness that makes the devil mistake the Tree of the Knowledge of Good and Evil, a sign of man's obedience to God, for a tree bearing fruit with the magical property of imparting higher knowledge.

The consequences of the new interpretation are severe for Eve. As Adam literalizes her creation, her status diminishes. The companion who is primarily valued for "Those thousand decencies that daily flow / From all her words and actions, mixt with Love / And sweet compliance" (8.601–3), the quotidian version of the exchange between heart and eye of the dream-vision, becomes the creature whose chief attraction is that she was made from his flesh and is, therefore, a part of him. Eve is in the process of becoming the woman of the exegetical tradition whose creation from the side of man argues for her subordinate place in the domestic hierarchy. Eve's sweet compliance will soon turn to subjugation.

Adam's last words before he falls echo his lament for the lost Eve and complete the identification between the woman and his rib:

> So forcible within my heart I feel
> The Bond of Nature draw me to my own,
> My own in thee, for what thou art is mine;
> Our State cannot be sever'd, we are one,
> One Flesh; to lose thee were to lose myself.
> (9.955–60)

Adam's echo of lines 912–16 is partial; to let necessity hold greater sway he changes "link of Nature" to "Bond of Nature," a subtle shift to a more absolute and indissoluble union.[46] The woman who was extracted from the man is drawn back into him. As his last free act, Adam reclaims the rib. His Fall is, in a sense, a Fall into literalness and into the standard assumptions of the commentaries where the rib is flesh and blood reality and where nature and necessity can hold sway.

Adam's lament is so intertwined with very human emotions that it is easy to overlook the shift in consciousness entailed by his reinterpretation of Eve's creation. The diatribe in Book 10, however, fully demonstrates the result of the new consciousness as Adam exploits the misogynous cliches of both the satirists and the exegetes. When he comes to feel the effects of his disobedience, Adam concludes that Eve is inherently vain and false because she was made from a "Rib / Crooked by nature" (10.884–85), a bare bone whose bent shape resembles the mazy folds of the serpent and allies the woman with the demonic world. Here for the first time Adam invokes the moral connotation of left and right: the rib was "More to the part sinister from me drawn" (10.886). Through the Latin etymology Eve becomes a left-handed creature, the weaker vessel, made from the weaker side of man, and inclined to evil deeds, a "fair defect / Of Nature" (10.891–92). He reviles her as the creature of a superfluous rib given him only for the express purpose of preventing his mutilation: "Well if thrown out, as supernumerary / To my just number found" (10.888–89). Adam's fallen exegesis takes the naturalistic premise that Eve was created from an extra rib to its logical conclusion. Woman is as uncanny as a supernumerary rib, "a novelty of Earth" (10.891) and Adam comes unwittingly close to finding himself surprised by Eve as Satan was by Sin.

Although Adam's diatribe allies the creation of Eve with its parodic, nightmare version, the birth of Sin, he omits one crucial element in his exegesis. Sin is born in the violence of searing pain ("dim thine eyes, and dizzy swum / In darkness, while thy head flames thick and fast / Threw forth" [2.753–55]), but Adam never raises the question of pain nor implies that he was put to sleep so as not to feel the extraction of the rib. He is "abstract," drawn away from himself while Eve is created, but there is no reason to believe that he is in that state for any other purpose than to participate in the dream-vision. It seems that even while Adam reviles the very origin of woman, he does not associate it with surgery or the conditions of childbirth after the Fall. Perhaps it is Milton's final critique of the tradition that, unlike so many a pious commentator, he finds no place for pain in the creation of Eve. The beneficent anaesthesia ascribed by the exegetes to Adam's sleep occurs only at the expulsion when he is told that he must leave the Garden:

> *Adam* at the news
> Heart-strook with chilling gripe of sorrow stood,
> That all his senses bound.
>
> (11.263–65)

He is frozen, mercifully anaesthetized so as not to feel the pain of the terrible punishment. His bound senses are curiously reminiscent of the description in Sylvester's Du Bartas of the bound senses of Adam cast into a deep sleep so that God might extract a rib from his side. Milton unequivocally reserves the potential pain and horror so often associated with the creation of woman for man's exile from Paradise.

The significance of the dream-vision of the creation of Eve in Book 8 recedes from Adam's imagination during the temptation until it is completely obscured by the Fall. Eve's creation undergoes one more reinterpretation as it is incorporated into Christian typology. If before Raphael greeted Eve with "*Hail* / . . . the holy salutation us'd / Long after to blest *Mary*, second *Eve*" (5.385–87), the terms in which he addressed the first Eve were exclusively terrestrial and devoid of typology:

> Hail Mother of Mankind, whose fruitful Womb
> Shall fill the World more numerous with thy Sons
> Than with these various fruits the Trees of God
> Have heap'd this Table.
>
> (5.388–91)

When the work of redemption begins, however, Eve who seemed to be the sum and source of all beauty on earth is supplanted by Eve who will bear the seed of man's deliverance from the Fall.[47] At their reconciliation Adam remembers God's curse on the serpent that adds the new typological meaning to Eve as the mother of all living:

> thy Seed shall bruise
> The Serpent's head; piteous amends, unless
> Be meant, whom I conjecture, our grand Foe
> *Satan*, who in the Serpent hath contriv'd
> Against us this deceit.
>
> (10.1031–35)

At the same time Adam becomes a type of Christ when he ascends the Mount of Vision and the dream-vision of the hieroglyphic of human love is emended by the vision in Book 11 and Michael's narrative in Book 12. The parallel between the new vision and the dream-vision of Eve's creation is underscored by the Archangel as he prepares to educate Adam for life in exile:

> Ascend
> This Hill; let *Eve* (for I have drencht her eyes)
> Here sleep below while thou to foresight wak'st,
> As once thou slep'st, while Shee to life was form'd.
>
> (11.366–69)

Witnessing the suffering and evil of future generations and learning of the divine love that will pay the penalty for mankind, Adam's dream-vision of terrestrial love cedes to the waking vision that is like the visionary sleep of prophecy of the biblical Patriarchs. And as the Christian vision of history is revealed to Adam, Eve's creation must be implicitly glossed by the analogy of the birth of the Church from the side of Christ, second Adam.[48] Where before Adam saw his heart wounded by the arrows of Cupid and a beautiful woman created, in the new vision he learns of "those written Records pure, / Though not but by the Spirit understood" (12.513–14), the only uncorrupted part of the Church, and of the faith and works that will guide him and his descendants from the terrestrial world to the Paradise within. After the Fall, the creation of Eve, Adam's fullest vision of the Garden of Eden, is meaningful only in the light of the higher vision of the atonement of Christ that saves the earth and human life from complete surrender to the shadows of Death and Hell.

The Fall is a victory for the standard exegeses and a defeat for the radical version of the creation of woman that Adam narrates to Raphael. Milton secularizes Eve's creation without recourse to naturalism and at the same time makes an innovative purge of the nearly ubiquitous belief that the birth of woman from the side of the sleeping man justifies her subordination, if not outright misogyny. In distinct opposition to the tradition which relegates Eve to an inferior status, Milton elevates her so that her birth stands at the focal point of Adam's life in Eden. So long as he interprets her creation as an emblem of human love defined by mutual exchange and resists the temptation of the false exegeses of Milton's contemporaries, Adam is fit to live in the Garden. But the Fall perverts the meaning of the dream-vision and in this change

Eve actively participates. She accepts Satan's false notion that Godhead can be found in a fruit, rather than in love, and leads Adam to acquiesce as he reinterprets her creation as a physical bond whose reality lies in the rib, not in the exchange of spirits that move his heart and open his eyes. It is no small part of the pathos of Eve's Fall that she tempts Adam by offering him a corrupted version of his dream in which she becomes a delusion who, seeming to offer him the means "To open Eyes, and make them Gods who taste" (9.866), closes his eyes to the beauties of Paradise and blocks his way to the celestial realms. Born to lead man to the human joys by which he might transcend his earthly limitations, the fallen Eve undoes her own creation.

Notes

1. For a judicious appraisal of Milton's knowledge of rabbinic sources, see Cheryl H. Fresch, "'As the Rabbines Expound': Milton, Genesis and the Rabbis," *Milton Studies* 15 (1981): 59–80. See also Golda Werman "Milton's Use of Rabbinic Material," *Milton Studies* 21 (1985): 35–47.

2. *The Babylonian Talmud*, trans. Jacob Schachter, ed. I. Epstein, 34 vols. (London: Soncino Press, 1935), 5: pt. 4, Sanhedrin 4, 39a. J. M. Evans, *"Paradise Lost" and the Genesis Tradition* (Oxford: Oxford University Press, 1968), 43–44 and 262–63, gives a useful background study for some of the exegetical motifs discussed here, but he does not make a systematic study of Milton's choices as I attempt to do. See also Cheryl H. Fresch, "The Hebraic Influence upon the Creation of Eve in *Paradise Lost*," *Milton Studies* 13 (1979): 181–99.

3. *"Rashi" on the Pentateuch: Genesis*, trans. James H. Lowe (London: Hebrew Compendium Publishing Co., 1928), 60.

4. *Midrash Rabbah*, trans. H. Freedman, ed. H. Freedman and Maurice Simon, 10 vols. (London: Soncino Press, 1939), 1: Bereshith 17.7.

5. Hieronymus Zanchius, *De Operibus Dei intra spacium sex dierum creatis . . .* (Hanover, 1597), 647, has: "Nam ait Moses, *Deum fecisse cadere hunc somnum super Adamum*. Fuit igitur supernaturalis & divinus: id quod etiam confirmatur verbo, *Cadere fecit super Adamum*. Fuit igitur de Caelo & ex alto. Naturalis enim somnus ascendit potius abo imo, in altum dum scilicet a vaporibus, qui e ventriculo ascendunt ad caput, in capite excitatur." The same supernatural sleep occurs to others in the OT, Zanchius notes, p. 649: "Talis fuit somnus, quo correptus Abraham, audivit a Domi-

no, quid futurum esset de suo semine, Genes. 15. Non dissimili somno affectus fuit Iacob, cum vidit scalam e Caelo, in terram usque pertingentem, Genes. 28." For a survey of Renaissance commentary on the creation of Eve, see Arnold Williams, *The Common Expositor: An Account of the Commentaries of Genesis 1527–1633* (Chapel Hill: University of North Carolina Press, 1948), 85–93.

6. John Salkeld, *A Treatise of Paradise. And the principall contents thereof: Especially of the greatnesse, situation, beautie, and other properties of that place* . . . (London, 1617), 169–70.

7. *De Operibus Dei*, 653: "Sicut enim in sua ecstasi, videt muliere e sua costa formari; sic experrectus a somno, ex adductione huius foeminae ad se per manun Jehovae, facile intellixit, eam sibi in uxorem offerri."

8. St. Augustine, *De Genesi ad Litteram*, ed. Joseph Zycka, in *Corpus Scriptorum Ecclesiasticorum Latinorum* (Vienna: F. Tempsky, 1894), 28: bk. 9. 19. For a study of the typology of Eve's creation, see Mother Mary Christopher Pecheux, "The Second Adam and the Church in *Paradise Lost*," *ELH* 34 (1967): 173–87, and Evans, *Genesis Tradition*, 100–101. Luther, who denies the validity of a typological reading, limits Adam's foreknowledge to the institution of marriage which requires that men leave their mothers and fathers for the sake of their wives: "There were no fathers and mothers yet, and no children, nevertheless, through the Holy Spirit, Adam prophesies this way about the life of married people." *Lectures on Genesis*, trans. George V. Schick, in *Luther's Works*, ed. Jaroslav Pelikan, 54 vols. (St. Louis: Concordia Publishing House, 1958), 1:139.

9. John Calvin, *Commentaries on the First Book of Moses Called Genesis*, trans. John King, 2 vols. (1948; repr., Grand Rapids, Mich: William B. Eerdmans, 1963), 1:135.

10. Andrew Willett, *Hexapla in Genesim: that is, a Sixfold Commentary upon Genesis* . . . (Cambridge, 1605), 37.

11. "The Sixth Day of the First Weeke," *The Divine Weeks and Works of Guillaume de Saluste Sieur Du Bartas*, trans. Joshuah Sylvester, ed. Susan Snyder, 2 vols. (Oxford: Oxford University Press, 1979), 1:1019–30.

12. *Lectures on Genesis*, in *Luther's Works*, 1:129.

13. *Paradise Lost*, in *Complete Poems and Major Prose*, ed. Merritt Y. Hughes (New York: Odyssey Press, 1957). This edition is used throughout.

14. Evans, *Genesis Tradition*, 263, notes that the immediate source of the dream-vision is probably Henry More's *Conjectura Cabbalistica*, where Adam is cast into a sleep, dreams the creation of Eve and wakes to find it true.

15. *Midrash Rabbah*, Bereshith 18.2. See also Evans, *Genesis Tradition*, 44, for the Midrashic commentary on the rib.

16. St. Thomas Aquinas, *Summa Theologiae*, trans. Edmund Hill, 60 vols. (New York: Blackfriars and McGraw-Hill; London: Eyre and Spottiswoode, 1964), 13:1a.92.3.

17. John Calvin, *Commentary on the Epistles of Paul the Apostle to the Corinthians*, trans. John Pringle, 2 vols. (Grand Rapids, Mich.: William B. Eerdmans, 1948), 1:357.

18. Daniel Rogers, *Matrimoniall Honour: or, The mutual Crowne and comfort of godly, loyall, and chaste Marriage* (London, 1642), 254–55.

19. *Religio Medici*, in *The Prose of Sir Thomas Browne*, ed. Norman Endicott (New York: New York University Press, 1968), 80. In *Christian Doctrine* Milton himself argues for female subjection on similar grounds: "Gen. ii, 22: *he made that rib which he had taken from Adam into a woman*. It is wrong for one single part of the body—and not even one of the most important parts—to disobey the rest of the body, and even the head, this, at any rate, is the opinion of God: Gen. iii, 16: *he shall rule over you.*" Trans. John Carey, ed. Maurice Kelley, in *Complete Prose Works*, 7 vols. (New Haven: Yale University Press, 1973), 6:782. Here Milton concludes that woman is a diminution of man because of the postlapsarian curse, without distinguishing between the fallen and unfallen states as he does in the poem where the curse cannot logically provide a gloss for Eve's creation.

20. Zanchius, *De Operibus Dei*, 650, has: "Rursus, unam tantum ab Adamo accepit costam, no plures; ne plus sibi imperii, quam par sit, in mulierem usurpet vir: quasi tota sit sumta ex viro. Ideo meminisse debet vir, in muliere non esse e suo, nisi costam una & aliquid carnis: totum reliquum additu illi a Deo fuisse."

21. David Pareus, *In Genesin Mosis Commentarius* . . . (Geneva, 1614), col. 431: "Voluit enim mulierem potius ex viro sumere, quam ex terra condere aut ex nihilo creare, ut non tantum naturae similitudine, sed etiam cognationis effectu primi conjuges arctius inter se devincti essent: idemque effectus mutui amoris in omnes conjuges diffunderetur. Hoc argumento Apostolus hortatur viros, ut diligant & foveant uxores suas, sicut sua ipsorum corpora." This reading is ultimately derived from St. Augustine who argues that God deliberately chose to Create Eve out of Adam's body in order to bind them in the "affection of kinship." *The City of God*, trans. Gerald Walsh and Grace Monahan, in *Fathers of the Church*, ed. Roy J. Deferrari, et al. (New York: Fathers of the Church, 1951), 14:289.

22. Pareus, *In Genesin Mosis Commentarius* . . . , col. 430, reads: "Probabile multis videtur fuisse ex sinistro latere costam detractam, ubi cor est, ut inter virum & uxorem vigeret cordialis amor & voluntatum intima consensio." Genesis, of course, does not specify to which side the rib belonged. See Sister Mary Irma Corcoran, *Milton's Paradise with Reference to the Hexameral Background* (Washington, D.C.: Catholic University of America Press, 1945), 65, for a discussion of the preference among the commentators for the left or right side of Adam. See also Roland Mushat Frye, *Milton's Imagery and the Visual Arts: Iconographic Tradition in the Epic Poems* (Princeton: Princeton University Press, 1978), 260–61, for the choice of right or left in the pictorial tradition.

23. Francis Quarles, *Hadassa: or the History of Queene Ester*, in *The Complete Works in Prose and Verse of Francis Quarles*, ed. Alexander B. Grosart (1880; facs. repr., New York: AMS Press, 1967), 2:50.

24. Zanchius, *De Operibus Dei*, 651: "Costa, robur significat: caro, infirmitatem. Ut igitur de robore viri communicatum est muliere; sic decuit viru imbecillitate mulieris, quae nomine *carnis* significatur, participari: ac proinde fortiorem debere compati imbecilliori; & plus ei tribuere honoris: hoc est, quod 1 Pet. 3 vers. 7 docet."

25. Alexander Ross, *An Exposition of the Fourteene first Chapters of Genesis, by way of Question and Answere* (London, 1626), 54.

26. Nicholas Gibbon, *Questions and Disputations Concerning the Holy Scripture; wherein are contained, briefe, faithfull, and sound expositions* . . . 2 vols. (London, 1602), 1:97.

27. For a discussion of the use of the rib in misogynous tracts, see Kester Svendsen, *Milton and Science* (Cambridge: Cambridge University Press, 1956), 183–84, and Katherine Rogers, *The Troublesome Helpmate: A History of Misogyny in Literature* (Seattle: University of Washington Press, 1966), 100–142. For the debates on the worth of women and their background, see Francis Utley, *The Crooked Rib: An Analytical Index to the Argument about Women in English and Scots Literature to the End of the Year 1568* (Columbus: Ohio State University Press, 1944), 3–90; Louis B. Wright, *Middle-Class Culture in Elizabethan England* (Chapel Hill: University of North Carolina Press, 1935), 465–507; Carroll Camden, *The Elizabethan Woman: A Panorama of English Womanhood, 1540–1640* (Houston: Elsevier Press, 1952), 17–30 and 241–63.

28. Browne, *Religio Medici*, 80.

29. *The Scholehouse of Women: wherein every man may reade a goodly prayse of the condicyons of women* (London, 1560), sig. B4v.

30. For a modern version of the defense of women through a feminist reading of Genesis, see Phyllis Trible, *God and the Rhetoric of Sexuality* (Philadelphia: Fortress Press, 1978), 72–143.

31. Heinrich Cornelius Agrippa von Nettesheim, *A Treatise of the Nobilitie and Excellencye of Womankynde*, trans. David Clapam (London, 1542), sig. A7r.

32. The rib offers the defenders of women other opportunities to counter-attack the misogynists. Daniel Tuvill, *Asylum Veneris, or A Sanctuary for Ladies* . . . (London, 1616), 8, says that the rib is not crooked but an arch, which is the fairest and firmest form of architecture. Ester Sowernam, [pseud.] *Ester hath hang'd Haman; or, An answere to a lewd Pamphlet, entituled, The Arraignment of Women* . . . (London, 1617) 3, rearranges the argument that claims that woman is only a fraction of man. Following the philosophic axiom that states that that which gives a quality to something must in itself be more abundant in that quality, she asks if woman is crooked for being made of the rib, how much more crooked is man who possesses all the rest of them?

33. Salkeld, *A Treatise of Paradise*, 177. For various solutions to the problem, see Williams, *The Common Expositor*, 90–91.

34. Andreus Rivetus, *Operum Theologicorum*, 2 vols. (Rotterdam, 1651), 1:100. "Et certe non est leve argumentum ad probandum costam illam fuisse unam ex necessariis ad corpus Adami, quia si fuisset superflua, & extra naturam ejus, vere dici non posset Evam ex Adamo fuisse formatam, nec dixisset Adamus Evam fuisse *os ex ossibus suis*."

35. Calvin, *Commentaries on the First Book of Moses*, 1:133. Calvin may here be drawing on rabbinic commentary. The *Talmud*, Sanhedrin 39a, raises the question whether it was just of God to take Adam's rib and finds that Eve was more than fair compensation for his loss. God's action is compared to that of a thief who steals a silver pitcher and replaces it with one made of gold.

36. *Lectures on Genesis*, in *Luther's Works*, 1:130.

37. Cheryl H. Fresch, "'And Brought Her Unto the Man': The Wedding in *Paradise Lost*," *Milton Studies* 16 (1982): 21–33, notes that both Milton and the rabbis place great emphasis on the beauty of Eve and that the word "adorned" is repeated several times in the poem to describe the woman when she is presented to Adam.

38. St. Augustine, *The City of God*, trans. Gerald G. Walsh and Daniel J. Honan, in *Fathers of the Church*, 24:464.

39. *Luther's Works*, 1:132.

40. Zanchius, *De Operibus Dei*, 1:651: "Ergo tam si spectes totam humani generis generationem ex Eva: quam totius Ecclesiae propagationem, accommodatissime usus est verbo aedificandi."

41. *An Hyme in Honour of Love*, in *Edmund Spenser's Poetry*, ed. Hugh Maclean (New York: W. W. Norton, 1968), lines 12–13.

42. See Manfred Weidhorn, *Dreams in Seventeenth-Century English Literature* (The Hague: Mouton, 1970), 151–53, for Eve's creation narrated as a love-dream lyric.

43. For the relation of spirits, heart and eye formulated and popularized by the *stilnovisti* of the *trecento*, see Maurice Valency, *In Praise of Love: An Introduction to the Love-poetry of the Renaissance* (New York: Macmillan, 1958), 218–22. Robert Burton, *The Anatomy of Melancholy*, Everyman (1932; repr., New York: Dutton; London: Dent, 1964), 3:65, sums up the commonplace: "The most familiar and usual cause of love is that which comes by sight, which conveys those admirable rays of beauty and pleasing graces to the heart."

44. For a study of the prelapsarian relationship of Adam and Eve as defined by reciprocity, see my article, "Fit Help: The Egalitarian Marriage in *Paradise Lost*," *Mosaic* 17, pt. 1 (Winter 1984): 29–48. Diane Kelsey McColley, *Milton's Eve* (Urbana: University of Illinois Press, 1983), discusses the radical difference between Milton's portrait of Eve and the attitudes of his predecessors. McColley reaches a conclusion somewhat different from my own. She argues, pp. 34–56, that in *Paradise Lost* Milton offers an altered version of the domestic hierarchy in which Eve is subordinate to Adam but without losing power and dignity thereby. I believe, however, that the marriage of Adam and Eve before the Fall is not founded on a qualified domestic hierarchy but on a particular kind of egalitarianism. See also Elizabeth Ely Fuller, *Milton's Kinesthetic Vision in "Paradise Lost"* (Lewisburg: Bucknell University Press, 1983), 156–63, for an analysis of prelapsarian hierarchy. James Grantham Turner, *One Flesh: Paradisal Marriage and Sexual Relations in the Age of Milton* (Oxford: Oxford University Press, 1987) appeared while this essay was already in press.

45. The difficulty of assigning preeminence to Adam because he was created first was not unknown to the exegetes. Matthew Griffith, *Bethel: or a Forme for Families* (London, 1633), 240–41, notes that priority signifies nothing since the animals were created before Adam and Eve but do not hold lordship over mankind.

46. For a possible source of the "Bond of Nature" and the "link of Nature," see John Reichert, "'Against His Better Knowledge': A Case for Adam," *ELH* 48 (1981): 105.

47. For the Mary-Eve typology, see Mother Mary Christopher Pecheux, "The Concept of the Second Eve in *Paradise Lost,*" *PMLA* 75 (1960): 359–66.

48. In her article, "The Second Adam and the Church in *Paradise Lost,*" 184, Mother Mary Christopher Pecheux notes the parallel relation between Adam's vision in Books 11 and 12 and his vision at Eve's creation: "The 'sum of earthly bliss' which Adam found in the nuptial bower as the fruit of his union with Eve is subsumed now into the endless joy which the elect share in the spirit of love which is the bond between the Father and the Son." The typology of divine love ought not to be used, however, to gloss the dream in Book 8 until after the Fall. The "opening" of Adam's side, which Mother Mary Christopher Pecheux (177) links to the *apercuit* of the Vulgate for the piercing of Christ's side, is initially linked to the opening of the cell of fancy, Adam's internal sight. Only after Book 11, when the mind's eye has been darkened and man prepares himself for redemption, is it appropriate to read the opening of Adam's side as a type of the wounding of Christ on the Cross.

Milton and the Ranters on Canticles

NOAM FLINKER

L ess than 20 years before Milton first published *Paradise Lost*, a group of antinomian radicals known as Ranters had achieved a great deal of notoriety.[1] Although these people held views that were almost universally condemned by their contemporaries, there is a curious parallel between their approach to sexuality and the Song of Songs and that of Milton's Adam. In *Paradise Lost*, Milton implicitly criticizes the Ranters' assumption that Adam's fall was irrelevant, yet when Adam uses a Ranter approach to Eve in his love song, he is in some sense insisting upon the validity of the Ranters in a prelapsarian world. That is, some of the positions presented by men such as Abiezer Coppe and Laurence Clarkson seem to be without objection for Adam.

Christopher Hill has made it clear that Milton should be read in the context of the radical political ideas that were an important part of his public world during the Interregnum. Hill stresses Milton's revolutionary background in the epics where he sees the poet "grappling with problems set by the failure of God's cause in England."[2] He points to a great many parallels between the Ranters and Milton that suggest the importance of examining the nature of their contemporary relations. The character of Satan, for instance, provides an area of thematic and ideological congruity between the Ranters and *Paradise Lost* "with . . . emphasis on fate, chance and necessity . . .[and] denial of the divine providence which Milton is asserting" (397). On another level, Hill might perhaps have seen Ranter antinomianism in Satan's soliloquy that concludes "Evil be thou my good."[3] None of this is problematic since the use of Ranter materials is confined to Satan. Hill does not extend his probings of the intertextual space occupied by *Paradise Lost* and certain Ranters beyond what can be seen as Milton's conscious adaptation of a particular ideological line for rhetorical purposes. He summarizes: "I am suggesting only that one possible source for Milton's conception of the rebel angels is the people he had encountered, whose activities had done (in his view) harm to the cause he believed in, although their ideas started from premises alarmingly close to his" (398).

Joan S. Bennett has extended this consideration of Miltonic interest in radical seventeenth-century political and theological discourse to a prelapsarian aspect of *Paradise Lost*. She deals primarily with antinomians less radical than the Ranters whom she understands Milton to have rejected: "Some antinomians—the Ranting sort—Milton condemned, as in his sonnet 12: 'License they mean when they cry liberty.'" Nevertheless, her discussion of Adam and Eve as "the first persons who had to deal with this dilemma of total spiritual liberty"[4] could be seen as an indication of Milton's partial sympathy for all antinomian views. Milton's sonnet need not blind us to the sympathies he may have felt with well-meaning sectarians who were guilty of confusing license and liberty, but whose political and religious tendencies were not wholly unlike his own.

The following analysis is concerned with the way Ranters like Abiezer Coppe and Laurence Clarkson were as closely interested as Milton in biblical texts from Canticles which they read both with and without the allegorical explanations of hundreds of years of commentary. As Coppe and Clarkson alluded to intertexts from Canticles, they communicated a direct sexual energy that is nonetheless charged with spiritual intensity. When Milton had Adam sing a love song to Eve in language that refers back to similar intertexts, he was in some sense granting his hero an approach to love that underlines the similarities of his revolutionary sympathies. Although Milton the libertarian who defended personal and intellectual freedom in the 1640s was not as radical as some of the sectaries who embraced his doctrines, his ideals and principles had much in common with them. This is not to identify Milton with Clarkson's antinomian views, but it is to suggest that despite some of his obvious objections to such positions, he had a basic sympathy for their spirit. It is thus useful to see Milton's reconsideration of some Ranter positions in the prelapsarian human conditions in *Paradise Lost*.

Any consideration of Ranter ideas requires a methodological caveat that signifies more than the presence of obscure texts of difficult accessibility. In one sense, attention to the Ranters demands of its students a recognition of the essential orality of the material treated. We must assume that most mid-century English readers who knew about the Ranters in any detail had access to oral reports about the sect that were never recorded in print. Those written texts that have been preserved are somewhat one-sided in their condemnation of the group. Most of the extant publications are attacks and thus can hardly serve as objective sources. Even works written by Ranters themselves must be examined carefully to insure that the author was in fact a Ranter at the time the piece was written. In a great many of the works the writer refers to himself as a "late fellow Ranter."[5] Such texts are suspect because the speaker may well be interested in discrediting the group whose tenets he no longer accepts. This leaves very few texts that can provide dependable evidence about the group, and in these the air of secrecy in the written discourse often suggests that the writer is hiding as much as he is revealing. Presumably a contemporary who wanted to hear more about these ideas would have been forced to contact the writers and attend meetings of the sect for himself. Today we must be wary not to assume that the surviving texts provide us with more than a series of fragments about the essence of the group's ideas.

Basic to Ranter doctrine is an insistence on liberty that most contemporaries must have regarded as blasphemous and licentious. The explicit testimony that we have is often colorful and sensational. Gilbert Roulston, who referred to himself as "a late Fellow-Ranter" on the title page of *The Ranters Bible*, described a Ranter gathering which supposedly took place on November 16, 1650:

A great Company of these new Generations of Vipers, called Ranters, were gathered together near the Soho as Westminster, where they exercised themselves in many royatous and uncivil actions; and after some hours spent in feasting and the like, they stript themselves quite naked, and dansing the Adamites Curranto, *which was, That after 2. or 3. familist Giggs, hand in hand, each man should embrace his fellow-female, in the flesh, for the acting of that inhumane* Theatre *of carnal copulation which is so gloriously illustrated in the sacred Scriptures, to be one of the greatest sins, in bringing them to the very brinks of perpetual damnation; in defence of which abominable and lascivious act, they hold it a tenent lawful, to lie with any woman whatsoever: These are a sort of* Ranters, *called by the name,* Of the Familists of Love, *who would have all things common, and hold it a* Paradice *to live so, because their Discipline allowes, to court naked, in which they blush no more, then* Adam *at his first Creation,* Gen. 2.5. (2)

Although none of the Ranter texts that have been preserved provides explicit support for such a report, the suggestions are not in conflict with the views they did profess. Especially striking is the comparison between the Ranters and Adam, since the liberty that a man such as Abiezer Coppe claims is that of unfallen Adam, or rather, of Christians who see themselves as beyond sin because of Christ and thus capable of committing any act in purity. For Milton's Adam, however, Roulston's testimony contains nothing that is objectionable. Only after his fall would nudity and unabashed sexuality become sinful.

Canticles provided the Ranters with a series of important texts used to articulate their view of the world. Although other biblical quotations also recur frequently, references to Solomon's Song appear in contexts that are clearly important yet which do not yield up their significance in an ordinary or straightforward manner. Although the allusions can be taken allegorically, understood sexually they help to intimate the Ranter doctrines about the relationship between sexual experience and spiritual liberty. In some sense, then, both the natural and spiritual levels of the intertexts from Canticles are essential for an understanding of Ranter discourse.

Abiezer Coppe was definitely a Ranter in 1649 when he published *Some Sweet Sips of Some Spirituall Wine* as well as his *A Fiery Flying Roll* and *A Second Fiery Flying Roule*. Nigel Smith describes *Some Sweet Sips* as "fiercely critical of formalised religion . . . and excitedly Antinomian, but also stressing the sublimity of God in man and in nature. It is Coppe's first deeply pantheistic statement."[6]

Coppe's discourse establishes recurrent motifs that seem to be urging a traditional approach to religious spirituality as opposed to carnal experience. When this facade disappears momentarily, however, the underlying ideology is revealed. For example, Coppe twists Paul's allegory of Hagar and Sarah (Galatians 4:21–31) into libertine doctrine: "*Isaac* is the heire, (the son of the *freewoman*[)], not *Ismael* the son of the *bondwoman* . . . but the son of the *freewoman* who is free, and very free too — is also free from persecuting any — so, and more then so, the son of the *freewoman* is a Libertine — even he who is of the *freewoman*, who is borne after the Spirit."[7] Chapter IV concludes with a sentiment to which Milton might have assented at first: "Thus saith the Lord, I will recover my Vineyard out of the hands of all *Husbandmen* and be *Pastor* my Self, and my people shall know no Arch-Bishop, Bishop, &c. but my Self. This you will believe and assent to (dear hearts, at first dash;) But they shall know no Pastor (neither) *Teacher*, *Elder*, or *Presbyter*, but the Lord, that Spirit" (21 [Smith, 56]). The radical nature of the political position here does not become clear before the rejection of "the Sword of the Lord Generall" (i.e., Cromwell) at the very end of the chapter.

Some Sweet Sips refers back to the Song of Songs in order to communicate a message that nonetheless remains quite unclear much of the time. Chapter III of Epistle II begins with an appeal to the reader to awaken to a new world of natural beauty and light:

WEll, once more; Where be you, ho? Are you *within*? Where be you? What! Sitting upon a *Forme*, without doors, (in the Gentiles *Court*,) as if you had neither life nor soul in you? Rise up, rise up, my Love, my fair one, and *come away*; for lo, the Winter is past, the raine is over and gone, the flowers appear on the earth, the time of the singing of birds is come, and the voice of the Turtle is heard in our land, And (let him that hath an eare to heare, heare what the Spirit saith) the figtree putteth forth her green figges, and the vines with the tender grape give a good smell: *Arise* my love, my fair one, and *come away*, *Cant.* 2.10, 11, 12, 13.

The day breaks, the *shadowes* flie *away. Rise* up, my Love, and
come away.

Come with me from *Lebanon,* with me from *Lebanon,* from
the top of *Amana,* look from the top of *Shenir,* and *Hermon,* from
the Lyons dens, from the mountains of the Leopards. Come with
me, *Rise,* let us be going.

Awake, awake, put on thy beautifull garments. Awake thou that
sleepest and arise from the dead, and Christ shall give thee *light.*

Awake, awake thou that sleepest in security, in the cradles of
carnality. Arise from the dead. (15–16 [Smith, 53–54])

Here the traditional garb consists of the references to Canticles that
seem to conform to standard allegorical interpretations of the biblical
poem as a love song between Christ and the Church. This, however,
would make the speaker in Coppe's text into a Christ figure urging
the Church to relinquish its hold on dead flesh and embark upon some
new spiritual venture associated with natural splendor and beauty.

Although there is no explicit indication in *Some Sweet Sips* of the
sexual level of the intertexts from Canticles, there is a curious irony
to the constant rejection of the carnal. The occasional references to liber-
tinism suggest that the accusations of "late fellow Ranters" about the
sexual nature of Ranter practices may have been justified to some ex-
tent. Coppe's insistence upon the pejorative nature of the carnal must
be understood in the context of his total vision. It is part of his policy
to subvert language in order to suggest the real nature of truth. A voice
in his text advocates a series of shifts, each of which connotes an in-
crease in spirituality: "Here is the voyce of one crying; Arise out of
Flesh, into *Spirit*; out of *Form,* into *Power*; out of *Typs,* into *Truth*; out
of the *Shadow,* into the *Substance*; out of the *Signe,* into the thing *Signi-
fied.*"[8] Although this longing to transcend the earthly may seem to
conform to Puritan orthodoxy, the voice sets up a whole series of an-
tinomian heresies. Since the aim of the voice is to move from sign to
signified, there is a point in the text that words and language itself must
be abandoned as mere signs. The meaning of language is thus related
to its words or signs, but the voice commands the listener to arise "out
of the Signe, into the thing Signified" and thus intimates that one can

get at the signified without sign or language. The relationship between word and meaning is seriously questioned.

This prepares the way for Coppe and his fellow Ranters to establish their own procedures for subverting biblical language with no sense of commitment to traditional understandings of meaning. While his frequent references to libertinism suggest a positive orientation to carnal experience, he continually rejects the flesh. He explains that the spiritual condition of a particular action is determined by the spirit of the doer, not by the action itself. Thus he can be pure in doing something which would be wrong for a less spiritually prepared person. Later in *Some Sweet Sips* he explains to his "Cronies at Oxford" that "there be five Tenses or Times: there is a Time to be merry [*To be merry in the Lord*] and that is the Present Tense with some, to others the Future" (37 [Smith, 62]). His merrymaking is in the present while others must wait until some point in the future before they can begin. Elsewhere he describes this merrymaking as a return *"Home, to the Inside,* heart, *Graine.* To the finest wheate-flower, and the pure bloud of the grape; To the fatted calfe, ring, shoes, mirth, and Musicke, &c. which is the *Lords Supper indeed"* (46 [Smith, 66]).

The intertext from Canticles is therefore very much like the Ranter position it is meant to articulate. It seems to have a traditional allegorical meaning, yet the speaker in Coppe's text undermines the validity of such an interpretation both directly and implicitly. He establishes himself as part of God and includes the whole spectrum of English Christianity from *"The Kings . . .* and the *Bishops* & the *Priests"* to "the *Seekers,* and the *Family of Loves"* (8 [Smith, 50]), in his personal disclaimer that simultaneously denies and claims divinity: "I am, or would be nothing. But by the grace of God I am what I am" (7 [Smith, 49–50]). Although other Ranter texts allude more directly to the sexual level of Canticles, in *Some Sweet Sips* Coppe was more secretive about such clear articulation.

The connection between Canticles and sexuality is somewhat clearer in Coppe's *Fiery Flying Roll,* published a little later in 1649. There he describes various sexual escapades: "and clip't, hug'd and kiss'd them, putting my hand in their bosomes, loving the she-Gipsies dearly . . . yet I can if it be my will, kisse and hug Ladies, and love my neighbours

wife as my selfe, without sin."⁹ Later he explains: "And then again, by
wanton kisses, kissing hath been confounded; and external kisses, have
been made fiery chariots, to mount me swiftly into the bosom of him
who my soul loves, [his excellent Majesty, the King of Glory.] Where
I have been, where I have been, where I have been, hug'd, imbrac't,
and kist with the kisses of his mouth, whose loves are better then wine,
and have been utterly overcome therewith, beyond expression, beyond
admiration" (13 [Smith, 108]). This section of Coppe's work is much
less hesitant about articulating the relationship between spirituality and
lust. Likewise the explicit references to Canticles manifest the simul-
taneous spirituality and sexuality in a verse such as: "Let him kiss me
with the kisses of his mouth for thy love is better than wine."¹⁰

Nor is the association between spirituality and sexuality from Canti-
cles limited to Coppe. In a pamphlet written while he was still a Ranter,
Laurence Clarkson quotes Canticles to justify adultery and other for-
bidden acts:

> Observe not the act nakedly, as the act, for we find the Prayer
> and Prayses of some to be pure, though to others impure: impure
> to those acting, in relation to the title his apprehension, his Con-
> science in the improvement of them is defiled and condemned for
> a Swearer, a Drunkard, an Adulterer, and a theef.
>
> When as a man in purity in light, acts the same acts, in rela-
> tion to the act, and not to the title: this man [no this man] doth
> not swear, whore, nor steal. . . . as it is said, *Thou art all fair my
> Love, there is no spot in thee.* Observe, all fair my love; in thee is
> beauty and purity, without defilement: my love my dove is but
> one, thou one, not two, but only one, my love: Love is God and
> God is Love; so all pure, all light, no spot in thee.¹¹

The love described in Canticles ("Thou art all fair, my love; there is
no spot in thee" 4:7) appears here as part of Clarkson's insistence upon
the spirit of imagination. He indicates that actions are not inherent de-
terminers of morality. Two similar acts can have entirely different sig-
nificance depending upon the thinking of the actors during the action.

Ten years later, Clarkson looks back at his career as a Ranter and
ignores anything elevating and admirable about the experience. Instead

he focuses upon the degradation and manipulativeness of his sexual exploits. In one memorable passage he recalls his misuse of the kind of preaching he described in the previous pamphlet:

> so coming to *Canterbury* there was some six of this way, amongst whom was a maid of pretty knowledge, who with my Doctrine was affected, and I affected to lye with her, so that night prevailed, and satisfied my lust, afterwards the mayd was highly in love with me, and as gladly would I have been shut of her, lest some danger had ensued, so not knowing I had a wife she was in hopes to marry me, and so would have me lodge with her again, which fain I would, but durst not, then she was afraid I would deceive her, and would travel with me, but by subtilty of reason I perswaded her to have patience, while I went into *Suffolk*, and setled my occasions, then I would come and marry her, so for the present we parted, and full glad was I that I was from her delivered . . . and then I heard the maid had been in those parts to seek me, but not hearing of me, returned home again, and not long after was married to one of that sect, and so there was an end of any further progress into *Kent*.[12]

In the same pamphlet he explains that Solomon had been central to his errors: "and indeed *Solomons* Writings was the original of my filthy lust, supposing I might take the same liberty as he did, not then understanding his Writings was no Scripture" (26 [Smith, 181]).

Lodowick Muggleton records a similar view about the source of Ranter sexual practices:

> for whoever is in *Solomons* spirit; doth not know the true God, nor the right devil, for *Solomon* knew neither of them, though he was a wise man in things of nature, but ignorant of spiritual and heavenly wisdom; for *Solomons* wisdom hath the Ground-work of much lust of the flesh and idolatry; for the Ranters practice was grounded upon *Solomons* practice, who knew so many women, so the Ranters thought they might have the same liberty, seeing wise *Solomons* Writings were owned for Scripture-record; thus they continued many of them in their practice of lust till many

of them were weary of it, as *Solomon* was when he was old, and then they left off that practice, and turned Quakers; and so fell to be the greatest idolaters of any, as *Solomon* did to his Heathenish Wives, drew his heart away from the worship of *Moses*, to worship idols.

So is it with those Ranters that are turned Quakers, they are become absolute Heathen idolaters, for when they were *Puritaines*, so called, they were zealous for the letter of the Scriptures, and did practice a good life as near as they could to the letter, but after they fell to the practice of lust, being encouraged by *Solomons* writings, they left that legal worship and civil practice the law tied them unto, and followed *Solomons* practice of lust.[13]

Muggleton's impression of the relevance of Solomon (and his Song) on Ranter practices speaks for itself. Although this may represent no more than Muggleton's prejudiced views of a rival sect, it is significant that both he and Laurence Clarkson, his former Ranter convert, explicitly connected Solomon and the Ranters. By attacking Solomon and his works, the Muggletonians were discarding what they regarded as a dangerous, corrupting text from biblical canon. Their sense of the power of Canticles to corrupt believers is additional evidence of the importance of a simultaneously sexual and spiritual understanding of this biblical book in the minds of the Ranters and their critics.

Additional evidence for the connection between Canticles and Ranter sexual practice can be found in an anonymous song recently discovered:

> As I was walking on a day, itt thus did come to passe
> A gallant Citty I expied Jerusalem new itt was
> A gallant Citty to behold wherein was pastures greene,
> A waterie fountaine was therein 2 bankes it run between,
> The gates therof they were nott shutt by day nor yet by
>   night,
> And ere the neerer I did come the more itt shined bright
> And fain I would enter therein and gott the gates within,
> Where Ball my nagge might have a dras-(?)* or therin
>   I might swim

And e're the More I sought to gett into these Meadows
  greene,
A while for to refresh myself or sleepe those Hills between,
The more the gates were closed too, which did mee much
  annoy,
But if I had gott in therto I'me sure I had gott a Boy,
But since thus basely from this place I am repulsed soe
The nought but cry and call for Plagues to wheresoere
  I goe,
O God confound them suddainly their Creditts bring to
  thrall,
And all that is to bee consum'd, O God consume itt all.

*Possibly *draught*[14]

The speaker's desire to "sleepe those Hills between" corresponds to the words of the beloved in Canticles: "he shall lie betwixt my breasts" (1:13). The speaker presents Jerusalem as a woman with whom he wants to make love and have a child. Although the sexual imagery is quite direct, the use of Canticles combines the holy and the sexual in a vision that incorporates both into a strange amalgam of ambiguity. The city appears as a pastoral sexual paradise that is somehow closed to the speaker. His only recourse is to ask God to "consume it all," perhaps as an expression of jealousy and frustration. In any case, the paradise that is in some sense lost for the speaker is not unlike Milton's Eden insofar as it encompasses the spiritual and the sexual in terms of Canticles. The speaker in the poem stresses apocalypse, likewise an important aspect of the Ranter community which expected the beginning of the end of days in the late 1640s or early 1650s. Like similar texts by Coppe and Clarkson, this poem refers to the nexus between Canticles, sexuality, and spirituality within the Ranter community, while it simultaneously calls for the apocalyptic destruction expected at the end of days.

During the two decades that separated the publication of Ranter works by Coppe and Clarkson and that of *Paradise Lost*, the English political scene changed radically. Coppe's expectation of imminent apocalypse in 1649 had lost much of its urgency long before the Restoration made it clear that the hopes of many English Protestants for the establishment of God's kingdom on earth had been premature. *Paradise Lost* shifts the imminent expectation of the Interregnum to a sense of an inner paradise that somehow consoles its readers for the loss of Eden. A comparison between Milton's Eden and the promises of Coppe and Clarkson suggests that, like the Ranters, Adam and Eve enjoyed a liberty that assumed innocence. When Satan's machinations ruined them, he also foredoomed the entire revolution, but with an important difference. Adam's similarities to the Ranters end with the Fall. The "Paradise within . . . happier farr" (12.587) has no equivalent in Ranter practice which in some sense had tried to deny the fallen condition.

Clearly certain parallels exist between Milton's Adam and Ranter presentation of holiness and sexuality through Canticles. These in some sense provide a Miltonic revision of revolutionary radical ideas in a biblical context that eliminates the most obvious objections to Ranter practice. Thus the various indications of Ranter public adultery are irrelevant in Eden since Adam's only sexual partner is Eve. On the other hand, Adam's love for Eve is articulated in terms that suggest a passage from Canticles. It is one of the earliest indications in the epic of Adam's confusion between two kinds of love. On one hand he is committed to Agape, love of God and the consequent obedience demanded of humanity. Nevertheless he is also in the grip of Eros, deeply, even irrationally, in love with Eve. Although there is nothing tainted about the coexistence of these two loves, a dynamic tension develops between them which provides motivation for the fall in Book 9.

At the beginning of Book 5 of *Paradise Lost*, Adam awakens Eve from her Satanic dream and in so doing evokes the same intertext from Canticles that Coppe used to develop his metaphor of spiritual awakening. He sings:

> Awake
> My fairest, my espous'd, my latest found,
> Heav'ns last best gift, my ever new delight,
> Awake, the morning shines, and the fresh field
> Calls us, we lose the prime, to mark how spring
> Our tended Plants, how blows the Citron Grove,
> What drops the Myrrh, and what the balmie Reed,

How Nature paints her colours, how the Bee
Sits on the Bloom extracting liquid sweet.
(5.17–25)

The connections between this passage and Canticles (2:10-13 and 7:11–12)
are well known to Milton scholarship.[15] Adam's use of Solomon's
words says something about the biblical poem just as it tells us about
the love he feels. The significance of Milton's use of the biblical inter-
text is further complicated by the specific use of the same intertext by
Coppe as well as by the general Ranter interest in Solomon's Song as
a biblical warrant for their rites and views.

In a mythic sense Adam can be understood to have inspired Solomon
to compose Canticles thousands of years later. Solomon's Song is then
somehow about the relations between Adam and Eve. Thus when the
lover in Canticles invites the beloved to "go forth into the field" to "see
if the vine flourish" (7:11–12), he is evoking Adam's song to Eve. On
a human level this makes Canticles a text about man's love for woman
and her no less impassioned response. Just as Milton's epic is quite ex-
plicit about sexuality and lovemaking before the Fall, so it provides an
interpretation of Canticles that is equally straightforward about sexual-
ity in the biblical text. This is not, however, to reject a spiritual or alle-
gorical reading of Canticles. In his divorce tracts Milton had been quite
definite about the way sexual and romantic love provide a model for
spiritual love: "and in the Song of Songs, which is generally beleev'd,
even in the jolliest expressions to figure the spousals of the Church with
Christ, [wisest *Salomon*] sings of a thousand raptures between those
two lovely ones farre on the hither side of carnall enjoyment." He cites
this as an instance by which "we may imagine how indulgently God
provided against mans loneliness."[16] Milton had no use for the fears of
sexuality expressed by most Protestant biblical commentators on Can-
ticles.[17] He saw Eros as an integral part of the human condition which
led to Agape when properly experienced. Similarly, *Paradise Lost* inti-
mates that the sexual love of Adam for Eve is part of a process that
leads eventually to the sacrifice of the Son and the resultant Christian
redemption. Adam's erotic love is a type of Christ's agapic love for the
Church and humanity. The intertext from Canticles thus suggests the

typological methodology of reading that informs all of *Paradise Lost*. The type prefigures the antitype, yet is no less real and earthy as it does so. Such typological language is the "Signe" that Coppe wanted to transcend, but which Milton recognized was essential to human existence and understanding.

The potential of Adam's love for Eve is made more intense when Eve responds to the love song with an account of a similar song that she has heard in her dream. Satan's Cavalier parody of Adam's song, analyzed by Howard Schultz,[18] represents the manipulative, sexist approach to love of all kinds. Adam ignores the Satanic perversions of the dream song which substitutes idolatry for the spiritual potential of his own poem. Satan's song thus presents Eve with a bogus type of spiritual temptation:

> Here, happie Creature, fair Angelic *Eve*,
> Partake thou also; happie though thou art,
> Happier thou mayst be, worthier canst not be:
> Taste this, and be henceforth among the Gods
> Thy self a Goddess, not to Earth confind.
>
> (5.74–78)

Adam's love song to Eve is thus ironic on different levels. It is a passionate call to Eve that anticipates Adam's failure to realize the difference between the values of human and divine love. At this level the irony is partially established by the reader's consciousness of the traditional fulfillment of the lover's love for his beloved in Canticles, i.e., Christ's love for the Church. On another level, the irony results from an awareness of the ways in which Canticles was seen by Ranters such as Coppe and Clarkson. The vision of these radical antinomians is spiritualized by Adam in Book 5 when he internalizes their attempt to see sexuality and holiness as part of a unified process. A revision of Ranter doctrine in the context of unfallen Adam suggests that as long as love for Eve leads Adam toward God, as does the Son's love for the Church, sexual Eros is holy and commendable. There is no necessary distinction between the sexual and the holy for Adam before he eats the fruit. Nevertheless, the possibility of confusion remains an option throughout the epic. Indeed, it is this that makes Satan's task feasible and finally successful.

Viewing Adam as Ranter, a reader could thus consider the love song to Eve in the context of Coppe's entreaties: "Rise up, rise up, my Love, my fair one, and *come away* . . ." or of Clarkson's argument: *"Thou art all fair my love, there is no spot in thee.* . . . Love is God and God is Love; so all pure, all, light, no spot in thee."[19] That is, in addition to the sexual aspects of the Ranter rites, there were clear entreaties for spiritual awakening as well. If Adam is akin to Coppe and Clarkson, he is also conscious of the spiritual implications of his words that will inspire Solomon. As long as he perceives the values of holy and sexual love as consistent, he cannot fall.

When Adam surrenders his monistic unity for the dialectically opposed worlds of Satan and God, he falls like Clarkson into total Muggletonian rejection of Solomon and a reconsideration of his love for Eve in selfish, manipulative terms. After eating the fruit, Adam regards Eve as a sexual object:

> For never did thy Beautie since the day
> I saw thee first and wedded thee, adorn'd
> With all perfections, so enflame my sense
> With ardor to enjoy thee, fairer now
> Then ever, bountie of this vertuous Tree.
>
> (9.1029–33)

Later on, he can only recall her part in his deliberate fall. His understanding of love has lost the mixture of Eros and Agape that characterized it before the fall. His excuse for eating the fruit is selfless love for Eve, but only a little while after the act he begins to scold and blame her:

> Is this the Love, is this the recompence
> Of mine to thee, ingrateful *Eve*, exprest
> Immutable when thou wert lost, not I,
> Who might have liv'd and joyd immortal bliss,
> Yet willingly chose rather Death with thee:
> And am I now upbraided, as the cause
> Of thy transgressing? not enough severe,
> It seems, in thy restraint: what could I more?
> . . . .

and perhaps
I also err'd in overmuch admiring
What seemd in thee so perfet, that I thought
No evil durst attempt thee, but I rue
That errour now, which is become my crime,
And thou th'accuser. Thus it shall befall
Him who to worth in Woman overtrusting
Let her will rule; restraint she will not brook,
And left t'her self, if evil thence ensue,
Shee first his weak indulgence will accuse.

(9.1163–70,77–86)

Perhaps a sense of Adam as refined Ranter can thus clarify some of the ironies implicit in his perceptions of himself and his love. A proper understanding of his typological relationship to God and the Son would have made it clear that Satanic imitation of the Son's sacrifice by eating the fruit would be a confusion of roles. Had he been able, in the Ranter fashion of Coppe and Clarkson, to maintain the Eros as well as the Agape that is implicit through Canticles in his love song to Eve, he could have remained in Eden. Instead he confused the way to unite his loves and betrayed them both, like Clarkson in his *Lost Sheep Found*. The inspiration Adam brings Solomon remains unfulfilled in Book 5 and irrelevant after the eating of the fruit in Book 9. Adam is still the only potentially perfect Ranter, but he misunderstands the nature of his happiness and then destroys it. The redemption yet available to him no longer owes anything to the Ranter vision.

Notes

1. For a history of the Ranters including a bibliography of original sources, see A. L. Morton, *The World of the Ranters: Religious Radicalism in the English Revolution* (London: Lawrence & Wishart, 1970).

2. Christopher Hill, *Milton and the English Revolution* (New York: Viking Press, 1978), 345.

3. *Paradise Lost* 4.110. All citations from Milton's poetry are to *The Complete Poetry of John Milton*, ed. John T. Shawcross, rev. ed. (Garden City, N.Y.: Doubleday and Co., 1971).

4. Joan S. Bennett, "'Go': Milton's Antinomianism and the Separation Scene in *Paradise Lost*, Book 9," *PMLA* 98 (1983): 389.

5. E.g., Gilbert Roulston, who referred to himself as "a late fellow RANTER" on the title page of *The Ranters Bible, Or, Seven several Religions by them held and maintain'd* . . . (London, 1650). Another pamphleteer, one J. M. identified himself as "(a deluded Brother) lately escaped out of their snare" on the title page of *The Ranters Last Sermon* . . . (London, 1654).

6. Nigel Smith, "Introduction," *A Collection of Ranter Writings From the Seventeenth Century* (London: Junction Books Ltd., 1983), 12. I shall provide bracketed references to this important anthology whenever Smith has reprinted the text under consideration.

7. Abiezer Coppe, *SOME Sweet Sips of Some Spirituall Wine, sweetly and freely dropping from one cluster of Grapes, brought between two upon a Staffe from Spirituall Canaan (the Land of the Living; the Living Lord.) TO Late Egyptian, and now bewildered Israelites* (London, 1649), 17–18 [Smith, 55].

8. *Some Sweet Sips*, 2–3 [Smith, 47–48].

9. *A Second Fiery Flying Roule: To All the Inhabitants of the earth; specially to the rich ones* . . . (London, 1649), 11 [Smith, 106–7]. Although this pamphlet has its own title page, it is bound together with *A Fiery Flying Roll* in the British Museum copy (Thomason Tracts). Page 11 is misnumbered 9 in the original.

10. Song of Songs 1:2. All biblical citations in my text are to the King James translation.

11. L[aurence] C[larkson], *A Single Eye: All Light, no Darkness; or Light and Darkness One* . . . (London, 1650), 10 [Smith, 170]. Clarkson acknowledged writing this pamphlet published under the initials L. C. in *The Lost Sheep Found* (London, 1660), 26 [Smith, 181]. There he described his previous life and various beliefs along with a great many details about his Ranter experience, including his refusal to admit having written *A Single Eye* when confronted by a committee of Parliament (30 [Smith, 184]). Testimony from *The Lost Sheep Found* must, of course, be regarded as similar to works of other "late fellow Ranters" and does not have the same testimonial validity as *A Single Eye* which was written when Clarkson was still a believing Ranter.

12. *The Lost Sheep Found*, 22–23 [Smith, 178–79].

13. Lodowick Muggleton, *A Looking-Glass for George Fox the Quaker, and other Quakers; Wherein they may see themselves to be Right Devils. In Answer to George Fox his Book Called Something in Answer to Lodowick Muggletons Book, which he calls The Quakers Neck broken* (London, 1668) [corrected on title page from 1667], 63–64.

14. Anne Laurence, "Two Ranter Poems," *Review of English Studies* 31 (1980): 59.

15. H. J. Todd pointed out that "Addison has observed the similarity of this address to that of Solomon, Cant. ii.10, &c." *The Poetical Works of John Milton* . . . 3rd ed. (London, 1826), 2:374. Merritt Y. Hughes (John Milton, *Paradise Lost: A Poem*

290 □ *Noam Flinker*

in Twelve Books [Indianapolis: Odyssey Press, 1962], 113) and Alastair Fowler (*The Poems of John Milton* [London: Longmans, 1968], 675) also have appropriate comments about the allusion. Diane Kelsey McColley (*Milton's Eve* [Urbana: University of Illinois Press, 1983], 92–98) discusses the relevance of the reference in terms of the vast tradition of medieval and Renaissance commentary. She stresses the typological force of the material from Canticles and points out that "The Song of Songs is, after all, an impassioned love poem; and one finds in Milton's use of it none of the strain to disembody or reembody the divine lovers that one finds in the allegorical annotations" (97).

    16. *Tetrachordon*, in *Complete Prose Works of John Milton*, gen. ed. Don M. Wolfe (New Haven: Yale University Press, 1959) 2:597. There is a similar reference to Canticles (8:6–7) in Milton's *Doctrine and Discipline of Divorce*: "but this pure and more inbred desire of joyning to it self in conjugall fellowship a fit conversing soul (which desire is properly call'd love) *is stronger than death*, as the Spouse of Christ thought, *many waters cannot quench it, neither can the flouds drown it*" (2:251).

    17. Cf. the words of Nathaniel Homes as quoted by George L. Scheper in his "Reformation Attitudes Toward Allegory and the Song of Songs," *PMLA* 89 (1974): 558: "away, say we, with all carnal thoughts, whiles we have heavenly things presented us under the notion of Kisses, Lips, Breasts, Navel, Thighs, Leggs. Our minds must be above our selves, altogether minding heavenly meanings."

    18. Howard Schultz, "Satan's Serenade," *Philological Quarterly* 27 (1948): 24–26.

    19. *Some Sweet Sips*, 15 [Smith, 53]; *A Single Eye*, 10 [Smith, 170].

Milton's Floating Couch:
The White Devil
of Paradise Regained

CHRISTOPHER GROSE

Neither *Samson Agonistes* nor *Paradise Regained*, of course, ends
with the verbal act which seals the personal or vocational
identity of Milton's protagonists. In *Paradise Regained*, the
narrator is free to carry on when the central struggle is concluded, and
the Son and Satan have left the stage; along with the briefest of dismis-
sals for the Son ("Home to his Mother's house"), there is the angel
chorus, and just before that the peculiar banquet for the poem's hero.
It is a meal uncomfortably reminiscent of the kind of thing at which
Milton had once said he was neither skilled nor studious:

> So Satan fell; and straight a fiery Globe
> Of Angels on full sail of wing flew nigh,
> Who on their plumy Vans receiv'd him soft
> From his uneasy station, and upbore
> As on a floating couch through the blithe Air,
> Then in a flow'ry valley set him down
> On a green bank, and set before him spread
> A table of Celestial Food, Divine,
> Ambrosial, Fruits fetcht from the tree of life,
> And from the fount of life Ambrosial drink,
> That soon refresh'd him wearied, and repair'd
> What hunger, if aught hunger had impair'd,
> Or thirst; and as he fed, Angelic Choirs
> Sung Heavenly Anthems of his victory

Over temptation and the Tempter proud.
(4.581-95)[1]

The aftermath of the Son's heroic deed is full of disturbing features. If we have read well, I think we cannot help worrying about those "plumy Vans," the blitheness of the local air, and (most of all, perhaps) the downright unMiltonic ease of that "floating couch." Like all Miltonic analogy, this one carries us toward ourselves, in the direction of this world and our own creature comforts; if there's no brandy and slippers, it's still more than a little decadent, the way "fiery Globe/ Of Angels" gets pictured, all too like that "pomp of winning Graces" suddenly attending Eve just as she leaves Adam and Raphael to their astronomical men's talk. And the problem of this scene is compounded by its placement. The son's victory over Satan has just involved a most impressive fusion between speech and actual, not merely evident, plot: "he said and stood" (4.561). Having vanquished Satan through this radical union of speech with metaphysical reality, why should Milton go on? And why, specifically, does he once again put these realms asunder, reverting to an externally-based narrative in this almost melodramatic turn to the spectacle of Satan's fall, "smitten with amazement" (4.562)[2] The description of the banquet begins with what looks like a second brief narrative of Satan's fall, presented with the finest dovetailing: "So Satan fell; and straight . . ." And because of our relocation of the real plot in metaphysical or spiritual territory just a moment ago, it becomes difficult to accept these delicacies as something offered only to the Son. Despite the narrator's severity in forcing personal distinctions (almost gloatingly at 580), it is not easy to refer the "him" of two lines later to anyone but the original subject of this sentence. Indeed, I would claim that we can confidently sort out these references only after the fact, when once again (in 594-95) Milton tells us who did what to whom, in this passage and also in the epic as a whole. Satan may be safely "debelled," but Milton *lingers* on the fate of the Adversary. He makes it difficult not to feel relief: here's the *tour de force* Milton really wanted to write, real epic at last! The more eagerly the poet disposes of his *dramatis personae* in space—Satan with his "crew, that sat consulting" (577), and the Son of God necessarily somewhere (anywhere!) else—

the greater our difficulty in deciding who is where. In short, I would argue that until recently in the brief epic, it has been hard *not* to read well, thanks to the active presence of this poem's bard, the divine protagonist himself; the divine Son's own critical pressures in *Paradise Regained* prevent any easy or exclusive application of this material to Jesus' experience. But here, the scene is conspicuously free from the kind of interpretive aids which Milton has hitherto supplied; no tell-tale "as seemed," no click of harpies' wings. As readers, we are on our own now, working without much help in a literary counterpart to the Son's own wilderness, following his and Satan's departure—if a Miltonic Satan ever *could* entirely disappear.

Almost from the beginning, of course, it was commonplace for readers to patronize or virtually ignore the Satan of Milton's brief epic, primarily because he did not quite measure up to his splendidly eloquent predecessor. Here, he was a depressed and world-weary figure who too clearly reflected the misfortunes or mistakes of his author, an altogether unworthy opponent for the Son, whose "heroic" victory consequently struck many readers as more than a little hollow, even downright uninteresting. In some of the recent scholarship on *Paradise Regained*, Satan has shown signs of the Antaean strength he possessed for Luther and other reforming authors.[3] It seems that he can be taken seriously again, either because there is more of his predecessor in him than we might have thought, or (more promising) he is a fit antagonist after all, a dialectician more or less in command of his strategies and seeking to undermine the very identity of his opponent. In fact, there are important connections between the Satan of *Paradise Regained* and his great predecessor, together with some signs that Milton has deepened his conception in at least one respect. If Satan is a strategically skillful speaker, we must also account for a new and evasive verbal *honesty*, an almost compulsive need to keep on talking, as though he were Samson in the old "effeminate" days—to translate and revise his speech. If he is no longer the grandly titled "father of lies," he is a *talker*, a chatty sophisticate like Comus or Belial, given an instinct for truthtelling found in *Paradise Lost* only in the unpremeditated speech of first awakening or the semi-privacy of Mt. Niphates. As in *Paradise Lost*, it is Satan's fate to experience forever that "desire / To see thee and approach thee"

(1.383–84), just as he had done with Eve alone in the garden. But in a more subtle and curious way than the earlier poem, the brief epic suggests that Satan's well-known literalism, the particularity of his language, his lyric propensity—all these actually involve the attempt to abstract himself from his own evil, to forget. So he dreams on of the angels' "mild seats" as a species of Heaven, and he postures grandly about his fear of a "ris'n" enemy (2.125, 127); he will speak of the Fall from Heaven as though it never took place, and he gets picky about the historical agenda and the providential means with which "that fatal wound / Shall be inflicted by the Seed of *Eve* / Upon my head" (1.53–55). But the talk is never quite convincing; and as the last example suggests, Satan literally cannot forget his "hated habitation" (1.47) any more than he can forget himself, here or in *Paradise Lost*.[4]

Far from making Satan's overweening memory the occasion for pathos, Milton makes it conceptually and stylistically central; it becomes the brief epic's idea of Satan. Unlike his predecessor, he serves as our memory too, or at least our raw, unheroic memory. In the Adversary's very first speech, Milton suggests that he provides our contact with the human "ages" now being reviewed in such different fashion—in an uninvolved way no reader could possibly manage—by the divine Son. Satan claims to have witnessed the Son's entire career, in and also outside history; he has heard the prophesies of the Messiah, of the Annunciation, and of course the early "private" career, to which the present encounter serves as culmination: "From that time seldom have I ceas'd to eye / Thy infancy, thy childhood, and thy youth, / Thy manhood last, though yet in private bred" (4. 507–09). It is Satan, indeed, who offers the poem's first explicit reminder of Genesis 3:15 and the "oracle" so embarrassing to himself (1.53–55). Within the work too, he is the original witness; his entire function can be summarized in the words of the narrator immediately following the first account of the Baptism: "That heard the Adversary" (1.33). This poem's Satan seems composed of what he has "seen, or by relation heard" (2.182); he is almost literally a creature of tradition, and the pervasiveness of tradition is a central preoccupation of the poem. The brief epic's first sustained use of Scripture occurs during the Son's memory of his mother's speech, where—together with the seemingly unexceptionable shepherds and a "glorious Choir / Of

Angels"—we discover, of all things, a "vested Priest" standing right there before "Just *Simeon* and prophetic *Anna*" (1.242–43, 255–57). Here as in *Paradise Lost*, the sources of tradition are located "Fast by the Oracle of God" (*PL* 1.12) and its practice entangled in false worship "with Temple, Priest, and Sacrifice" (3.83). And Satan is its vehicle, whether he is considered as a character, mode of behavior, or institution. It is he and not the Son himself who ventures to quote the "Sovran voice" at Jordan (1.84–85), while we are scrupulously denied access to this text. (This has not deterred intelligent readers from accepting the quotation as authentic, and even attributing it to the Son—one of the many interesting lapses in the poem's critical history.) And the Adversary has plenty of assistance, from those intelligence reports and "councils" to the behavior of the "new-baptized."

A common complaint about *Paradise Regained* is that, for whatever reason, Satan has arrived too late to pose anything like an adequate test for Milton's heroic Son. And in keeping with the supposed "degeneration" of Satan in *Paradise Lost*, the world-weary antagonist is sometimes thought to become even more demoralized, if this is possible, as the work proceeds. But in both of Milton's epics as in Reformed theology, Satan is irrelevant considered simply as a dramatic spectacle—innocent victim, heroic rebel, grand combination of Elizabethan villain and epic hero, what you will. To apply a distinction from *Paradise Lost*, if Satan ever was "actual," he is now within us, "in body" (*PL* 10.587); in both works he waits "day and night for [man's] destruction" (*PL* 2.505). In large measure, the difficulty of the brief epic is due to misunderstandings about how Milton puts Satan within us. This Adversary, I would claim, plays a twofold part, as an embodiment of the Son's memory in all its detail, but also as a worse-than-fallible early witness and scribe. As a vestigial "conscience" (in the seventeenth-century sense), Satan resembles the Chorus and the other visitors to Samson, vocalizing and expatiating upon the Son's memories and early consciousness in general, presenting what in *Samson Agonistes* are called the protagonist's "thoughts."[5] As the bystanders to this encounter, we witness the ritualized aftermath of a biographical struggle never really enacted within the poem, but instead rehearsed in the Son's memories of Book 1—the nearest thing here to the intensity of Satan's soliloquy on Mt. Niphates.

But more importantly for the reader of *Paradise Regained*—for the late-Reformation, nonMessianic observer, at any rate—the Adversary functions as the prime onstage recipient and echo of the emerging author's words; he stands for the divine protagonist's early public, a prominent character in both poems of Milton's final volume. Thus viewed, the scene of *Paradise Regained* becomes what Milton considered to be the narrow verge between the tradition-bound antecedents of this crucial moment in human history and its equally traditionalizing reception. In it, Milton writes the history of the inner "motions" which precede and eventuate in the Gospel. But *Paradise Regained* is more wide-ranging than its companion partly because it seems to incorporate, in addition, that future conversation with the "gentiles"—in effect, with us—to which the Adversary refers toward the end of the poem. Like the Book of Judges for *Samson Agonistes*, the familiar source of Milton's myth is synecdochically included within the work, a distant aftermath of the authentic events we witness, a creation of the public to which I have referred. It is as though Milton were coupling Luke's account with an epitome of Acts, say, or Paul's epistle to the Galatians; the epic encompasses the early, but for Milton also a kind of paradigmatic history of the Church of the world. Thus the poem's ambiguous allusion to the eventual "fame" of Andrew and Simon, on the one hand, and its insistence (more emphatic than in *Paradise Lost*) that the central action was performed "in secret" and consequently "unrecorded left through many an age" (1.15–16). In reading Milton's brief epic, we are witnessing nothing less than the divine Son's glimpsing of providential "means," including the fact of his own human suffering; but we do all this, I would submit, in the company of tradition's own special guardian, the "white devil."[6]

Luther's name for the keeper of traditions and the expert in their strange powers of fascination was meant to distinguish him from the "black" devil, who wears the kind of easy label ("error," or "devil") that makes him less a threat than a cartoon figure. The real Adversary, of course, "does not want to be as black as he is painted," Luther had written; "he would like to shine in the beautiful garment of God's Word."[7] Satan consequently "adorns himself with such an angelic, yes, such a divine form and appearance, just as he makes a god of himself when he speaks to Christ in Matt. 4:9" (*Luther's Works*, 24:312). Tak-

ing his seat "not in a stable or in a pigpen or in a congregation of un-
believers, but in the highest and holiest places possible, namely in the
temple of God," the white devil is a specialist, as Luther sees it, in cus-
tom and the impossible claims of the Law—in general, the whole area
of spirituality, where he "peddles his deadly poison as the doctrine of
grace, the Word of God, and the Gospel of Christ, in the guise of an
Angel or even God himself" (Luther's Works, 26:25). And the white devil's
primary technique is fascination, bedazzlement, a form of deception con-
sistently described as visual: "he stirs up dust, hoping to raise a cloud
before our eyes so that we cannot see the light. In the cloud he dazzles
us with will o' the wisps to mislead us" (Luther's Works, 40:262). He
seeks to "lead us off our path by his flying brands and flames" (Luther's
Works, 40:70). Under such circumstances—and especially in a church—it
is the Christian's difficult task to "receive [God's] Word without stop-
ping to gaze at its external beauty or equipment," "for [God] permits
no false prophets to attempt anything except something external, such
as works, and subtle minute discoveries about external things" (Luther's
Works, 20:73; 40:80). If Milton's Satan were conceived along these lines,
it would explain the extraordinary extent of his involvement or over-
lapping with the whole range of the work's characters, including the
Son—an artistic development with interesting and perhaps not altogether
manageable implications for the role and actual behavior of the epic
historian himself.

2

In Paradise Lost, we are lucky. We have the occasionally clairvoyant
bard (together with several assistants) to jog us out of our amazement,
to remind us that for all the visual fascination of the first book, it is
really the ear of that belated peasant which is getting charmed, the reader
of the poem who is tricked into thinking that he sees things. In Para-
dise Regained this kind of interpretive assistance is rather quickly removed,
and with it our grasp of God's "permissive will." It is relatively early
that we are offered the fully explained version of how the Satanic wiles
fit with the divine plan: whatever the Adversary's intentions, we are

dealing with a "contrary" fulfillment of the "purpos'd Counsel pre-ordain'd and fixt / Of the most High" (1.127–28). Briefly but unmistakably, Milton points to the fullness of the Son's trial "Through all temptation" (1.5) and the plenary verification of the central promise declared in the Scriptural *protevangelium*.[8] And as in *Paradise Lost* he does so by surrounding the Satanic perspective with a sort of governing doctrinal field, the divine "prospect high" (*PL* 3.77). But in the brief epic this is the last such interpretive intrusion on the part of the narrator. His subsequent clarifications are both more limited in extent and also more clearly pathetic—they are responses from the human community rather than a critic's authoritative exposition.[9] Before long, Satan gives instructions to stage-management to a "chosen band / Of Spirits likest to himself in guile / To be at hand, and at his beck appear, / If cause were to unfold some active Scene / Of various persons, each to know his part" (2.236–40). Innocuous though it seems at the moment, the incident involves an irreversible attachment of staging to demonic agency. From this point on, we are virtually left to our own devices, allowed to explore this literary wild with the assistance of two rival guides who *aren't* the poet; and the more talkative of our two guides is now evidently in charge of scenery, as though Belial and Mammon had joined forces in a latter-day reprise of the council in Hell. Only Satan figures to benefit from a gradual retirement of the narrator as expository assistant, and he can be said to displace the narrator as the purveyor of the story in its external aspect—the visible world of *Paradise Regained*. Bound to full authenticity in presenting material previously "unrecorded," the poet has become an adjunct of Milton's own white devil. If the Miltonic orator can command words to fall "into their own places" in the fashion of "nimble and airy servitors," as Milton wrote in the *Apology against a Pamphlet*, the brief epic extends his verbal powers into the realm of visible, apparently real, events (*Complete Prose*, 1:949).[10]

Milton's presentation of the setting helps make the point. Earlier, we were better readers; when we first meet the proto-Wordsworthian "aged man in Rural weeds" (1.314), the parenthetic formulae remind us that first appearances are superficial; Milton actually indulges our curiosity only to rebuke it, in this way making his story's manifold particulars problematic, even irrelevant:

Full forty days he pass'd, whether on hill
Sometimes, anon in shady vale, each night
Under the covert of some ancient Oak,
Or Cedar, to defend him from the dew,
Or harbor'd in one Cave, is not reveal'd.

(1.303–7)

There are indications elsewhere that Satan is literally involved with the "dark shades and rocks" of the wilderness (194), just as he seemed to inhabit the mists and exhalations of *Paradise Lost*; and these particulars are qualified only by the Son. Once the Adversary's servitors are in place, however—once Satan has posed the ultimate challenge to such critical resistance—it is hard to see how a reader can easily forget them, so programmatically are they introduced as to variety of persons and indeterminateness of form or "part." And I believe that Milton is at some pains to keep this quasi-authorial supervision in mind as we proceed. In the middle of the second book, the Son dreams of Elijah while sleeping in a "hospitable covert . . . / Of Trees thick interwoven" (2.262–63). Within twenty lines, he has waked and entered a similarly enclosed area, determined to rest at noon. For him (and temporarily for us) it is a scene of easily resisted temptation; the shade is

High rooft, and walks beneath, the alleys brown
That open'd in the midst a woody Scene;
Nature's own work it seem'd (Nature taught Art)
And to a Superstitious eye the haunt
Of Wood Gods and Wood Nymphs; he view'd it round.

(2.292–97)

For the time being we share the Son's vision, and experience something like the bard's clairvoyance. Whatever our problems with the later prospects and panoramas—and these persist virtually to the end of the poem—the Son's view of these matters at any rate does *not* involve a "Superstitious eye." Even so, however, the "active scene" continues to unfold—to be fallen is to forget. It is a massive recollection of classical fable and learning from the earlier exchange with Belial, from the similes and especially the catalogue of the earlier epic's first book, and beyond that, from the mythographical speculations of Milton's youthful reading: those "stripling youths" compared to Ganymede and Hylas, then nymphs "of *Diana's* train." Naiades bringing fruits and flowers retrieved "from *Amalthea's* horn, / And ladies of th'*Hesperides*" (2.352–57). All these pleasant things, Milton suggests (with his usual willingness to strive in literary wealth and luxury) were fairer than their fictional predecessors; and as he does in *Paradise Lost*, the poet extends the figural references downward historically into the relatively recent grail romances cited by Hughes. Moreover, the creatures change in perceptual status; until now relatively inert visual objects, they break into movement and controlled activity, a parodic animation of the Nativity Ode's "serviceable angels." And it is all attended by a distinctly Lydian music: "And all the while Harmonious Airs were heard / Of chiming strings or charming pipes, and winds / Of gentlest gale *Arabian* odors fann'd / From their soft wings, and *Flora's* earliest smells" (2.362–65).[11] Given the Adversary's instructions in stage-management, it is a passage involving collusion between narrative and Satanic art, the narrator himself now one of the Tempter's "airy servitors." The seemingly objective description precedes a speech (by the Adversary) which then refers to and incorporates it (368–77); and in fact that speech is singularly bare, concluding with the disclaimer that his actors were all "Spirits of Air," all those classical deities and half-reified literary allusions, in a fascinating (and for Milton a deeply-rooted) pun, "Thy gentle Ministers" (2.374–75). In this way, the real Satan of *Paradise Regained* is nothing a reader can be done with quite so soon in the narrative. As a character, he is denied much of the sympathy which bathes him in the earlier epic, and he is pronounced "foil'd / In all his wiles" more often and more variously than many readers care to remember. But Milton's conception of the antagonist and the brief epic's structure permit a brilliant and literally fascinating resilience. Even more insidious than the white devil of Luther, this Satan is at once a practitioner of deceit and himself susceptible to fascination; it is because he can still "contemplate and admire" that he seems to secure the narrator's own cooperation, and so retains for the poem's readers, if not for his onstage audience, the kind of influence which makes his evil almost irresistible. What seems bound to impress us, paradoxically, is the almost compulsively reflexive practice of his inexhaustible imagination—something rather different, to be sure, from what Harold Bloom has called the "strong poet" in Milton.[12]

For the collusion I have referred to continues, now without the disclaimers, as is clear if we consider that view from Niphates (3.251–66). Even if we remember the band of maskers, it is different not to think of this as a real mountain, not just a vision of "Nature taught Art." It is right there before the Son's eyes, something to point to, an independent, objective phenomenon of the sort Milton points to elsewhere (2.337) in a formula like "He spake no dream." But the apparently objective grandeur of the introduction to this rather long section of the poem, "It was a Mountain," seems to point to the results of a fiat; it has the effect of validating or authorizing the scene to which Satan, in charge of the visible plot, now brings the Son. This section of the poem can be seen as an extenuation of catalogue, with the difference that all the name-dropping seems to flesh out a real, geographically verifiable landscape. The poety is dedicated to the reader's own vulnerability to "subtle minute discoveries about external things," as Luther had put it. And to judge from the poem's critical history, Milton has succeeded admirably. Many of the poem's readers have become the kind of audience Satan would have the Son to be: fixated by the dazzle of world geography, philosophical schools, and even by mere shapes and forms—marching formations in the shapes of rhombs, crescents, stars. Like those pilgrims at Golgotha (PL 3.476–77), we delight in the familiarity of an actual Mt. Niphates, and would climb it if we could; a recent editor has attempted to visualize the view from its summit as though we were reading the Times Atlas of World History.

For his part, Milton's divine Son (like the Lady of Comus) is meant to be a far more imaginative and rhetorically talented character than he seems willing to demonstrate. More consistently than any reader (or at least any reader on record), the Son answers the challenge in the poem's extensive appeal to the mind's eye; in keeping with the Reformers' association of traditions with the Church's "external beauty or equipment," we seem to see things in Paradise Regained only when the Son is not speaking, only when he calls us out of our amazement with the Adversary's fictive talk. He reminds us that it is Satan's speech, evidently seconded by the narrator, which actually applies all this ornament, creates the view from Niphates. He arrests Satan's words, and *catches* things like "noblest" or "glorious" amidst the welter of particulars. Part of what he recognizes in pointing to the theologically centrifugal nature of Satan's appeals, is that all this visual material, like the Pandemonium of *Paradise Lost*, is a verbal spectacle, heroic catalogue at close quarters, culminating here again with a concrete and "visible" temple, wrongly (or very ambiguously) called "thy Father's house" (4.552). If we read and in any way yield to this poem, few of us indeed will be sufficiently undistracted to recognize the force and aptness of that decisive "I never lik'd thy talk" (4.171).

It is only partially true, however, to say that the Son himself is the chief practitioner of what is commonly regarded as Milton's own late, spare style. A central problem with the poem's structure and Milton's conception of Jesus is perfectly illustrated by the well-known anomaly near the end of the poem, when the Son suddenly becomes marvelously, uncharacteristically inventive, a development which results in something oddly close to the lyric virtuosity of Jonson's Sir Epicure Mammon:

> Nor doth this grandeur and majestic show
> Of luxury, though call'd magnificence,
> More than of arms before, allure mine eye,
> Much less my mind; though thou should'st add to tell
> Thir sumptuous gluttonies, and gorgeous feasts
> On *Citron* tables or *Atlantic* stone;
> (For I have also heard, perhaps have read)
> Their wines of *Setia*, *Cales*, and *Falerne*,
> *Chios* and *Crete*, and how they quaff in Gold,
> Crystal and Murrhine cups emboss'd with Gems
> And studs of Pearl. . . .
>
> (4.110–20)

It is an almost gratuitous bit of authorship in Satan's own kind (the "Office mean," Milton had called a similar indulgence in *Paradise Lost* [9.39]): a passage which permits us not even a distant prospect of architectural configurations, but an almost dizzying close-up of materials and adornments of drinking-cups. He is an expert in antique porcelains, we discover to our surprise, and he proves it by scrutinizing what Michael had called the "Arts that polish Life" (*PL* 11.610).

For the critic, the difficulty of the moment is suggested in Milton's parenthetic "I have also heard, *perhaps* have read," and the implications of that awful programmatic word for the speech (some would say the whole poem), "unmov'd." It is the uncommittedness of this strange figure that makes him an expository or bardlike figure; and it is easy to draw conclusions which are unrelated either to the actual range of his performance or to the Christology informing the poem. The work seems to involve a process of review that is recognizably related to the last phase of learning as Milton had described it in the seventh Prolusion and *Of Education*: the phase devoted to frequent reviews or retirements "for memories sake" until they have "confirm'd, and solidly united the whole body of their perfected knowledge, like the last embattelling of a Romane legion" (*Complete Prose*, 2:406–7). At such a point, possessed of a "universall insight into things," one might almost forget the curricular underpinnings of divine contemplation. There can be little question that Milton thought of his curriculum, including its oddly described last phase, with relation to traditional Christology. Two years earlier, he had described the Son (and other teachers of the Church) in the specifically literary terms appropriate to the *recapitulator generis humanae*, who possessed all literary gifts and commanded the whole range of styles otherwise divided among the teachers of His church. The Son of *Paradise Regained* too is imagined as uniquely gifted; a single or dominant style, like Milton's or Luther's "vehemence," would signal a character altogether different from one in literary as in other ways "perfect." Thus our impression that the Son's literary talents remain almost completely latent, and our sense of anomaly or parody when he momentarily deviates into lyricism while remaining "unmov'd," and beats Satan at his own dazzling game of verbal microscopy.[13] And his historical consciousness too is recapitulatory; he is "revolving" all these traditions, literary and prophetic texts to the point of mastery or "authority"; we are well beyond their ideological claims when he can say of them so remotely that "I have also heard, perhaps have read." His much-discussed "Think not but that I know these things; or think / I know them not" (4.286–87) consequently points to something much more specific, perhaps even technical, than the Son's well-known reticence or reserve. There seems to be gaps in the hero's information as to how he should throw off his "obscurity" and (in his seemingly incomplete phase) "openly begin" (1.288), as to how complete an analogue is to be found in Uzze-an Job. But the work remains faithful to the uniquely recapitulatory consciousness of its subject. The Son is indeed the soul of wit, in his text-minded and humorless way a literary version of Prince Hal, composed "of all humors that have showed themselves humors since the old days of goodman Adam to the pupil age of this present. . . ."[14]

For all his conceptual rigor, however, Milton knew as well as Shakespeare that there was much to be said on behalf of his Falstaff. If decorum is indeed "the grand masterpiece to observe," both the divinely recapitulatory character and the fictional setting—Jesus on the threshold of his public ministry—lend themselves to effects on the very outskirts of Milton's own sphere of artistic influence. The Son's omnicompetence, that unique and divine "talent," may well be literary death to hide. But more to the point, it is not easy to see how his perfect memory, or a mere facility in doubling stylistically with Satan can finally negate the Adversary's influence over us.[15] And the later portions of the poem in particular challenge us to remember that band of nimble and airy servitors, the ordering of Satan's masque-like spectacle; this is no easy matter when Milton and Satan alike ask us to spectate—to "behold a wonder" or "look on mee"—like the confused night-wanderers of those epic similes in *Paradise Lost*. For all his depressive tendencies, Satan lingers unidentified almost to the end of the poem, perhaps even surviving his ostensibly definitive fall. As Milton presents it, that "floating couch" is literally a part of the reception of the Son's victory, all the better for its resemblance to the reader's armchair which now furnishes so many of our most helpful readings of Milton. If we can resist the couch, it is because of the dissociative, necessarily nonreferential words like "celestial"—the term Milton applies (in *Paradise Lost*) to light, just as we are sorting out fundamental confusions between the "sovran vital Lamp" and the true (or inward) locus of inspiration. And "divine" and the reiterated "ambrosial" are here too with their world-abandoning pressures, together with the powerful repetition "tree of life . . . fount of life" (4.589–90). To negotiate this successfully, we must have become what Milton would have called "self-suspicious" readers and for good reason—the divine Son, not the narrator of *Paradise Regained*, has shown us the way.[16] And so, perhaps, the Son has indeed been "fully tried" in the typological sense that the reader too is included as the third Adam; the work can involve the ultimate verification of Scripture's central promise, that inward, Protestant displacement of those central incidents in the ancient faith, the Passion and the Harrowing.

The general effect here ought to be close to the way in which the narrator of *Paradise Lost* so abruptly reorients us near the end of Book 1. There, words like "aery" and "incorporeal" (as applied, respectively, to "spirits" and "forms") prevent a literal reading of the fallen angels' size- and shape-shifting, and help to suggest that their "strait'n'd" circumstances have less to do with numbers, size, or physical confinement than with the constrictions of the Hell within them. But the earlier part of *Paradise Regained* is in many respects closer to the eleventh book of the earlier epic—to the visions and their eventual replacement by Michael's and Adam's collaborative hermeneutics. And eventually in the brief epic, the visual fascination of the poem is so expertly or wholeheartedly indulged that we may easily forget what the Son has taught. The general loss of critical resistance extends to the poet himself, and seems bound to affect all but the most heroic readers. Like the appearance of demonic swords drawn from Cherubic thighs in Hell (*PL* 1.663–66), divine history here answers Satan's words, if indeed they are not anticipated by Mammon's own kind of visual effects. Unlike Uriel "once warned," we get drawn yet again into sensuous particulars, feeling that "sharp sleet of arrowy showers" (3.324), and forgetting all about the orderly ranks of Milton's own archers. Faced with the dazzle of human traditions, our vigilance flagging since the retirement of the poem's uniquely perfect respondent, we can only hope that the divine Son somehow manages to remain "unobserv'd." The ending of *Paradise Regained* provides Milton's most radical test for his audience, by challenging us to improve upon the poet's own performance. Here, only the fittest of us will remember to apply the admonition of 1642: "the author is ever distinguisht from the person he introduces" (*Complete Prose*, 1:880).

Notes

First presented in honor of Joseph H. Summers at the Le Moyne Forum, and again here, this essay later appears as a chapter in my book, *Milton and the Sense of Tradition* (New Haven: Yale University Press, 1988).

1. Milton's poetry is quoted from the text of Merritt Y. Hughes, ed., *John Milton: Complete Poems and Major Prose* (New York: Odyssey Press, 1957); references to *Paradise Lost* in the text will be indicated by *PL*, followed by book and line numbers.

2. Editors have frequently commented upon the relative scarcity of allusions and echoes in *Paradise Regained*; Newton thought it "composed from memory and with no help from other books" (H. J. Todd, ed., *The Poetical Works of John Milton, with Notes of Various Authors*, 5th ed. [London, 1852], 3:202). Several parallels have been cited, however, for Milton's account of the Son's descent, including Apuleius's description of Psyche (IV), Ovid's *Metamorphoses* (IV–V), and Giles Fletcher's *Christ's Triumph on Earth*. See Todd, 3:195, and notes of John Carey in *The Poems of John Milton*, ed. John Carey and Alastair Fowler (London: Longmans, 1968), 1076–77, 1163–64. On Milton's treatment, Thyer comments acutely that "There is a peculiar softness and delicacy in this description," a quality he finds appropriate, given the dangers from which the Son has just been removed. More interesting is his general point that Milton has "throughout the work thrown the ornaments of poetry on the side of errour, whether it was that he thought great truths best expressed in a grave unaffected style, or intended to suggest this fine moral to the reader, that simple naked truth will always be an overmatch for falsehood, though recommended by the gayest rhetoric, and adorned with the most bewitching colours" (Todd, 3:195, 168–69).

3. The problem is well summarized by D. C. Allen, *The Harmonious Vision: Studies in Milton's Poetry* (Baltimore: The Johns Hopkins University Press, 1954), 110–13. Woodhouse found Satan "shorn of his grandeur," but essentially the same as his predecessor ("The Theme and Pattern of *Paradise Regained*," *University of Toronto Quarterly* 25 [1955–56]: 171–73). Satan's strategies are shrewdly traced in recent studies by Stanley E. Fish ("Inaction and Silence: The Reader in *Paradise Regained*," in *Calm of Mind: Tercentenary Essays on "Paradise Regained" and "Samson Agonistes" in Honor of John S. Dieckhoff* [Cleveland: Case Western Reserve Press, 1971], 25–47; and "Things and Actions Indifferent: the Temptation Plot in *Paradise Regained*," in *Milton Studies* 17 [1983]: 163–85); and Georgia Christopher (*Milton and the Science of the Saints* [Princeton: Princeton University Press, 1982], 199–224).

4. Arnold Stein seems to me quite right in saying that in *Paradise Regained* Satan is "more nearly domestic . . . He is fascinatingly wrong, essentially inept" (*Heroic Knowledge: An Interpretation of "Paradise Regained" and "Samson Agonistes"* [Minneapolis: University of Minnesota Press, 1957], 16); Stein's way of putting it allows us to focus at once upon the human and the sinister, *influential* sides of Satan. Annabel Patterson has recently suggested that Satan is "driven by the need to know the truth and . . . tormented by ambiguity . . . in the divine Word itself" ("*Paradise Regained*: A Last

Chance at True Romance," *Milton Studies* 17 [1983]: 202). See also Lawrence Hyman, *The Quarrel Within: Art and Morality in Milton's Poetry* (Port Washington, N. Y.: Kennikat Press, 1972), 83–89.

5. The eighteenth-century critic Richard Meadowcourt found the Son's soliloquy a blemish in the poem; it was "long, and low, and unpleasing"; more specifically, he observed that it was "made up of several Circumstances which are before related, and partly repeated over again in a soliloquy of the Virgin *Mary* in the second Book" (*A Critique on Milton's "Paradise Regained"* [London, 1732], repr., ed. Joseph Anthony Wittreich, Jr. [Gainesville: Scholars' Facsimiles and Reprints, 1971], 28–29).

6. In describing the "double scripture" available under the gospel, Milton writes that "the external scripture, particularly the New Testament, has often been liable to corruption and is, in fact, corrupt. This has come about because it has been committed to the care of various untrustworthy authorities, has been collected together from an assortment of divergent manuscripts, and has survived in a medley of transcripts and editions. But no one can corrupt the Spirit which guides man to truth, and a spiritual man is not easily deceived." (*Christian Doctrine*, trans. John Carey; *Complete Prose Works of John Milton*, ed. Don M. Wolfe et al. [New Haven: Yale University Press, 1953-], 6:587–88).

7. *Luther's Works*, ed. Jaroslav Pelikan (St. Louis: Concordia, 1963), 24:264.

8. For an expert discussion of the *protevangelium*, see Georgia Christopher, "The Verbal Gate to Paradise: Adam's Literary Experience in Book X of *Paradise Lost*," *PMLA* 90 (1975): 69–77.

9. In the fullest of these collective identifications, just after the Son's account of the Baptism, the narrator marks the speech itself—and not the historical or merely visible emergence of Jesus from Jordan—as the actual rise of "our morning star," alluding to Jesus' own interpretive recollection in Revelations 22:16.

10. Roger H. Sundell treats the poem's divided exposition in "The Narrator as Interpreter in *Paradise Regained*," *Milton Studies* 2 (1970): 83–101.

11. For a discussion of Milton's Lydianism, see my article "The Lydian Airs of *L'Allegro* and *Il Penseroso*," *Journal of English and Germanic Philology* (1984): 183–99.

12. Harold Bloom, *The Anxiety of Influence* (New York: Oxford University Press, 1973), 11, 19–20, 26.

13. See Stanley E. Fish, "Inaction and Silence," 40.

14. *1 Henry IV*, 2.4.89–91; I quote from *William Shakespeare: The Complete Works*, gen. ed. Alfred Harbage (New York: Viking, 1969).

15. On the question of the Son's memory and consciousness, see Barbara K. Lewalski's useful discussion in *Milton's Brief Epic* (Providence: Brown University Press, 1966).

16. Writing to the unknown friend in 1633, Milton enclosed the "Petrarchian stanza" (now Sonnet VII), specifically "that you may see that I am something suspicious of my selfe" (*Complete Prose*, 1:320).

Index

312 ☐ *Index*

A Fine Tuning offers rich and wide-ranging studies, both traditional and new, on the problems and possibilities of thinking about and reading the incomparable poetry of George Herbert and John Milton. Louis Martz writes eloquently on the generous ambiguity of Herbert's *Temple*, while Diane McColley discusses the poem as hierophon: "Herbert's poems, begotten in liturgy, are borne on the wings of music." Michael Schoenfeldt examines Herbert on the art of submission; Sidney Gottlieb compares the two endings of *The Church*; Thomas Hester describes visual shapes; and Chauncey Wood gives an Augustinian reading of "The Pulley." The studies of Milton's poetry are equally wide-ranging, beginning with Barbara Lewalski's fundamental and still controversial arguments about generic multiplicity and ending with Christopher Grose's analysis of the insidious tempter of *Paradise Regained* attempting to displace the narrator. In diverse ways, both Marshall Grossman and William Shullenberger interrogate Milton's troubling poem, "The Passion," in fresh and provocative discourse of deep structure and language. Alinda Sumers broadly surveys Protestant commentaries while Noam Flinker argues on the basis of Milton's parallelling of contemporary Ranter antinomian texts, that Canticles provides the proper intertext for Adam's song. Fannie Peczenik demonstrates that, in his depiction of the creation of Eve, he severely criticizes prevailing contemporary beliefs.

This spirited collection constitutes a warm and appropriate tribute to Joseph H. Summers, whose outstanding studies of Herbert and Milton still stand as the best books of their kind. Illuminating the volume are a witty and graceful tribute to Summers by Russell Peck and a bibliography of Summers' works.

Mary A. Maleski has held an NEH summer fellowship at Princeton University and is director of the Le Moyne College Forum on Religion and Literature and director of the Le Moyne College Honors Program. She is currently Associate Professor of English at Le Moyne College.

mRts

meðieual & Renaissance texts & stuðies
is the publishing program of the
Center for Medieval and Early Renaissance Studies
at the State University of New York at Binghamton.

mRts emphasizes books that are needed —
texts, translations, and major research tools.

mRts aims to publish the highest quality scholarship
in attractive and durable format at modest cost.